lege

ɹ

'ail's

Isabella Livingston is a graphic-design historian.
She is a senior lecturer at Falmouth College of Arts,
Cornwall, UK, where she has taught since 1993.

Thames & Hudson world of art

This famous series provides the widest available range of
illustrated books on art in all its aspects. If you would like
to receive a complete list of titles in print please write to:

Thames & Hudson
181A High Holborn, London WC1V 7QX

In the United States please write to:
Thames & Hudson Inc.
500 Fifth Avenue, New York, New York 10110

Moved from Ref to Circ
August - 2013

Printed in Singapore

The Thames & Hudson Dictionary o

Alan and Isabella Livingston

Graphic Design and Designers

504 illustrations, 58 in color

 Thames & Hudson world of art

For Suzanne

First published in paperback in the United States of America in 1992 by Thames & Hudson Inc., 500 Fifth Avenue, New York, New York 10110

thamesandhudsonusa.com

Revised edition 2003

Library of Congress Catalog Card Number 2001093714
ISBN 0-500-20353-9

Previously published as *The Thames and Hudson Encyclopaedia of Graphic Design and Designers*

Text pages designed by Derek + Fred Birdsall
Typeset by Omnific

Printed and bound in Singapore by C.S. Graphics

Contents

A reader's guide to the use of this book

The aim of the *Dictionary of Graphic Design and Designers* is to present a concise compendium of information on not only the leading figures in graphic design since 1840 but also on the artistic movements and technical advances of the period, thereby helping to show how the development of graphic design relates to the history of fine art and illustration. This broad contextual approach is intended to show how graphic design, far from being on the fringes, has been at the heart of artistic developments during the past 160 years.

All information is given in a concise form and while there are more than 750 entries, the choice is of necessity selective; this is particularly so with the leading figures of contemporary graphic design, from amongst whom only a few of the most influential have been chosen. This choice of the more radical and important practitioners in the field today provides clear indications of likely developments in graphic design over the next decade and beyond.

The huge range of entries is outlined in the **subject index** (opposite), which is intended to help the reader draw parallels between entries that may appear some distance apart in the alphabetical order; such interrelationships are further indicated by the **cross references** in the text, which appear in SMALL CAPITALS.

Black-and-white **illustrations** have been selected to provide as complete a visual record as possible of the subjects discussed, while the colour illustrations on pp. 65–72 reveal the particular significance of colour in certain areas of graphic design.

The **chronological chart** on pp. 232–35 suggests the links between major artistic movements and the designers, companies and technical inventions of greatest significance in each period.

A **bibliography** giving details of some of the most fundamental and informative sources on this subject is to be found on pp. 236–37. **Acknowledgments** for the illustrations appear on pp. 238–39.

Tissi, Rosmarie
Toorn, Jan van
Tscherny, George
Tschichold, Jan
Valicenti, Rick
VanderLans, Rudy
Velde, Henry Clemens
van de
Vermeulen, Rick
Vignelli, Massimo
Vivarelli, Carlo L.
Weingart, Wolfgang
Widmer, Jean
Wright, Edward
Wunderlich, Gert
Wurman, Richard Saul
Wyman, Lance
Yokoo, Tadanori
Zwart, Piet

Journals/Magazines
Advertising Arts
Ark
Commercial Art
Design
Emigre
Eye
Fleuron, The
Fortune
Fuse
Gebrauchsgraphik
Graphis
Harper's Bazaar
Idea
i-D
I.D.
Merz
New Graphic Design
Octavo
Pan
Penrose Annual, The
Poster, The
Savoy, The
Studio, The
Typographica
Typography
U&lc
Ver Sacrum
Vogue
Yellow Book, The

Movements/Styles
Art Deco
Art Nouveau
Arts and Crafts
Movement
Chap Book Style
Constructivism
Cubism
Dada
De Stijl
Futurism
International
Typographic Style
Jugendstil
Modernism/Modern
Movement
New Typography
New Wave
New York School
Plakatstil
Pop Art
post-modernism
Private Press
Movement
Psychedelia
Punk
Suprematism
Surrealism
Vienna Secession
Vorticism

National Summaries
American graphic
design
British graphic design
Dutch graphic design
French graphic design
German graphic design
Japanese graphic design
Swiss Style/Swiss
graphic design

**Organizations/
Societies/Schools**
Alliance Graphique
Internationale (AGI)
American Institute of
Graphic Arts (AIGA)
Art Directors Club of
New York
Arts and Crafts
Exhibition Society

Art Worker's Guild
Aspen International
Design Conference
Association
Typographique
Internationale
(ATypI)
Bauhaus
Century Guild
Chartered Society of
Designers (CSD)
Design and Industries
Association (DIA)
Design Council
Designers and Art
Directors Association
(D&AD)
Deutscher Werkbund
Double Crown Club
Federal Art Project
(FAP)
Federal Design
Improvement
Program
ICOGRADA
ISO
Pira
Royal Designers for
Industry (RDI)
Ulm Hochschule für
Gestaltung

**Other Influential
Figures**
Albers, Josef
Apollinaire, Guillaume
Beddington, Jack
Doesburg, Théo van
Gray, Nicolette
Gropius, Walter
Hoffmann, Josef
Jones, Owen
Katsumie, Masaru
Lewis, Wyndham
Loewy, Raymond
Mackintosh, Charles
Rennie
Marinetti, Filippo
Tommaso
Muybridge, Eadweard
Neurath, Otto
Pick, Frank

Talbot, William Henry
Fox
Warde, Beatrice

Poster Artists
Aleksiun, Jan Jaromir
Auriol, Georges
Bernhard, Lucian
Berthon, Paul
Bonnard, Pierre
Carlu, Jean
Chéret, Jules
Colin, Paul
Cooper, Austin
Erdt, Hans Rudi
Gipkens, Julius
Grasset, Eugène
Hassall, John
Hohlwein, Ludwig
Klinger, Julius
Leete, Alfred
Lenica, Jan
Leupin, Herbert
Loesch, Uwe
Mlodozeniec, Jan
Mucha, Alphonse
Newbould, Frank
Nicholson, Sir William
Orazi, Emmanuel
Penfield, Edward
Pryde, James
Purvis, Tom
Quernec, Alain Le
Reed, Ethel
Rhead, Louis
Savignac, Raymond
Stankiewicz, Eugeniusz
Starowieyski,
Franciszek (Jan Byk)
Steinlen, Théophile-
Alexandre
Swierzy, Waldemar
Taylor, Fred
Tomaszewski, Henryk
Toulouse-Lautrec,
Henri de
Troxler, Niklaus
Villemot, Bernard

kern
kerning
laid paper
lamination
laser printer
Latin
layout
Letraset
letterpress
ligature
lining numerals/figures
linocut
Linotype
literals
lithography
logotype
loose-leaf binding
lower case
Ludlow Type
    Composing Machine
machine-coated paper
machine-finished paper
machine-glazed paper
majuscules
measure
mechanical
Mechano-Faktura
    (Theory of)
MICR
minuscules
Modern Face
modern figures
Monoline
Monotype
mouse
non-lining numerals/
    figures
OBR
OCR
offset litho/offset
    photolithography
old face/old style
old style
    numerals/figures
optical spacing/
    optically even
    spacing
ornament
outline letter
Paintbox
Pantone System
paper sizes

PC (Personal
    Computer)
perfect binding
photocomposition
photoengraving
photogram
photogravure
photolithography
Photo-Mechanical
    Transfer/PMT
Photoshop
Pica, Pica em
pictogram/graph
pie graph/chart
planographic
point
prelims
printer's flowers
printer's ornament
proof correction marks
quad
quad/quadrat
QuarkXPress
quarto
quire
rag paper
RAM (Random Access
    Memory)
ranged left/ragged right
ranged right/ragged left
ream
rebus
relief printing
ROM (Read Only
    Memory)
Roman
Roman numerals
saddle-stitching
sans serif
screen printing
script
section-sewn binding
serif
set
shaded letter
side-stitching
signage
silk screen process
slab serif
small capitals
solarization
stress

swash characters
symbol
symmetric typography
tabular work
trademark
transitional type
type
typeface
typeface classification
type family
type-height
    (height-to-paper)
type mark-up (TMU)
type measurement
type nomenclature
typographer
typography
U&lc, U/lc
unjustified
upper case
Venetian
Venn diagram
Vox Classification of
    Typefaces
windows
woodcut
wood engraving
wove paper
WYSIWYG
x-height

Typeface Designers
Benton, Morris Fuller
Burns, Aaron
Carter, Mathew
Cooper, Oswald
Excoffon, Roger
Frere-Jones, Tobias
Frutiger, Adrian
Gill, Eric
Goudy, Frederic W.
Hoefler, Jonathan
Johnston, Edward
Koch, Rudolf
Krimpen, Jan van
LettError
Middleton, Robert
    Hunter
Morison, Stanley
    Arthur
Novarese, Aldo
Reiner, Imre

Renner, Paul
Trump, Georg
Wolpe, Berthold
Zapf, Hermann

Typefaces
Albertus
Baskerville
Bell
Bembo
Bodoni
Caslon Old Face
Century
Cheltenham
Clarendon
Cooper Black
Didot
Folio
Franklin Gothic
Futura
Garamond
Haas Grotesque
Helvetica
Imprint
Ionic
Microgramma
Optima
Perpetua
Plantin
Rockwell
Template Gothic
Times New Roman
Univers

A

8vo London-based graphic design consultancy established in 1985 by Mark Holt (b.1958) and Hamish Muir (b.1957). Holt studied at Newcastle Polytechnic, followed by three years in San Francisco as a freelance designer. Muir trained at Bath Academy, Corsham, before spending a year at the Kuṅstgewerbeschule, Basle under Wolfgang WEINGART. Their associate Michael Burke is an English designer/ teacher based in Stuttgart. 8vo designed and published their own eight-volume typographic journal *Octavo* (1986–92) as a reaction against the fashion-led TYPOGRAPHY of the early 1980s. *Octavo* adopted a critical and analytical perspective on current typographic conventions, with later issues demonstrating the technological and creative possibilities of electronic typesetting and page make-up systems. The influence of the APPLE MAC-INTOSH COMPUTER is apparent in issue number 7. Primarily concerned with the effective transmission of information, 8vo reject the manipulation of type to make illustrations or contrived word-pictures. In their use of SANS SERIF typefaces and dismissal of unnecessary decorative elements they acknowledge the underlying tenets of the INTERNATIONAL TYPO-GRAPHIC STYLE and the design philosophy espoused by the influential Swiss journal NEW GRAPHIC DESIGN. However, 8vo's determination to break new ground in the design of electronically generated typography is evident in projects such as their CORPORATE IDENTITY for Uden Associates, a London film and television production company. The inherent discipline of 8vo's design approach has attracted major international clients including Zanders Paper, Germany, American Express Europe, the Museum Boymans-van Beuningen, Rotterdam, and the architectural practice Nation Fender.

A,B,C system of standard paper sizes

International system originally established by the German standards institution (DIN) and subsequently adopted by the International Standards Organization (ISO) in Switzerland. The 'A' series covers stationery and books; the 'B' series is an alternative intermediate range normally used for posters and wall-charts, etc.; the 'C' series is exclusively intended for envelopes. The 'A' sizes are based on a rectangle one square metre in area (just over one square yard; the basic A0 sheet). The sides of all sheets are in the proportion of 1:1.4142, with these proportions remaining constant however many times the sheet is folded. The sizes shown are as trimmed and are indicated in millimetres.

A0	1189 × 841	B0	1414 × 1000
A1	841 × 594	B1	1000 × 707
A2	594 × 420	B2	707 × 500
A3	420 × 297	B3	500 × 353
A4	297 × 210	B4	353 × 250
A5	210 × 148	B5	250 × 176
A6	148 × 105	B6	176 × 125
A7	105 × 74	B7	125 × 88
A8	74 × 52	B8	88 × 62
A9	52 × 37	B9	62 × 44
A10	37 × 26	B10	44 × 31

C0	1297 × 917	Specials:	
C1	917 × 648	DL	220 × 110
C2	648 × 458	C7/6	162 × 81
C3	458 × 324		
C4	324 × 229		
C5	229 × 162		
C6	162 × 114		
C7	114 × 81		

July from **8vo**'s 1992 calendar for Zanders Paper.

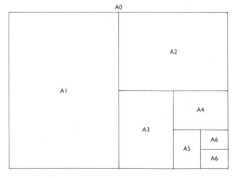

A,B,C system of standard paper sizes: 'A' series.

Adigard, Erik (b.1953) Artist and designer of computer graphics who, with Patricia McShane, founded the San Francisco–based M.A.D. (McShane/Adigard Design) in 1989. Adigard was born in Brazzaville, Congo, and studied initially at the Ecole des Beaux-Arts de Montpellier, France and then at Censier, University of Paris. Following that he moved to the US, where he graduated from California College of Arts and Crafts and exhibited as a painter before turning to the electronic arts. M.A.D. create innovative and idiosyncratic design solutions for a range of graphic, illustration, advertising and multimedia projects. Clients include *Wired*, *Vogue*, *Mother Jones*, Lotus, Microsoft and Sony. Experimental interactive projects for *Wired*'s website LiveWired and M.A.D.'s own website 'Funnel' feature in the San Francisco Museum of Modern Art's permanent collection. The studio produced the graphic identity for the International Design Conference, Aspen (1999). Winners of numerous awards, including the 1998 Chrysler Award for Innovation in Design. Adigard coproduced *Architecture Must Burn* with Aaron Betsky (2000).

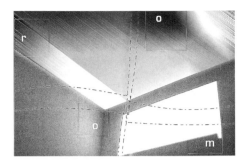

Spread from **Adigard**'s design for the book *Architecture Must Burn*, 2000.

Adobe Systems Incorporated American software company founded in 1982 in San Jose, California. Their font and printing software programs (including PHOTOSHOP) are in widespread use throughout the graphics and desktop-publishing industries.

Advertising Arts Influential American magazine committed to promoting modernist developments in advertising and graphic art. Published throughout the 1930s, *Advertising Arts* was a supplement to the trade magazine *Advertising and Selling*. It made no apology for using progressive ideas in art, science and design in the service of commerce.

Agha, Mehemed Fehmy (1896–1978) Russian-born and educated in Kiev and Paris, Agha brought the visual language of modernist European design to the American magazine. Worked as a graphic artist in Paris and then for German *VOGUE* in Berlin. In 1928 met the publisher Condé Nast, who invited him to become art director of American *Vogue* in New York, where he also assumed responsibility for the design of both *Vanity Fair* and *House & Garden*. Employed by Condé Nast until 1943. His asymmetric layouts displayed a bold use of typographic elements and an innovative approach to the content and arrangement of photographic images. He was among the first to introduce colour photographs and bled-off pages (see BLEED) to the modern magazine.

Agha's cover design for *Vanity Fair*, December 1929.

Four of the symbols **Aicher** designed for the 1972 Olympic Games.

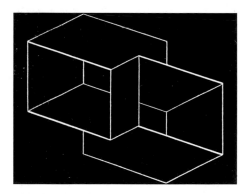

One of a series of 'Structural Constellations' designed by **Albers** between 1953 and 1958.

Upper- and lower-case letters from the **Albertus** typeface.

ABCDEFGH
abcdefgh

AGI See ALLIANCE GRAPHIQUE INTERNATIONALE

Aicher, Otl (1922–91) German graphic designer and typographer who led the visual design group of the 1972 Olympic Games, Munich. Studied at the Akademie der Bildenden Künste, Munich, before establishing a graphic design practice in Ulm, 1948. Co-founder, and from 1962 until 1964, vice-chancellor of ULM HOCHSCHULE FÜR GESTALTUNG. Aicher combined a rational design approach with an intuitive use of colour and movement to produce compelling graphic imagery. This is apparent in the CORPORATE IDENTITY and SIGNAGE programme he prepared for the German town of Isny in the late 1970s. Corporate work for major industrial concerns included schemes for Braun, Lufthansa, Blohm & Voss and Erco. Created Rotis, a typeface that combined the characteristics of SERIF and SANS SERIF alphabets (1988).

AIGA See AMERICAN INSTITUTE OF GRAPHIC ARTS

airbrush Painting implement, resembling a large fountain pen, which is powered by compressed air to produce a finely controlled spray of paint or ink. Successful airbrushing depends on the skilful application, and then removal, of cut-out adhesive 'masks', which ensure that the spray of colour is accurately directed at the area left exposed. Airbrushing is a technique capable of great subtlety in tonally graded effects. Used by commercial illustrators and fine artists, its potential for super-realism means that it is employed in photographic retouching.

Albers, Josef (1888–1976) German artist, designer and educator who developed theories relating to the emotional and perceptual impact of colour, line and geometric forms. His BAUHAUS principles influenced generations of design students. Studied in Berlin, Essen and Munich before joining the Bauhaus, from 1920 until 1923 as a student and then as a teacher, later director, on the preliminary course. Emigrated to the US in 1933 where he held numerous academic posts including professor at Black Mountain College, North Carolina, 1933–49, and professor at Yale University School of Art, 1950–60, where he established the graphic design programme. At Yale he also worked on a series of abstract paintings, collectively entitled *Homage to the Square*. Disciplined and subtle compositions in flat colours, they consisted of three or four squares set inside one another. Albers' ideas on colour relationships are explored in his book *Interaction of Colour*, 1963.

Illustration for a poster, by **Aldridge**, for a gala evening of the National Council for Civil Liberties, 1968.

Cover for the November 1954 issue of *Fortune* magazine, designed by **Allner**.

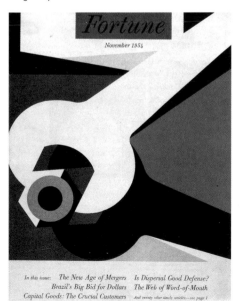

Albertus Family of typefaces (Albertus, Albertus Light, Albertus Bold, Albertus Titling) designed by Berthold WOLPE for the MONOTYPE Corporation, England, 1932–40. The individual characters end in a distinctive thickened terminal, rather than a traditional SERIF form. Albertus has been successful as a typeface for DISPLAY SETTING and for SIGNAGE in architectural applications.

Aldridge, Alan (b.1943) Influential graphic artist during the 1960s explosion of pop culture in Britain. As fiction art director of Penguin Books, London (see Sir Allen LANE) between 1963 and 1967 he brought a brash humour and fantasy to paperback art. In addition to his own surreal, often grotesque, AIRBRUSH illustrations, he commissioned many strikingly original photographs taken in unusual locations. Also produced a number of memorable covers for *The Sunday Times* colour supplement during the 1960s and early 70s. Edited both volumes of *The Beatles Illustrated Lyrics* (1969 and 1971) and was responsible, along with George Perry, for *The Penguin Book of Comics* (1967). Since the mid-1970s has collaborated with airbrush artist Harry Willock in designing and illustrating numerous children's books.

Aleksiun, Jan Jaromir (b.1940) Polish avant-garde artist who has challenged and developed the traditions of the Polish poster school. From 1959 until 1966 studied fine arts at Wroclaw, where he was later elected rector of the university. Since the late 1960s he has collaborated with Eugeniusz STANKIEWICZ. Brings his personal vision as a painter and printmaker to the art of the poster, producing shadowy and surreal images, often with a mythological undercurrent. Winner of numerous awards including a bronze medal at the 1978 Warsaw Poster Biennale.

Alliance Graphique Internationale (AGI)
Association of graphic designers founded in Paris by a small group of French and Swiss designers. The first annual meeting took place in 1951, since when they have taken place in different European cities. The original European membership has now been extended to include distinguished practitioners worldwide. Membership is by invitation and is restricted to individuals with an acknowledged international reputation. AGI regularly organizes exhibitions of members' work, often illustrating a particular cultural or educational theme.

Allner, Walter H. (b.1909) BAUHAUS-trained designer, typographer and painter who studied with Josef

ALBERS, Vasily Kandinsky, Paul Klee and Joost SCHMIDT. Assistant to Piet ZWART in the Netherlands (1930). After the closure of the Bauhaus (1933) he settled in Paris, first working as an assistant to Jean CARLU and then becoming a partner in Ommium Graphique and art director for the publisher Formes, Editions d'Art Graphique et Photographique. Paris editor of GRAPHIS from 1945 until 1948. Moved to the US in 1949 where he undertook design and consultancy work for many major companies, including Johnson & Johnson, 1954–55 and RCA Records, 1965–67. In 1960 he designed the posters for the national Traffic Safety Campaign by the Outdoor Advertising Association of America. Influential art director of FORTUNE magazine 1963–74. Participant in the exhibition '50 Years Bauhaus', which toured museums worldwide, 1968–70. International president of AGI, 1974.

alphabet Set of letters or characters, arranged in a fixed sequence, used to write language. In typesetting a full set of characters of one size of TYPEFACE in hot metal, or a full range of sizes in PHOTOCOMPOSITION, is called a FONT/FOUNT.

American graphic design From the 1860s with the creation of the first advertising agencies, to the 1880s when the LINOTYPE and MONOTYPE typesetting machines were developed, the US established a tradition of creative and technical ingenuity that continued throughout the 20th c. The ideals of the ARTS AND CRAFTS MOVEMENT in England were embraced by four great US type designers and printers: Daniel Berkeley UPDIKE, Frederic W. GOUDY, Bruce ROGERS and William Addison DWIGGINS. From the early 1930s to the end of the Second World War the American graphic design community was enriched by an influx of important European designers fleeing from the deteriorating political situation in Europe. Notable amongst these were László MOHOLYNAGY, who founded the Institute of Design, Chicago, in 1937 and Herbert BAYER, who settled in New York. During the early 1940s the CONTAINER CORPORATION OF AMERICA broke new ground by commissioning fine artists like Ben SHAHN and Henry Moore to design advertisements. This link between fine art and design practice was the forerunner to CCA's later, and even more influential campaign, 'Great Ideas of Western Man'. The 1950s were years of affluence and a dramatic growth in advertising, with Madison Avenue in New York becoming the advertising centre of the world. The design offices created by Charles Eames, Raymond LOEWY and Henry Dreyfuss pioneered a multidisciplinary approach to design problems. Such popular magazines as *Look* and *Life* provided important outlets for illustrators and photographers. By the end of the decade some significant young designers were emerging: Paul RAND, William GOLDEN, Robert BROWN-JOHN, Ivan CHERMAYEFF, Tom GEISMAR, Saul BASS and Henry WOLF. During the 1960s the development of colour television presented a mass medium to be explored. The psychedelic imagery of the period counterbalanced the INTERNATIONAL TYPOGRAPHIC STYLE that was still visible in many major corporate brochures and visual identity programmes. A more intuitive and eclectic typographical and illustrative style, developed by designers like Herb LUBALIN and Milton GLASER of PUSH PIN STUDIO, manifested itself from the late 1960s onwards. Experimentation followed, in which POP ART, ART NOUVEAU, ART DECO and Victorian nostalgia were all assimilated, with no single style dominating. A creative distinction also emerged between the West and East Coasts, with the West appearing more vital and experimental, while the East continued to look to Europe in its pursuit of a functionalist philosophy. Whilst the 1970s were distinctive for their lack of any real design innovation or direction, the skills of the graphic designer were increasingly applied to communicating political and social issues. This period of conservatism was followed by a decade of dramatic growth in the design business coupled with an exploration of POST-MODERNISM and the ideas generated by Wolfgang WEINGART, an influential teacher in Basle. A 'new wave' of designers led by April GREIMAN on the West Coast sought to combine new technological developments with a freer, more humanistic interpretation of the International Typographic Style.

American Institute of Graphic Arts (AIGA) Founded in New York in 1914, the AIGA is the oldest and largest organization in the US devoted to the interests of creators and users of the graphic arts. It is non-profit making and through exhibitions, seminars, competitions and publications endeavours to 'do all things which would raise the standard and the extension and development towards perfection of the graphic arts in the US'. In 1974 the US Department of Transportation commissioned the AIGA to design a master set of user symbols for universal use. An advisory committee of five prominent graphic designers, chaired by Thomas Geismar of CHERMAYEFF & GEISMAR INC. and including Rudolph de HARAK, Seymour CHWAST, Massimo VIGNELLI and John Lees, researched and evaluated each symbol. The final set was designed by COOK AND SHANOSKY ASSOCIATES.

American Type Founders Company (ATF)
US company that has made an outstanding contribution to the design and production of forms of TYPEFACE in the 20th c. Created in 1892 after a number of type foundries merged, the consortium stabilized a traditional industry undermined both by rampant design piracy and the development of the LINOTYPE and MONOTYPE mechanized typesetting systems during the 1880s. Within a decade ATF was a major force in the production and distribution of foundry, or hand-set, metal type. Will BRADLEY became a consultant to the company, designing typefaces, ornaments and an influential series of magazines called *The American Chap Book*. Frederick W. GOUDY, Morris Fuller BENTON and Lucian BERNHARD were among the many type designers who contributed to the success of ATF.

ampersand Symbol (&) used in place of the word 'and'. Originally derived from the Latin *et* (and).

Anglo-American Point System British and American unit of TYPE MEASUREMENT adopted in America in 1886 and in Britain in 1898. Based on a standard unit of 0.3515mm (0.013837in).

animation Film-making technique that creates the illusion of movement by the rapid projection of a series of sequential still images, produced from drawings, photomontage, or three-dimensional models. During the 1920s and 30s the American studios of Warner Brothers, MGM, and Walt Disney transformed the cartoon film from a primitive comic strip into a hugely successful narrative form. Many graphic designers have exploited the potential of animation for commercial, informational and political purposes. Since the early 1980s, computer-generated animation has increasingly contributed to pop videos and television commercials.

antique paper Non-calendered printing paper with a rough, lightly sized surface used mainly for booklets, folders and stationery. When the lines from the paper-mould are clearly visible it is called 'antique laid', otherwise it is known as 'antique wove'.

Apollinaire, Guillaume (1880–1918) French poet and influential avant-garde critic. Observed that 'catalogues, posters, advertisements of all types, believe me, they contain the poetry of our epoch'. His singular contribution to early 20th-c. typographic developments is his book of visual poems entitled *Calligrammes* (1917), in which he attempted to inte-

grate word and image. His 'image' poems are composed of words and letterforms formally arranged to convey a visual design or image relating to the content. Along with the Italian Futurist poet Filippo MARINETTI, Apollinaire was an early exponent of the expressive use of typography to heighten the meaning of language.

appearing size Term applied to the perceived difference in size of letters from different TYPEFACES but with the same point size (*see* TYPE MEASUREMENT). This results from the variation in X-HEIGHT in relation to the height of the ASCENDER and the depth of the DESCENDER.

ABCDEFGHIJKLMNOPQ
abcdefghijklmnopq
14pt Garamond

ABCDEFGHIJKLMNOPQ
abcdefghijklmnopq
14pt Walbaum

There is an obvious difference in the **appearing size** of the typefaces Garamond and Walbaum.

The Bleeding-Heart Dove and the Fountain, an 'image' poem from *Calligrammes* (1917), composed and arranged by **Apollinaire**.

Front cover of issue 23 of *Ark*.

Poster designed by Robert Bonfils for the Paris 1925 'Exposition Internationale des Arts Décoratifs et Industriels Modernes', which gave its name to **Art Deco**.

Apple Macintosh (Mac) Computer Launched in January 1984, the first computer to achieve commercial success with a WIMP (WINDOWS Icon MOUSE Pull-down-menus) interface. The user-friendliness of the graphics interface allows users to get to grips with the machine without the need to learn a complex command language. Images and text can be created quickly and cheaply, while the designer stills retains control. The Apple Mac was launched with a number of software packages, most notably Mac Write, Mac Draw and Mac Paint, which were quickly adopted, revolutionizing graphic design practice. Subsequently, more sophisticated packages such as Hyper Card, Microsoft Word, Aldus FreeHand, Aldus PageMaker and QuarkXPress were made available and became industry standards. A programme of continuous technical updating has ensured that Apple Mac is one of the most widely used computers in graphic design.

Arabic numerals The numerals 1, 2, 3, 4, 5, 6, 7, 8, 9, 0 originated in India *c.* AD 500 and were introduced to Europe *c.* 1100 by the Arabs. They did not achieve widespread usage until *c.*1400. *See* ROMAN NUMERALS

Ark Journal produced at the Royal College of Art, London, between 1950 and 1976. Initiated by the School of Graphic Design, it chronicled British designers' move away from historicism and nostalgia toward an increasing awareness of contemporary developments in advertising, photography and typography in Europe and America. *Ark* provided good opportunities for such emerging designers at that time as David GENTLEMAN and Alan FLETCHER.

Arsovski, Mihajlo (b.1937) Graphic designer based in Zagreb, influential in bringing international standards of design to Yugoslavia. Worked with Zagreb University Student Centre, producing posters and books for its gallery, theatre and publishing group. His posters demonstrate his ability to manipulate letterforms in a powerful and original manner. Co-operated in the design of Yugoslavian trade and cultural pavilions throughout the world.

art Abbreviation for ARTWORK (US).

Art Deco Luxurious, international style of decoration that flourished *c.* 1918–39 in fashion, interiors, architecture, ceramics and industrial design. Named after the 1925 World's Fair in Paris ('Exposition Internationale des Arts Décoratifs et Industriels Modernes'). Utilized bright, vibrant colours along with a distinctive range of motifs – floral, figurative and geometric. Sources go back to the early 20th c., when designers were searching for an alternative to the overwhelming influence of ART NOUVEAU and its reliance on curvilinear natural forms. In graphic design Art Deco was less ornate than in other fields but displayed a strong emphasis on striking geometric shapes and patterns. The bold rectilinear typefaces of the period, which provided improved legibility, were in stark contrast to the florid creations of Art Nouveau. Artists like A.M. CASSANDRE in France and E. McKnight KAUFFER in England created posters of great originality and exuberance, with the lettering carefully integrated as an important graphic element.

Art Directors Club of New York Founded in 1920, the Art Directors Club of New York was formed for the purpose of developing and maintaining high creative standards in visual communications. Its annual exhibition, 'Advertising and Editorial Art', is a prestigious national event, attracting thousands of entries.

Art Nouveau Decorative style in architecture, furniture, consumer products, fashion and graphics throughout Europe and the US for two decades from about 1890. Known as JUGENDSTIL ('young style') in Germany and as 'Stile Liberty' in Italy (after the Liberty retail business in London). The significance of Art Nouveau is much greater than an acknowledgment of its characteristic organic fluidity and floral motifs would imply. It was an important catalyst in setting aside 19th-c. historicism and contributed to the development of early concepts of MODERNISM. Whilst the roots of the style are complex, there are obvious links with the ARTS AND CRAFTS MOVEMENT, the Pre-Raphaelites, Celtic ornament and Japanese WOODCUT prints. Although originally trained as fine artists, many Art Nouveau poster designers were quick to exploit the potential of CHROMOLITHOGRAPHY, thus making the style widely accessible. The asymmetrical typographic style and the ornate forms of TYPEFACE associated with Art Nouveau imagery were still apparent throughout the 1920s, with a late revival occurring during the psychedelic 1960s. Influential designers were Jules CHERÉT, Eugène GRASSET and Alphonse MUCHA in Paris, Aubrey BEARDSLEY, Walter CRANE and the BEGGARSTAFF BROTHERS in England, Louis RHEAD and Will BRADLEY in America, Henry van de VELDE and Jan TOOROP in Belgium, Gustav KLIMT and Koloman MOSER in Austria and the young Peter BEHRENS in Germany.

art paper Good-quality printing paper with a smooth surface created by applying an even coating of china clay compound on one or both sides of the sheet. CAST-COATED PAPER, which is the best quality, results when an ink-absorbent coating is laid on top of a paper that has previously been machine-coated. A hot glazing drum provides a final polish. Brush-coating utilizes a revolving cylindrical brush to apply the coating, which is then smoothed by flat brushes as it moves across a rubber apron. Machine-coating, the cheaper alternative to cast-coating and brush-coating, produces a printing surface of inferior quality. See IMITATION ART PAPER, MACHINE-COATED PAPER

Arts and Crafts Exhibition Society In 1888 a splinter group from the ART WORKER'S GUILD formed the Combined Arts Society, later renamed the Arts and Crafts Exhibition Society, with the objective of organizing regular exhibitions of the decorative arts. With Walter CRANE as its first president the Society played an active role in spreading the arts and crafts ethos to Continental Europe and America. The Society's international influence was confirmed by its involvement in the English contribution to a number of international exhibitions, notably Turin in 1902, St Louis in 1904, and Ghent in 1913. The significance of the Exhibition Society declined rapidly after the First World War.

Arts and Crafts Movement Movement in the decorative arts and architecture that emerged in Britain during the 1870s in response to the dehumanizing working conditions and debased products of the Industrial Revolution. Initiated by the Socialist reformer William MORRIS who was much influenced by the philosophy of John Ruskin, the movement embraced artists, architects, designers, craftworkers and writers. In relation to book design and production, the shoddy typography, inferior paper and poor presswork of much contemporary printing were rejected in favour of a medievalist approach that revered fine craftsmanship, traditional techniques and the use of natural materials. Encouraged the establishment of the PRIVATE PRESS MOVEMENT including Morris's own KELMSCOTT PRESS, which reverted to a hand press in its attempt to recreate the standards of 15th-c. printers. Morris researched medieval types and produced three Gothic-inspired typefaces. Unfortunately the private presses' emphasis on medieval standards tended to overlook the requirements of convenience, legibility and economy. The movement's legacy to the 20th c., particularly to the BAUHAUS, is its concern for craft skills and the understanding of materials. See ART WORKER'S GUILD

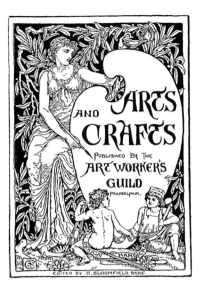

Walter Crane's cover design for the first issue of the American **Art Worker's Guild** magazine, *Arts and Crafts* (1893).

artwork Term applied to illustrative, diagrammatic and photographic material (i.e. material that is not typeset) prepared for reproduction by a designer or artwork technician. When all type and design elements have been positioned, this camera-ready copy is also referred to as finished artwork or MECHANICAL. Finished artwork would normally include specifications for any detailed reproduction or printing requirements. Commonly abbreviated to art (US) or a/w.

Art Worker's Guild Spawned by the ARTS AND CRAFTS MOVEMENT, the Art Worker's Guild was formed in London in May 1884 after a merger of the St George's Art Society and The Fifteen. Provided a forum for designers, architects and craftsmen concerned with the decline in standards of workmanship, including those in the printing industry, since the Industrial Revolution. The first master of the Guild was the sculptor George Blackall Simonds; later masters included Walter CRANE (1888 and 1889), who designed the Guild's symbol and stationery, and William MORRIS (1892). A group from the Guild contributed to the formation of the ARTS AND CRAFTS EXHIBITION SOCIETY.

ascender That part of certain lower-case letters (b, d, f, h, k, l, t) which extends above the X-HEIGHT.

Ascenders of lower-case letters in the Gill Sans typeface.

Ash, Stuart See GOTTSCHALK + ASH INTERNATIONAL

Ashendene Press Established in England in 1894 and directed by C.H. St John Hornby, the Ashendene Press was one of the outstanding products of the PRIVATE PRESS MOVEMENT. Ashendene books were lavish productions created according to 15th-c. standards, with bold types, wide margins, coloured initials and a frequent use of vellum. The press was famous for its use of the Subiaco type, designed by Emery WALKER and Sidney Cockerell and based on the FONT used by Sweynheym and Pannartz at Subiaco, Italy, from 1464.

'Ashley' See HAVINDEN, ASHLEY

Aspen International Design Conference
Important design conference held annually at the Aspen Institute of Humanistic Studies in Colorado, US. Originating in 1951, the conference is an integral part of the Institute's commitment to debate between leading figures in government, business and education on the social, philosophical and intellectual ideas that have shaped the 20th c. Walter Paepcke of the CONTAINER CORPORATION OF AMERICA and Herbert BAYER were amongst the founders of the conference.

Association Typographique Internationale (ATypI) Founded in Lausanne, Switzerland, in 1957, ATypI provides an important forum for typesetting-system manufacturers, typographers and lettering designers. While seeking 'to bring about a better understanding of typography', the primary objective of ATypI has been to improve copyright protection for each individual TYPEFACE. The annual Congress meets in a different country each year.

asymmetric typography Modern typographic design style formulated in Germany during the 1930s that rejects the traditional arrangement of type on a central axis (symmetry) and advocates the functional, dynamic placement of typographic and visual elements. Asymmetric design strives to create a visually balanced arrangement of contrasting elements. The principles were expounded by the Swiss Jan TSCHICHOLD in his influential *Typographische Gestaltung*, 1935, published in America and Britain as *Asymmetric Typography*, 1967. See NEW TYPOGRAPHY, SYMMETRIC TYPOGRAPHY

ATF See AMERICAN TYPE FOUNDERS COMPANY

Auriol, Georges (1863–1939) French ART NOUVEAU poster artist, based in Paris during the 1880s and 90s. Friend and contemporary of Henri de TOULOUSE-LAUTREC and the Swiss artist Théophile-Alexandre STEINLEN. Designer of the calligraphic TYPEFACE Auriol for the French foundry DEBERNEY & PEIGNOT.

author's corrections Corrections or changes made by the author after the final, approved text has been typeset. See PROOF CORRECTION MARKS, LITERALS

a/w Abbreviation for ARTWORK.

Awazu, Kiyoshi (b.1929) Graphic, exhibition, film and theatre designer and teacher. Avant-garde contributor to the creative renaissance in JAPANESE GRAPHIC DESIGN in the late 1960s and 70s. His designs for posters, books, magazine covers, etc. successfully combine the traditional Japanese quality of poetic expression with a European graphic directness and sophistication. Awazu's deeply personal images reflect a belief that the individual must challenge the increasing sterility of modern life. Wide-ranging practitioner who created a playground for Expo '70, Osaka, and designed the Gaudí exhibition, Tokyo and Okinawa, 1978 and the Great Japan Exhibition, London, 1982.

Ayer, N.W. & Son First major advertising agency, established in Philadelphia, US, in 1869. Represented the interests of its clients, buying newspaper space on their behalf and charging a fixed commission. By 1900 it had expanded to become a 'full-service' agency, having pioneered the hiring of specialist copywriters and art directors in the 1880s and the exploitation of market research.

B

B series of paper sizes See A, B, C SYSTEM OF STANDARD PAPER SIZES

backslanted Any typeface that slants backwards towards the left. The effect can be achieved on many computerized typesetting systems.

Examples of the calligraphic typeface **Auriol**.

Backslanted letters from the Isometric typeface.

British stamp designed by **Bailey** in 1964 to commemorate the 20th International Geographical Congress.

Smiley face created for State Mutual Life Assurance by **Ball** in 1963.

Lithograph by Théo **Ballmer** advertising an exhibition in Basle entitled '100 Years of the Photograph' (1927).

Bailey, Dennis (b.1931) British designer, illustrator and teacher, based in London. Assistant editor of GRAPHIS magazine, Zurich, 1956. Worked in Paris 1960–64 specializing in advertising and publishing. Art director of Town magazine, London, 1964–66. Designed UK stamps for the 20th International Geographical Congress, 1964. Since 1967 has run his own design and illustration practice covering book and magazine design, posters and exhibition graphics. Tutor in typography and graphic design at the Central School of Art and Design, London, 1957–60, Chelsea School of Art, London, 1970–81, and Middlesex Polytechnic during the late 1980s. Elected RDI in 1980.

Ball, Harvey (1921–2001) American graphic designer who created the eponymous yellow 'smiley face'. Ball trained at the Worcester Art Museum School, Massachusetts, thereafter establishing his own design and advertising agency in Worcester. The smiley face (1963) was created for State Mutual Life Assurance, following the merger of two insurance companies. Never having applied for copyright, Ball subsequently enjoyed the way the symbol was embraced by the music scene, the advertising industry and street culture. In 1998 Ball founded the World Smile Corporation to promote smiley products and to distribute profits internationally to children's charities.

Ballmer, Théo (1902–65) Swiss designer, teacher and pioneer of the INTERNATIONAL TYPOGRAPHIC STYLE. Studied under Ernst KELLER at the Kunstgewerbeschule, Zurich and for a short time at the BAUHAUS in Dessau. Ballmer's significance rests on the work he produced during the late 1920s and early 30s. His rigorous use of the GRID combined with his pursuit of DE STIJL principles provided an early indication of how graphic design would develop in Switzerland after the Second World War. An influential teacher at the Kunstgewerbeschule, Basle for over three decades, from 1931.

Ballmer, Walter (b.1923) Swiss-born designer who has spent most of his career in Italy. After training at the Kunstgewerbeschule, Basle, Ballmer worked in Lucerne and for Studio Boggeri in Milan. In 1956 joined Olivetti, Milan, working for the department of advertising, industrial design and public relations. Remained at Olivetti until 1981, carrying out many acclaimed corporate design and advertising projects, including exhibitions and murals. His work combines Swiss typographic discipline with Italian flair.

bank paper Thin, tough, uncoated paper similar to BOND PAPER but slightly lighter. Suitable for typewriting, carbon copies and for designers' layouts.

bar chart/graph Graphic representation of different values using horizontal or vertical bars. When more than one value is to be illustrated (using either colour or tone), a 'segmented' bar chart may be utilized.

general product category identification —— 9

manufacturer identification number

product identification number

bar code (Optical Bar Code Recognition, OBR) Ubiquitous pattern of vertical lines on packaging, books, magazines, etc., scanned by computer-linked optical sensors. Shops and supermarkets increasingly rely on the effectiveness of the device for efficient stock control. Patterns normally include an indication of the product category, the manufacturer's identification number and the product identification number.

Barnbrook, Jonathan (b.1966) English-born designer and typographer. Studied at Central Saint Martin's College of Art and Design, London (1985–88) and at the Royal College of Art, London (1988–90). Inventive type designer renowned for designing fonts that subvert (and often combine) the historical classification of typefaces from different periods. The early 1990s was a particularly prolific time for Barnbrook, when he created such fonts as Exocet (1991), Manson (1992, retitled Mason after protests received by EMIGRE, the publisher), Drâylon (1997), Prozac (1997) and Nixon (1994). Joined Tony Kaye Films as a director (1992). Barnbrook's advertising work (including directing commercials for Nike and Toyota) subsidizes personal projects, which have an overtly political dimension. Launched own font foundry, Virus (1997). Designed Damien Hirst's book *I want to spend the rest of my life everywhere, with everyone, one to one, always, forever, now* (1997). Created multifaceted identity for Beams, a Japanese fashion retailer and record label (2000).

Example of a **bar code** showing the basic components of the 'European Article Number' (EAN) system.

Example of the typeface Bastard by **Barnbrook** (1990).

Page layouts by **Baron** from *Harper's Bazaar*, 1997.

Letters from the **Baskerville** typeface.

ABCDEFGH
abcdefgh

Poster by **Bass** for the 1955 film
The Man with the Golden Arm.

Baron, Fabien (b.1959) French art director trained and worked in Paris before moving to New York in 1982, where he quickly established a reputation as an innovative magazine designer. Appointed creative director of *Italian Vogue* in 1988, a post that required him to work in New York and Milan. Retired to New York in 1990 to set up his own studio, Baron & Baron Advertising, and to oversee the re-launch of *Interview* magazine. Following position as creative director (1992–99) of *Harper's Bazaar*, Baron attracted international acclaim. Baron's page layouts are cool and memorable, underpinned by an endlessly inventive approach to typography and lettering. His studio has worked with some of the best-known brands in the fashion world, including Calvin Klein, Giorgio Armani and Issey Miyake. Creative director of *Sex* (1992), Madonna's controversial book. Appointed honorary ROYAL DESIGNER FOR INDUSTRY in 2000.

Baskerville Important 18th-c. TRANSITIONAL TYPEFACE designed by John Baskerville (1706–75), a Birmingham writing master who subsequently established himself as a printer, having made a fortune from the art of japanning. From the outset he sought to improve the quality of English printing and typography. To achieve this Baskerville experimented with inks and papers and designed his own typeface, which has generous proportions and wide, open characters. The ITALIC was specifically designed to match the ROMAN, with some of the italic capitals betraying a calligrapher's flourish. Baskerville is one of the most readable text faces, its popularity confirmed by its wide availability on numerous typesetting systems.

Bass, Saul (1920–96) Graphic designer responsible for numerous innovative and memorable title sequences and promotional pieces for films. Studied at the Art Students League, and from 1944 to 1945 at Brooklyn College, New York, with Gyorgy KEPES. After a period employed as a freelance designer and art director in New York moved in 1946 to Los Angeles. Worked for several agencies before establishing Saul Bass Associates. Enjoyed highly productive collaborations with the film makers Otto Preminger and Alfred Hitchcock. Bass's technique for film titles was to reduce the array of predictable images to a minimum of graphic elements. Early examples include Preminger's films *The Man with the Golden Arm* (1955) and *Anatomy of a Murder* (1959). Also directed special sequences in feature films, such as the shower scene in Hitchcock's *Psycho*, 1960. Bass produced many successful CORPORATE IDENTITY programmes including United Airlines, Quaker Oats, AT&T and Warner Communications. Designed posters and graphics for the Los Angeles Olympics, 1984. US Art Director of the Year in 1957 and was elected to ART DIRECTORS CLUB OF NEW YORK Hall of Fame in 1978.

Bauhaus (German: 'building house') German design school that attempted to create a new unity between art and industry by rejecting any division between decorative and constructional techniques. The Bauhaus was the most important educational enterprise underpinning the development of the MODERN MOVEMENT in architecture. Its origins and aspirations relate to many of the ideas pursued by the ARTS AND CRAFTS MOVEMENT and the DEUTSCHER WERKBUND. Founded in Weimar in 1919, under the direction of the architect Walter GROPIUS, the Bauhaus produced a manifesto that declared, 'The complete building is the ultimate aim of all the visual arts.' This overriding commitment to architecture encouraged the exploration of new ideas associated with DE STIJL and Russian CONSTRUCTIVISM. Designers and craftsmen and women worked towards the removal of conventional subject barriers; the staff included Johannes ITTEN, Paul Klee, Vasily Kandinsky and László MOHOLY-NAGY. Although graphic design was not specifically included in the curriculum at Weimar, constituent elements like photography and typography were taught, most particularly by Moholy-Nagy. In the first publication of the Bauhaus press, *Staatliches Bauhaus in Weimar, 1919–1923*, Moholy-Nagy wrote: 'Typography is a tool of communication. It must be communication in its most intense form. The emphasis must be on absolute clarity.' This commitment to a NEW TYPOGRAPHY was integral to the Modern Movement's wish to explore different ways of living, particularly in relation to developing technologies. Following a period of intense political and economic pressure the Bauhaus was forced to move to Dessau in 1925, relocating the following year to a building designed by Gropius. The move produced a further shift towards Constructivism and functionalism, with Moholy-Nagy and Josef ALBERS assuming responsibility for the preliminary course, whilst former student Herbert BAYER became head of the new department of typography and advertising. Throughout the productive and successful Dessau period, Moholy-Nagy and Bayer gave the Bauhaus journal, books and projects a distinctive visual identity. In 1928 Gropius, Marcel Breuer, Moholy-Nagy and Herbert Bayer resigned to pursue their own work. Hannes Meyer, a Swiss archi-

tect, was appointed director. Bayer's replacement was Joost SCHMIDT who broadened the principles established by Bayer, achieving particular success in the area of exhibition design. Continuing difficulties with the Dessau municipal authorities forced Meyer to resign in 1930. His successor was the distinguished architect Ludwig Mies van der Rohe, who created a short-lived stability before Nazi-dominated Dessau City Council withdrew all staff contracts in 1932. In a last desperate attempt at survival, Mies van der Rohe moved the Bauhaus to an empty telephone factory in Berlin. Political harassment continued, culminating in the seizure of the building by the Nazis in April 1933. The Bauhaus came to an abrupt end in July 1933 when the staff voted to dissolve the School with effect from the following month. The ideas and the subsequent achievements of Bauhaus staff and students, particularly in the US, have had a profound influence on architecture, design, and educational developments. The emphasis on rationality, the reliance on the GRID, the commitment to SANS SERIF typefaces, and the link with contemporary art movements provided an important springboard for the New Typography and the later INTERNATIONAL TYPOGRAPHIC STYLE.

Oskar Schlemmer's 1922 design for the **Bauhaus** seal.

Bawden, Edward (1903–89) Versatile and prolific English designer, illustrator and printmaker, particularly from work in LINOCUT, with a graphic style that combined a gentle humour and a strong sense of pattern. From 1922–25 trained at the Royal College of Art, London, under Paul NASH, where he met Eric RAVILIOUS. Much-travelled war artist during the Second World War. In addition to numerous and masterful book illustrations, Bawden worked over many years for the Curwen Press, Shell, Fortnum & Mason, National Westminster Bank and London Transport.

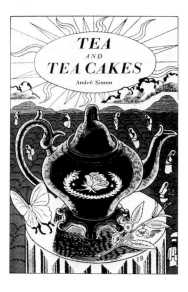

Book jacket designed by **Bawden** for the Wine and Food Society c. 1947.

Invitation to the last Bauhaus party in Weimar, March 1925, designed by **Bayer**.

His output during a seven-decade career embraced wallpapers, murals, textiles, posters, pattern papers and advertisements. Awarded a CBE in 1946, elected RDI in 1949 and RA (Royal Academy, London) in 1956.

Bayer, Herbert (1900–85) Austrian-born graphic and exhibition designer, architect, photographer and painter who pioneered MODERNISM in European and American design. Apprenticed to the architect Schmidthammer in Linz before moving to Darmstadt in 1920 to work for the architect Emanuel Margold. From 1921–23 studied at the BAUHAUS, Weimar, under Kandinsky and MOHOLY-NAGY. Developed quickly into a designer of wide-ranging abilities, designing a series of bold, functional typographic banknotes (inflation currency) for the State Bank of Thuringia in 1923. When the Bauhaus moved to Dessau in 1925, Bayer was appointed head of the new department of typography and advertising. His influence was immediate, as he used Bauhaus publications as a vehicle for radical typographic ideas. Advocated the use of SANS SERIF typefaces as the typographic expression of the age and with his geometric 'universal' alphabet (1925), which was never cut as a typeface, proposed the abolition of capital letters. In 1928 he left the Bauhaus to set up a studio in Berlin where he undertook advertising, typography, exhibition design, painting and photography. In 1930 he collaborated with GROPIUS, Moholy-Nagy and Marcel Breuer on the design of the DEUTSCHER WERKBUND exhibition in Paris and in 1931 with Gropius and Moholy-Nagy on the 'Building Workers Union Exhibition' in Berlin. Produced a typeface, Bayer-type, for the Berthold foundry, Berlin in 1933. His commitment to progressive ideas was apparent in his use of photography and photomontage in advertising and editorial design work. During the late 1920s he became art director of *VOGUE* magazine, whilst his colour photographic covers for the magazine *die neue linie*, 1930–36, demonstrate an extraordinarily creative imagination. Political unrest in Europe forced him to move to New York in 1938, becoming consultant art director throughout the war years to the advertising agencies J. Walter Thompson and Dorland International. Designed and contributed to the influential 1938 Bauhaus exhibition at the Museum of Modern Art, New York. In 1946 Bayer moved to Aspen, Colorado, becoming a leading educator at the Aspen Institute, for which he designed a series of buildings (he was one of the founders of the ASPEN INTERNATIONAL DESIGN CONFERENCE). Also began a long association with CONTAINER CORPORATION OF AMERICA, eventually in 1956 becoming chairman of its design department. Contributed to CCA's widely acclaimed 'Great Ideas of Western Man' advertising campaign and the ambitious *World Geo-Graphic Atlas* (1953). In addition to his own design achievements, Bayer was a leading commentator on the history and achievements of the Bauhaus.

Beall, Lester (1903–69) Contributor to the MODERN MOVEMENT in AMERICAN GRAPHIC DESIGN before the influx of European immigrant designers in the late 1930s. During the 1950s and 60s was responsible for numerous major CORPORATE IDENTITY programmes. Self-taught as a designer, although in 1926 received a doctorate in art history from the University of Chicago. Brought an understanding of European avant-garde art movements, including CONSTRUC-TIVISM, DADA and SURREALISM, to the practice of design. Worked as a freelance designer in Chicago before establishing his own New York practice in 1936. Between 1937 and 1941 produced a series of eight silkscreen posters for the Rural Electrification Administration which, with their strong flat colours and geometric simplicity, remain potent and enduring images. In 1951 Beall moved to a Connecticut farm where he produced corporate images for clients including International Paper Company, Martin Marietta and Connecticut General Life Insurance Company. He was an early innovator in the develop-ment of the DESIGN MANUAL as a method of controlling the disparate elements of a corporate identity scheme. A major figure in American design, becoming in 1937 the first American graphic designer to be honoured with a solo exhibition at the Museum of Modern Art, New York.

Beardsley, Aubrey (1872–98) Largely self-taught English ART NOUVEAU illustrator whose powerful and original black-and-white imagery symbolized the decadence of the 1890s. The grotesqueness of his characters was offset by a delicacy of line and tautness in design, probably derived from Japanese prints. First major commission in 1892, when he illustrated a new edition of Malory's *Morte d'Arthur*. In 1893 *The STUDIO*, England's leading Art Nouveau magazine, featured work by Beardsley in its first issue. He gained notori-ety through his controversial illustrations for Oscar Wilde's *Salomé* (1894) and for *The YELLOW BOOK*. Became art editor of *The Yellow Book* in 1894 but was forced to resign in 1895 in the aftermath of Wilde's public humiliation. In 1896 became art editor of the new magazine *The SAVOY*; the eight volumes of this fine publication are evidence of his maturing style. Beardsley's death from tuberculosis prematurely ended a unique talent.

Two posters designed by **Beall** in 1937, part of his series for the Rural Electrification Administration.

A version of *The Climax*, one of **Beardsley**'s illustrations to *Salomé*, first published in *The Studio* in 1893.

Beck's London Underground map, 1933.

One of the advertising posters commissioned by
Beddington for Shell c.1937; this example incorporates a
painting by Paul Nash.

Poster for the Lyceum production of Don Quixote, designed
in 1895 by the Beggarstaff Brothers.

Beck, Henry C. (1903–74) Designer of London
Underground diagrammatic map, a watershed in the
representation of public transport information and
an icon in British graphic design. Beck, a draughtsman
with London Transport, submitted a redesign of the
route guide in 1931. The design was given a trial printing in early 1933 after Frank Pick became vice-chairman and chief executive of the newly created London
Passenger Transport Board. The guide used geographical distortion (an enlargement of the central area in
relation to the outlying districts) with all routes
simplified to verticals, horizontals and 45° diagonals.
This clear diagrammatic solution proved immensely
popular with the public. Beck reworked numerous
subsequent editions until 1959 when the last map
bearing his name was printed.

Beddington, Jack (1893–1959) Innovatory British
design manager responsible for the enlightened publicity policy of Shell-Mex BP Limited during the 1930s.
Disliked the differentiation between art and design,
believing that 'the most effective of poster artists
were great artists in their own right'. Worked for
Shell-Mex 1927–38 and by commissioning highly
regarded British artists, including Rex Whistler, Paul
NASH and Edward BAWDEN he encouraged the production of posters that combined striking imagery,
expressive typography and clever headlines.

Beeke, Anthon (b.1940) Leading figure in development of the new-wave graphic design that emerged in
the Netherlands during the late 1970s and early 80s.
Conventions were overturned and the distinction
between function and decoration eroded. Whilst
working for TOTAL DESIGN in Amsterdam Beeke's freer,
more intuitive approach contrasted with the distinguished functional tradition of Total. Designed advertising, books, magazines, stamps, packaging and a
provocative series of posters for the Globe Theatre,
Eindhoven (1977–84). Established his own studio in
1981 in Amsterdam. His capacity for generating startling imagery is evident in the art direction of View on
Colour, a trend-forecasting magazine for the design
and fashion industries (launched in 1992). Beeke's
playfulness and invention have also been applied to
complex informational problems, including an unconventional SIGNAGE system for the Rotterdam Central
Library and a number of brochures and directories
for the Dutch Postal Service (PTT).

Beggarstaff Brothers, The William Nicholson
(1872–1949) and his brother-in-law James Pryde

(1866–1941) were respected British academic painters who adopted the pseudonym in 1894 to provide anonymity for their activities as poster artists. Until 1899 their collaboration produced bold and vigorous images which were to prove enormously influential for the illustrators of the 1920s, 30s and 40s. However, the conservatism of clients resulted in only a dozen of their posters being printed at the time. The famous poster designed in 1895 for Henry Irving's production of *Don Quixote* at the Lyceum Theatre, London, was rejected by Irving, only being printed some years later as a limited edition for collectors. The Beggarstaffs were influenced by Henri de TOULOUSE–LAUTREC but their style was distinct. Developed a collage technique that produced flat simplified shapes, often requiring the viewer to visualize missing contours. Colours were few and strong, lettering when used was hand drawn and integrated into the design. The immediacy of their sparse designs starkly contrasts with the florid ART NOUVEAU images of contemporary posters.

Behrens, Peter (1868-1940) Distinguished German architect and designer. Born in Hamburg, he trained as a painter at the Karlsruhe School of Art (1886-89) and under Ferdinand Brütt in Düsseldorf (1889). Began his career producing graphic design in the ART NOUVEAU style. In the late 1890s designed for several influential German journals including *Jugend, Die Insel* and *Der Bunte Vogel*. From 1903 until 1907 he directed the Düsseldorf School of Arts & Crafts. Behrens' significance lies in his reaction to Art Nouveau. Embracing the ideals of the ARTS AND CRAFTS MOVEMENT he sought a visual language to express the modern age of mass production. The turning point in his career came in 1907 when Emil Rathenau, director of the giant electrical corporation Allgemeine Elektricitaets Gesellschaft (AEG), invited him to Berlin to assume responsibility for all visual manifestations of the company including architecture, design of products and printed material. His subsequent design of AEG electrical goods is the first example of a coordinated industrial design programme for a major corporation. He created a visual unity in the printed material by the consistent use of typestyles, the famous honeycomb LOGOTYPE and by his concern for classical proportion in the arrangements of compositional elements. This visual co-ordination of AEG's activities is generally recognized as the earliest CORPORATE IDENTITY programme. Behrens became a founder member of the DEUTSCHER WERKBUND in 1907. In 1908 he created four typefaces for the Klingspor foundry (Behrensschrift, Behrens Antiqua, Behrens Cursiv, Behrens Mediäval). As AEG's architect he was responsible for the important 1909 turbine factory. Some of the century's leading architects were employed as assistants in his office: Walter GROPIUS, Ludwig Mies van der Rohe and Le Corbusier.

Bell Important ROMAN text TYPEFACE cut by Richard Austin for John Bell's British foundry in 1788. Generally regarded as the first British MODERN FACE, the design was part of the move towards more sharply cut letters which developed at that time. There is an obvious influence from the innovatory design developed by the Frenchman Firmin DIDOT in 1784 when he introduced a truly modern typeface with vertical STRESS and a marked contrast between the thick and thin strokes. Bell's design is less severe than the usual modern face, the SERIF strokes are bracketed, and offers a cursive ITALIC in the style of BASKERVILLE.

ABCDEFGH
abcdefgh

Letters from the **Bell** typeface.

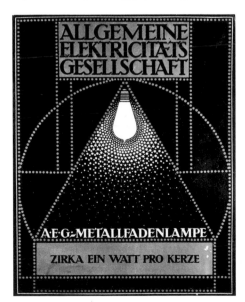

Behrens designed this poster for AEG electric light bulbs in c. 1910.

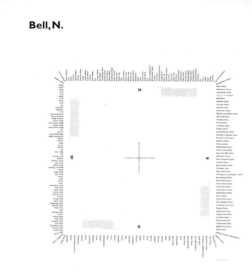

Screenprinted banqueting roll designed by Nick **Bell** for The British Council, 1999.

Bell, Nick (b.1965) British graphic designer, trained at the London College of Printing (1984–87) where, since 1990, he has been influential as a visiting tutor. The graphic-design journal EMIGRE (ISSUE 22, 1992) was dedicated to his activities and those of his students at the LCP. Bell's graphic-design practice was responsible for designing the college's prospectus and logo (1997–98). Immediately upon graduation, Bell worked for Siobhan KEANEY (1987–88). Both designers were influenced by the work of Dutch designer Gert DUMBAR who had been head of the graphic-design department at the Royal College of Art, London (1986–87). Bell is acclaimed for numerous, unconventional cover designs for the Virgin Classics labels, which challenged the design conventions of the classical-music industry. Since 1997, Bell has been a partner in UNA (London), a design group that is the London arm of the Amsterdam-based practice founded in 1987. This move further confirmed his alignment with the aesthetics of DUTCH GRAPHIC DESIGN. Key aspects of his practice include the subtle integration of image and type and his experiments in the process of communication. In 1997 he became art director of graphic-design journal, *EYE*. Under the editorship of John L Walters he subsequently became creative director. Bell's design has been exhibited in the British Council touring exhibition 'Lost & Found: Critical Voices in New British Design' (1999/2000). He has been featured in many publications including the important *Typography Now: The Next Wave* (1991). Bell and UNA have won numerous awards in Europe and America, including the Design Centre Essen's award for High Quality Design (2000).

ABCDEFGH
abcdefgh

Bembo, the first old face.

Benton's 1908 News Gothic typeface.

ABCDEFGH
abcdefgh

Bembo ROMAN text TYPEFACE, so called because it was originally used in Cardinal Bembo's book *De Aetna*, published by the Venetian printer Aldus Manutius in 1495. Cut by the punch-cutter Francesco Griffo, it is accepted as the first OLD FACE, and provided a model for European type design over the next two centuries. Bembo has an oblique STRESS and oblique top SERIF form in the lower case. The capitals are shorter than each ASCENDER of the lower case.

Benton, Morris Fuller (1872–1948) Prolific American type designer. Worked for many years with AMERICAN TYPE FOUNDERS COMPANY, latterly as chief designer. They commissioned Benton to design a number of popular SANS SERIF alphabets in the first decade of the century including Franklin Gothic (1903–12) and News Gothic (1908). Thereafter produced many SERIF, sans serif, DISPLAY and SCRIPT alphabets for ATF.

A 'mechano-faktura' design by **Berlewi** entitled *Composition in Red and Black* (1922).

Bernhard's prize-winning poster design for Priester matches, 1905.

Berlewi, Henryk (1894–1967) Polish-born contributor to the development of modern typography. Traditional art training in Antwerp and Paris, encountering CUBISM at the École des Beaux-Arts in Paris about 1912. In 1920 attended lectures given by El LISSITZKY in Warsaw. Went to Berlin in 1922 and over the next two years developed his theory of 'mechano-faktura' (mechanical reproduction), which sought to eliminate any three-dimensional illusions from his work. Berlewi created compositions by placing simple geometric forms and typographic elements on a ground, according to mathematical principles, using only red, black and white. In 1924 returned to Warsaw to become a partner in the innovative advertising agency Reklama Mechano, committed to bringing fine art forms into a commercial context. Moving to Paris in 1927, Berlewi surprisingly became involved in figurative painting. Pursued his mechano-faktura theories again after the Second World War.

Bernhard, Lucian (1883–1972) German poster and type designer. Born Emil Kahn, adopting the pseudonym in 1905. Largely self-taught, studying for brief periods at Akademie der Kunst, Munich, and in Berlin. Career launched in Berlin after winning a poster competition for Priester matches in 1905. Influenced by the work of the BEGGARSTAFF BROTHERS in England, particularly in his dramatic simplification of form, use of flat colours, and in the strength and placement of his illustrations. Bernhard's handling of type was outstanding. As a prolific TYPEFACE designer – for example, Fraktur (1913), Antiqua (1911) and Cursive (1925) – lettering was skilfully integrated within his poster and packaging designs. In 1910 he collaborated with Hans Sachs on the establishment of the magazine *Das Plakat* (see PLAKATSTIL), later renamed *Gebrauchsgraphik*. From 1914 to 1918 he produced many typographic posters on behalf of the German war effort. In 1920 he was appointed as the first professor of poster design at the Akademie der Kunst, Berlin. Following a move to New York in 1923, Bernhard combined teaching at the Art Students League and New York University, with his practice as a graphic and interior designer under the banner of Contempora (co-founded with Rockwell Kent, Paul Poiret and Bruno Paul). In 1928 he began a long professional relationship with AMERICAN TYPE FOUNDERS COMPANY, thereafter designing many popular typefaces including the SANS SERIF Gothic (1929–30) and Fashion (1929), and the SCRIPT Tango (1933).

Berthon, Paul (1872–1909) French ART NOUVEAU poster artist and decorator. After initial training as a painter in Villefranche moved to Paris in 1893, studying under Eugène GRASSET at the École Normale d'Enseignement du Dessin. His compositions are characterized by a strong sense of design and bold contours, complemented by a limited palette of analogous colours. His archetypal Art Nouveau images of young women in idealized floral settings, reflecting the influence of Grasset and Alphonse MUCHA, were popular on posters, magazine covers (*The POSTER*, May 1899) and interior decorative panels.

Bierut, Michael (b.1957) American graphic designer. Studied at the University of Cincinnati's College of Design, Art, Architecture and Planning, graduating in 1980. Joined VIGNELLI Associates in 1980, subsequently becoming vice-president of graphic design. Partner (1990) in PENTAGRAM, New York. Bierut's graphic output defies superficial categorization. He demonstrates an impressive level of graphic skill and invention, constantly challenging and re-examining established graphic conventions. This approach can be seen in his poster for the Next Wave Festival, Brooklyn Academy of Music (1995) and in the visual identity and architectural graphics for the Minnesota Children's Museum (1995). Through his involvement with the AIGA and education (since 1993 he has taught at the Yale School of Art), Bierut endeavours to strengthen the dialogue between graphic designers, design critics and the public. Co-editor of *Looking Closer: Critical Writings on Graphic Design* (1994) and *Looking Closer 2* (1996). He is also contributing editor to *I.D.* and *Interiors* magazines. Elected to the AGI in 1989. His work is represented in various museum collections, including the Museum of Modern Art, New York.

Bierut's environmental graphics for the Minnesota Children's Museum, 1995.

Catalogue cover designed by **Bill** for the 1944 'Concrete Art' exhibition at the Basle Museum of Art.

konkrete kunst

10 einzelwerke ausländischer künstler aus basler sammlungen
20 ausgewählte grafische blätter
30 fotos nach werken ausländischer künstler
10 œuvre-gruppen von   arp
                         bill
                         bodmer
                         kandinsky
                         klee
                         leuppi
                         lohse
                         mondrian
                         taeuber-arp
                         vantongerloo

kunsthalle basel   18. märz-16. april 1944

Bill, Max (1908–94) Swiss architect, painter and sculptor as well as graphic, exhibition and industrial designer. Pre-war pioneer of the INTERNATIONAL TYPOGRAPHIC STYLE. Studied silversmithing at the Kunstgewerbeschule, Zurich (1924–27), then at the BAUHAUS, Dessau (1927–29). Central figure in the Zurich Group, which included Josef MÜLLER-BROCKMANN. In 1931 Bill adopted Theo Van DOESBURG's concept of 'concrete art', which advocated a universal art of absolute clarity. In attempting to apply a purist aesthetic and impose a strict visual discipline on disparate design elements, Bill employed modular grids and mathematical progressions. During the 1930s and 40s he often utilized Akzidenz Grotesque, a SANS SERIF typeface, in his posters. In 1950 Bill became involved with the design of buildings and planning of curriculum for the ULM HOCHSCHULE FÜR GESTALTUNG, becoming its first rector (1951–57) and director of the departments of architecture and product design.

Binder, Joseph (1898–1972) Austrian-born designer instrumental in the development of MODERNISM in America during the late 1930s and 40s. Studied at the State School of Applied Arts in Vienna under its director Alfred ROLLER. His 1924 award-winning *Musik und Theaterfest* poster for the Buro des Festes, Vienna, demonstrates an early ability to refine and reduce pictorial elements, achieving a controlled geometric severity which was to become more marked in his mature work. In 1934 he emigrated to the US and in 1939 designed the poster for the New York World's Fair. His reputation was further enhanced following successes in poster competitions organized by the Museum of Modern Art for agencies like the National Defence, the United Nations and the American Red Cross. Designed covers for *FORTUNE* and *GRAPHIS* magazines. In the 1940s and 50s Binder produced powerful graphic statements including a series of memorable recruitment posters for the US forces.

binding methods Ways of securing pages of book or brochure on left-hand edge (spine). Detachable, loose-leaf methods include a slide-on plastic spine, metal ring binders inside an outer cover, or a plastic comb binding inserted through a series of punched holes. Permanent, more traditional methods include saddle-stitching (usually two wire staples through the centrefold of each double spread), side-stitching (staples punched through the book on the left-hand side, slightly to the right of the spine), section-sewn (traditional method with individual sections collated and sewn together at the spine using thread), perfect-binding (no staples or sewing required, pages are glued together and attached to the inner spine of the cover; as used in paperbacks).

Birdsall, Derek (b.1934) British graphic designer and typographer. Trained at Wakefield College of Art, 1949–52 and Central School of Art and Design, London, 1952–55. A principal of BDMW Associates, London, 1960–65, designing the first of the famous Pirelli calendars in 1964. Birdsall's work consistently displays a taut visual and typographic order. He has designed literature for Lotus cars, CORPORATE IDENTITY schemes for both Dorothy Gray cosmetics and United Overseas Bank, Singapore, a number of Monty Python books and many Penguin book jackets. He has art directed *Town, Twen, Nova* and *Connoisseur* magazines and in 1988 was appointed consultant to the colour magazine of the *Independent* newspaper, London. Throughout the 1970s edited and designed a number of books including *A Book of Chess* (1974) and *The Technology of Man* (1978). Design consultant to Mobil Oil Corporation, United Technologies Corporation and IBM Europe. Founder partner of Omnific Studios, London in 1978. In 2000, assisted by

One of the US forces recruitment posters designed by **Binder** (1941).

Birdsall's July 1968 cover design for *Nova* magazine.

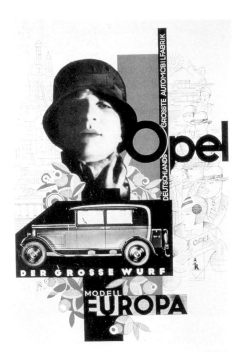

Modell Europa, an example of **Bittrof**'s design work for Opel, 1928.

Text printed in **Black Letter** typeface.

𝔔uod tũ audiſſet dauid:deſcendit in preſidiũ.Philiſtijm autem venientes diffuſſi ſunt in valle raphaim.Et cõ-ſuluit dauid dñm dicens.Si aſcendã ad philiſtijm·et ſi dabis eos ĩ manu mea? Et dixit dñs ad dauid. Aſcende: q̃a tradens dabo philiſtijm in manu tua. Venit ergo dauid ad baalphara-ſim:et percuſſit eos ibi et dixit.Diuiſit dñs inimicos meos corã me:ſicut di-uiduntur aque.Propterea vocatũ ẽ no-men loci illi⁹ baalpharaſim.Et reliq̃-runt ibi ſculptilia ſua:q̃ tulit dauid et

---

John Morgan of Omnific, he redesigned the Church of England's *Common Worship* prayer book. ART DIRECTORS CLUB OF NEW YORK gold award for his book *Shaker Design*, 1987. Visiting Professor of Graphic Arts and Design, Royal College of Art, London 1987–88.

Bittrof, Max (b.1890–1972) German graphic designer whose career and output reflects the dramatic cultural and political changes of mid-20th-c. Germany. Born in Frankfurt-an-der-Oder, Bittrof trained at Krefeld and Wuppertal–Elberfeld, combining a printing apprenticeship with evening classes. Settled in Frankfurt-am-Main, where he contributed to the aesthetic experiments of the NEW TYPOGRAPHY during the 1920s, although without much evident concern for the theoretical basis underpinning the movement. In 1923 he became co-founder of the German Association of Graphic Designers (BDG) – a professional body that continues to represent the interests of German designers. Bittrof is acclaimed for his influential work for car manufacturer Opel (1927–29), for whom he designed an integrated CORPORATE IDENTITY programme and an extensive range of promotional material that relied upon a rational modernist vocabulary of SANS SERIF typefaces, elemental forms and photomontage. His contemporary influence can be gauged by the inclusion of a fourteen-page article on his work in the December 1928 issue of GEBRAUCHSGRAPHIK. Bittrof's commitment to a modernist design aesthetic was undermined by the Nazi distrust of the New Typography and, in 1934, he created the GOTHIC typeface Element in direct contradiction to the principles of the New Typography. Following World War II, Bittrof produced banknote and stamp designs for West Germany and established a long design association with the electronics company Telefonbau and Normalzeit, Frankfurt. His influence spread when he began teaching graphic design at Westend, a private school in Frankfurt, in 1960.

Black Letter Category of TYPEFACE created by German printers from the 1450s onwards to simulate the Gothic handwriting practised by scribes during the earlier decades of that century. The development of Black Letter reflected the spread of printing south across the Alps, with the individual characters gradually becoming lighter and more ROMAN in response to national and regional handwriting styles. Despite poor legibility when characters are grouped, Black Letter remained popular, particularly in Germany, up to the beginning of the Second World War. (Also known as GOTHIC, Fraktur, Textura, Old English.)

Blechman, R.O. (b.1930) American illustrator and animator, born Brooklyn, New York. Self- taught, graduating in history from Oberlin College, Ohio, 1952. Published *The Juggler of Our Lady* in 1952, since when his distinctive line drawings have appeared widely in magazines, books, advertisements, murals, animated films and TV commercials. His editorial work for *Esquire, Time* and the *NewYork Times* regularly demonstrates an ability to present complex social issues in a memorable graphic form. Executed three murals for the US pavilion at Expo '67 in Montreal and for the Hall of Man, Museum of Natural History in 1977. In 1974 he produced his first cover for *The New Yorker* magazine. Advertising commissions have included work for Sony, Volvo and Olivetti. His animated films often tackle biblical themes, as in his 1978 film *No Room at the Inn.* He has been a director of New York animation studio The Ink Tank since 1978, winning an Emmy in 1984 for 'outstanding individual achievement in animation programming'. In 1991, became the sole cover artist for American literary journal *Story*. Blechman's genius is to combine his comic storytelling talents with a unique and instantly recognizable graphic style. *Behind the Lines* (1980) is Blechman's own account of his career up to that time.

Illustration by **Blechman** for a Grossmont District Hospital advertisement, 1988.

bleed That part of a printed image which extends beyond the normal illustration area to the trimmed edge of a book or magazine page. Also known as 'bled off'.

blind embossed Raised surface impression created by die-stamp being pressed into surface of paper or card. Called 'blind' because the die-stamp is not inked or foiled.

Bodoni Popular MODERN FACE designed about 1785 by Giambattista Bodoni (1740–1813), an innovative printer and type designer of Parma, Italy. Like the BELL typeface, Bodoni was heavily influenced by Firmin DIDOT's modern face, designed in 1784. Many 20th-c. versions, while varying in detail from the original, retain the essential characteristics of Bodoni's innovation. The STRESS is vertical. Each SERIF is flat and unbracketed, with the sharp contrast in stroke weight emphasized by the thin hairline strokes.

body matter/text Text matter or reading matter in any publication, distinct from the headings or DISPLAY setting.

body type Term for type sizes, normally from 6 to 14 POINT, used for text setting or reading matter.

ABCDEFGH
abcdefgh

Part of the **Bodoni** typeface.

Bold
Medium

Medium and **bold** versions of the Helvetica typeface.

Poster for the magazine *La Revue Blanche*, designed in 1894 by **Bonnard**.

Boom's dust jacket for the book *Otto Treumann*, 1998.

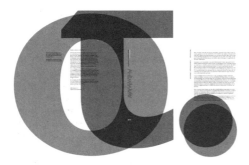

bold, bold face Bold TYPEFACE, normally heavier, blacker version of standard weight of the same typeface/FONT.

bond paper Originally used for government bonds and legal documents, bond paper is a strong, evenly finished paper normally used for stationery requirements such as writing and typing. It also provides a reasonable printing surface.

Bonnard, Pierre (1867–1947) French painter who designed a few influential ART NOUVEAU posters. Closely associated with TOULOUSE-LAUTREC and a member of the Nabis group of painters who were interested in the decorative arts. In 1888 studied painting at the École des Beaux-Arts and at the Académie Julian in Paris. His most famous posters were for *France Champagne* (1891) and *La Revue Blanche* (1894). Stylistically indebted to the formal devices of Japanese prints, Bonnard employed flat planes of colour, japonist silhouettes and arabesques. Along with Toulouse-Lautrec and Jules CHÉRET, paved the way for the modern advertising poster.

book face Style and weight of TYPEFACE suitable for large areas of reading matter, e.g. CASLON or TIMES NEW ROMAN.

Boom, Irma (b.1961) Dutch graphic designer. Educated at the AKI Art School in Enschedé, Holland, where she studied painting before transferring to graphic design. Worked for SDU Ontwerpgroep in The Hague, the organization responsible for producing all printed material for the Dutch government, where clients included the PTT (the Postal, Telegraph and Telephone authority), Rand voor de Kunst (the Dutch Arts Council) and the Holland Festival. Since 1990 Boom has practised as a freelance designer in Amsterdam. She is particularly acclaimed for her highly experimental approach to the design of books and catalogues, whereby the material form of the book is explored and pushed to its limits. An example of her treatment of the book as a beautiful object is *thinkbook* (1996), a 2136-page commemorative volume documenting the history of Dutch multinational Steenkolen Handels Vereniging (SHV Holdings). Boom has taught at various academies in Holland and America including Yale School of Art in New Haven, where she has been since 1992.

border Continuous, ornamental elements which combine to produce a frame or rule for highlighting text or illustration. The individual repetitive devices

Cover of *The Chap Book* magazine, by **Bradley**, 1894.

Poster designed by **Brattinga** entitled 'Chris de Moor – The Man Behind the Design of PTT' (the Dutch Post Office), 1960.

(rules, dots, flowers, etc.) are normally available in a range of sizes to match the POINT size of each TYPEFACE.

Bradley, Will (1868–1962) Celebrated American graphic designer and art editor. Self-taught, he was influenced by the British ARTS AND CRAFTS MOVEMENT. Began as an errand boy for a Michigan newspaper and spent a period as an apprentice engraver before becoming a typographic designer with a Chicago printing company. Between 1894 and 1896 he designed eighteen covers for the technical journal *The Inland Printer*, which demonstrate his familiarity with Arts and Crafts imagery, ranging from the heavy ornamentation of William MORRIS to the delicate sinuous contours of Aubrey BEARDSLEY. These covers and his series for *The Chap Book* (1894) herald the arrival of ART NOUVEAU in America. In 1895 he established the Wayside Press, producing books, advertisements and his own short-lived literary journal *Bradley: His Book* (1896). During this period he discovered the Boston Public Library collection of books printed in colonial New England. The robust and vigorous style of these publications with their CASLON OLD FACE types and bold WOODCUT illustrations revealed a new design direction which became known as the CHAP BOOK STYLE. During the early 1900s Bradley acted as a consultant to AMERICAN TYPE FOUNDERS COMPANY, producing forms of TYPEFACE and ORNAMENT and writing and designing their series of twelve magazines *The American Chap Book*. After 1907 he concentrated upon editorial design, making a valuable contribution to the development of the modern magazine as art editor of *Collier's* magazine and art director of the Hearst chain of publications in the 1920s. Retired in 1930.

Brattinga, Pieter (b.1931) Dutch graphic designer, educator and author. Professor and chairman of the department of advertising design and visual communication at Pratt Institute, New York, 1960–63. Editor, and sometime designer, of a series of experimental publications called *Quadrat Prints* for Steendrukkerij de Jong and Company, Hilversum, 1957–74. Since 1964 he has been a partner of Form Mediation International, Amsterdam, designing catalogues, posters and exhibitions for the Rijksmuseum Kroller-Muller, Otterlo; also designed the Museum's exhibitions of the work of DE STIJL (1982) and Vincent Van Gogh (1990). Design consultant to the Dutch State Mines. Recipient of the Grafische Cultuurprijs in 1998. His books include *A History of the Dutch Poster 1890–1960* (1968) with Dick Dooijes, and *Sandberg, A Documentary* (1975) with Ad Petersen.

Part of the commemorative wall 'Biddy Mason: Time and Place' (1989) designed by de **Bretteville**.

Bretteville, Sheila Levrant de (b.1940) Graphic designer and teacher concerned with the visual presentation of social issues, particularly relating to women. Graduated in art history from Bernard College, New York, 1962, and in graphic design from Yale University, New Haven, 1964. She created the first design programme for women at California Institute of the Arts (1971) and founded the Women's Graphic Center at 'The Woman's Building' (1973), a centre for female culture in Los Angeles. From 1981–91 she led the department of communication design and illustration at Otis Art Institute of Parsons School of Design, Los Angeles, where she established the Brooklyn Design Workshop, which provides an opportunity for student designers to work on alternative, non-profit-making projects. During the 1980s she ran her own graphic design studio in Los Angeles with clients including Olivetti, Warner Bros, and the *Los Angeles Times*. Publications designed include *Chrysalis*, a quarterly magazine which addresses female issues, and two books documenting Judy Chicago's *The Dinner Party* (1978/79). Designed a commemorative wall in California, 'Biddy Mason: Time and Place' (1989). In 1991 became director of the graduate programme on graphic design, Yale University.

'Britain Can Make It' exhibition Held in London in 1946, this was a British government initiative to promote good design to manufacturers and the public. Supported by Sir Stafford Cripps, director of the Board of Trade of the post-war Labour government. Designed by James Gardner, the exhibition displays acknowledged a link between 'contemporary' design and the imagery of SURREALISM, providing a foretaste of the graphic style and wit associated with the 1951 FESTIVAL OF BRITAIN.

British graphic design From the 1850s graphic art in Britain increasingly reflected the decorative and extravagant excesses of Victorian taste. This drift towards vulgarity and shoddy workmanship was challenged by William MORRIS who emphasized the need for a return to medieval standards of printing and book production. His campaign achieved momentum and widespread recognition in 1890 when he established the KELMSCOTT PRESS. The ART WORKER'S GUILD and the ARTS AND CRAFTS EXHIBITION SOCIETY were also sympathetic to Morris's ideals. The launch of *The STUDIO* magazine in 1893 provided a focus for ART NOUVEAU in England. There was a foretaste of future educational developments when the Central School of Arts and Crafts, London was established in 1896 'to encourage the industrial application of decorative arts'. In the early 1900s Britain failed to embrace the MODERN MOVEMENT, with the legacy of Morris and the ARTS AND CRAFTS MOVEMENT still apparent in the consistent emphasis on tradition and craftsmanship. The DESIGN AND INDUSTRIES ASSOCIATION (DIA) was founded in 1915, with an opening exhibition at the Whitechapel Gallery, London, on 'Design and Workmanship in Printing'. Poster artists like the BEGGARSTAFF BROTHERS, John HASSALL and Dudley HARDY gained widespread popularity, with Frank PICK at London Transport providing new commercial opportunities for artists. In 1916 Pick commissioned a London Transport typeface from Edward JOHNSTON. A potent image of this period was Alfred LEETE's First World War *Your Country Needs You* recruitment poster, which featured Lord Kitchener. The 1920s saw the emergence of progressive advertising agencies, like S.H. Bellsoll and W.S. Crawford, where Ashley HAVINDEN quickly became an influential art director. The most innovative poster artist throughout the 1920s and 30s was E. McKnight KAUFFER, determinedly pursuing European developments in MODERNISM. Typographic design at this time was dominated by Stanley MORISON and Beatrice WARDE and their type development programme at the MONOTYPE Corporation. Morison's emphasis on tradition was instrumental in Britain's rejection of the INTERNATIONAL TYPOGRAPHIC STYLE. The creation of the Society of Industrial Artists (later known as the CHARTERED SOCIETY OF DESIGNERS) in 1930 provided a forum for professional debate. In the mid-30s the influx of a group of European émigrés including F.H.K. HENRION and Hans SCHLEGER was to provide an input of radical thinking. At the outset of the Second World War the Ministry of Information (MOI) became a major design patron for an emerging generation of designers, including Milner GRAY,

Henrion, Schleger and George Him. Abram GAMES worked for the public relations department of the War Office, creating many distinguished posters. The FESTIVAL OF BRITAIN (1951) dominated the early 1950s, with its influence most apparent in the typographic vogue for early 19th-c. DISPLAY faces. The late 1950s saw a move away from commercial art to the professional practice of graphic design, apparent in the CORPORATE IDENTITY programmes carried out by newly created practices like Hans Schleger Associates, and Henrion Design Associates. These groups signalled the demise of the individual design 'stars' of earlier decades. The swinging 1960s produced POP ART and PSYCHEDELIA. By contrast, public sector design initiatives gained increased prominence: Jock KINNEIR's road and motorway SIGNAGE systems were followed by an outstanding corporate identity programme for British Rail by DESIGN RESEARCH UNIT (1964) and by the Post Office's adventurous stamp design programme initiated in 1966. The establishment of the DESIGNERS AND ART DIRECTORS ASSOCIATION (1962) encouraged new standards of excellence in graphic design and advertising. This coincided with the arrival of several influential US designers to Britain including Robert BROWN-JOHN, Bob GILL and Lou KLEIN. Fletcher, Forbes and Gill, the forerunner of PENTAGRAM, was established in 1962. The late 1960s signalled a period of growth for graphic design practice with the establishment of a number of important consultancies. Many major corporate design schemes were initiated throughout the 1970s with design becoming more aligned with big business. British advertising achieved international recognition, with the surreal Benson & Hedges cigarettes campaign (by Collett Dickenson Pearce) and the 1979 Conservative Party general election campaign (by Saatchi & Saatchi) being of particular note. The visual manifestations of PUNK in the late 1970s were partially a response to the growing influence of corporate attitudes within all branches of design activity. Throughout the 1980s many small groups emerged to challenge the major consultancies. Design and style became synonymous, with an increase in retail design and the establishment of lifestyle magazines like *i-D* and *The Face*. The art director of *The Face*, Neville BRODY, achieved widespread acclaim for his adoption of POST-MODERNISM in typography and editorial design. The growth in popularity of the APPLE MACINTOSH COMPUTER made design more accessible to non-professionals, whilst it created new standards of production efficiency in design studios. British advertising continued to produce quality work, with television commercials and pop videos exploring new imagery made possible by developments in computer animation. The early 1990s saw a contraction in the design business, resulting in the decline, if only temporary, of the major design consultancies.

Brno: International Biennale of Graphic Design Originating in 1964, this exhibition is held every two years in Brno, Czechoslovakia, and provides an opportunity to survey contemporary graphic design practice within a broad political and social context. It is supported by a lecture programme. A distinguished jury awards the grand prix, the gold, silver and bronze medals.

Symbol of the **Brno International Biennale**.

Brodovitch, Alexey (1898–1971) American editorial art director and photographer. Born in Russia, Brodovitch worked in Paris designing and illustrating store displays, advertising, books and theatrical sets before moving to America in 1930. Established and directed the department of advertising design at what is now the Philadelphia College of Art, 1930–38. Also freelanced for the N.W. AYER advertising agency and other clients. Following an invitation from the editor, Carmel Snow, he became art director of *HARPER'S BAZAAR* in 1934. Remained for twenty-five years, redefining the role of the art director and introducing new ideas in editorial graphics and photography. His dynamic layouts combined bold typography with adventurous fashion and reportage photography, from great photographers like Man RAY, Henri Cartier-Bresson, Richard Avedon and Irving Penn. In a continuing search for innovation he commissioned covers and editorial illustrations from artists and illustrators including A.M. CASSANDRE, Herbert BAYER and Salvador Dali. Brodovitch's significance lies in his ability to organize the sequential flow of a magazine by controlling the juxtaposition of images on each double spread. Throughout his time at *Harper's Bazaar* he also freelanced, designing advertisements for Saks of Fifth Avenue, New York,

February 1939 cover design of American *Harper's Bazaar*, by **Brodovitch**, celebrating the New York World's Fair.

Cover and inner sleeve for Cabaret Voltaire's 1984 record *Micro-Phonies*, designed by **Brody**.

1939–41, producing photographic books and designing the short-lived, but innovative, large-format magazine *Portfolio* (1950–51). Brodovitch was an influential teacher, holding classes at his home-based design laboratory in the 1930s, and at the New School for Social Research, New York, during the 1940s. His protégés included Otto STORCH and Henry WOLF, appointed as Brodovitch's successor at *Harper's Bazaar* in 1958.

Brody, Neville (b.1957) British art director, graphic designer and typographer. Trained at the London College of Printing, 1976–79. Early work as record cover designer at Al McDowell's practice Rocking Russian and for the independent labels Stiff Records and Fetish Records. From 1981–86 art editor of British style magazine *The Face*, for which he designed the geometric *Typeface Six* (1986). His POST-MODERNISM, in the aftermath of PUNK, challenged most of the conventions in editorial design. Designed and manipulated many images and varieties of TYPEFACE into new, often illegible, shapes and proportions. Cover designer for the London weekly guide *City Limits* 1983–87. In 1987 designed *Arena* (a lifestyle magazine for men) in a distinctly neutral, less frenetic typographic style. Formed in the late 1980s, his London design practice attracts corporate and fashion projects from abroad. One of the new generation of designers to embrace the creative potential of the APPLE MACINTOSH, he has also designed four new fonts for LINOTYPE. His ideas are outlined in *The Graphic Language of Neville Brody* (1988), and *The Graphic Language of Neville Brody 2* (1994). An exhibition of his work was held at the Victoria & Albert Museum, London, 1988. Partner with Erik SPIEKERMANN in FontWorks, a company specializing in the supply of typefaces for computerized PostScript printers. Since 1990 Brody has art directed *Fuse*, an interactive type magazine.

Brownjohn, Robert (1925–70) American graphic designer. A founder of the design office, Brownjohn, Chermayeff & Geismar, established in New York in 1957. The practice gained a reputation for typographic invention and a fresh approach to image-making, particularly in the design of book jackets and record covers. Brownjohn studied painting and design under László MOHOLY-NAGY and architecture under Serge Chermayeff. In 1958 the partners designed a major exhibition, 'Streetscape' for the US pavilion at the Brussels World's Fair. When Brownjohn left in 1960, to join J. WALTER THOMPSON, London, the practice was renamed CHERMAYEFF & GEISMAR INC. During his time in

Peace poster designed by **Brownjohn** in 1970.

Brun's advertising poster for Maryland cigarettes, 1950.

England, Brownjohn's visual wit was a major influence on British graphic designers. Towards the end of his brief career his design of film title sequences gained widespread acclaim, with those for the James Bond film *Goldfinger* (1964) being of particular note.

Brun, Donald (b.1909) Swiss graphic and exhibition designer. Began his career in a graphic design studio in Basle whilst also studying at the Allgemeine Gewerbeschule. Further training in Berlin at the Akademie für Freie und Angewandte Kunst before returning to Basle to establish a practice in 1933. Acclaimed over four decades for the gentle humour of his posters, Brun's output displays an impressive range of techniques. His exhibition design includes two pavilions for the Swiss National Exhibition, Zurich 1939, stands at the Brussels World's Fair (1958) and the Lausanne Expo (1964). In addition he is a regular contributor to the annual Schweizer Mustermesse in Basle. Teacher at the Kunstgewerbeschule, Basle 1947–74. Founder member of AGI.

Bubbles, Barney (1942–83) London-based designer. Born Colin Fulcher, he is renowned for his distinctive contribution to the graphic design associated with the British independent music scene during the late 1970s and early 80s. Brought an informed awareness of 20th-c. art and design movements (particularly Russian CONSTRUCTIVISM and FUTURISM) to post-PUNK imagery. His significance has been difficult to assess because of his refusal to sign work. He committed suicide in 1983.

Logotype designed by **Bubbles** in 1977 for Ian Dury's Blockheads.

Opening woodcut illustration by **Burne-Jones** for the 1896 Kelmscott Press edition of *The Canterbury Tales*.

Burne-Jones, Sir Edward (1833–98)

Pre-Raphaelite painter, illustrator and designer of stained glass, tapestry and tiles. Close friend of William MORRIS whom he met at Exeter College, Oxford. Designed stained glass and hangings for Morris's home, the Red House (1860). In 1861 involved in the establishment of Morris's decorative arts company. His output as an illustrator was primarily through Morris's KELMSCOTT PRESS. *The Works of Geoffrey Chaucer* (1896), a magnificent 565-page volume which was four years in production, contained eighty-seven WOODCUT illustrations by Burne-Jones. In 1897 he became an honorary member of the VIENNA SECESSION.

Burns, Aaron (1922–91)

American typographic designer in the forefront of the technological revolution in TYPEFACE design and manufacture. During the late 1940s he was employed by several New York studios, including briefly – as assistant to Herb LUBALIN – at the advertising agency Sudler and Hennessy (1948). In 1952 he became director of The Composing Room, New York, an important type house which set and sold type commercially and was instrumental in improving standards of advertising typography. Responsible for numerous guides dedicated to educating designers about type and technology. The first, *typography* (1961), concentrated on the expressive potential of typography freed from the constraints of hot metal. Worked for the innovative type shop TGC in New York where he produced *The TGC Handbook of Linofilm Technology*. In 1970, along with Herb Lubalin and Edward Rondthaler, founded the INTERNATIONAL TYPEFACE CORPORATION (ITC) which developed typefaces for PHOTOCOMPOSITION and DIGITIZATION. In the late 1980s collaborated with Herman ZAPF on the development of style guides for the non-professional, with the aim of ensuring that effective typographic communication is achieved with the new technology and personal computers.

Burtin, Will (1908–72)

BAUHAUS-influenced graphic and exhibition designer. Trained as a typographer and designer at the Werkschule, Cologne, Germany, where he later taught. Emigrated to the US in 1938. Married the graphic designer Cipe PINELES in 1961. Designed exhibition units for the Federal Pavilion at the 1939 New York World's Fair. From 1943–45 involved in the American war effort producing training manuals and exhibitions for the Office of Strategic Services and the US Army Air Corps. In 1945 Burtin became art director of *FORTUNE* magazine, where he devised innovative solutions to the problems of graphically presenting complex technical information. In 1949 established his own design practice in New York with clients including Union Carbide, Eastman Kodak, the Smithsonian Institution and Upjohn Pharmaceutical Company. Through the design of *Scope*, the Upjohn journal for physicians, and his award-winning exhibitions, Burtin made important advances in making scientific knowledge more accessible. For an Upjohn exhibition in 1958 he created a model representing the structure and functions of a human cell enlarged one million times, enabling the public to walk around inside it. Other models concerned with human science followed, including one of the human brain (1960). He was American President of AGI and in 1971 was awarded a gold medal and a retrospective exhibition by AIGA.

Device by **Caflisch** for the Swiss Booksellers' and Publishers' catalogue cover, c. 1950.

'Beautiful writing requires gaiety for its execution': an example of **calligraphy** by Alfred Fairbank, British teacher, type designer, calligrapher and founder in 1952 of the Society for Italic Handwriting.

Letters from the **cameo** version of Gill Sans typeface.

C

C series of envelope sizes See A, B, C SYSTEM OF STANDARD PAPER SIZES

CAD See COMPUTER-AIDED DESIGN

Caflisch, Max (b.1916) Swiss book designer and typographer who trained as a compositor's apprentice 1932–36. Studied typography and calligraphy in Zurich and Basle, receiving additional practical training from Jan TSCHICHOLD and Imre REINER. Art director of the Benteli AG publishing house in Switzerland 1941–62 where he adopted a restrained classical approach to typography. Responsible for numerous award-winning book designs and for the creation of the TYPEFACE Columna (1955). Taught typography at the Kunstgewerbeschule, Zurich, 1962–81. In 1965 he received two gold medals at the Leipzig Book Exhibition and again in 1970 was awarded the Golden Letter for the 'best designed book of the world'.

caliper Thickness of a sheet of paper or board measured in microns (millionths of a metre) or mils (thousandths of an inch).

calligraphy 'Beautiful writing', derived from the Greek words *kalli* and *graphos*. The craft of calligraphy requires an understanding of formal penmanship and a respect for traditional materials and tools. The classic text on Western calligraphy is Edward JOHNSTON's *Writing & Illuminating & Lettering* (1906). A new generation of practitioners in Europe and the US is now challenging the emphasis on medieval standards and exploring new forms of expression. Great 20th-c. calligraphers, in addition to Johnston, include Rudolf KOCH, Imre REINER, William Addison DWIGGINS, Berthold WOLPE, and Herman ZAPF.

cameo Term applied to a TYPEFACE in which individual characters are reversed white out of a solid or shaded background.

camera-ready Generic term for ARTWORK that is ready for reproduction by the process camera prior to printing.

Cuisine Electrique, a luminous poster by **Carlu**, 1935.

capital letters/capitals Term for the larger letters in a FONT of type, e.g. A, B, C, D, E, F, G, etc. The term derives from their use as inscriptional lettering on the capitals (or heads) of Roman columns. In typographic usage often abbreviated to 'caps'. Also known as upper case or majuscules. See SMALL CAPITALS

Carlu, Jean (1900–97) French graphic designer and illustrator. Began training as an architect but, at the age of eighteen, lost his right arm in an accident. Thereafter focused on commercial art, exploiting a feeling for architectural form and familiarity with modern European art movements. Employed the geometry and symbolic imagery of CUBISM to produce direct, concise images which display an almost scientific exactness. During the 1920s and 30s became established, alongside A.M. CASSANDRE and Paul COLIN, as a leading French poster artist. As artistic and technical advisor to the French Information Service, visited the US in 1940 to organize an exhibition on the theme of 'France at War' at the New York World's Fair. After learning that the Germans had invaded Paris, remained to produce some of his finest work in the US. Created terse, potent images to support the war effort including the first US defence poster, entitled *America's Answer – Production* (1941), which won a medal from the ART DIRECTORS CLUB OF NEW YORK and was voted poster of the year. Carlu also contributed to the innovative advertising campaigns of CONTAINER CORPORATION OF AMERICA and his designs include a poster series for Pan American Airways, 1947–48. In 1953 returned to France, becoming consultant to various companies including Air France, Larousse and Firestone France. Retired in 1974.

Carson, David (b. 1956) American graphic designer whose influential POST-MODERN graphic style served to radically challenge the conventions of traditional editorial and advertising design during the late 1980s and the 1990s. Originally trained as a sociologist, Carson's formal design education was confined to workshops in America and Switzerland. After periods teaching sociology and as a world-ranking professional surfer, he developed his experimental and intuitive approach whilst working as designer and art director on a number of youth-oriented magazines, including *Transworld Skateboarding* (1983–87), *Musician*, *Beach Culture* and *Surfer*. In 1992 he launched *Ray Gun*, a music and style magazine that brought his work to an international audience and had a huge impact on a generation of young designers. Carson playfully manipulates and blurs text and image to reflect and amplify content and meaning, encouraging closer engagement from the viewer. His style employs asymmetrical layouts, pages of densely layered images, and fragmented typefaces of contrasting weights, sizes and forms. He left *Ray Gun* in 1995 to establish David Carson Design, New York, attracting such clients as Nike, Microsoft, Levis, Xerox, Armani. Produced two books with Lewis Blackwell, *The End of Print* (1995) and *David Carson:2nd sight* (1997). A multimedia solo exhibition of his work was held at Die Neue Sammlung Museum, Munich (1995) and subsequently travelled to Dusseldorf, Paris, London and America. Carson collaborated with William Burroughs on a short film that accompanied the exhibition.

Carter, Mathew (b.1937) TYPEFACE designer who works in US and Britain. Originally trained as a punch cutter and typefounder at Enschedé. Cut replacement punches for the Fell collection at Oxford University Press. Freelanced in England before going to US in 1960. Worked as typographic consultant to Crosfield Electronics, 1963–65 before becoming a staff designer at Mergenthaler Linotype, New York, where he created new faces and converted existing ones for PHOTOCOMPOSITION. Returned to London in 1971 to freelance, continuing to work for Linotype. Designed the type family Bell Centennial, commissioned in 1978 by AT&T for use in US telephone directories. Typographic consultant to Her Majesty's Stationery Office (HMSO) 1980-84. Co-founder and creative director of Bitstream Inc., Massachusetts, producing fonts for computerized image-setting. Increasingly committed to the development of programmes to improve the design and typographic performance of amateur personal computer programs. Type designs include Snell Roundhand, Cascade Script, Helvetica Compressed, Olympian and Galliard.

cartridge paper Strong, general-purpose paper with a rough or matt surface which is suitable for drawing, endpapers and book jackets. OFFSET cartridge is specially made for printing. It is a well-sized paper and perfectly even-sided.

Casey, Jacqueline (1927–92) American graphic designer who trained at Massachusetts College of Art before working as a fashion illustrator and advertising, editorial and interior designer. In 1955 joined the Office of Publications (Design Services Office) at Massachusetts Institute of Technology (MIT), working with Muriel COOPER who was then Design Director. Casey's work acknowledges the influence of the GRID established by the post-war graphic design masters in Switzerland. As Director of Design Services many of her posters have been created to publicize exhibitions organized by the MIT Committee on the Visual Arts. She often uses strong elemental imagery, manipulated from letterforms. Exhibitions of her work have been held at MIT, at the Chelsea School of Art, London (1978) and the London College of Printing (1980). Member of AGI.

Caslon Old Face ROMAN TYPEFACE designed by William Caslon of London about 1725. Based on the Dutch types of the late 17th c., then in general use among British printers. Caslon's type initiated a revival in British typographic standards. The characters are of generous proportions, with the rather steeply inclined ITALIC offering a wide range of SWASH capitals.

ABCDEFGH
abcdefgh

Carter's ITC Galliard typeface.

ABCDEFGH
abcdefgh

Part of the **Caslon Old Face**.

Advertising poster for Dubonnet by **Cassandre**, 1932, which ran for about twenty years.

Cassandre, A.M. (1901–68) Pseudonym adopted by the poster artist Adolphe Jean-Marie Mouron. Born in the Ukraine, he migrated to Paris during the First World War. Studied painting at the École des Beaux Arts and the Académie Julian. Learnt the techniques of poster production whilst working for the lithographic printer, Hatchard et Compagnie. Between 1923 and 1936 responsible for a series of classic and enormously influential advertising posters that assimilate different elements of the language of MODERNISM, particularly CUBISM and Purism. Amongst the most famous are *Étoile du Nord* (1927), *Dubonnet* (1932) and *Normandie* (1935). Characteristics of his work are bold geometric abstraction, broad planes of restricted colour, dynamic composition and masterful integration of letterforms and image. In 1927, along with Charles Loupot and Maurice Moyrand he cofounded L'Alliance Graphique, which was disbanded in 1935 after Moyrand's death. TYPEFACE designer for the French typefoundry DEBERNY & PEIGNOT including Bifur (1929), Acier Noir (1936) and the popular Peignot (1937). In 1936 honoured by the Museum of Modern Art, New York, with an exhibition. Worked in the US during the late 1930s, producing exceptional posters for CONTAINER CORPORATION OF AMERICA and N.W. AYER. Commissioned by fellow Russian Alexey BRODOVITCH to design covers for *HARPER'S BAZAAR*. Returned to France in 1939, concentrating for the next three decades on painting, theatre and ballet design. Cassandre's original output represents a major contribution to the development of 20th-c. graphic design.

cast-coated paper High-quality ART PAPER with glossy, enamel-like surface, suitable for fine HALFTONE and colour reproduction. The thick ink-absorbent coating of china clay and adhesive is added to a pre-coated paper base. A final polish is achieved by passing the paper round a hot glazing drum. See COATED PAPER, MACHINE-COATED PAPER

casting-off Term applied to method of calculation used to establish the amount of space (number of lines, pages, etc.) a manuscript will occupy when set in a specific TYPEFACE at a given size and measure.

Cato, Ken (b.1946) Australian graphic designer and art director. After studying at the Royal Melbourne Institute of Technology, worked in a number of advertising and design studios before establishing Cato Hibberd Design, with his British partner Terry Hibberd in 1970. The practice evolved into Cato

Design, Melbourne, with offices in Sydney, Tokyo, Singapore, Hong Kong, Auckland and Los Angeles. Specializing in packaging, CORPORATE IDENTITY and editorial design, Cato commissions outstanding photographers and illustrators to satisfy the design requirements of his international clients. A founder member and chairman (1980) of the Australian Writers and Art Directors Association. His work has been exhibited at the BRNO: INTERNATIONAL BIENNALE OF GRAPHIC DESIGN and the ART DIRECTORS CLUB OF NEW YORK. Editor of *First Choice* (1989), a selection of work by his fellow members of AGI. Author of *Cato Design* (1995) and *Design by Thinking* (2000).

CCA *See* CONTAINER CORPORATION OF AMERICA

CD/ROM *See* ROM (Read Only Memory)

Century Popular MODERN FACE specially created for the American *Century Magazine*. Cut in 1894 by L.B. Benton and T.L. de VINNE. Used in the magazine from 1895, the slightly condensed characters are economical in their use of space and easily read in the smaller sizes. One of the first typefaces specifically designed to meet the exacting standards of high-speed quality printing.

Century Guild ARTS AND CRAFTS MOVEMENT guild formed in London in 1882 'to render all branches of art the sphere, no longer of the tradesman, but of the artist'. Led by the architect Arthur Heygate MACKMURDO, the group included the designer-illustrator Selwyn IMAGE. The graphic design of the Guild was less medievalist than the work of William MORRIS and the KELMSCOTT PRESS, and instead employed fluid, organic patterns pre-dating ART NOUVEAU by about ten years. *Hobby Horse,* the Guild's influential magazine, was meticulously produced and printed under the supervision of Emery WALKER at the Chiswick Press. This commitment to quality printing was a reflection of Mackmurdo's enthusiasm for book design and the emerging PRIVATE PRESS MOVEMENT. The Guild was disbanded in 1888.

Chancery Italic/Script Cursive handwriting style developed by the Papal Chancery in Rome during the 15th and 16th c. This *Cancellaresca* with its flourished ASCENDER and DESCENDER design provided the model for the subsequent development of the ITALIC TYPEFACE.

Logotype designed by **Cato** for the Graphic Arts Services Association of Australia (1988).

ABCDEFGH abcdefgh

Part of the **Century** modern face.

Selwyn Image's title-page woodcut for the January 1886 edition of *Hobby Horse*, the magazine produced by the **Century Guild** between 1884 and 1888.

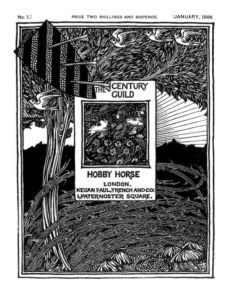

Will Bradley's 1905 cover design for *The Printer Man's Joy*, an example of **Chap Book Style**.

Letters from the **Cheltenham** typeface.

ABCDEFGH
abcdefgh

Chap Book Style American graphic design style of the late 1890s, closely associated with Will BRADLEY, which sought to recreate the vigour and integrity of early colonial printing. Characteristics included the use of Old Style CASLON types, naive WOODCUTS, wide letterspacing and in particular the avoidance of excess ornamentation.

Chartered Society Of Designers (CSD)
Foremost British professional society which endeavours to establish standards of practice and conduct. Formed in London in 1930, it was originally known as the Society of Industrial Artists, subsequently becoming the Society of Industrial Artists and Designers.

Cheltenham ROMAN TYPEFACE designed in America by Bertram G. Goodhue in 1896 and introduced to Britain in 1902. More suitable for DISPLAY purposes than for text setting, the Cheltenham range offers numerous CONDENSED, ITALIC and BOLD variations.

Chéret, Jules (1836–1932) Major French poster artist often described as the father of the modern poster (he designed more than a thousand). Apprenticed as a lithographer from 1849, his career paralleled the development of colour LITHOGRAPHY. Attended evening classes in drawing at the École Nationale de Dessin. Briefly visited England in 1854 where the techniques of lithography and CHROMOLITHOGRAPHY were well advanced. His first major poster commission on his return to Paris was for Offenbach's operetta, *Orphée aux Enfers* (1858). Worked in London 1859–66 designing posters for the music hall, theatre and circus as well as book covers for the publisher Cramer. A successful collaboration with the perfume manufacturer Eugène Rimmel, for whom he designed packaging, resulted in the establishment of a lithographic press in Paris in 1866. The press enjoyed early acclaim for the poster *La Biche au Bois* featuring Sarah Bernhardt. The famous Loïe Fuller poster for the Folies Bergère (1893) is typical of Chéret's work. It illustrates a central figure of graceful, animated beauty engulfed by swirling drapery and brilliant streaming colours. His female creations became idolized archetypes for the Gay Nineties. In 1881 Chéret sold his press to the Imprimerie Chaix, retaining artistic control. In 1889 he was honoured with a major one-man exhibition and a gold medal at the International Exhibition, Paris. The French government awarded him the Legion of Honour in 1890.

Tom Geismar, a founder member of **Chermayeff & Geismar Inc.**, designed this Mobil Oil logotype in 1964.

Poster by **Chéret** (1893) showing the famous Loïe Fuller at the Folies Bergère.

Chermayeff & Geismar Inc. Leading New York design practice that is particularly renowned for CORPORATE IDENTITY programmes and exhibition design. Originated in 1957 as Brownjohn, Chermayeff & Geismar Associates, the group reformed as Chermayeff & Geismar Inc. after Robert BROWNJOHN left for London in 1960. Current partners also include John Grady and Swiss graphic designer Steff GEISSBUHLER. Ivan Chermayeff (b.1932) and Tom Geismar (b.1931) met as students at Yale University, New Haven, graduating in the mid-1950s. During the early years with Brownjohn the group produced clever designs for book jackets and record covers, often resorting to typographic solutions and collage effects. The early 1960s brought widespread recognition following an important corporate design scheme for the Chase Manhattan Bank (1959). Since then the group has been responsible for hundreds of corporate identity programmes ranging from Mobil Oil (1964, implemented 1965) and Xerox (1965) to the Museum of Modern Art, New York (1970), and the Lincoln Centre, New York (1988). Their innovative approach to exhibition design is apparent in the 1958 exhibit 'Streetscape', produced for the US Pavilion at the Brussels World's Fair. Later important exhibitions include US government pavilions at Expo '67 in Montreal and Expo '70 in Osaka, and the Smithsonian Institution's 'Nation of Nations' exhibition for the Bicentennial celebrations. As an illustrator Chermayeff has been responsible for advertisements and posters for numerous clients including the Public Broadcasting System and the Museum of Modern Art. Chermayeff and Geismar were founding partners of Cambridge Seven Associates, an architectural and multidisciplinary design group in Cambridge, Massachusetts. In 1973 Geismar chaired an important AIGA advisory committee on transportation signs and symbols (see COOK AND SHANOSKY ASSOCIATES). Chermayeff has served as Andrew Carnegie Visiting Professor of Art at the Cooper Union School in New York. In 1979 Chermayeff and Geismar jointly received an AIGA gold medal and in 1983 were awarded the Japan Design Foundation's first international design award.

chromolithography Traditional printing technique based on the principles of LITHOGRAPHY, associated with the production of posters from the 1850s to the 1930s. Each colour to be printed was hand-drawn on to a lithographic 'stone', with the final multicoloured image resulting from the build-up of successive, individual colour printings.

End Bad Breath.

End Bad Breath, a 1967 woodcut poster by **Chwast** protesting against US involvement in the Vietnam War.

Chwast, Seymour (b.1931) American illustrator and graphic designer who works in advertising, publishing, packaging, corporate design, animated films and record covers. A founding principal of the influential PUSH PIN STUDIO. Studied at New York's Cooper Union School, graduating in 1951. Worked in advertising and publishing until in 1954, along with Milton GLASER, Reynolds Ruffins and Edward Sorel, he established Push Pin. By 1958 Ruffins and Sorel had left the group, leaving Chwast and Glaser to maintain a partnership which lasted over two decades. Chwast produced witty and highly inventive design solutions, finding inspiration in the naive imagery of primitive and children's art, comic books and Victorian typography. Originator and art director 1955–81 of *Push Pin Graphics,* the studio magazine which became an experimental showpiece and which he continued after his collaboration with Glaser had ended. A master at creating expressive letterforms for specific projects, some of which were later developed into novelty typefaces. Illustrator of over a dozen children's books. During the early 1980s he worked in partnership with Herb LUBALIN and Alan PECKOLICK. Awards include the St Gauden's medal from Cooper Union (1972), where he has served as visiting professor, and the AIGA medal (1985). Elected to Hall of Fame OF ART DIRECTORS CLUB OF NEW YORK, 1983. One-man exhibition at Galerie Delpire, Paris 1974 as well as many group shows.

Poster produced by **Cieslewicz** in 1964 to advertise a theatre production of Kafka's *The Trial*.

Cieslewicz, Roman (1930–96) Polish-born graphic designer, poster artist and art director. Studied at the Academy of Fine Arts, Krakow, before moving to Warsaw where he worked for publishers, government agencies and CWF Central Film Distributors. Quickly established a reputation as an outstanding designer of cultural posters. Between 1959 and 1963 designed *Ty i Ja* magazine, Warsaw. Moved to Paris in 1963, working as an art director for *VOGUE* 1966–67 and *Elle* 1967–69. From 1969 to 1972 he was art director of the Mafia publicity agency. His potent images have a disturbing and hypnotic quality, resulting from a masterful use of PHOTOMONTAGE and COLLAGE. Cieslewicz has received many awards, including a special prize for cinema posters at Cannes, 1973 and a Grand Prix for poster art, Paris, 1979. His advertising work for Charles Jourdan (1982) and his posters for Centre Georges Pompidou, Paris from 1975–83 are of particular interest.

Clarendon EGYPTIAN TYPEFACE originated by the English foundry R. Besley & Co. in 1845, with a SLAB SERIF character. The bracketed serifs are slightly

ABCDEFGH
abcdefgh

Letters from the **Clarendon** typeface.

Poster for the *Revue Nègre*, by **Colin** (1925).

thinner than the main strokes. Overall the typeface is quite heavy, making it useful for DISPLAY purposes or as a BOLD headline face in a text setting.

coated paper General term for printing papers that have their surface coated with a fine layer of china clay. Coated papers provide an excellent printing surface for fine HALFTONE and colour reproduction. *See* CAST-COATED PAPER

Cohen, Elaine Lustig (b.1927) Pioneering female graphic designer who incorporated the aesthetic vocabulary of European modernism into American graphic design during the 1950s and 60s. After training as a painter, developed her design skills working with Alvin LUSTIG (whom she married in 1948). Following Lustig's premature death in 1955, she took control of the studio and between 1955 and 1961 produced a distinctive series of covers for publishing houses Meridian Books and New Directions. With their strong concepts, abstract forms and typographic invention, they represented a break from the prevailing tradition of pictorial illustration in book-jacket design. Her ability to summarize the content of a text in the cover design was further aided when, working for architects including Eero Saarinen and Philip Johnson, she produced signage schemes intended to express a building's character. Designed many posters and catalogues for New York–based arts organizations, including the American Center for the Arts, the Lincoln Centre, the Whitney Museum of American Art and the Jewish Museum. Married Arthur A. Cohen, publisher of Meridian Books; in 1973 they established Ex Libris, New York, a bookshop and gallery specializing in rare volumes of the European avant-garde. In 1995 her contribution to graphic design was acknowledged by an exhibition at the Cooper Hewitt, National Design Museum, New York.

Colin, Paul (1892–1985) Prolific designer of ART DECO posters and theatre sets. Alongside A.M. CASSANDRE and Jean CARLU, a master of the modern French poster. Trained as a painter, later turning to design after his appointment as graphic and set designer at the Théâtre des Champs Elysées, Paris, in 1925. Created a vast number of posters, possibly up to 2,000 and up to 800 set designs. He was also responsible for French propaganda posters during the Second World War. Founder and director of the famous Paul Colin School of Design, Paris. Continued to produce striking and memorable work into the 1970s.

collage Technique in which found fragments of paper, newsprint and fabric are arranged and glued together to form an original composition. The random nature of collage has been exploited to powerful effect by many designers and illustrators, with early innovators like the BEGGARSTAFF BROTHERS and Kurt SCHWITTERS being of particular note. SURREALISM employed collage to highlight bizarre visual relationships and provided a rich legacy still apparent in current illustration, advertising and pop videos.

collotype Photomechanical printing process suitable for finely detailed reproductions. Although not utilizing a HALFTONE screen, the process gives the impression of continuous tone. The printing surface is prepared by pouring a light- sensitive emulsion of gelatin on to a sheet of plate glass, which is then dried in an oven. Collotype is a delicate, rarely used process suitable only for short-run production.

colophon Publishing term: (a) typographic or emblematic device identifying the printer or publisher, usually featured on the spine and/or title page of a book, or (b) information placed at the end of a book or on the reverse of the title page, giving details of the publisher, printer, place and date of publication.

colour For the use of colour in graphic design, see specially extended entry and colour illustrations pp. 64–72.

Commercial Art Monthly British publication that sought to present the best in commercial art and advertising. Originating in 1922 it was taken over by *The STUDIO* in 1926. The title changed to *Commercial Art and Industry* in 1932, then to *Art and Industry* in 1937, and finally to *Design for Industry* shortly before its demise in 1959.

composition size Term applied to those TYPEFACE sizes, normally 6 to 14 POINT, used in setting of text matter.

computer Machine that can be controlled by a program of instructions to accept and process data. The data supplied is a signal from a COMPUTER INPUT DEVICE such as a keyboard pointing device, disc or tape. The results of a user's action are signals to a COMPUTER OUTPUT DEVICE which is seen as information on a screen, printer or the creation of a file on a disc or tape.

computer-aided design (CAD) Process of using a COMPUTER to assist in the design of physical objects. CAD packages allow the user to manipulate and produce two- and three-dimensional representations of objects. These can be as simple as a two-dimensional drawing or as complex as a three-dimensional view of the object. CAD has been used by architects to produce site plans and visualizations and by engineers to produce diagrams of components and assemblies. Graphic designers have recently found CAD packages useful for creating sophisticated drawings and renderings of three-dimensional objects. Once produced these can be inserted into documents using a DESKTOP PUBLISHING package or output on a printer or video recorder.

computer graphics Representation of information in a graphic form using a COMPUTER. Usually the output is printed, displayed on a screen, or output to video tape. The quality of the image produced is dependent on the resolution of the COMPUTER OUTPUT DEVICE. Screen resolution is dependent on the number of pixels (very small elements of an image) that can be displayed horizontally and vertically, whereas printer resolution is described by the number of dots that can be printed per inch. Computer graphics differ from COMPUTER AIDED-DESIGN in that CAD is the use of a computer to assist in the design process whereas computer graphics use a computer throughout the production of a graphic design.

computer input device Device that sends data to a COMPUTER. The most common types of input device in current use are a keyboard and/or MOUSE.

computer I/O (input/output) device Peripheral unit to a COMPUTER that can be used as either an input device or an output device. For example, disc and tape devices that can be read from (offering no facility for user modification) or written to (interactive, enabling user modification) are I/O devices.

computerized composition/typesetting Computer-controlled method of type composition. The COMPUTER can be programmed to facilitate all the functions after keyboarding and up to the production of setting. Details such as type size, measure, format and punctuation rules are readily accommodated.

computer languages Artificial languages designed to allow human beings to communicate with a programmable machine. Normally used to produce fast efficient programs using instructions that are close to the machine's own processing mechanisms. Low-level languages are used by those wishing to control the basic processes of a machine. High-level languages, more in tune with how human beings solve problems, vary from those for general use to those designed to assist with a specific task such as page layout, data-base construction or animation.

computer output device Device that receives data from a COMPUTER. The most common types in current use are monitors/screens, plotters, printers and video recorders.

computer terminal COMPUTER INPUT/OUTPUT DEVICE used to communicate with a remote computer. Terminals do little processing of information, merely sending commands, usually via a keyboard, and receiving the results on a screen. The operator may also request the computer to process files stored on disc or tape and relay results to output devices other than the terminal's own screen.

condensed Term used to describe narrower, com-pressed version of a TYPEFACE with standard propor-tions. The individual characters are also set closely together.

Constructivism Radical Russian art movement that developed shortly before the Bolshevik Revolution in 1917. In an attempt to redefine the role of the artist and contribute to the 'construction' of a new commu-nist state, a group of artists rejected the 'art for art's sake' concept underpinning SUPREMATISM and directed their energies to socially useful activities like industri-al, graphic and theatre design, photography and film. Led by Vladimir Tatlin (1885–1953), Alexander RODCHENKO and El LISSITZKY, the movement's non-figurative visual vocabulary relied upon brightly coloured shapes, often made from materials like glass, sheet metal and cardboard. Committed to taking their work into the streets, Rodchenko and Lissitzky embraced COLLAGE, photography, PHOTOMONTAGE, bold lettering design and new printing techniques. The expressive quality of Constructivist typography with its reliance on SANS SERIF faces gave the revolution a potent identity. Constructivist ideas had a profound influence on the educational ethos of the BAUHAUS, subsequently extending across Europe through publi-cations, exhibitions and exchange visits. During the early 1920s the Soviet government became increas-ingly concerned about the movement, stressing the need for a pictorial art in the service of the State.

Container Corporation of America (CCA) Leading American manufacturer of paperboard and corrugated fibre packaging, founded in 1926 by the Chicago industrialist Walter P. Paepcke (1896–1960). Paepcke chose to differentiate his company by adopt-ing an enlightened and highly innovative advertising policy that aligned CCA with experimentation and excellence in the visual arts. In 1936 he initiated a long association with N.W. AYER, the advertising agency, and their art director Charles Coiner. In the same year he appointed Egbert Jacobson as director of the new CCA design department, the first of several directors who have ensured CCA remains in the forefront of corporate advertising. Jacobson created the LOGOTYPE, which was applied to a redesigned sta-tionery range. CCA is recognized as the first American company to establish a CORPORATE IDENTITY programme. In 1937 A.M. CASSANDRE designed a series of innovative advertisements that married powerful images with pithy, concise copy. The foremost artists and designers worked for CCA, including Fernand Léger, Man RAY, László MOHOLY-NAGY, Gyorgy KEPES and

ABCDEFGH
abcdefgh

Condensed letters from the Univers Light typeface.

Container Corporation of America symbol, redesigned by Ralph Eckerstrom (1957).

Symbols for customs and baggage lockers, designed in 1974 for the United States Department of Transportation by **Cook and Shanosky Associates**.

Austin **Cooper**'s 1933 lithograph poster advertising the 'Exhibition of British Industrial Art in the Home'.

Herbert BAYER, who served as a consultant designer for many years. During the war Jean CARLU and Herbert MATTER joined Bayer and Jacobson in the striking 'Paperboard Goes to War' campaign. In 1950 Paepcke initiated the enormously successful 'Great Ideas of Western Man' campaign. A year later he played a leading role in establishing the ASPEN INTERNATIONAL DESIGN CONFERENCE. CCA modernized its identity in 1957 with a revised logo developed by design director Ralph Eckerstrom. John MASSEY became director of design in 1964 and brought both HELVETICA and the INTERNATIONAL TYPOGRAPHIC STYLE to CCA, imposing a visual discipline upon all printed communications. In 1966 the commitment to design excellence was extended to clients through the experimental Center for Advanced Research in Design, an independent studio providing design services to external organizations.

Cook and Shanosky Associates Graphic design practice founded in New York in 1967, moving to Princeton, New Jersey in 1977. Partners are Roger Cook (b.1930) who trained at the Pratt Institute, New York and Don Shanosky (b.1937) from Philadelphia College of Art. They worked together before establishing this small but influential studio. Highly regarded in the fields of CORPORATE IDENTITY, annual reports and symbol design. They produce rational, elegant design solutions with restrained typography and often powerful photographic imagery. In 1974 they were commissioned by an AIGA committee led by Tom GEISMAR to design pictographic symbols for a transportation SIGNAGE system to be applied across the US. The project established a clear and uniform visual communication system that crosses language and cultural barriers.

Cooper, Austin (1890–1964) Canadian-born poster designer who trained and practised in Britain. Trained at Cardiff College of Art and the Allan Frazer College of Art, Arbroath 1909–10. In 1910 moved to London, studying in the evenings at the City & Guilds School. Thereafter worked for a short time in Canada as a commercial artist, interrupted by war service in Europe. Settled in London in 1922, where over the next two decades he established a reputation as a poster designer. His approach throughout the 1920s became increasingly pictorial, with his work for, amongst others, the London Underground, the Empire Marketing Board and the LNER (London and North Eastern Railway) receiving widespread public acclaim. His book *Making a Poster* (1938) was published by Studio in the popular 'How to do it' series.

The fat face roman **Cooper Black**.

ABCDEFGH
abcdefgh

Cooper Black Popular FAT FACE ROMAN designed by the American type designer Oswald COOPER in 1921. Based on early 19th-c. advertising styles and on Cooper's other roman type, Cooper Old Style, the sheer bulk of Cooper Black means that the enclosed inner spaces (counters) of each character are very small. Its weight requires that it be used sparingly and for DISPLAY purposes only. There is also a CONDENSED face, and a shaded version, called Cooper Hilite.

Cooper, Muriel (1925–94) American graphic and book designer. Her contribution to graphic design was recognized in 1986 when the AIGA awarded its Design Leadership Award to the three graphics groups that she founded and led at Massachusetts Institute of Technology. Design director MIT Office of Publications (Design Services) 1952–58; design and media director, later special projects director MIT Press 1966–78; in 1975 appointed to the Architecture Department at MIT, subsequently establishing the influential Visible Language Workshop, a research unit concerned with the impact of the technological revolution on graphic communication. Many of the five hundred books designed, art directed and produced at the MIT Press were award winners - of particular note are *The Bauhaus* (1969) by Hans M. Wingler, *Learning from Las Vegas* (1972) by Robert Venturi, Denise Scott-Brown and Stephen Izenour, and *Is anyone taking any notice?* (1973) by Donald McCullin. In addition, Cooper was a principal in Muriel Cooper Media Design, Cambridge, Massachusetts, from 1958. Member of AGI.

Cooper, Oswald (1879–1940) American TYPEFACE designer based in Chicago. The rapid growth of the advertising industry in the early 1900s, combined with the emergence of the LINOTYPE and MONOTYPE typesetting machines, fuelled a demand for new typefaces. By commissioning designers like Cooper, AMERICAN TYPE FOUNDERS COMPANY was instrumental in satisfying this demand. Working as a partner in the practice Bertsch & Cooper, he provided a lettering and typesetting

Muriel **Cooper**'s 1972 cover design for *Learning from Las Vegas* by Venturi, Scott-Brown and Izenour, published by the MIT Press.

Poster designed by Oswald **Cooper** for the Chicago Group of the AIGA.

service to the communication industries. Two of his typefaces are of particular note; Cooper Old Style for Barnhart Bros & Spindler 1919–24, and the popular COOPER BLACK for the same company in 1921. The *Book of OZ* (1949) was a commemorative volume celebrating Cooper's typographic achievements.

copperplate printing INTAGLIO printing process normally used for the short-run production of invitations and business cards. Produces a distinctive, slightly raised impression with fine sharp lines and excellent dense solids.

copyfitting See CASTING-OFF

Crane's title-page design for his influential publication *Line & Form* (1900).

corporate identity Process whereby the design elements of an organization are utilized to maximum effect in order to communicate what it does and how it does it. Corporate identity can embrace products, services, environments, and the means of internal and external communication. Application of the corporate identity is often controlled by a DESIGN MANUAL. The first major corporate identity was the scheme produced by Peter BEHRENS for the German electrical company Allgemeine Elektricitaets Gesellschaft (AEG) in 1907.

Council of Industrial Design See DESIGN COUNCIL

Cranach Press German PRIVATE PRESS founded at Weimar in 1913 by Count Harry Von Kessler (1868–1937). The superb Cranach Press *Hamlet* (1928) reveals the widespread influence of the English revival of quality book production. The 255 copies of *Hamlet* were printed on a hand press, most on paper made by Kessler and the French sculptor Aristide Maillol. English artists employed by Kessler included Edward Gordon Craig, Eric GILL and Edward JOHNSTON. Craig took seventeen years to produce the WOODCUT decorations for *Hamlet.*

Crane, Walter (1845–1915) British illustrator and designer. Commissioned in 1863 to illustrate his first major work, *The New Forest.* Thereafter he produced many covers and illustrations for novels and children's books, primarily for the publisher Routledge. From 1870 his prolific output and technical virtuosity, combined with a deep knowledge of Japanese and antiquarian styles, brought widespread acclaim. Influenced by the work of William MORRIS and Edward BURNE-JONES, his earlier output contributed to the reputation of the Pre-Raphaelites in England and abroad. Crane's wide-ranging activities extended to designs for tiles, vases, wallpapers, mosaics and stained glass. In 1884 he was a founder member of the ART WORKER'S GUILD, becoming Master in 1888 and 1889. Led the breakaway group that established the influential ARTS AND CRAFTS EXHIBITION SOCIETY (1888). Illustrated *The Story of the Glittering Plain* (1894), which was produced by the KELMSCOTT PRESS. Crane's commitment to the ARTS AND CRAFTS MOVEMENT was confirmed by his activities as a socialist and the many designs and illustrations he contributed to trade union activities. Throughout the 1890s he held a number of senior posts in British design education, culminating in his appointment as principal in 1898 of the newly created Royal College of Art, London. This period coincided with the growth of his reputation in Europe. Following his appointment as an honorary member of the VIENNA SECESSION in 1897, he designed a cover for the German ART NOUVEAU journal *Jugend* (1898). Two volumes of his collected lectures, *The Bases of Design* (1898) and *Line & Form* (1900) have a lasting relevance.

Crouwel, Wim (b.1928) Dutch graphic designer, exhibition designer and educator. Trained at the Academy of Arts and Crafts, Groningen, 1947–49 and the Institute for Arts and Crafts in Amsterdam 1951–52. Established a design practice in 1952 and during late 1950s collaborated with designer Kho Liang Ie. In 1963 he became one of five founding partners of TOTAL DESIGN, so called because it was the first multidisciplinary design practice in the Netherlands. Since 1964 responsible for many posters, catalogues and exhibitions for the Stedelijk Museum, Amsterdam, where he has been honoured with an exhibition (1979). Produced functional, inventive solutions utilizing the geometry of the GRID. In 1967 he launched *New Alphabet* within the Quadrat-Print series of journals produced by the Hilversum printer, Steendrukkerij de Jong. This radical typographic experiment proposed new letterforms suitable for

Radical alphabet designed by **Crouwel** in 1966 to meet the new technological demands of the cathode-ray tube and television screen.

reproduction by a TYPE composition system using a cathode-ray tube. Awarded the Ordre Leopold II for his contribution to the Benelux pavilion at the 1958 Brussels World's Fair. Also worked on the Dutch pavilion at the 1970 Osaka World's Fair. Taught in Hertogenbosch at Royal Academy of Arts and Crafts until 1957 and at Amsterdam's Institute for Arts & Crafts (1957–63). In 1965 he began a long association with Delft University of Technology, becoming a professor in 1972. Throughout this period continued as a consultant with Total Design. Secretary General of ICOGRADA (1963–66). Has won many prizes for his posters and book design. Since 1980 he has been involved with the management of the Museum Boymans-van Beuningen in Rotterdam, initially as a commission member, subsequently as director.

CSD *See* CHARTERED SOCIETY OF DESIGNERS

Cubism Art movement that emerged in France between about 1906 and 1909. Developed by Pablo Picasso and Georges Braque, it evolved from the theories and later work of Paul Cézanne. 'Analytic' Cubism (1909–12) abandoned traditional perspective, endeavouring to explore the multidimensional facets of an object rather than express it in a flat two-dimensional manner. The elimination of colour and the application of COLLAGE emphasized the 'idea' of the object. 'Synthetic' Cubism (1912–14) revived an interest in colour, texture and tactile quality. The introduction of ephemera, lettering and newsprint to explore the relationship between illusion and reality created a new visual language that has since been used by many designers and illustrators.

Curwen, Harold (1885–1949) Master printer at the Curwen Press, Plaistow, England, renowned for its quality printing. Assumed control of the family business in 1913. Closely involved with the emergent DESIGN AND INDUSTRIES ASSOCIATION, which was concerned to eradicate shoddy standards of production. In a purge of his TYPEFACE collection and in response to government appeals for type metal to sustain the war effort, he disposed of his stock of over two hundred types, retaining only CASLON OLD FACE. After two years of printing entirely in this typeface he slowly extended the range, beginning with Imprint and Goudy's Kennerley. The press was responsible for many fine books, with high typographic standards developed under the guidance of the typographer Oliver SIMON. Amongst the finest is *Urne Buriall and the Garden of Cyrus* (1932) with illustrations by Paul NASH.

Poster for a **Dada** recital in The Hague, 1923, designed by Kurt Schwitters and Théo van Doesburg.

Danziger's poster advertising the 'New York School' exhibition at Los Angeles County Museum of Art, 1965.

D

Dada Literary and visual art movement that developed in Switzerland during 1916. Responding to the futility of the First World War a group of poets and artists set out to ridicule established values and beliefs. Pioneered in Zurich by the poets Tristan Tzara and Hugo Ball and the artist Hans Arp, the movement quickly spread to other major cities like New York, Paris and Berlin. The need to shock required new forms of visual communication with bold typography, COLLAGE and PHOTOMONTAGE emerging as favoured techniques. Kurt SCHWITTERS utilized rubbish and ephemera in his 'Merz' collages, while photomontage techniques were brilliantly employed by the Berlin Dadaists Raoul Hausmann, John HEARTFIELD, and George GROSZ. Dada was a liberating influence that challenged and overturned many social and artistic conventions. Ceasing to be effective after 1922, Dada was a forerunner of SURREALISM, which emerged in Paris in 1924.

daguerrotype, daguerreotype Early photographic process invented by Louis J.M. Daguerre (1799–1851) in 1839. The process is activated when a silver-coated copper plate, made light-sensitive with iodine (or iodine and bromide), is exposed in a camera. After exposure the final image is created on the plate through the chemical reaction of mercury vapour with the light-sensitized silver compounds.

Danziger, Louis (b. 1923) American graphic designer and photographer. Began as a fifteen-year-old apprentice in the art department of a New York printer. Influenced by the German journal GEBRAUCHS-GRAPHIK. Studied under Alvin LUSTIG at the Los Angeles Art Center School of Design (1947), returning to New York in 1948 to train briefly under Alexey BRODOVITCH at the New School for Social Research. Avoids transitory and fashionable solutions in his quest for restrained, intelligent design concerned with order and clarity of communication. Worked for the magazine *Esquire* (1948) before establishing a freelance design and consultancy practice in Los Angeles with clients including the CONTAINER CORPORATION OF AMERICA and the advertising agency The Dreyfus Company. Designed all the promotional material for the 1955 ASPEN INTERNATIONAL DESIGN CONFERENCE, whilst in the same year the Society of Typographic Art, Chicago, organized a one-man exhibition of his work. After becoming design consultant

Cover of *New York* magazine, November 1970, designed by **Davis**.

De Stijl magazine cover from April 1917 by Vilmos Huszar.

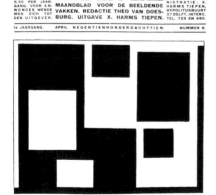

to the Los Angeles County Museum of Art in 1957, Danziger created a series of elegant exhibition catalogues and posters. Corporate design consultant to the Atlantic Richfield Company 1978–86 and for the 1984 Los Angeles Olympic Games. Taught at the Los Angeles Art Center School, 1956–62 and again from 1988, Chouinard Art Institute 1963–72, subsequently becoming director of graphic design at the California Institute of the Arts, Valencia, 1972–88. Exhibited in many major shows in the US. Member of AGI and AIGA.

Davis, Paul (b.1938) American designer/illustrator whose work has appeared in books, magazines, posters, record covers and advertising. Studied at the School of Visual Arts in New York, later establishing his reputation at the PUSH PIN STUDIO. Influenced by American folk art, he first emerged in the magazine *Push Pin Graphic* with a series of painted wooden panels that revealed targets superimposed upon primitive figures. Davis has evolved a distinctive graphic style involving a dramatic use of naturalistic painted imagery. The impact of his work is often heightened by a clever integration of lettering.

De Stijl (The Style) Dutch art movement and magazine originated by the painter and designer Théo van DOESBURG in 1917. De Stijl, which influenced the international avant-garde throughout the 1920s, was committed to a unity of the arts. Attracting artists, designers and architects, the movement sought an abstract objectivity through the use of the rectangle and a reliance on primary colours in association with black, white and grey. Other leading names associated with De Stijl were the painter Piet Mondrian, the architect and furniture designer Gerrit Rietveld, Bart van der LECK, Vilmos HUSZAR and Piet ZWART. The graphic and typographic design of De Stijl was very disciplined, employing forms of SANS SERIF TYPEFACE, with straight lines, tight rectangular blocks, and innovative asymmetrical layouts. The magazine became increasingly purist, its typographic conventions providing a foretaste of the INTERNATIONAL TYPOGRAPHIC STYLE. Van Doesburg introduced De Stijl ideas to BAUHAUS students and staff when he lived in Weimar from 1921 to 1923; the movement and magazine effectively came to an end in 1931 with his premature death.

Deberny & Peignot French foundry that has played a leading role in typographic developments throughout this century. The poster designers Eugène GRASSET and Georges AURIOL worked for the foundry,

designing forms of TYPEFACE with ART NOUVEAU characteristics. The major influence on the company's
creative achievements was Charles Peignot (1897–
1983), who commissioned A.M. CASSANDRE to design a
number of typefaces throughout the 1930s. The Swiss
designer Adrian FRUTIGER moved to Paris in 1952, helping Deberny & Peignot to transfer classic typefaces
to the newly emerging filmsetting systems. In 1957,
in response to a commission from Peignot, Frutiger
produced UNIVERS, the phenomenally successful SANS
SERIF face. Peignot's international status was confirmed when he was elected president of the newly
created typeface protection organization, ASSOCIA-
TION TYPOGRAPHIQUE INTERNATIONALE. Still active and
innovative, Deberny & Peignot continues to develop
designs for today's sophisticated technological typesetting systems.

Delaunay, Sonia (1885–1979) Russian painter, fashion and textile designer and poster artist. Born in the
Ukraine, she studied anatomy and drawing at the
Kunstakademie, Karlsruhe, 1903–4, before moving to
Paris to train as a painter at the Académie de la
Palette, Paris (1905). She then worked as an independent painter and graphic artist, moving into stage
and textile design after the First World War. Married
painter Robert Delaunay in 1910; the couple travelled
widely in Europe, working for brief periods in Nantes,
Spain and Portugal. In 1913 she created a brightly
coloured abstract illustration for *La Prose du
Transsibérien* by Blaise Cendrar, which folded out to a
length of two metres. From 1921 to 1939 the
Delaunays were based in Paris, followed by a final year
together in the Auvergne. During the 1920s she
opened a number of avant-garde boutiques that sold
her clothes, fabrics and furnishings. Following her husband's death in 1941, Delaunay worked in Grasse
1942–44 before moving back to Paris for the remainder of her life. A prolific and versatile talent, her
posters, illustrations and textile designs display a distinctive use of strong colours and rhythmic geometric
forms. Her understanding of the emotional power of
colour and movement is well illustrated by her
Chocolat posters for Chocolat Bensdorp (1916–22).
Productive throughout a long life, her 'Simultané'
playing card designs (*c.* 1959) were produced by the
Deutsches Spielkarten Museum, Bielefield in 1964.
UNESCO commissioned her to produce a poster for
'International Women's Year' in 1975.

Four of the 'Simultané' playing cards designed by **Delaunay**
in *c.* 1959.

Depero, Fortunato (1892–1960) Italian futurist
who extended his activities as a painter, writer and
theatre designer into the area of graphic and advertising design. Depero explored the dynamic visual language of FUTURISM using strong colour, flat planes,
repetitive forms and diagonal composition. Aside
from creating graphic material to promote the activities of the movement, he experimented in typography, poster and magazine design for commercial
clients. His 1927 book *Depero Futurista* was notorious
for its use of two large chrome nuts and bolts that
bind together its pages. This early example of exploring the physicality of the book as an art object displayed all the inventiveness of futurist typography and
design. Depero spent a brief but highly productive
period in New York (1928–30), a city that exuded the
intensity of experience and energy demanded by such
futurists as MARINETTI. Here he designed covers and
created illustrations for numerous magazines, including *Vanity Fair*, *VOGUE* and *The New Yorker*. He also produced advertisements for commercial organizations,
such as millinery shop De Marinis and Lorie. His
contribution was to prove influential in promoting
modernist aesthetics in American graphic design.

descender The part of a LOWER CASE letter that appears below the X-HEIGHT.

Descenders in the Gill typeface.

Design British journal launched in London by the Council of Industrial Design (now the DESIGN COUNCIL) in 1949. Featuring product and graphic design, the journal provides British industry with informed comment on national and international developments. The masthead was created in 1962 by Ken GARLAND, the journal's art director.

Design and Industries Association (DIA) British design organization established in London in 1915. Based on the model of the DEUTSCHER WERKBUND, the association was open to practitioners, educators and the general public. Its main aim was to improve the standards of design in British industry. Although embracing a 'fitness for purpose' philosophy in its earlier years, the association found it difficult to distance itself from the tradition of the ARTS AND CRAFTS MOVEMENT. During the 1930s there was a clearer commitment to the development of the MODERN MOVEMENT in Europe. With its promotion of machine production and appropriate materials, combined with a rejection of superfluous decoration, the DIA was instrumental in improving the standards of British printing before the Second World War. Members like Harold CURWEN, Frank PICK and Sir Francis MEYNELL helped spread the message that 'Nothing need be ugly'. Still in existence, the DIA's campaigning role was largely overtaken when the Council of Industrial Design was created in 1944.

Design Council British government-sponsored organization with a brief to promote design. Began as the Council of Industrial Design (1944), renamed the Design Council in 1972. Early propagandist initiatives included the 'BRITAIN CAN MAKE IT' exhibition (1946) and the launch of DESIGN magazine (1949). Following its successful involvement in the 'FESTIVAL OF BRITAIN', the Council established the Design Centre in London in 1956 and initiated its Annual Design Awards in 1957. Following a major operational review in 1994 it was restructured with a brief to 'improve the UK's competitiveness through the better use of design'.

design manual Document that specifies the operational guidelines for the application of a CORPORATE IDENTITY. Produced by the designers of the identity, the manual provides the client organization with a quality-control system to ensure that each visual component (TYPEFACE, LOGOTYPE, colours, SIGNAGE, uniforms) is used correctly. Visual parameters are established, with examples of 'right' and 'wrong' applications to ensure that the identity is effective in a national and international context.

Design Research Unit (DRU) Influential British multidisciplinary design consultancy. Established in 1943, with the design historian Herbert Read as its first manager. DRU's main contribution to British post-war design has been in the development of major CORPORATE IDENTITY programmes. Successful schemes, such as those for the photographic company Ilford (1946–66), British Rail (1956–66) and the rubber company Dunlop (1962), were important in highlighting the role of design within large organizations. The outstanding creative influences on DRU during its first three decades were Milner GRAY, the architect Misha Black and June FRASER.

Designers and Art Directors Association (D&AD) Leading British design and advertising association established in London in 1962 to improve creative standards in the UK. Membership is restricted to those whose work is accepted for inclusion in the D&AD exhibition and *Annual*. Its education programmes are supported by top practitioners and are designed to introduce newcomers to the pressures and expectations of professional practice.

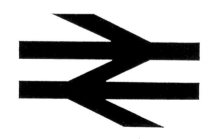

Design Research Unit produced this symbol as part of its corporate identity scheme for British Rail, 1956–66.

Designers Republic

EP cover *Punk Skunk Funk* for Supercharger by The **Designers Republic** in 1998.

Designers Republic, The British design consultancy, based in Sheffield. Established in 1986 by Ian Anderson, a philosophy graduate from Sheffield University. Originally influenced by the work of Malcolm GARRETT and subsequently inspired by technology, corporate culture and Manga Comics, the designers are consummate image-makers for the club scene and music industry. Their complex visual 'sampling' and mutation of popular culture challenges prevailing attitudes to consumerism and advertising, an approach that is evident in a series of didactic banners (on consumerism, food, death, religion, etc.) they produced for the show 'Customised Terror' at New York's Artists Space (1995). The success of their technologically led aesthetic has enabled The Designers Republic to apply their creative philosophy to such major youth-oriented corporations as Sony, Nike and MTV.

Desktop Publishing (DTP) Small-scale production of typesetting and graphics produced by microcomputers offering page-make-up programmes. The increasing sophistication of DTP systems has made professional standards of reproduction available to a diverse range of producers and audiences. By mixing text with visual material, DTP systems facilitate the production of CAMERA-READY ARTWORK, for photographing and printing. The ability to preview the final design and page layout enables changes to be made before printing on a laser printer.

Deutscher Werkbund Alliance of manufacturers, retailers and designers formed in Munich in 1907 to improve the quality of German industrial products. Influenced by the functional ideas of the ARTS AND CRAFTS MOVEMENT in England, the Werkbund sought to apply them to the requirements of mass production techniques. The architect Hermann Muthesius, who was instrumental in establishing the Werkbund, argued for standardization and the benefits of exploiting the potential of a machine ethic. Other major figures involved were the architects Peter BEHRENS and Henry van de VELDE. Behrens' work for AEG, covering architecture, product design, graphic design and typography, epitomized the Werkbund ethos. The first major exhibition of the Werkbund took place in Cologne in 1914 with buildings specially designed by Walter GROPIUS and van de Velde. Increasingly identified with the design philosophy of the BAUHAUS, a touring exhibition entitled 'Form without Ornament' (1924) spread the Werkbund message to a wider public. Eventually crushed by the Nazis in the mid-1930s the Werkbund enjoyed a limited revival after the Second World War.

diagram Graphic device in which complex statistical concepts of time, space, performance, location, etc. are presented in a condensed visual form. The presentation of such information was significantly improved following the development of the ISOTYPE system by Otto and Marie Neurath. The numerous diagrammatic conventions and techniques available to the designer reflect the diversity of information problems. See BAR CHART, PIE GRAPH, VENN DIAGRAM

Didot First MODERN FACE cut by Firmin Didot of the famous French printing and publishing dynasty, c. 1784. The significance of this ROMAN TYPEFACE is evident in the mathematical precision of the characters, with their vertical STRESS, fine unbracketed SERIF forms, and marked contrast between thick and thin strokes. Influenced the development of BODONI in Italy and BELL in England. Remains popular in France for books and text setting.

ABCDEFGH
abcdefgh

Letters from the **Didot** typeface.

Didot Point System European unit of TYPE MEASURE-MENT established by the Parisian typefounder François-Ambroise Didot in 1775. It is based on a standard unit of 0.3759mm (0.0148in).

digitization Process of converting an illustration or TYPEFACE outline into a set of small lines that a COMPUTER can process to reproduce the original image. This differs from a scanned image, which is comprised of a colour or monochrome specification of each element of a grid placed over the original image.

DIN Abbreviation of Deutsche Industrie Norm, a set of industry standards established in Germany in the 1920s, which subsequently led to the development of the International Standards Organization (ISO) recommended paper sizes. DIN standards still apply in the rating of film speeds. See A, B, C SYSTEM OF STANDARD PAPER SIZES

DiSpigna, Tony (b.1943) Italian-born typographic and lettering designer whose work embraces advertising, CORPORATE IDENTITY, publishing and film titles. Graduate from New York City Community College and Pratt Institute, where he later taught. Joined LUBALIN Smith Carnase in 1969, contributing to the practice's inventive use of type and calligraphy. In 1973 he established a New York studio, which he maintained for five years before becoming vice-president of Herb Lubalin Associates. In 1980, again opened his own studio. TYPEFACE designs include Serif Gothic, Playgirl, Lubalin Graph, Fattoni and WNET. Numerous awards from the New York Type Directors' Club and AIGA.

display matter/setting Typesetting that uses the full range of type sizes and weights to ensure that the information conveyed stands apart from continuous text setting. Advertisements, headings and titles are examples of display matter/setting designed to attract the reader's attention.

display size Size of TYPEFACE used for DISPLAY MATTER/SETTING. Display sizes are categorized as those over 14 POINT – that is, 3.5mm (c. ⅛in) cap height and above. Normally used as headings or titles within a page of text set in a COMPOSITION SIZE of type.

Distéfano, Juan Carlos (b.1933) Argentinian graphic and typographic designer responsible for the design of posters, books, annual reports and symbols. Trained at the Escuela Industrial de Artes Graficas and at the Academia de Bellas Artes 1951–54. During the late 1950s he worked in advertising before becoming director of the Visual Arts Centre of the Instituto Torcuato Di Tella where, along with Ruben Fontana, he designed posters using powerful, highly expressive typography. From 1971 until 1976 he and Fontana collaborated in their own studio. Concurrently, in 1973, Distéfano taught at the University of Buenos Aires and led the graphic design department of the Buenos Aires Municipal Research Centre for Mass Communication. During the late 1970s he redirected his talents towards the fine arts, specializing in drawing and sculpture. One-man shows of his design achievements were held in Buenos Aires in 1961 and 1979.

Doesburg, Théo van (1883–1931) Dutch painter, designer and art critic acknowledged as the main creative force behind the DE STIJL movement. Edited the didactic *De Stijl* magazine from 1917 until his death in 1931. From 1921 to·1923 lived in Weimar, Germany, using his home as a meeting place to spread the De Stijl philosophy to staff and students of the BAUHAUS. In 1922 he convened an International Congress of Constructivists and Dadaists in Weimar. Published a *Manifesto of Art Concret* in 1930, advocating an art of absolute purity and simplicity.

Lettering designed by **DiSpigna** for a US bicentennial stamp, 1976.

Title page for *De Stijl* magazine, vol. 4 (1921), designed by van **Doesburg**.

The use of colour in graphic design

Colour is used by graphic designers to differentiate products, to aid the communication of information and as a tool of persuasion, through the use of symbolic associations.

Victorian designers sought to overcome the limitations of monochrome printing by using excessive ornamentation, extreme tonal contrasts and discordant typography. In effect, crude typographic compositions with dramatic contrasts in type size and weight acted as a substitute for colour as designers strove for visual impact and novelty. Following the publication in 1856 of The Grammar of Ornament by Owen JONES, exotic decorative patterns, in an array of both subtle and garish colour combinations, began to appear in posters, packaging and magazines. The public's new aesthetic awareness was promoted by technical developments in CHROMOLITHOGRAPHY from the 1860s, which allowed the application of colour on popular magazine covers, advertising posters, labels and cartoons. In a great democratization of the printed image the public could enjoy wonderfully complex colour illustrations, while graphic artists began to realize the potential of certain colours to communicate unconsciously sensations, moods and concepts as diverse as aggression, joy, tranquillity, even femininity and masculinity.

Towards the end of the century followers of the ARTS AND CRAFTS MOVEMENT evolved a disciplined approach to visual imagery and typography, colour and ornament being used sensitively and with telling effect. The 'decorative honesty' espoused by William MORRIS, however, was soon challenged, not only by the curvilinear forms of ART NOUVEAU but also by the new design opportunities presented by the increasingly sophisticated chromolithographic process; in France especially the dazzling colour reproduction of theatre and music-hall posters, by artists including Jules CHÉRET and Henri de TOULOUSE-LAUTREC, enlivened what was often a drab urban landscape. Designers like Eugène GRASSET, Alphonse MUCHA and Koloman MOSER also exploited the technical and creative potential of the new medium. In England, meanwhile, the BEGGARSTAFF BROTHERS experimented with their COLLAGE technique, juxtaposing strongly delineated colour areas and white space in an entirely new way.

In the first decade of the 20th c. the potency of colour as a means of maximizing impact was exploited as never before by the German PLAKATSTIL designers, including Ludwig HOHLWEIN and Lucian BERNHARD. Strong, simple images became icons of design through the use of brilliant, unexpected colour combinations. An illusion of depth was created on the flat surface by using colours that advanced or receded depending on the context of the adjacent or surrounding colours.

After the First World War the followers of CONSTRUCTIVISM and DE STIJL explored dynamic typographic compositions complemented by the primary colours, red, blue and yellow. Blocks of colour were placed to maximize the visual effect of shapes created by the 'negative' space between formal compositional elements such as rules and lettering. The rapid technical developments of the period, combined with the increasing range and complexity of design commissions, contributed to the emergence of graphic design as a profession. During the mid-1920s and early 30s the crisp, penetrating purity of red contrasted with a dense, black typographic composition became a favoured colour combination for Jan TSCHICHOLD and other exponents of the NEW TYPOGRAPHY. Black and red remained popular throughout the evolution of the later, grid-dominated INTERNATIONAL TYPOGRAPHIC STYLE.

The geometric severity of many ART DECO designs facilitated a startling and original use of colour. The decorative appeal of Art Deco was enormous and was employed with vigour, the bold colour combinations evoking the flamboyance of the 1920s.

After the Second World War colour became an essential component of contemporary graphic design: colour magazines and Hollywood films were increasingly accessible and created new consumer demand. Innovations in printing technology enabled the production of photographic and illustrative imagery of unprecedented accuracy and realism. The significance of this new, consumer-led society was highlighted in the early 1960s by POP ART, of which such exponents as Andy Warhol employed flat, discordant colours and the imagery of throwaway consumer products, and revealed through super-enlargement that even the most lifelike photographs were made up of a series of dots. In the mid-1960s PSYCHEDELIA's clashing colours and swirling forms suggested a drug-induced, hallucinatory form of visual perception.

Since the mid-1970s designers, illustrators and art directors have had access to an unprecedented range of colours and hues which can be specified with absolute precision for reproduction by print, film, television and COMPUTER. Sophisticated market research aims to identify the psychological properties associated with colour, and colour forecasting techniques can predict those colours that will be attractive to different groups of consumers in the near future. Such information enables manufacturers and designers both to anticipate and determine this key element of popular taste. International public recognition of products and CORPORATE IDENTITY programmes can be strengthened by a consistent adherence to a distinctive combination of colours. During the early 1990s the sheer pervasiveness of colour reproduction stimulated a paradoxical revival of interest in the nostalgic and emotional appeal of black-and-white photographs and advertising commercials.

What is certain, however, is that the sometimes bewildering yet compulsively fascinating proliferation of colour images with which we are surrounded in our daily lives will continue, as ever-increasing public expectations are matched and exceeded by amazing technical advances.

1 **Chéret**, *Les Girard: L'Horloge Champs Elysées*, poster 1879.
2 **Bradley**, *The Twins*, cover for the May 1894 issue of *The Chap Book*.
3 J.H. McNair and F. and M. Macdonald (Scottish), *The Glasgow Institute of the Fine Arts*, 1895.
4 **Moser**, *Frommes Kalender*, poster c. 1898.
5 Oskar Kokoschka (Austrian), *Kunstschau*, 1908.

6 Ferdinand Andri (Austrian), poster for the XXVI Ausstellung Secession exhibition, 1906.
7 Fritz Ehmcke (German), advertising poster for Syndetikon glue, c. 1902.
8 Coles Phillips (American), *Light Consumes Coal*, 1915–16.
9 **Bernhard**, advertising poster for Bosch, 1915.

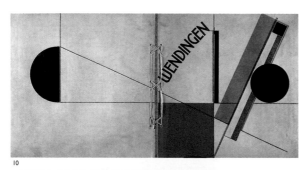

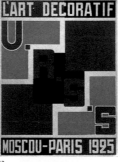

10 El **Lissitzky**, *Wendingen*, cover design, 1922.
11 Liubov Popova (Russian), *Work uniform design for actor no. 5*, 1921.
12 Dmitrii Bulanov (Russian), poster for Leningrad Advertisement Bureau promoting advertising on trams, 1926.

13 **Rodchenko**, cover of catalogue for Soviet section of Paris 1925 'Exposition Internationale des Arts Décoratifs et Industriels Modernes'.
14 Stenberg brothers (Russian), poster for the film *Springtime*, 1927.
15 **Schmidt**, poster for 1923 Bauhaus exhibition.
16 **Moholy-Nagy** and van **Doesburg**, cover of a Bauhaus book, 1925.

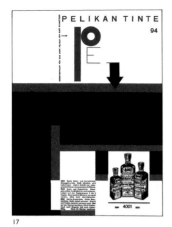

17 **Schwitters**, advertisement for Pelikan inks, 1924.
18 Karel Teige (Czechoslovakian), cover for
Red magazine, 1927.
19 **Stoecklin**, Der Buchdruck (Book Printing), 1922.
20 Man **Ray**, cover for André Breton's Le Surréalisme et
la peinture, 1928.

21 **Zwart**, page from a type catalogue for N.V. Druckerei
Trio, a printing firm in The Hague, 1929.
22 **Cassandre**, Casino advertising sign, c. 1930.
23 Le Corbusier (Swiss), cover for Des Canons, des
munitions?, 1938.

24

25

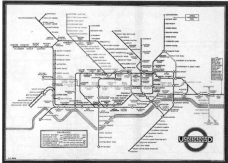

26

27

28

THE
intelligentsia
OF GREAT BRITAIN
BY DMITRI MIRSKY
(ci-devant Prince Mirsky)

including estimates of
Bernard Shaw   Eddington
H. G. Wells   Jeans
J. M. Keynes   Cole
G. K. Chesterton E. M. FORSTER
Bertrand Russell   *Lytton Strachey*
D. H. LAWRENCE   T. S. Eliot
Aldous Huxley   Dean Inge
Virginia Woolf
WYNDHAM LEWIS   Laski
Middleton Murry   **MALINOWSKY**
&c. &c.

We (the publishers) ask our friends to forgive us:
we don't agree with **everything**
~~Prince~~ MIRSKY says.

29

30

24 **Purvis**, *East Coast by L.N.E.R.*, 1925.
25 **Kauffer**, poster for London Underground, 1928.
26 **Beck**, London Underground map, 1933.
27 Max Ponty (French), Gitanes cigarette packet, *c.* 1930.
28 Paolo Garretto (Italian), August 1932 cover for *Fortune*.

29 **Morison**, *Intelligentsia of Great Britain* book cover,
    1935.
30 Shell poster commissioned by **Beddington** using an
    illustration by Graham Sutherland, 1934.

31

32

33

34

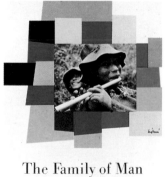

The Family of Man

The greatest photographic exhibition of all time—503 pictures from 68 countries—created by Edward Steichen for The Museum of Modern Art

Prologue by Carl Sandburg

35

36

31   **Pineles**, July 1949 cover for *Seventeen* magazine.
32   **Binder**, cover for *Graphis* no. 23, 1948.
33   **Brun**, *Geh Zum ACV*, poster 1950.
34   Walter **Ballmer**, cover for *Ali Rivista*, c. 1952.
35   Cover for *The Family of Man* exhibition catalogue
       by **Lionni**, 1955.
36   **Loewy**, Lucky Strike cigarette packet, 1940.

38

37

40

39

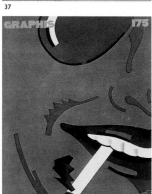

41

42

43

37   Wes Wilson (American), *The Association: Concert at the Fillmore Auditorium,* 1966.
38   **Glaser**, poster/record insert for Bob Dylan, 1967.
39   Andy Warhol (American), Velvet Underground record sleeve, 1971.
40   **Tomaszewski**, poster for the play *A Tale from Irkutsk,* 1967.
41   **Chwast**, cover of *Graphis* no. 175.
42   **Spencer**, cover for *Pioneers of Modern Typography,* 1969.
43   **Awazu**, concert poster, 1973.

44
45
46

47

48
49

50
51

44 Fifth poster from the series *Man and Environment* by van **Toorn**, 1985.

45 Logotype for British television's Channel 4 by **Lambie-Nairn**.

46 Katherine **McCoy**, cover of Cranbrook Academy of Art catalogue, 1983.

47 Trevor Jackson (British), Bass Records singles sleeve.

48 Pierluigi Cerri (Italian) of Gregotti Associati designed these 12ft (4 m) high letters for the Fiat Lingotto car plant, 1983–84.

49 **Brody**, cover for *The Face* no. 65, 1985.

50 **Computer**-generated slice from the Digital Equipment Corporation.

51 **VanderLans** and Licko, cover for Emigré 4, 1986.

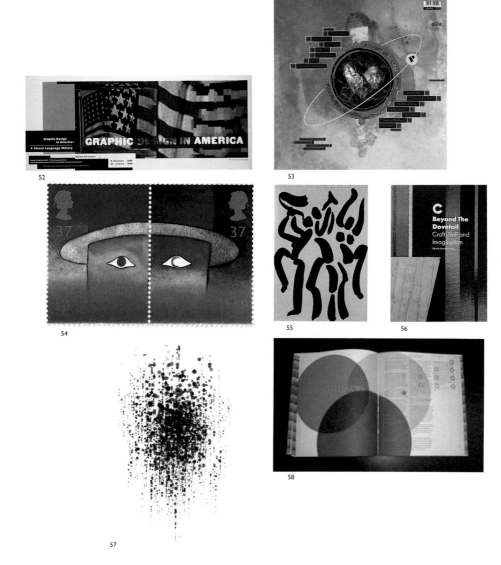

52 **Greiman**, *Graphic Design in America* exhibition poster and two billboard images, 1990.

53 Back of the sleeve by **Oliver** for the Pixies' record *Bossanova*, 1990.

54 British stamps designed by **Folon**, 1991.

55 **Troxler**, poster for South African Jazz Night, 1990.

56 **Pentagram** design for the Crafts Council by John Rushworth and Vince Frost, 1991.

57 Four Colors by John **Maeda**, designed for the book *Maeda@Media*, 2000.

58 Spread from *Licht Jahre, Zumtobel 2000–1950*, designed by Irma **Boom**, 2000.

Dorfsman, Lou (b. 1918) New York graphic designer who raised advertising and design standards within the broadcasting industry during forty-two years at the CBS Broadcasting Group. Whilst still a student at the Cooper Union School (1937–41) he produced exhibition designs for the New York World's Fair, 1939. After graduation he worked as a freelance designer 1941–45, then spent a brief period as art director in the Reiss Advertising Agency 1945–46. Joined William GOLDEN at CBS in 1946 as the radio division's art and creative director. After Golden's death in 1959 he was appointed creative director of the television network, later becoming director of design for the entire organization 1964–88. In 1966 he created all aspects of graphic information in the new CBS headquarters designed by the architect and designer Eero Saarinen. Since his retirement from CBS he has remained active as president of Lou Dorfsman Design. His achievements are confirmed by the twelve gold medals awarded by the ART DIRECTORS CLUB OF NEW YORK and by induction into its Hall of Fame (1978). In 1979 AIGA awarded him a gold medal. His work has been exhibited in one-man shows in America, Japan and Europe.

'Black History: Lost, Stolen or Strayed', the CBS television series, was heralded with this 1968 newspaper advertisement designed by **Dorfsman**.

dot-matrix printer COMPUTER-linked printing device that uses a pattern of dots to create printed characters. The image quality is relatively poor, and is generally unsuitable for reproduction purposes.

Double Crown Club Dining club founded in London in 1924 by Oliver SIMON and Hubert Foss with a membership of distinguished practitioners in book design and production. Members meet for 'the purpose of exchanging ideas on good printing'. Early attempts to crown the two most outstanding specimens of printing from the previous year foundered because unanimity could not be achieved. The club celebrated its 300th dinner in 1989.

Doves Press See WALKER, EMERY

Doyle Dane Bernbach Advertising agency formed in New York in 1949, later with offices worldwide, which helped to change the international face of advertising. The copywriter William Bernbach and graphic designer Bob Cage, two of the founders, developed a creative approach that required close collaboration between copywriter and art director working as members of a small team. This broke the tradition that gave copywriters overall creative control of an advertisement. The result was an intelligent,

Doyle Dane Bernbach produced this 1960 Volkswagen advertisement.

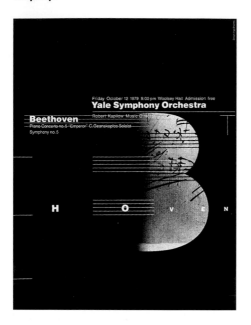

Poster for a Yale Symphony Orchestra concert in October
1979 by **Druckrey**.

'Postcode' stamps designed for PTT in 1978 by van Raalte
and **Dumbar**.

often witty integration of the verbal and visual elements; copy became more succinct and more focused to underpin an image that was both arresting and credible. The agency's approach spearheaded 'the new advertising'. It launched many outstanding art directors including Len Sirowitz, Helmut Krone, Bob Kuperman, Bill Taubin and Bert Steinhauser. Amongst highly influential, award-winning campaigns are those for the New York department store Orbach's, Levy's Bread and, most famous of all, Volkswagen.

drop cap Initial letter of the first word in a text setting that, because it is set in a larger size, extends into the lines of type below. Also referred to as a dropped initial.

THIS is an example of a three-line dropped initial, set in Gill Sans regular 8/10 pt, with the dropped caps set in Gill Sans light This is an example of a three-line dropped initial, set in Gill Sans regular 8/12 pt, with the dropped caps set in Gill Sans light This is an example of a three-line dropped initial, set in Gill Sans

Druckrey, Inge (b.1941) Since completing her graphic-design studies at the Kunstgewerbeschule, Basle (1965), Druckrey has pursued a diverse design and teaching career in Europe and America. Part of the 'new wave' of graphic designers that emerged in the late 1970s, her approach to established typographic conventions shows the influence of POST-MODERNISM. A visiting professor of design at Yale University, New Haven, she has produced numerous posters for museums, galleries and cultural events.

Dumbar, Gert (b.1940) Graphic designer and educator in the forefront of avant-garde Dutch design, responsible for a number of innovative private- and public-sector design projects. Born in Jakarta, Indonesia he studied painting and graphic design at the Royal Academy of Fine Arts in The Hague 1959–64 and at the Royal College of Art, London 1964–67. In 1967 joined industrial design group Tel Design Associates in The Hague, to develop a graphic-design department. The group produced an extensive and important CORPORATE IDENTITY for Nederlands Spoorwegan (Dutch Railways), which enjoyed international acclaim. He left Tel in 1977 to establish Studio Dumbar. A collaboration between the practice and TOTAL DESIGN produced the corporate identity for PTT, the Dutch Postal, Telegraph and

Telephone authority. Other important projects include the corporate identity programmes for ANWB (Dutch Automobile Association), Westeinde Hospital in The Hague and the award-winning SIGNAGE system for the Rijksmuseum. The studio has a staff of about fifteen, including partners Michel de Boer and Kitty de Jong. It fosters valuable links with design education, providing work experience opportunities for students from prestigious Dutch colleges, Cranbrook Academy, US and the Royal College of Art, London; Dumbar was professor of graphic design at the Royal College of Art 1985–87. He returned in 2000 as a visiting professor. Has served as chairman of the Dutch Graphic Design Association (GVN) and as president of the DESIGNERS AND ART DIRECTORS ASSOCIATION, London, 1987–88.

Dutch graphic design Holland has made a significant contribution to the history and development of graphic design, with the influence of certain key individuals extending internationally. In the 1890s and early 1900s ART NOUVEAU prevailed, with Jan TOOROP recognized as a major influence. After the First World War, two distinct strands of development emerged, with the radical ideas of DE STIJL counterbalanced by an adherence to the traditional typographic principles associated with Dutch book and type design. Piet ZWART, Paul SCHUITEMA and Willem SANDBERG were distinguished radical practitioners, with Jan van KRIMPEN representing classic typographic ideals. The Dutch ability to feed off international developments in design is evident in the experimental typographic work of Hendrik WERKMAN, who sought to explore and extend both De Stijl and the principles of CONSTRUCTIVISM. Throughout the 20th c. the willingness to combine craft skills with avant-garde ideas has given graphic design in Holland a distinctive quality. This is reflected in the pioneering achievements of a unique design patron, the Postal, Telegraph and Telephone authority (PTT): since the appointment of the enlightened Jean François van Royen as General Secretary in 1920, this major public-sector organization has used leading artists and designers to create an exciting visual identity. In the early 1960s TOTAL DESIGN in Amsterdam represented a new multidisciplinary approach to design problems, with Wim CROUWEL becoming an international figure over the next twenty-five years. Total created a new design awareness within the public sector, their success providing the platform for succeeding generations of designers to establish innovative design practices throughout

Holland. The avant-garde has flourished since the mid-1970s with the output of Anthon BEEKE and Jan van TOORN in Amsterdam and Gert DUMBAR in The Hague receiving widespread acclaim.

Dwiggins, William Addison (1880–1956)
American book and type designer, credited as the first to use the term graphic designer (1922). Although his greatest contributions were to the publishing house Alfred A. Knopf Inc. and to the Mergenthaler LINOTYPE Corporation, he also designed numerous limited editions for private presses. Studied under Frederic W. GOUDY at the Frank Holme School of Illustration, Chicago. Ran his own press in Cambridge, Ohio 1903–4, then followed Goudy to Hingham, Massachusetts, where his early work was in advertising. In 1923 he met the publisher Alfred A. Knopf, for whom he subsequently designed over three hundred books. Dwiggins's style, which inventively combines type, calligraphy, illustration and stencil forms, was largely responsible for the high visual standards at Knopf. Wrote, designed and illustrated a standard text, *Layout in Advertising* (1928). Designed many books for the Limited Editions Club. In 1931 he produced his celebrated edition of *The Time Machine* by H.G. Wells for the New York publisher Random House. During the late 1920s he was invited by Harry L. Cage of Mergenthaler to produce TYPEFACE designs. A twenty-seven-year association with the company produced outstanding types including Metro (1929–30), the text type Electra (1935) and Caledonia (1938), one of the most popular types in the US. Dwiggins is an honorary member of AIGA and the DOUBLE CROWN CLUB, London.

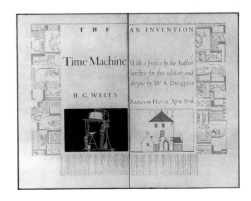

Title pages of *The Time Machine*, in the 1931 edition designed by **Dwiggins**.

E

Eckersley, Tom (1914–97) British graphic designer who established his reputation during the Second World War, maintaining a position of eminence, both as a practitioner and educator, over the ensuing three decades. Studied at Salford College of Art, Lancashire 1930–34. Worked in London 1934–40 in collaboration with Eric Lombers, designing for clients including

Poster by **Eckersley** for the General Post Office, 1952–53.

Title page of *Eckmann-Schriftprobe*, **Eckmann**'s 1901 book on letterforms.

London Transport and Shell. Cartographer with the Royal Air Force 1940–45, while continuing to design posters for public service agencies like the Ministry of Information and General Post Office. Established successful freelance practice after the war. Eckersley consistently demonstrated an ability to distil complex elements into bold graphic statements of great clarity. Awarded an OBE in 1949 for services to British poster design. Head of the graphic-design department at the London College of Printing 1957–76. Elected RDI in 1963. Awarded the CHARTERED SOCIETY OF DESIGNERS medal, 1990. Member of AGI and author of *Poster Design* (1954).

Eckmann, Otto (1865–1902) Pioneer JUGENDSTIL designer who began his career as a painter c. 1890. Studied in Hamburg, Nuremberg and at the Munich Academy. Abandoned painting in 1894 to concentrate on the applied arts and, in addition to his work as a graphic artist and TYPEFACE designer, he was responsible for furniture, ceramics, wallhangings and wallpaper designs. Produced illustrations for the influential German magazines PAN (from 1895) and *Jugend* (from 1896). Designed typefaces for the Klingspor foundry, Offenbach, including the popular ART NOUVEAU typeface EckmannSchmuck (1900). *Eckmann-Schriftprobe*, his book on letterforms, was published in 1901. From 1900 to 1902 he designed publicity material for AEG, the German electrical company that later employed Peter BEHRENS to establish their CORPORATE IDENTITY programme.

Edelmann, Heinz (b.1934) Influential and prolific German graphic and animated film designer and illustrator. Studied graphic arts at the State Academy, Düsseldorf 1953–58. Worked as a copywriter in an advertising agency 1958–59 before he set up practice in Dusseldorf in 1959, designing many posters for the theatre and the West German Broadcasting Institution. Thereafter created distinctive illustrations for the fashion magazine, *Twen* (see FLECKHAUS, Willy). During 1967 and 1968 he produced the drawings for *The Yellow Submarine*, the Beatles' acclaimed animated film. Highly inventive and technically outstanding, his imagery is both fantastical and disturbing. Subsequently moved to The Hague where he combined teaching at the Free Academy and the Royal Academy with his freelance practice. In the early 1980s he undertook a major redesign of book jackets for the Klett-Cotta publishing house, Stuttgart. Edelmann's wide range of techniques has also been frequently used in the illustration of children's books.

ABCDEFGH
abcdefgh

Egyptienne Bold, one of the range of **Egyptian** typefaces.

Symbol design by **Eksell** for the Mazetti food and confectionery company, 1956.

Egyptian Generic term for a range of heavy SLAB SERIF TYPEFACE designs. Primarily intended for posters and advertising requirements, the types display little variation of weight between the slab serifs and the vertical strokes. When first shown in 1815, and for some time thereafter, Egyptian typefaces were also referred to as 'antique'.

Eksell, Olle (b.1918) Versatile Swedish graphic, industrial and exhibition designer, illustrator, painter and sculptor. Formed Olle Eksell Design, Stockholm, in 1969. Significant both as a practitioner and promoter of design issues, his achievements have been closely linked to his output as an author. Writer and illustrator with the newspaper *Aftonbladet* from 1952. His design skills extend over CORPORATE IDENTITY, packaging, book design and exhibition displays. His *Corporate Design Programs* (1967) provided an early insight into the visual principles underpinning a successful corporate identity.

Elffers, Dick (1910–90) Dutch graphic and exhibition designer, illustrator and painter. Studied in Rotterdam at the Academy of Art 1929–33. His activities as a painter and designer were interrupted by the Second World War. In 1945 he established a studio in Amsterdam. His many memorable posters include

Cover illustration by **Edelmann** for a German translation of *Lord of the Rings*, 1969.

Elffers' famous poster *Vigilant Democracy* (1946).

Winter 1999 cover of *Emigre*.

U-Boats Out!, a classic First World War poster by **Erdt**.

Vigilant Democracy (1946) and numerous music and film images designed for the Holland Festival throughout the 1950s and 60s. He participated in the poster Biennale in Warsaw, 1968 and 1974. Exuding great vitality, Elffers' bold colours, inventive typography and patterns have been applied to book jackets and record sleeves. Exhibition design includes the Dutch pavilion in Auschwitz (1980).

em Typographic measurement derived from the square of each type size, e.g. a 10 POINT em is 10pts x 10pts, a 12pt em is 12pts x 12pts. A 12pt em (4.216mm or 0.166in) is traditionally referred to as a PICA EM. Line measurements and type areas are usually specified in pica ems.

embossing Process that uses die-stamps to create a raised impression on paper, cloth or board. Illustrations and lettering can be embossed to create a three-dimensional effect. A BLIND EMBOSSED impression is made without ink or foil.

Emigre American graphic-design journal based in Sacramento, California. Originally launched by Rudy VANDERLANS, Marc Susan and Menno Meyjes as a culture magazine for immigrants (1984). By 1986 both Susan and Meyjes had left and were replaced by Zuzana LICKO. Thereafter the editorial direction changed, and in 1988 a quarterly magazine on graphic design was produced. Since then *Emigre* has had a significant impact on the computer-generated revolution in graphic and typographic design. In 1993 the company published *Emigre (The Book); Graphic Design into the Digital Realm. Emigre*'s work has been exhibited widely in Europe and the US.

en Typographic measurement half the width of an EM.

endmatter Sections of a book that normally follow the main text, e.g. appendices, glossary, bibliography, index. See PRELIMS.

Eragny Press (1894–1912) Private press established in Hammersmith, London, by the painter, illustrator and wood engraver Lucien Pissarro (1863–1944). Son of the Impressionist painter Camille, he left France in 1890 to take advantage of the renaissance in book production inspired by the success of the KELMSCOTT PRESS, established by William MORRIS. Many of the beautiful books produced at the Eragny Press combined ART NOUVEAU–style WOODCUT illustrations with the Brook TYPEFACE designed by Pissarro in 1903.

July 1929 cover of *Harper's Bazaar*, designed by **Erté**.

Symbol design by **Excoffon** for the 1968 Grenoble Olympic Games.

Standard and **expanded** versions of the Helvetica typeface.

Erdt, Hans Rudi (1883–1918) Leading Berlin poster artist who worked along with Lucian BERNHARD, Julius GIPKENS and Julius KLINGER in developing an economical approach to poster design, which relied upon a simple message and bold shapes. Much of Erdt's work was done for the Berlin lithographic printers Hollerbaum and Schmidt. During the First World War his talents were used on behalf of the German war effort. His classic *U-Boats Out!* poster c. 1916 is a strong, highly reductive composition and displays a skilful manipulation of letterforms.

Erté (1892–1990) Russian-born illustrator and costume designer for theatre and film. Born Romain de Tirtoff, he established a reputation in Paris for his exotic illustrations and bold set designs. Moved to US in 1924 after signing an exclusive contract with the fashion magazine HARPER'S BAZAAR. This relationship continued until 1937, by which time he had produced many of the illustrations that have become archetypal images of ART DECO. Continued working into his nineties, with his prodigious output embracing costume design, jewelry, ballet sets, posters, books and editorial illustrations. Published his autobiography *Erté: Things I Remember* in 1975.

Excoffon, Roger (1910–83) Self-taught, versatile French graphic and TYPEFACE designer. Born in Marseilles, he moved to Paris to study painting, quickly becoming involved in the graphic arts. Established his own studio in 1947 while also working as design director of the typefoundry Fonderie Olive, Marseille. In 1956 jointly founded U&O, a successful advertising agency that handled many major accounts including Bally shoes and Air France. After U&O he set up his own consultancy, Excoffon Conseil, in 1972. His numerous posters display an impressive range of graphic techniques combined with a consistent typographic approach. Produced a number of DISPLAY typefaces for Fonderie Olive, including Banco (1951), Mistral (1953), Choc (1955), Diane (1956), Calypso (1958), Nord (1959) and his masterpiece Antique Olive (1962).

expanded/extended Wider and elongated version of a standard TYPEFACE design.

Medium
Expanded

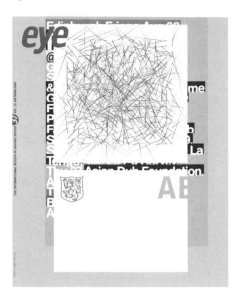

Cover design of **Eye**, Autumn 2000 (issue 37).

One of the black Penguin Classics covers introduced by **Facetti** in 1963.

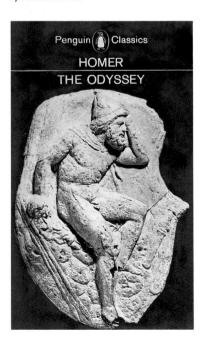

Eye International review of graphic design published as a quarterly magazine. Founded in London in 1990 by British graphic-design-historian Rick Poyner who remained editor until 1997. The magazine has made a significant contribution to the development of a critical and reflective writing on contemporary graphic-design issues. It seeks to challenge and extend graphic-design history by acknowledging the achievements of lesser-known designers.

F

Facetti, Germano (b.1926) Italian designer who was art director of Penguin Books, London, 1961–72. Training originally in architecture and art history in Milan, Facetti worked for the journals *Domus* and *Architectural Review* before assuming responsibility for the design of Olivetti's showrooms in Britain. His achievement at Penguin was to establish a cover design programme that redirected the distinguished typographic tradition of Penguin and Pelican books towards a more contemporary visual approach, with new illustrative and photographic opportunities. Facetti now works as a design consultant in Italy.

Farrow, Mark (b.1960) British graphic designer renowned for CD designs. During the early 1980s Farrow worked in Manchester as a freelance designer for Factory Records and the Haçienda nightclub. Moving to London in 1985, he quickly established a fruitful partnership with pop group The Pet Shop Boys. The collaboration, dedicated to challenging production and marketing conventions, produced a number of celebrated iconic covers, including *Suburbia* (1986), *Actually* (1987), *Bilingual* (1996). His company's work for other bands, such as Spiritualized and Manic Street Preachers, is equally bold and unconventional. Farrow Design's versatility extends beyond the music industry and is confirmed by his contribution (with Wilkinson Eyre Architects) to designing a new gallery, Making of the Modern World, for the Science Museum, London (2000).

fat face Term for those ROMAN TYPEFACE designs that exhibit an extreme contrast between their thick and thin strokes. BOLD faces originated in the early 19th c. and were much used in posters and advertising.

Federal Art Project (FAP) The Works Progress Administration (WPA), instigated by the Roosevelt government as part of the New Deal, was created in

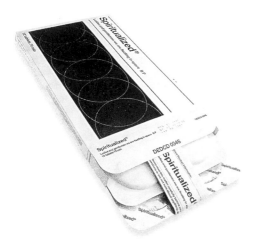

CD package designed by **Farrow** Design for Spiritualized's album *Ladies and Gentlemen We Are Floating in Space*, 1997.

ABCDEFGH
abcdefgh

Fat face Figgins Condensed No.2, designed in 1870.

Advertisement that appeared in the *New Yorker* for the magazine *Woman's Day*, by **Federico** (1953).

1935 to provide employment for millions left jobless by the Great Depression in the US. The WPA's Federal Art Project (1935–39) gave work to artists, writers, actors and musicians. A division of FAP was dedicated to poster production, presenting public service information on social issues such as health, education and housing, as well as advertising cultural events and the WPA programme. Drawing together illustrators, designers, painters and sculptors, the poster division created some 35,000 designs, of which about 2,000 have survived. The modernity of these posters (e.g. the work of Lester BEALL for the Rural Electrification Administration) contrasts strikingly with the naturalistic illustration that prevailed at that time. In part this was the result of the influence of avant-garde European art, but an additional factor was the widespread use of silkscreen printing, which produced bold, simple shapes and broad expanses of flat colour.

Federal Design Improvement Program
Established by the US government in 1974 to improve all aspects of design in the public service. Embracing architecture, interiors, landscaping and graphic communication, the initiative had a specific Graphics Improvement Program directed by Jerome Perlmutter. The first federal department to gain from the programme was the Department of Labor, with a cohesive CORPORATE IDENTITY developed by John MASSEY and the Center for Advanced Research in Design. Many other leading American designers were involved, as the programme extended to about forty different departments and agencies. The initiative brought to federal government the high visual standards and professionalism of design as practised in the private sector.

Federico, Gene (b.1918) American art director and graphic designer. Trained at the Pratt Institute, New York, 1936–38, and under Herbert BAYER at the Art Students League, New York, 1939-41. Following war service with the US Army, Federico worked for leading American advertising agencies including DOYLE DANE BERNBACH 1950–53, Douglas D. Simon 1953–58 and Benton & Bowles 1958–66. In 1967 he co-founded Lord, Geller, Federico, Einstein Inc., New York. Federico's work is distinctive for its directness, visual wit and consistent typographic elegance. His contribution to post-war American advertising and graphic design was confirmed by the award of the AIGA medal in 1987 and his induction in 1980 to the ART DIRECTORS CLUB OF NEW YORK Hall of Fame. Member of AGI.

Feininger's woodcut for the title page of *Europaeische Graphik*, 1921.

Festival of Britain symbol, designed by Abram Games.

Feininger, Lyonel (1871–1956) Expressionist painter, graphic artist and educator. Born in New York, he became an influential master of graphic printing at the BAUHAUS design school. Travelled to Hamburg in 1887 where he studied at the Kunstgewerbeschule. Produced humorous illustrations for newspapers before moving to Weimar in 1906, where he established a studio. His appointment at the Bauhaus in 1919, along with Johannes ITTEN and the sculptor Gerhard Marcks ensured that Expressionism and craft skills became dominant influences during the school's early years. Returned to America in 1936, teaching summer courses in California (1936) and at Black Mountain College, North Carolina (1945).

Fella, Edward (b.1938) American designer and educator. Originally trained as an apprentice commercial artist in a Detroit art studio (1957). Had a successful career as a designer before becoming a student at Cranbrook Academy of Arts in the mid-1980s. After graduating with an MFA he became a graphic-design tutor at California Institute of the Arts (CalArts) in Valencia, California (1987). Fella's irreverant approach to typography deconstructs and manipulates language and images in a free and poetic manner. His stream-of-consciousness ballpoint drawings are outstanding examples of a graphic imagination that finds limitless invention in the apparently random collision of words and phrases.

Festival of Britain (1951) Nationwide celebration commemorating the centenary of the Great Exhibition of 1851. The Festival proclaimed the 'British achievement in arts, sciences and industrial design'. Against a backdrop of post-war austerity it represented a surge of confidence in a better future. The major exhibition centre was the Royal Festival Hall on London's South Bank. Giving a lead particularly in the areas of architecture and technology, the Festival created many opportunities for an emerging generation of graphic designers, including F.H.K. HENRION, Milner GRAY and Abram GAMES, who created the Festival SYMBOL. A Typography Panel chaired by Charles Hasler introduced a Festival *Specimen Book* of approved lettering. The Festival alphabet was designed by Phillip Boydell.

Fili, Louise (b.1951) American designer of elegant book jackets, Fili draws upon European graphic design from the interwar period. Her interest in early vernacular forms of commercial art has been fuelled by

Fili's book jacket for *The Lover*, 1983.

Fior's P A I G C Unidade Guiné Cabo Verde political poster.

numerous trips to France and Italy. Fili's POST- MODERN retro style is highly individualistic and reveals an inventive approach to typography, initially fostered as a student employed in the college typeshop and then developed during a period working for Herb LUBALIN (1976–78). Fili was art director at Pantheon Books (1978–89) before leaving to establish her own studio.

filmsetting *See* PHOTOCOMPOSITION

finished art(work) *See* ARTWORK

Fior, Robin (b. 1935) London-born designer of politically committed graphic design who has created posters and pamphlets for numerous left-wing organizations in the UK and Portugal. Largely a self-taught designer, in 1955 he learnt printing techniques at evening classes taken by Edward WRIGHT at Central Saint Martin's School of Art and Design, London, where he began to teach part-time in 1958. Fior's career has been motivated by his concern for radical causes. During the 1960s he designed influential protest graphics for the Campaign for Nuclear Disarmament (CND), adopting a distinctive typographic modernism that revealed the influence of the INTERNATIONAL TYPOGRAPHIC STYLE. Ken GARLAND also made an important graphic contribution to this movement, and, in 1964, Fior joined Garland and others as a signatory to the original *First Things First* manifesto, which called upon graphic designers to direct their skills towards socially responsible design. In 1960 Fior redesigned the journal *Peace News* using Record Gothic and the German Akzidenz Bold typefaces; a design that was to influence Fior's student David HILLMAN in his later redesign of *The Guardian* newspaper. After moving to Lisbon in 1972, Fior was soon involved in designing political propaganda, particularly in support of groups demanding independence for Portugal's African colonies. He has played an important role in Portugal as a graphic-design practitioner and educator; since 1974 he has taught at the Centro de Arte e Comunicação Visual, Lisbon. In recent years Fior has experimented with typography, graphic form and the physical structure of the printed artefact to explore language's role. His involvement with bilingual projects in English and Portuguese has placed him in a unique position to engage with these issues.

Fiore, Quentin (b. 1920) American designer. Primarily self-taught, Fiore briefly attended drawing and painting classes in New York and at the New Bauhaus in Chicago. After early work experience

Flagg's famous First World War recruiting poster, 1917.

Cover design for *Twen* magazine by **Fleckhaus**, 1963.

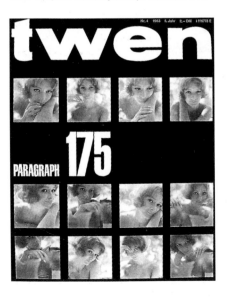

with Lester BEALL, he led a successful career working with a wide range of corporate clients throughout the 1940s and 50s. Fiore's international reputation derives from his design of a number of high-profile books. His work (as designer and coauthor) on two seminal texts by Marshall McLuhan, *The Medium is the Massage* (1967) and *War and Peace in the Global Village* (1968), was particularly inventive and greatly helped to present McLuhan's ideas to a global audience. Fiore's unexpected juxtaposition of text and image was also used to great effect in *Do it! Scenarios of the Revolution* (1970), a radical, political text written by underground leader Jerry Rubin and *I Seem to Be a Verb* (1970), a collaborative project on technology and the environment involving Buckminster Fuller, Jerome Agel and Fiore.

Flagg, James Montgomery (1877–1960)
Illustrator responsible for one of the great graphic icons of 20th-c. America: based on a contemporary British poster of Kitchener by Alfred LEETE, Flagg's First World War poster of Uncle Sam, *I want YOU for US Army* (1917), continues to be reproduced. Derived from a self-portrait, Flagg's poster was revived again during the Second World War. Born in New York, he trained at the Art Students League, with further periods of study in England and France. In total he produced some forty-six war posters, in his distinctive fluid style. A popular editorial illustrator, he worked for many of the leading US journals, including *Saturday Evening Post* and *Collier's*. He also wrote and illustrated several books, including *Celebrities* (1951).

Fleckhaus, Willy (1925–83) German art director renowned for his design of the post-teenage magazine *Twen*. First published in 1959, *Twen* quickly established an innovative approach to editorial design. Dynamic covers and page layouts were supported by powerful photography and excellent typography; during eleven years of publication Fleckhaus attracted contributions from many of the world's leading writers, photographers and illustrators. A gifted book designer, he designed superb book covers for the German publishing houses Suhrkamp and Insel. From about 1980 he art directed the *Frankfurter Allgemeine Magazin*. His significance and influence were acknowledged when he was appointed professor of graphic design, first at Essen (1974) and then at Wuppertal (1981). Fleckhaus's work has been recognized by inclusion in many exhibitions and by the award of the gold medal from the ART DIRECTORS CLUB OF NEW YORK.

Poster devised by **Fletcher** in 1985 for the 1986 exhibition '100th Anniversary of the Automobile'.

Letters from the **Folio** typeface.

ABCDEFGH
abcdefgh

Fletcher, Alan (b.1931) British graphic designer. Studied at Central School of Arts and Crafts, London (1950–51), the Royal College of Art, London (1953–56), and Yale University School of Architecture and Design, New Haven (1956). Remained in US for some years, working for the CONTAINER CORPORATION OF AMERICA and in 1958 for *FORTUNE* magazine, New York. Returned to London as a freelance designer, becoming founding partner in 1962 of Fletcher/FORBES/GILL, London. In 1965, following Bob Gill's departure and the arrival of Theo Crosby, the practice became Crosby/ Fletcher/Forbes and provided the foundation for the establishment of PENTAGRAM, London, 1972. Fletcher's approach to design relies on strong concepts, a sharp wit and an unerring sense of graphic style. Fletcher and Forbes shared the DESIGNERS AND ART DIRECTORS ASSOCIATION President's Award (1977) for outstanding contributions to design. Elected RDI in 1972. Left Pentagram in 1992 to continue his career as a freelance consultant. Inducted into ART DIRECTORS CLUB OF NEW YORK Hall of Fame (1994). Published *Beware Wet Paint* (1996) and *The art of looking sideways* (2001).

Fleuron, The (1923–30) British typographic journal edited by Oliver SIMON from 1923 until 1925, and thereafter by Stanley MORISON. Whilst contributing to the inter-war revival in British typography, *The Fleuron* was essentially a conservative influence, largely ignoring progressive typographic developments in Europe.

flexography Form of LETTERPRESS printing that uses rubber or flexible plastic plates. Most commonly used for printing on a wide range of packaging surfaces.

flow chart/flow diagram Graphic representation illustrating the sequential 'flow' of a process or activity.

Folio Popular SANS SERIF TYPEFACE designed by Konrad Bauer and Walter Baum and cut by the German foundry Bauer between 1957 and 1962. A range of weights is available.

folio (a) Resulting sheet or book size when a standard sheet size is cut or folded in half. (b) Printing term for page numbers.

Folon, Jean-Michel (b.1934) French-based graphic artist and illustrator. Born in Brussels, he studied architecture before specializing in design and illustration. Folon's haunting and melancholic drawings have appeared in many leading magazines including *Time, FORTUNE, GRAPHIS* and *The New Yorker*. His work constantly addresses the alienation of the individual in an increasingly technological age. Endlessly inventive within this theme his illustrations have been used extensively in posters, advertising and in animated sequences for film and television. Designed murals for a Métro station in Brussels (1974) and for Waterloo railway station in London (1975). Has exhibited in Europe and America, and received the ART DIRECTORS CLUB OF NEW YORK award 1966. Folon is now seeking to combine his commercial practice with more specifically fine art–based projects.

font (UK), fount (US) Traditional term in HOT METAL COMPOSITION for a complete set of alphabets relating to one size of TYPEFACE. Would normally include UPPER- and LOWER-CASE ROMAN, SMALL CAPITALS, upper- and lower-case ITALIC, upper- and lower-case BOLD, figures and punctuation marks. In PHOTOCOMPOSITION the definition of a font/fount is less clear, as the potential for reduction, enlargement and distortion enables the range of alphabet sizes supplied by a particular system to be expanded endlessly.

Forbes, Colin (b.1928) British graphic designer. Studied at Central School of Arts and Crafts, London 1948–51, before becoming a design assistant to Herbert SPENCER 1952–53. Head of the Department of Graphic Design, Central School of Arts and Crafts, 1958–61. In 1962 co-founded FLETCHER/Forbes/GILL, London, which became Crosby/Fletcher/ Forbes in 1965 with the arrival of architect Theo Crosby. The practice was absorbed into the newly created PENTAGRAM (1972). Forbes's approach is based on a belief that the solution is within the problem. His acclaimed posters include a series for Pirelli (1966–69) and the campaign against admission charges to British museums (1970). In 1978 he moved to the US, with overall responsibility for Pentagram's New York office. International president of AGI 1975–79. Forbes and Alan Fletcher shared the DESIGNERS AND ART DIRECTORS ASSOCIATION President's Award (1977) for outstanding contributions to design. Past president of the AIGA.

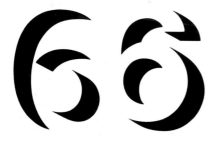

Zinc Development Association logotype for a die-casting conference, 1966, designed by **Forbes**.

July 1946 cover of **Fortune** designed by Ladislav Sutnar.

Fortune American monthly business magazine of industry and science, founded in 1930 by publisher Henry Luce and famous for exemplary standards in editorial design. For over forty years, beginning with the original art director Thomas M. Cleland, the magazine presented complex technical information in an accessible and visually elegant manner. The European émigré art directors who applied the design principles of MODERNISM at *Fortune* include Will BURTIN 1945–49, Leo LIONNI 1949–62 and Walter ALLNER 1962–74. Covers and illustrations were commissioned from Fernand Léger, Herbert MATTER, Ladislav SUTNAR, Herbert BAYER, Gyorgy KEPES and Lester BEALL.

Fougasse (1887–1965) Pseudonym for English humorous illustrator Cyril Kenneth Bird. Former Royal Engineer in the British Army who was invalided out of the war after being badly wounded at Gallipoli in 1916. Became a cartoonist following the success of the illustrations he produced during his convalescence. Famous for his Second World War poster campaigns *Careless Talk Costs Lives* and *Waste the Food and Help the Hun*. Art editor 1937–48 and editor 1949–53 of *Punch* magazine.

founder's/foundry type Top-quality metal type, cast and supplied by typefoundries for hand composition.

four-colour process Means of producing colour printing using four separate plates to print yellow, magenta, cyan (blue) and black. The plates are produced using a photographic technique that 'separates out' the yellow, magenta, cyan and black elements from the original image to be printed. The successive build-up of the four colours gives a convincing impression of full colour.

Fraktur Early form of BLACK LETTER, originating in Germany at the beginning of the 16th c.

François, André (b.1915) French illustrator and cartoonist. Born in Timisoara, Romania, he studied in Budapest and in Paris with A.M. CASSANDRE 1935–36. François has been an innovative and prolific illustrator for over five decades. Renowned for his advertising posters and covers for international journals including *GRAPHIS, Punch* and *The New Yorker,* he has also illustrated numerous books, many for children. Increasingly working in the areas of painting and sculpture, his versatility extends to designing theatre sets, having worked for a number of leading directors

WASTE THE FOOD
AND
HELP THE HUN

One of the famous Second World War posters designed by **Fougasse** to boost the Allied war effort.

Cover design for *Graphis* no. 106, by **François** (1963).

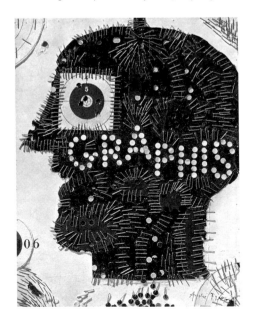

during the late 1950s and early 60s. Exhibitions of his work have been shown throughout the world. An Hon RDI, François was also awarded an honorary doctorate from the Royal College of Art, London in 1977. His many graphic achievements are celebrated in *André François* (1986).

Franklin Gothic Popular SANS SERIF TYPEFACE often used for headlines and DISPLAY setting. Designed by Morris Fuller BENTON, the full range of alphabets, including CONDENSED, wide and ITALIC, was issued by AMERICAN TYPE FOUNDERS COMPANY between 1903 and 1912.

ABCDEFGH
abcdefgh

Franklin Gothic typeface.

Fraser, Claud Lovat (1890–1921) British illustrator and theatre designer. Studied art at the Westminster School of Art, London, under Walter Sickert. Before the First World War he produced a series of hand-coloured chapbooks. After being invalided out of the army (1916), established a reputation producing book jackets for the Poetry Bookshop, illustrations for the Curwen Press (see Harold CURWEN), and graphics for Heal & Son and London Underground. His loose, linear style – achieved with a reed pen – evokes the robust WOODCUT illustrations of earlier centuries. In 1920 he designed the poster, sets and costumes for a production of *The Beggar's Opera* in London. Fraser's romantic, colourful images were particularly effective within the monochrome typographic setting of a well-designed book – as in his illustrations for *Pirates* (1921). *The Book of Lovat* (1923) by Haldane McFall summarized his brief but prolific career.

Fraser, Eric (1902–83) English illustrator and designer. Trained at Goldsmiths' College of Art, London 1919–23. He quickly established himself as a professional illustrator, his renowned association with *Radio Times* stretching from 1926 through to the early 70s. Fraser's work also featured in magazines like *VOGUE*, *HARPER'S BAZAAR*, *The STUDIO* and *The Listener*. His early illustrations reveal the influence of CUBISM and FUTURISM, with later works recalling the strength and

Eric **Fraser**'s Mr Therm symbol for the Gaslight and Coke Company, 1932.

Symbol of the Slinger Group designed by June **Fraser** in 1965.

Baynard Claudia initials for The Baynard Press, by **Freedman**.

contrast of fine, early WOODCUT prints. Created Mr Therm, a much-loved cartoon figure used by the British gas industry for over thirty years from 1932. During the 1930s and 40s he worked as a poster designer for London Transport, Shell, Guinness and the General Post Office. In later years he became more active as a book illustrator, working for publishers like the Folio Society, the GOLDEN COCKEREL PRESS and the Limited Editions Club (US). His illustrations for *The Lord of the Rings* (1977) are of particular note.

Fraser, June (b.1930) Graphic and packaging designer. Completed a graphic-design training at the Royal College of Art, London in 1957. From 1957 until 1980 worked for DESIGN RESEARCH UNIT, London, an early and influential multidisciplinary design practice, becoming a partner in 1963 and director in 1968. Projects at that time included award-winning packaging for Berkshire hosiery and Hoskyns computer software company and several large CORPORATE IDENTITY schemes. One of the first women to have a significant influence in British graphic design, in 1980 she joined John Lewis Partnership, London, as head of graphic design, responsible for the redesign of all own-brand packaging. Became head of industrial design at the DESIGN COUNCIL, London in 1984 – charged with the brief of promoting design to British industry – after which she set up as a design consultant in London. Served as president of the CHARTERED SOCIETY OF DESIGNERS, London, 1983–85.

Freedman, Barnett (1901–58) British illustrator and designer who produced many posters and book jackets for clients like London Transport, Shell, the General Post Office and Faber & Faber. During the early 1930s he was influential in reviving and popularizing colour LITHOGRAPHY as a medium for book illustration. Some of his most successful work was for the Limited Editions Club of New York, including *War and Peace* (1938) and *Anna Karenina* (1951). His classic stamps celebrating George V's jubilee in 1935 were widely acclaimed by philatelists and the general public alike. War artist (along with Edward BAWDEN and Edward Ardizonne) during the Second World War.

French graphic design Distinguished primarily for its contribution to the art of the poster. Throughout the halcyon days of the 1890s and early 1900s the organic and decorative potential of ART NOUVEAU was explored by a number of great poster designers, including Henri de TOULOUSE-LAUTREC, Pierre BONNARD, Jules CHÉRET, Eugène GRASSET and Alphonse MUCHA.

From the 1920s through to the Second World War a distinctively Gallic illustrative tradition evolved, most noticeably in the work of masters like Jean CARLU, A.M. CASSANDRE, and Paul COLIN. Many of their posters demonstrate a remarkable sophistication in conception and execution. Book illustration and advertising at this time were less distinguished, with a great diversity of styles. Post-war, Raymond SAVIGNAC and Bernard VILLEMOT perfected a style based on humour and graphic spontaneity. Although receiving widespread acclaim, much of the work produced during this period lacked the innovation and rigour associated with the output of Cassandre and his contemporaries. Typographically the 1950s and 60s were notable for the TYPEFACE designs of Roger EXCOFFON, and even more importantly, Adrian FRUTIGER. Frutiger's SANS SERIF type, UNIVERS (1957), has proved to be one of the most rational and successful type programmes of the 20th c. The political unrest of 1968 produced many spontaneous graphic statements of great vitality and inventiveness and encouraged a flourishing underground press. GRAPUS set out to challenge conventional commercial practice by working exclusively for worthy causes within the public domain. The established French tradition of visual wit and charm has been extended over the past twenty-five years by Roman CIESLEWICZ, a Polish emigrant. Cieslewicz's contribution is typical of an increasingly wide range of international influences, which whilst contributing to some outstanding work, make it more difficult to discern the uniquely French characteristics of earlier decades.

Frere-Jones, Tobias (b. 1970) American TYPEFACE designer. Trained at Rhode Island School of Design (1988–92) where he was influenced by contact with such leading designers as Inge DRUCKERY and Mathew CARTER. Whilst at college he developed a working relationship with the Font Bureau, Boston, a digital foundry. In 1991 he released (through FontFont) his first commercial typeface Dolores, named after his brother's rock band. Moved to Boston in 1992 to join the Font Bureau. Subsequently created such fonts as Garage Gothic (1992), inspired by the rough aesthetics of parking receipts and Interstate (1993–99), based on federal highway signage. Frere-Jones finds inspiration in diverse sources: Nobel (1993) is based on work by Dutch designer S.H. Roos and reveals Frere-Jones's fascination with typographic history; Pilsner (1995) was inspired by a French beer label and suggests the influence of his urban surroundings. Frere-Jones has also worked for *Fuse*, the journal of

experimental typeface design, for whom he made three fonts – Reactor (1993), Fibonacci (1994) and Microphone (1995). In 2000 he left Font Bureau, returning to New York to collaborate with Jonathan HOEFLER on such fonts as Lever Sans (2000) and Mercury (2000). He teaches at Yale School of Art.

Friedman, Daniel (1945–95) American graphic designer who graduated from Carnegie Institute of Technology, Pittsburg, Pennsylvania, 1967. Thereafter studied at the ULM HOCHSCHULE FÜR GESTALTUNG, West Germany, and at the Allgemeine Gewerbeschule, Basle, Switzerland. Identifying with the American New Wave (See POST-MODERNISM) that emerged in the early 1970s, Friedman attempted to challenge and redefine the functionalism underpinning the Swiss typographic tradition. His design solutions were

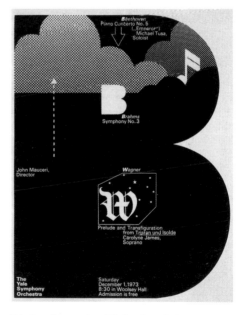

Friedman's poster for a Yale Symphony Orchestra concert, 1973.

Interstate typeface designed by **Frere-Jones**, 1993–99.

ABCDEFGH
abcdefgh

overtly expressive and often incorporated a determination to exploit the potential of electronic media. Returned to the US in 1970. Taught at Yale University, New Haven before becoming assistant professor at the School of Visual Arts, New York 1972–75. From 1975 to 1995 ran his own practice in New York City. His design autobiography *Dan Friedman: Radical Modernism* was published in 1994.

frontmatter American publishing term for PRELIMS.

Froshaug, Anthony (1920–84) British typographer and educator. Trained at the Central School of Arts and Crafts, London, 1937–39, specializing in drawing and engraving. During the Second World War he became a freelance printer, typographer and exhibition designer producing early British examples of progressive European typography influenced by Jan TSCHICHOLD. Moved to Cornwall, England, to set up his printing press, briefly returning to London 1952–53 to teach typography at the Central School of Arts and Crafts. From 1957 to 1961 was professor in graphic design and visual communication at the ULM HOCHSCHULE FÜR GESTALTUNG. Returned to England to teach at the Royal College of Art, London, 1961–64. Thereafter, worked as a part-time lecturer at a number of English art schools, with a period 1967–69 studying architecture at the Architectural Association School, London. In 1971 he re-established his printing press in London. His contribution to modernist typographic design is documented in *Anthony Froshaug: Typography and Text* (2000).

Frutiger, Adrian (b.1928) Swiss typographer and TYPEFACE designer. Trained at the Kunstgewerbeschule, Zurich 1948–52. Moved to Paris in 1952 following an invitation from Charles Peignot, of the typefounders DEBERNY & PEIGNOT. Quickly established his credentials as a type designer with his first major face, Méridien (1955). Frutiger's international reputation was established with UNIVERS, a SANS SERIF face. The success of Univers was based on its elegant simplicity supplemented by a family of twenty-one visually co-ordinated variations, including regular, BOLD, CONDENSED and ITALIC. Each variation was allocated a numerical code, rather than the conventional nomenclature describing weight and width. His many other typefaces include the OCR-B standard alphabet for optical recognition (1965–71), Serifa (1967), Iridium (1972), Glypha (1979) and Icone (1980). In addition to his type designing, Frutiger has worked in the areas of book design, calligraphy, logotypes and sculpture. He has been a consultant to IBM, the Stempel typefoundry, and the airports of Paris, producing lettering for the SIGNAGE at Charles de Gaulle airport during the early 1970s. (This alphabet subsequently appeared in 1976 as Frutiger, a sans serif family that used the numerical coding system first developed in Univers.) Frutiger's output continues unabated with his involvement in the production of typefaces for the ever-expanding range of technologically based typographic systems.

ABCDEFGH
abcdefgh

Distillation by **Froshaug** of the text of Bach's *Mass in B Minor*; his condensed version (1948), in which whole phrases are condensed into a single new word, fills only a few lines.

Frutiger designed the eponymous Frutiger sans serif typeface.

Fuel London-based design group founded in 1991 by Peter Miles, Damon Murray and Stephen Sorrell at the Royal College of Art. Their creative reputation was established at the RCA through their magazine *Fuel*, which adopted a visually aggressive stance on sensitive subjects with issues called 'Girl', 'Hype', 'USSR', 'Cash' and 'Dead'. Continuing critical acclaim has inevitably obliged the practice to embrace the opportunities and challenges presented by a diverse range of mainstream design and advertising campaigns for such names as Levi Strauss, MTV Europe and Sony. In 1998, Fuel designed Juergen Teller's book *GO-SEES*. The designers have directed television commercials and produced a series of short films called *Original Copies*, which combined live action with computer animation. In 2000, they designed and produced *Wow Wow*, a publication of website reviews, and also published *Fuel 3000*, a critical enquiry into the future.

Fukuda, Shigeo (b.1932) Pioneering Japanese designer whose work combines the traditions of Japanese culture with the wit and eclecticism favoured in the West. Since graduating from Tokyo National University of Fine Arts and Music (1956), he has embraced all aspects of graphic-design practice, with his posters receiving international acclaim. Appointed to carry out poster, SIGNAGE and PICTOGRAM design for Expo '70, Osaka and signage for the Sapporo Winter Olympics, 1972. Awarded the gold medal at the Warsaw International Biennale of Posters, 1972. As a leading representative of the increasing internationalism apparent in Japanese graphic design since the mid-1960s, he has shown his work in many group and one-man shows throughout the world. Member of AGI. Visiting professor at Yale University, New Haven during the late 1980s.

full colour Alternative term for FOUR-COLOUR PROCESS.

Fuse Journal of experimental typography founded by British designer Neville BRODY and writer Jon Wozencroft. Published sporadically since 1991, *Fuse* introduces innovative fonts (on disk) created by leading international type designers. The journal also provides a forum for debate on typographic issues and publishes posters that demonstrate diverse applications of selected fonts.

Badge by **Fuel** from their book *Fuel 3000*.

Silkscreen design by **Fukuda** advertising his exhibition at Keio Department Store, Tokyo, 1975.

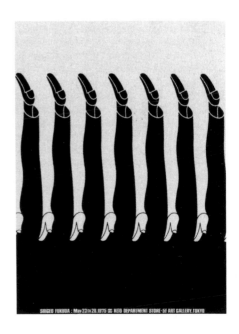

Paul Renner's **Futura** typeface.

ABCDEFGÀ
abcdefgh

Futura Classic German SANS SERIF TYPEFACE designed by Paul RENNER and originally issued by the Bauer type-foundry (1927–30). The characters exhibit a distinctive geometric quality throughout the full range of weights and variations. Futura is used for text and DISPLAY purposes.

Futurism Revolutionary art movement founded in 1909 by Italian writer and poet Filippo Tommaso MARINETTI. Conceived as a literary movement, it subsequently embraced all the arts including painting, sculpture, music and architecture. The first Futurist Manifesto, published in the French newspaper *Le Figaro* on 20 February 1909, advocated an uneasy mix of Italian nationalism, militarism and the 'new religion of speed', as expressed through cars and aeroplanes. Other significant Futurists included Umberto Boccioni, Giacomo Balla and Gino Severini. Futurism encouraged the emergence of the typographer/poet, challenging the tradition of the printed page and the predictable sequence of typographic information. Type elements and COLLAGE were used in a dynamic manner to create picture-poems, early forerunners of concrete poetry. Futurism's influence as a force for change declined rapidly after about 1915.

Futurism's founder, Filippo Marinetti, designed this cover for the 1915 Futurist Manifesto, *Mountains + Valleys + Streets x Joffre*.

Advertisement for Campari that appeared in 1923, designed by Fortunato Depero, an exponent of **Futurism**.

One of the posters designed by **Games** for the War Office, 1942.

G

Games, Abram (1914–96) British poster and graphic designer. Largely self-taught, having left St Martin's School of Art after two terms. Between 1932 and 1936 worked for Askew-Young, a London studio. Awarded first prize in a London County Council poster competition in 1936, enabling him to establish an eventually successful studio with clients including Shell, London Transport and the General Post Office. In 1939 Games joined the infantry, and was drafted to the War Office in 1941 to produce a Royal Armoured Corps recruiting poster. Persuaded the War Office to commission many instructional and educational posters and in 1942 was appointed to the newly created post of Official War Poster Designer. Left the War Office in 1946 having designed nearly a hundred posters and immediately resumed his freelance practice. His personal philosophy of 'maximum meaning, minimum means' gave his posters, advertisements, symbols and stamps a distinctive conceptual and symbolic quality. Games went on to produce hundreds of posters for private and public organizations in Britain and Israel. His symbols for the 1951 FESTIVAL OF BRITAIN (designed in 1948), BBC Television (1952) and the Queen's Award to Industry (1965) are of particular note. Visiting lecturer in graphic design at the Royal College of Art, London 1946–53. In 1957 he was awarded an OBE and in 1959 was appointed RDI. Awarded the DESIGNERS AND ART DIRECTORS ASSOCIATION President's Award 1991. *Over My Shoulder*, published in 1960, is his account of his career to that date.

Garamond Distinguished French OLD FACE ROMAN TYPEFACE designed by the Parisian engraver and typefounder Claude Garamond (1480–1561). The relatively large X-HEIGHT makes Garamond a popular choice for text setting. Garamond was the first of the classic typefaces to be revived by MONOTYPE in the early 1920s.

ABCDEFGH
abcdefgh

Monotype **Garamond** typeface.

Garland's cover design for the Galt Toys catalogue 1969–70.

Assorted images EP record sleeve for the group Magazine, designed by **Garrett** (1983).

Garland, Ken (b.1929) British graphic designer who trained at the West of England Academy of Art under Anthony FROSHAUG and Herbert SPENCER, and at the Central School of Arts and Crafts, London 1952–54. Art Editor of *DESIGN* magazine 1956–62, then established Ken Garland and Associates, London. In 1964 he published a manifesto entitled *First Things First* – signed by twenty-one other designers and photographers – which expressed concern that talents and resources were being squandered on consumer advertising, and that projects of benefit to social causes should be afforded a higher priority. Garland's body of work reflects this credo. Between 1962 and 1966 he produced striking posters for the Campaign for Nuclear Disarmament. Designed books for the Ministry of Technology, London 1962–67 and Cambridge University Press 1973–75 as well as CORPORATE IDENTITY programmes for Barbour Index 1962–73 and the toymakers James Galt 1962–82. During the 1980s responsible for elegant catalogues and posters for the Arts Council of Great Britain, which displayed a return to traditional typographic principles. The exhibition 'Ken Garland: A Retrospective' was held at Reading University (1997). His influence as a design educator derives from his role as an examiner to many UK institutions. Author of *Graphics Handbook* (1966) and *Illustrated Graphics Glossary* (1980).

Garrett, Malcolm (b.1956) British graphic designer and typographer who, along with contemporaries Neville BRODY and Peter SAVILLE, made a major impact on the visual identity of many aspects of the UK arts and entertainment industries during the late 1970s PUNK period and the 1980s. Studied typography at Reading University 1974–75 and graphic design at Manchester Polytechnic 1975–78. In 1977 he produced his first professional work, a record sleeve for the Manchester band Buzzcocks. Adopting the name Assorted images, he moved to London in 1978 to become consultant art director at Radar Records. Garrett was an early advocate of CORPORATE IDENTITY in the marketing of pop musicians. Assorted images (Ai) was incorporated in 1983 after Garrett formed a partnership with former *New Sounds, New Styles* editor Kasper de Graaf. Jamie REID and Steven Appleby are associate artists with the company. Ai is a multidisciplinary consultancy taking a special interest in APPLE MACINTOSH and other desktop computer systems. During the early 1990s Garrett began designing for international clients, including Bloomingdales in the US and Parco in Japan. In 1990 he created the poster for the annual Nippon graphic design exhibition and was the first European invited to judge the exhibition entries. Designer of *Understanding Hypermedia* (Cotton & Oliver, 1993) and *The Cyberspace Lexicon* (Cotton & Oliver, 1994). Garrett left Ai in 1994 to establish a multimedia design company AMX, where clients have included Barclays Bank and British Telecom. The exhibition 'Malcolm Garrett: Ulterior Motifs' was held at the Design Museum in London (1992). In 1997 he became a visiting professor at the London Institute. Appointed to the faculty of ROYAL DESIGNERS FOR INDUSTRY in 2000.

Gebrauchsgraphik Influential graphic-design journal first published in Germany in 1925. Successor of *Das Plakat,* a monthly journal that promoted German poster art. Wide-ranging in content, *Gebrauchsgraphik* comments on current developments in graphic design, illustration, photography and advertising. The title was extended to *Novum Gebrauchsgraphik* in 1972.

Geismar, Tom See CHERMAYEFF & GEISMAR INC.

Geissbuhler, Steff (b.1942) Swiss graphic designer. Studied at the Allgemeine Gewerbeschule, Basle, under Armin HOFMANN and Emil RUDER 1958–64. Worked with the Geigy pharmaceutical company, Basle 1964–67, before moving to the US where he joined the architectural and planning consultancy Murphy/Levy/Wurman, Philadelphia, 1968–71. In New York he became a freelance designer before working for Anspach/Grossman/Portugal 1973–74. Since then

his career has developed with CHERMAYEFF & GEISMAR INC. New York, becoming a partner in 1979. From 1967 he taught at the Philadelphia College of Art, becoming chairman of the graphic-design department in 1973. His achievement has been to apply the discipline of his original Swiss training to the commercial demands of American corporate design. A gifted draughtsman, his prolific and varied output embracing LOGOTYPE designs, CORPORATE IDENTITY programmes and posters demonstrates a consistent search for new means of communication. His typographic experimentations contributed to the emergence of POST-MODERNISM in the 1980s. President of the New York chapter of AIGA, 1985–86.

Gentleman, David (b.1930) Designer, illustrator, painter and lithographer whose work challenges the traditional divisions between graphic design, illustration and printmaking. Studied at the Royal College of Art, London 1950–53. Prolific designer of British postage stamps since the issue of his first set in 1962; of particular note are the Sir Winston Churchill issue (1965) and those celebrating the Battle of Britain (1965) and Social Reformers (1976). Produced the cover engravings for the New Penguin Shakespeare and has designed posters for the National Trust and London Transport. Responsible for the design of a platform-length mural installed at Charing Cross Underground Station, London. In recent years he has written and illustrated an acclaimed series of travel guides. Member of AGI and in 1989 elected Master of the Faculty, RDI.

Geissbuhler's logotype for the Alvin Ailey American Dance Theater, 1983.

Platform-length mural for Charing Cross Underground Station, designed in 1979 by **Gentleman**.

German graphic design From the mid-1890s the ART NOUVEAU style spread throughout Germany. Known as JUGENDSTIL, it was more restrained than in other European countries as is evident in the work of Otto ECKMANN and Josef Sattler. Nevertheless, the century opened with designers determined to establish a new approach to design practice and to encourage stronger links between art and industry. The DEUTSCHER WERKBUND, formed in 1907, was acclaimed for its efforts to improve the standard of design in everyday products. The wide-ranging output of the architect and industrial designer Peter BEHRENS epitomized many of the aspirations of the Werkbund. German poster art at this time achieved international success through the work of Ludwig HOHLWEIN, Lucian BERNHARD, Julius GIPKENS, and Hans Rudi ERDT. The German war effort used the skills of many of these designers. Before the First World War, Count Harry Von Kessler's CRANACH PRESS and Rudolf KOCH, the calligrapher and type designer, were influential in bringing the ideals of the British ARTS AND CRAFTS MOVEMENT to German book design and printing. In the inter-war years, Kurt SCHWITTERS and Berlin DADA

artists John HEARTFIELD and George GROSZ experimented with techniques, including PHOTOMONTAGE and COLLAGE, to produce shocking imagery. In the early 1920s the intellectual and artistic ferment of Berlin also attracted El LISSITZKY and László MOHOLY-NAGY. The 1920s were dominated by the legendary BAUHAUS school, established by Walter GROPIUS in 1919 to further the principles established by the Deutscher Werkbund. SANS SERIF TYPEFACE designs began to achieve widespread acceptance, with Paul RENNER'S FUTURA being of particular note. With the rise of Nazism in the 1930s a number of designers including Herbert BAYER, László Moholy-Nagy, Jan TSCHICHOLD, Hans SCHLEGER, F.H.K. HENRION and Berthold WOLPE were forced into exile. During the late 1940s Germany took the first steps towards its spectacular recovery. The ULM HOCHSCHULE FÜR GESTALTUNG, founded in 1949, pursued many of the ideas promulgated by the Bauhaus. Max BILL was director from 1951–56, with Otl AICHER taking over in the early 1960s. In the GDR the pre-war traditions in book production, typeface design and wood engraving were revived. Major West German figures to emerge in the 1960s were Anton STANKOWSKI, Willy FLECKHAUS and Hans HILLMANN, whilst Hermann ZAPF has consolidated his reputation as one of the great type-designers of the century. Germany's ability to encourage and accommodate radical ideas is again evident in the success of the innovative group RAMBOW/LIENEMEYER/VAN DE SAND, which emerged in Frankfurt during the early 1970s. Graphic design in Germany throughout the 20th c. reflects a distinctive national ability to exploit the creative tension between tradition and innovation.

Gerstner, Karl (b.1930) Swiss graphic designer, typographer and painter. Has been based in Basle throughout his career, beginning his studies in graphic design at the Allgemeine Gewerbeschule 1945–46. Worked as a junior designer with Fritz Buhler 1946–49. Collaborated with Max Schmidt 1949–53, producing promotional material for the Geigy pharmaceutical company. Established Bureau Basle design studio 1953–59 before founding the Gerstner + Kutter advertising agency in association with Markus Kutter (1959). In 1962, industrial designer Paul Gredinger joined with Gerstner and Kutter to form the GGK agency. The design philosophy of the agency reflected Gerstner's commitment to the rational principles evolved by the BAUHAUS and post-war SWISS STYLE graphic design. An ambitious programme of expansion in the 1970s coincided with an increasingly international approach to advertising problems. The

Gerstner's typographic record cover design for Bech Electronic Centre, Zurich, 1962.

original typographic discipline evolved to embrace the superb photography and advertising copy headlines demanded by multinational clients like Volkswagen, IBM and Swissair. Gerstner retired from GGK in 1970 to pursue his interests as a writer and artist. In 1959 Gerstner and Kutter produced *The New Graphic Art*, a seminal book outlining key developments in graphic design up to the 1950s. Gerstner's books on typography and language include *Designing Programmes* (1963) and *Compendium for Literates* (1970).

Gill, Bob (b.1931) American designer and illustrator. After training at the Philadelphia Museum School of Art 1948–51, Gill returned to his native New York to work as a freelance designer. Drafted into the US army for two years, he resumed his career in 1954, winning an ART DIRECTORS CLUB OF NEW YORK gold medal for a CBS television title (1955). His concise and ironical illustrations appeared in *Esquire, Architectural Forum* and *FORTUNE*. Moved to London in 1960, and became a founding partner, along with Alan FLETCHER and Colin FORBES, of Fletcher/Forbes/Gill (a forerunner of PENTAGRAM) 1962–67. He had a one-man show at the Stedelijk Museum in Amsterdam 1968, thereafter spending his time designing, writing and illustrating children's books and directing industrial and documentary films. After returning to New York in 1975, Gill became involved in a wide range of projects, including films and the production of multi-media events.

Gill, Eric (1882–1940) Sculptor, letter-cutter, TYPEFACE designer, illustrator. Trained at Chichester School of Art, England. In 1902 attended evening classes in lettering, run by Edward JOHNSTON at the Central School of Arts and Crafts, London. Abandoned his ambition to become an architect in favour of letter carving, initially working as Johnston's assistant (1903). Between 1905 and 1909 designed numerous initial letters and title-pages for Count Harry von Kessler's CRANACH PRESS in Germany. Gill's pre-eminence as a sculptor and letter-cutter led to typeface commissions from Robert Gibbings at the GOLDEN COCKEREL PRESS and later from Stanley MORISON at MONOTYPE. His relationship with Gibbings dates from 1925, and led to the design of initial letters, illustrations and a text type for the exclusive use of the Press. The latter undoubtedly influenced Gill when he designed PERPETUA, a fine classical face, for the Monotype Corporation. His illustrative initials for the four volumes of *The Canterbury Tales* (1928–31)

and *The Four Gospels* (1931) are superb examples of book art. Gill's involvement with the Monotype Corporation culminated in the production of Perpetua and its related ITALIC Felicity (1925–30) and the Gill Sans range (1928–30). Gill Sans was subsequently selected by the London and North Eastern Railway for all printing and publicity material. Other typefaces of note are Solus (1929), Bunyan (1936), recut by Linotype as Pilgrim in 1953, and Joanna, a SERIF face originally designed for Hague & Gill in 1930. Gill's famous *Essay on Typography* (1931) was printed in Joanna. His *Autobiography* (1940), published a month after his death, confirmed his respect for craftsmanship and his life-long campaign against 'aesthetic snobbery'. Elected RDI in 1936.

Magazine illustration for *Town* magazine, 1968 by Bob **Gill**, to show how pipe smoking improves one's image.

Illustration by Eric **Gill** for the final issue of *The Fleuron*, 1930.

Gipkens' First World War poster for an 'Exhibition of Captured Aircraft', Berlin 1917.

Advertisement for Geigy Pharmaceuticals by **Giusti**.

Gipkens, Julius (b.1883) Self-taught German poster artist, associated with a distinguished group of Berlin poster designers including Hans Rudi ERDT, Julius KLINGER and Lucian BERNHARD. Established an extensive commercial practice in Berlin, where he undertook much work for the lithographic printers Hollerbaum und Schmidt. During the First World War he designed posters for the German war effort, many emphasizing the need for the restrained use of scarce resources. His fluid rococo drawing style often contrasted with the reductive imagery favoured by Bernhard and Erdt.

Giusti, George (1908–91) Born in Milan, Giusti spent much of his career in the US working in all aspects of graphic communication. Trained at the Royal Academy of Fine Arts, Milan. Between 1930 and 1937 maintained a practice in Zurich, Switzerland. Emigrated to US where in 1939 he established a studio in New York. Designed posters, publicity material and exhibitions for government agencies. Giusti's simplified, symbolic imagery was successfully utilized during twelve years as design consultant for Geigy Pharmaceuticals. Produced many memorable cover designs for the magazines *Time, FORTUNE* and *Holiday*. In 1958 elected Art Director of the Year and in 1979 inducted into the ART DIRECTORS CLUB OF NEW YORK Hall of Fame. Member of AGI.

Glaser, Milton (b.1929) Prolific and versatile New York designer and illustrator whose name is synonymous with PUSH PIN STUDIO, which he co-founded with Seymour CHWAST and Edward Sorel in 1954. Best known for witty and eclectic designs for book and record covers, magazines and posters, Glaser's work extends to CORPORATE IDENTITY, packaging, exteriors, interiors and exhibitions. Trained at the Cooper Union Art School 1948–51, subsequently travelling on a Fulbright scholarship to the Academy of Fine Arts, Bologna, where he studied etching under Giorgio Morandi 1952–53. President of Push Pin Studio until 1974 when he established Milton Glaser Inc., New York. In 1983 along with Walter Bernard he founded WBMG, a publications design firm. Amongst a host of magazines designed by Glaser are *Paris Match, L'Express, Esquire* and *Village Voice* where he was vice-president and design director 1975–77. Along with Clayton Felker, he established *New York Magazine* (1968), holding the posts of vice-president and design director until 1976. During three decades Glaser has created over three hundred posters, including his famous Bob Dylan image, a graphic icon of the 1960s. Since 1978 he has been engaged on a large project for the Grand Union Company, the US supermarket chain, including exteriors, interiors, advertising and packaging. Other projects include a 180m (600ft) mural for the New Federal Office, Indianapolis (1974) and an exhibition for the Triennale di Milano's International Exhibition, Milan, 1987–88. In 1987 he was responsible for an international Aids symbol and poster for the World Health Organization. Glaser has lectured at the Pratt Institute and, since 1961, at the School of Visual Arts, New York. In addition to illustrating numerous books, his design work is reviewed in *Milton Glaser: Graphic Design* (1973) and *The Milton Glaser Poster Book* (1977). President of the ASPEN INTERNATIONAL DESIGN CONFERENCE in 1989. Former vice-president of AIGA.

G/M² Term used to denote the substance of paper by weight. It is an abbreviation for 'grammes per square metre'.

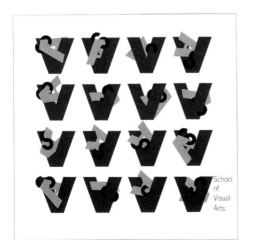

Examples from **Glaser**'s Houdini typeface; as lines are progressively removed, the letters 'disappear'.

Catalogue cover designed by **Glaser** for the School of Visual Arts, New York.

Goffin, Josse (b.1938) Belgian designer/illustrator and teacher whose work embraces advertising, publication design and television titling. Studied design in Brussels before moving to Paris to work in advertising. In 1962 he established a freelance practice in Brussels. His exquisitely coloured illustrations often describe a disconcerting array of fantasy figures and objects. Clients include Union chimique belge, Office du tourisme belge and the French publishers Plon et Hachette. He has collaborated with the prominent German art director Olaf LEU and worked for numerous magazines in Europe and America.

Golden, William (1911–59) Influential art director at the Columbia Broadcasting System, New York, for over two decades. Responsible for establishing the pioneering CBS CORPORATE IDENTITY, which was primarily founded on consistently excellent graphic communication. Educated at a vocational high school in New York, where he was introduced to commercial design and photo-engraving. After a period at the *Los Angeles Examiner,* where he learnt about advertising layout, he returned to New York and spent a year with M.F. AGHA at Condé Nast Publications. Joined CBS Radio Network in 1937, becoming creative director in 1946. During the Second World War Golden and his wife, the designer Cipe PINELES, worked in Paris on an army magazine entitled *Overseas Woman.* Resumed his career at CBS where, in 1946, he was joined by Lou DORFSMAN. In 1951 CBS president Frank Stanton recognized the importance of design by appointing him creative director of advertising and sales promotion. Golden created the famous CBS 'eye' SYMBOL that represents both the viewer's eye and the lens of a camera (1951). He commissioned artists like Ben SHAHN to illustrate advertisements. Golden also designed for political causes, including posters for US presidential candidate Adlai Stevenson. Nominated Art Director of the Year in 1959 by the ART DIRECTORS CLUB OF NEW YORK, shortly before his premature death.

Golden's 'eye' symbol for CBS, designed in 1951.

Golden Cockerel Press Founded by Harold Taylor in 1920, part of the British PRIVATE PRESS MOVEMENT. Robert Gibbings, the printer and engraver, took charge in 1924 and moved the press from Berkshire to London. Books produced by the press were memorable for their excellent typography and illustrations, by Eric GILL and David Jones amongst others. The outstanding achievement was *The Four Gospels* (1931), containing superb WOOD ENGRAVING illustrations by Gill. From 1936 the press was directed by Christopher Sandford and it continued publishing during and after the Second World War.

Wood-engraved chapter heading by Eric Gill for *The Four Gospels* (1931), produced by the **Golden Cockerel Press**.

Gorham's illustration for an article on Georgian furniture in *Nova* magazine, 1973.

Gorham, John (1937–2001) British graphic designer and illustrator. Briefly studied at Harrow School of Art, thereafter mainly self-taught. During 1960s worked in the publicity department of the *Daily Mirror* and *Sunday Mirror* newspapers, later with *The Sunday Times,* and then as art director at Cassons advertising agency, London. Since establishing his freelance practice (1969), Gorham has worked alone, maintaining a determined independence. His numerous posters, CORPORATE IDENTITY schemes, book jackets and stamps are quintessentially English in style, displaying a consistent visual wit and typographic elegance. It is this quality of conception and execution that has attracted numerous awards throughout the world. Tutor at Royal College of Art, London during the early 1980s. Edited *The English Difference* with Paul Jennings (1974). Member of AGI. In 1993 he was awarded the DESIGNERS AND ART DIRECTORS ASSOCIATION (D&AD) President's Award for outstanding service to design and advertising.

Gothic Alternative name for BLACK LETTER TYPEFACE. Also used in US as an alternative term for GROTESQUE typefaces.

Gottschalk + Ash International Leading firm of design consultants established in 1965 in Montreal, later opening studios in Toronto, Zurich and Milan. Founded by Swiss-born Fritz Gottschalk (b.1937) – who studied at Kunstgewerbeschule, Zurich and in Basle – and the Canadian Stuart Ash (b.1942), a graduate of Ontario College of Art. Gottschalk + Ash International specialize in graphic design, CORPORATE IDENTITY, packaging, product design and architectural graphics. Adopting a SWISS STYLE of graphic design they put forward functional and intelligent solutions. Impact is achieved through the dynamic interplay of typographic elements and colour. Amongst numerous corporate identity programmes produced are those for VIA (Canadian Railway), and the New York Stock Exchange. In 1985 Gottschalk designed the new Swiss passport. Internationally acclaimed, the firm has received awards in Switzerland, Canada and the US. Exhibitions of work were held at Montreal Museum of Fine Art (1968) and CONTAINER CORPORATION OF AMERICA (1975).

Logotype for Kultur Förderungsgesellschaft Zürichsee (a Zurich-based arts organization) designed by Fritz Gottschalk of **Gottschalk + Ash International** in 1988.

Goudy Old Style, a typeface designed in 1915 by **Goudy**.

ABCDEFGH
abcdefgh

Goudy, Frederic W. (1865–1947) Prolific American type designer and printer. His remarkable output includes popular typefaces like Copperplate Gothic (1901), Kennerley (1911) and Goudy Old Style (1915). A varied early career embraced clerking, bookselling, printing and teaching. Moving to Chicago in 1899 to become a freelance designer, he taught the young William Addison DWIGGINS at the Frank Holme School of Illustration. After moving to New York in 1906 he dedicated himself to type design and manufacture. In 1920 he was appointed consultant to the Lanston MONOTYPE Corporation of Philadelphia. Left New York in 1923 to establish the Village Letter Foundry at Marlboro on the Hudson River. Overall, Goudy's faces are somewhat inconsistent, their distinctive characteristics making them more suitable for advertising and DISPLAY purposes than for book setting. His books include *The Alphabet* (1908), *Elements of Lettering* (1921) and *Typologia* (1940).

graph Visual representation of the relationship between different factors as expressed on unitized vertical and horizontal axes. See BAR GRAPH/CHART, PIE GRAPH/CHART

graphic design Generic term for the activity of combining TYPOGRAPHY, illustration, photography and printing for purposes of persuasion, information or instruction. William Addison DWIGGINS first used the term 'graphic designer' in 1922, although it did not achieve widespread usage until after the Second World War.

Graphics Improvement Program (US)
See FEDERAL DESIGN IMPROVEMENT PROGRAM

graphics tablet Interactive COMPUTER device consisting of flat, electronically sensitive board and electronic pen. The pen is used to select a graphic/ alphanumeric option, from those available on the board, for display on the VDU screen. Thereafter image composition and manipulation are possible.

Graphis Trilingual design journal first published in Switzerland by Walter HERDEG in 1944. Committed to covering the outstanding achievements in applied art in general and graphic design in particular. With editorial offices in New York and Zurich it remains influential in encouraging progressive developments and fostering new talent.

Grapus Graphic-design co-operative founded in Paris during 1970. The three founders, Pierre Bernard (b.1942), Gérard Paris-Clavel (b.1943) and François Miehe (b.1942), met at the École Nationale Supérieure des Arts Décoratifs and later studied separately in Poland, under the master poster artist Henryk TOMASZEWSKI at the Academy of Arts, Warsaw. They combined to produce subversive posters during the political turmoil that paralysed France in May 1968. Between 1968 and 1970 Bernard and Paris-Clavel collaborated on a research project at L'Institut de L'Environment on the imagery of political propaganda. Although Grapus found itself aligned with the objectives of communist and socialist organizations, it steadfastly maintained an independent perspective. In the early years the group created

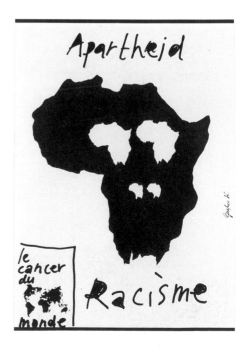

Anti-apartheid poster designed by Pierre Bernard for **Grapus** (1986).

posters and publicity campaigns for left-wing groups and publications. Responsible for a corporate image for CGT, the French trade union, 1975. They have also produced a wealth of startling images for social and cultural organizations including Amis de la Terre, Amitiés Franco-Vietnamiennes, Centre Georges Pompidou and La Comédie Française. Pierre Bernard's chilling 1986 anti-apartheid poster quickly became a graphic-design icon. During the mid-1970s the Grapus partners were joined by Jean-Paul Bachollet and Alexander Jordan, Miehe leaving in 1978 to teach. During the 1980s they also worked on large-scale CORPORATE IDENTITY projects, including the new image for the Louvre in Paris, 1989. Grapus was disbanded in January 1991 to reform as three separate design practices.

Grasset, Eugène (1841–1917) Swiss-born pioneer of ART NOUVEAU book and poster design. Emigrated to Paris in 1871 after studying architecture in Zurich. Initially worked as a textile designer but in 1878 began creating ornamental letters. Illustrated Abbé Drioux's *Les Fêtes Chrétiennes* (1880). His major early achievement resulted from an 1881 commission by printer Charles Gillot to design and illustrate *L'Histoire des Quatre Fils Aymon* (1883). Its innovative design and masterly integration of illustration and typography established a benchmark in book design and printing. He received his first poster commission in 1886. His distinctive style, relying upon thick black contour lines and muted flat colour, revealed a debt to medieval art and Japanese WOODCUT prints. He enjoyed much popular appeal, his reputation rivalling those of Alphonse MUCHA and Jules CHÉRET. Between 1889 and 1892 HARPER'S BAZAAR commissioned cover designs, which were printed in Paris and transported to New York for binding. Grasset also designed stained glass and jewelry. In 1900 he produced an Art Nouveau typeface for Peignot Frères. An influential professor of decorative arts at the École Normale d'Enseignement du Dessein, he also published specimen books and articles on design. Grasset was an honorary member of the VIENNA SECESSION.

gravure *See* PHOTOGRAVURE

Gray, Milner (1899–1997) British graphic, exhibition and industrial designer. Founder member of the Society of Industrial Artists, London (now the CHARTERED SOCIETY OF DESIGNERS) in 1930. Founder partner of DESIGN RESEARCH UNIT, London from 1943, remaining as a consultant up to the early 1980s. Contributed product designs to the 'BRITAIN CAN MAKE IT' exhibition, London (1947) and the SIGNAGE system for the FESTIVAL OF BRITAIN exhibition (1951). Master of the Faculty of ROYAL DESIGNERS FOR INDUSTRY 1955–57 and British president of the AGI 1963–71. Through his numerous public offices Gray contributed significantly to an improved public awareness of design practice in the UK.

Gray, Nicolette (1911–97) Influential British writer on lettering. After graduating from Oxford University she researched Dark Age inscriptions at the British School of Rome (1931). Author of an extensive body of internationally acclaimed works on the history and expressive qualities of lettering. Taught lettering at the Central School of Art and Design, London 1964–81. In 1962 she produced a relief in wood for a wall of the Shakespeare Memorial Library, Stratford-upon-Avon. Also designed and inlaid mosaic inscriptions for Westminster Cathedral. Publications include *Nineteenth-Century Ornamented Typefaces* (1938, revised 1976), *Lettering on Buildings* (1960), *Lettering as Drawing* (1970) and *A History of Lettering* (1986).

Poster designed by **Grasset** for an exhibition of his own work, 1894.

Above, range of gift packaging designed for Austin Reed Ltd by Milner **Gray** in 1954.

Below, **Greiman** created a one-page poster (folded) to form issue 133 of *Design Quarterly* (1986), 'Does It Make Sense?'

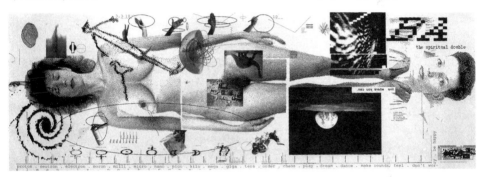

Greiman, April (b. 1948) American graphic designer whose highly innovative work reflects a witty synthesis of SWISS STYLE graphic design, the colours and culture of California and the multilayered effects made possible by technology. Trained at Kansas City Art Institute 1966–70. Postgraduate studies with Wolfgang WEINGART and Armin HOFMANN at the Kunstgewerbeschule, Basle 1970–71. For the next five years she was based in New York and Connecticut, teaching at the Philadelphia College of Art and designing for clients including the Architects Collaborative, Boston, and Anspach/ Grossman/ Portugal. In 1976 commissioned by Emilio Ambasz to create the catalogue and posters for the 'Taxi Project', a competition and exhibition held at the Museum of Modern Art, New York, concerned with the design and manufacture of an economical, non-polluting taxi. Moved to Los Angeles in 1976 where she quickly became a leading figure in emergent NEW WAVE graphic design. An appointment to direct the visual communication programme at the California Institute of the Arts (1982) provided opportunities to experiment with video and computers. Collaborating with photographer Jayme ODGERS she created widely acclaimed publicity material for the Institute. Approaches the page as if it were three-dimensional space within which typographic, photographic and formal elements playfully juxtapose, overlay, tilt and recede in a dynamic balance. She has designed for Esprit, Xerox Corporation, *Wet* magazine, Benetton, Optica and the 1984 Los Angeles Olympic Committee. In *Hybrid Imagery: the Fusion of Technology and Graphic Design* (1990), Greiman examines a range of her design work spanning thirteen years. Designed US stamp commemorating the 19th Amendment (1995). Joined PENTAGRAM in 2000, establishing new office in Los Angeles. Member of AGI, New York Type Directors Club and AIGA.

Grignani's 1964 cover for *Idea* magazine.

'Cheers, Comrade – the proletariat is disarmed!',
April 1919 magazine cover by **Grosz**.

grid Layout device used by graphic designers and typographers to achieve a visual order and consistency on the printed page. Pre-printed grid sheets indicating column widths, picture sizes and margins provide a disciplined framework for the placing of diverse visual components. The grid is synonymous with the rational approach of SWISS STYLE graphic design after the Second World War.

Grignani, Franco (b.1908) Italian painter, graphic designer and photographer who trained as an architect at the Politecnico, Turin 1929–33. Concerned to develop his own visual vocabulary, Grignani experimented in the field of optical dynamics from c.1950 through to the early 1970s. His studies in perception and the effects of movement and illusion on signs and patterns have subsequently been applied to many advertisements, symbols and book jackets. His one-man exhibitions have explored and extended the relationship between fine and applied art.

Gropius, Walter (1883–1969) German architect and educator. After studying in Munich and Berlin 1903–7, worked in the office of Peter BEHRENS 1908–10. Influential member of the DEUTSCHER WERKBUND; his pre-First World War factory designs were internationally acclaimed. In 1919 he was appointed director of the applied and fine arts schools in Weimar, combining them to form the legendary Das Staatliches BAUHAUS. The influence of the Bauhaus on graphic design is largely attributable to Gropius's ability to attract outstanding talents to Weimar, including Josef ALBERS, Herbert BAYER, László MOHOLY-NAGY, and Joost SCHMIDT. Gropius resigned from the school in 1928 to practise architecture in Berlin. Emigrated to England in 1934, moving to the US in 1937. From 1937 to 1952 he taught architecture at the Graduate School of Design, Harvard, Massachusetts.

Grosz, George (1893–1959) Berlin-born graphic artist renowned for his powerful satirical illustrations that exposed the decadence of German society after the First World War. He trained in Dresden from 1909 before serving in the army, from which he was court-martialled for insubordination. Early associate of the Berlin DADA artists John HEARTFIELD and Kurt SCHWITTERS. Following an invitation to teach at the Art Students League in New York, Grosz moved to America in 1932. Remained there for the rest of his career, his work becoming increasingly conservative. He returned to Berlin a few months before his death.

ABCDEFGH
abcdefgh

Letters from the Berthold **Grotesque** typeface.

Grotesque Term used to describe the early forms of SANS SERIF TYPEFACE dating from the 1850s onwards. In the US the term GOTHIC is also used to describe grotesque typefaces.

H

Haas Grotesque Original name for HELVETICA TYPEFACE.

Haggerty, Mick (b.1948) British graphic designer and illustrator, now resident in the US. Studied at the Central School of Art and Design, London, moving to Los Angeles in 1973. Initially worked with designer Rod Dyer, before establishing a partnership, 'Art Attack' (1975), with John Kehe. When the partnership dissolved Haggerty developed a freelance practice, working mainly for clients in the entertainment industry. His eclectic approach to image-making reflects his fascination with comics, graffiti and cheap ephemera. A superb draughtsman, his versatility and mastery of pastiche are well suited to the demands of art directors working in the record business or for magazines like *Vanity Fair, LA Style* and *Time*. His album covers for such performers as David Bowie, Simple Minds, Jerry Lee Lewis and Orchestral Manoeuvres in the Dark have received widespread acclaim in a notoriously critical industry. Since the early 1980s he has become involved in the art direction of promotional videos for a number of major groups.

A **halftone** illustration (below) is shown by enlargement (bottom) to to be made up of a series of dots.

halftone Continuous tone image (photograph or illustration) that has been converted for reproduction using the HALFTONE PROCESS.

halftone process Photochemical process that converts a continuous tone image into a series of minute, graduated dots. This dot pattern, which facilitates the printed reproduction, is created by photographing the original through a halftone 'screen'. The crossed lines of the screen break the image into black dots, which vary in size according to the tonal range of the original.

Harak, Rudolph de (b.1924) American designer and educator active in graphic, exhibition and product design. Self-taught, working initially as a painter and illustrator in Los Angeles. In 1950 moved to New York to establish a design studio. De Harak has explored the rational principles of SWISS GRAPHIC

Symbol designed for the Canadian Association for Retarded Children by **Harder** (1964).

Promotional poster for *Hard Werken* magazine, 1981.

DESIGN in his search for clarity in visual communication. The 350 paperback covers he designed for McGraw-Hill Publishers in the early 1960s, using a GRID and a uniform SANS SERIF TYPEFACE, proved a watershed in American book-jacket design. Founding principal of Cambridge Seven, an architectural and design practice in Massachusetts (1962). In 1969 he was joined by Al Corchia to form Corchia de Harak Inc. As a designer of exhibitions, De Harak created the pavilion 'Man, his Planet and Space' for the Canadian government at Expo '67 Montreal, and, along with Cambridge Seven, the US pavilion at Expo '70 in Osaka. Responsible for SIGNAGE for a wing of the Metropolitan Museum of Art. Member of the important US advisory committee on transportation signage, chaired by Tom GEISMAR. Appointed professor of design at Cooper Union School, New York from 1979 and has taught at many other US design colleges. In addition, he has designed a series of clocks, some of which are held in the Museum of Modern Art collection. Member of AIGA and past US president of AGI.

Harder, Rolf (b. 1929) German-born graphic designer who emigrated to Canada in 1955 and has done much to heighten international awareness of the quality and variety of Canadian design. Studied at the Hamburg Academy of Fine Arts 1948–52. Worked in advertising in both Hamburg and Montreal, where in 1959 he founded Rolf Harder Design. In 1964 won a competition to create a symbol for the Canadian Association for Retarded Children with a PICTOGRAM showing an interdependent adult and child. Along with Ernst ROCH established Design Collaborative, Montreal, 1965–77; the practice quickly achieved prominence through CORPORATE IDENTITY programmes, LOGOTYPE designs, posters and design for publications. He is conscious of his responsibility in contributing to an aesthetically enriching environment, producing rational and imaginative solutions. In 1977 founded the design consultancy Rolf Harder & Associates, Montreal. Designed some forty postage stamps for Canada Post and a number of award-winning book designs. Recipient of over a hundred national and international design awards. Member of AGI and AIGA.

Hard Werken (1980–93) Dutch graphic-design studio that grew out of the magazine *Hard Werken*, published in ten issues (1978–82). Based in Rotterdam, the founder members included Rick Vermeulen, Gerard Hadders and Willem Kars. Breaking the rational, modernist rules of Dutch graphic design,

Gaiety Girl theatre poster designed in 1895 by **Hardy**.

the studio adopted diverse and unconventional approaches, typically using witty anarchic typography, staged photography, shocking colours and a seemingly disorganized layout. Throughout the 1980s the designers produced many startling posters for arts organizations; other clients included the Dutch PTT and the publisher Bert Bakker for whom they created a series of book jackets. An exhibition of their work was held at the Kunsthal, Rotterdam (1995). In 1993 the studio merged with the more commercial Belgian practice Ten Cate Bergmans to become Inzio Design Group.

Hardy, Dudley (1866–1922) English painter, book and magazine illustrator and poster designer. Born in Sheffield, the son of a marine painter, he studied in Düsseldorf, Antwerp and Paris. A prolific illustrator with a rapid, spontaneous style, although the quality of his output was variable. His more successful work included a series of opera sketches in *Punch*. Celebrated for his humorous, animated posters including the very popular theatre poster *Gaiety Girl* (1895) and the *Yellow Girl* advertisement for a weekly newspaper. Influenced by French poster artists, particularly Jules CHÉRET.

Harper's Bazaar Quality monthly magazine for women, founded in 1867 by Harper and Brothers, New York, and sold to the Hearst Corporation in 1913. Gained a reputation for innovative editorial design by employing the most gifted designers and photographers. Between 1924 and 1937 ERTÉ was exclusively contracted to design covers and fashion illustrations. Alexey BRODOVITCH was art director from 1934 until 1958, after which Henry WOLF took over until 1961. During this period the magazine overturned conventions in photography, typography and page layout.

Hart's Rules Abbreviated title for Horace Hart's *Rules for Compositors and Readers at the University Press, Oxford*. A popular set of rules that provides the basis for the typographic HOUSE STYLE of many printers and publishers, covering, amongst other matters, spelling, spacing, hyphenation and punctuation.

Cover of **Harper's Bazaar** for the issue of 1 March 1938, designed by A.M. Cassandre.

Skegness is So Bracing (1909), a famous advertisement by **Hassall** for the London and North Eastern Railway.

Poster designed in 1936 that formed part of **Havinden's** campaign for the Milk Marketing Board.

Hassall, John (1868–1948) Prolific British poster designer famous for his classic 1909 poster *Skegness is So Bracing*. After training at the Antwerp Academy and the Académie Julian, Paris, he became a painter and illustrator in black and white. From the early 1890s he drew for *Sketch* and designed many trade and theatre posters. A popular illustrator of children's books, he also published two volumes supporting the British war effort during the First World War. His long career extended through to the Second World War, with a last poster entitled *Save Poland*.

Havinden, Ashley (1903–73) British advertising designer known simply as 'Ashley'. Worked for the London advertising agency W.S. Crawford for forty-five years, joining as a nineteen-year-old trainee, becoming director of art and design in 1929 and vice-chairman 1960–67. Under his influence Crawfords became a leading British advertising agency during the 1920s and 30s. Along with Margaret Sangster (later to become his wife) as account executive and G.H. Saxon Mills (who had been Stanley MORISON's secretary) as copywriter, Ashley produced many innovative advertising campaigns. Influenced by CUBISM, FUTURISM and BAUHAUS typography, by the mid-1920s he was developing a new typographic language for his advertisements. The 1925 Chrysler campaign, which used bold SANS SERIF typefaces and a dynamic combination of text and illustration, was enormously successful, inspiring a host of imitators. During the 1930s he produced influential campaigns for the Milk Marketing Board, Simpson of Piccadilly, the General Post Office and Eno's Fruit Salts. His post-war activities included work for Liberty, DAKS, Wolsey and Pretty Polly. In 1933 he began to design rugs and tapestries, some of which were used by Simpson. Created two varieties of TYPEFACE for MONOTYPE, Ashley Crawford (1930) and the heavy brush script known as Ashley Script (1955). In 1947 elected RDI (Master of Faculty 1967 and 1969) and in 1951 received an OBE for services to graphic design. President of the Society of Industrial Artists (now the CHARTERED SOCIETY OF DESIGNERS) in 1953 and President of AGI 1957–60. Author of *Line Drawing for Reproduction* (1933, '41), *Advertising and the Artist* (1956).

Heartfield, John (1891–1968) German graphic artist, member of the Berlin DADA group. Studied at the Munich Kunstgewerbeschule 1909–12. In 1916 he changed his name from Helmut Herzfelde as a protest against anti-British propaganda. Along with his brother Wieland Herzfelde began publication of a

Hurrah, the Butter is Finished! (19 December 1935). **Heartfield** produced this poster, showing an ordinary German family eating nuts and bolts, garden tools and a bicycle, in response to Goering's remarks that 'Iron makes the regime strong, butter and dripping makes its people fat'.

Part of the popular **Helvetica** typeface.

ABCDEFGH
abcdefgh

Henrion Design Associates' KLM logotype (c. 1964).

radical anti-war journal *Neue Jugend* (1916), transforming it into a vehicle for experimental typography. The brothers collaborated with George GROSZ at Der MalikVerlag, a publishing house for left-wing literature and inexpensive novels. As art director at Malik Heartfield designed powerful book jackets, combining arresting typography with startling photographic imagery. He and Grosz experimented with the new medium of PHOTOMONTAGE from around 1916. Heartfield became the acknowledged master, using the device as a polemical weapon to satirize the emergent Nazi party. Between 1918 and his flight to Prague in 1933 he created many pro-Communist posters. Left Prague for London in 1938 where he designed book jackets for Lindsay Drummond and photomontages for *Picture Post* and *Lilliput*. Finally moved to Leipzig, East Germany in 1950 and during the 1960s created anti-Vietnam War photomontages.

Helvetica Ubiquitous SANS SERIF TYPEFACE designed by Max Miedinger and Edouard Hoffman and issued by the Swiss type foundry Haas in 1957. Based on Akzidenz Grotesque, an alphabet popular at the turn of the century, it was originally called Haas Grotesque/New Haas Grotesque, but was retitled Helvetica after release in Germany in the early 1960s. Its legible, clear-cut characters have ensured its continuing international popularity.

Henrion, F.H.K. (1914–90) Graphic, industrial and exhibition designer, pioneer of CORPORATE IDENTITY in Britain. Born in Nuremberg, Germany, he adopted British nationality in 1946. Studied in Paris with Paul COLIN where he became familiar with the posters of A.M. CASSANDRE and modern-art developments, particularly SURREALISM. between 1936 and 1939 he worked in Paris and London designing posters, packaging and exhibitions; finally emigrated to England in 1939, where an early commission was the design of a Smoke Abatement Exhibition (1939). During the war established his reputation through posters and exhibitions designed for the Ministry of Information and the US Office of War Information in London. An early exponent of PHOTOMONTAGE and COLLAGE, which he often incorporated into surreal compositions. During the 1940s and 50s he worked for advertising agencies and publishers and contributed to TWO FESTIVAL OF BRITAIN pavilions, for which he was awarded an OBE. In 1951 Henrion Design Associates was founded, becoming HDA International in 1972. As a leading consultancy in corporate identity the practice was responsible for many enduring schemes including

Blue Circle Cement, London Electricity Board, British Leyland and KLM (Royal Dutch Airlines). During the mid-1960s he began a fruitful collaboration with Alan Parkin, a Cambridge mathematician: together they advocated a rational, systematic approach to problem solving in corporate design and published *Design Co-ordination and Corporate Image* (1967). In 1982 Henrion became a consultant to Henrion, Ludlow & Schmidt, corporate identity specialists. A respected spokesperson for his profession, Henrion was president of AGI and Master of the Faculty of RDI (1972–73). Also an influential teacher, lecturing at the Royal College of Art, London, 1955–65 and leading the faculty of visual communication at the London College of Printing 1976–79.

Herdeg, Walter (1908–95) Swiss designer and publisher. Throughout the 1930s he was an innovator in the use of PHOTOMONTAGE in his posters. His major contribution to graphic design was as publisher of the Swiss journal *GRAPHIS*, for which he designed a number of early covers.

Hillman, David (b.1943) British designer with an international reputation in editorial design. Trained at the London College of Printing 1959–61. Art editor of *The Sunday Times*, London 1966–68, then art director and deputy editor of the influential UK style magazine *Nova* 1968–75. Prior to becoming a partner in PENTA-GRAM in 1978, he spent a year as art director of the French newspaper *Le Matin de Paris*. Since joining Pentagram he has redesigned numerous publications including *The Guardian, New Statesman & Society* and *City Limits*. His field of operation has widened significantly in the past decade with a number of award-winning CORPORATE IDENTITY programmes and retail design projects. Member of AGI.

Hillmann, Hans (b.1925) German graphic designer and illustrator. From 1948 until 1953 trained at the Staatliche Werkakademie in Kassel where he began his freelance career, moving to Frankfurt in 1956. Throughout the 1960s and early 70s he produced promotional material for the film distributors Neue Filmkunst Walter Kirchner, Göttingen. His celebrated posters frequently juxtapose and manipulate images, using a range of techniques such as photography, COLLAGE, painting and illustration. He has also produced illustrations for magazines, including *Twen*, book designs for Fischer Verlag and his 'picture stories'. In 1982 he published *Flypaper*, a crime story written by Dashiell Hammett, which Hillmann retells using black-and-white watercolour illustrations. Since 1961 he has taught graphic design at the Hochschule für bildende Kunst in Kassel.

Cover for *Graphis* magazine by **Herdeg** (1947).

David **Hillman** front page for *Le Matin de Paris* newspaper (24 February 1977).

Hans **Hillmann**'s 1967 poster for Eisenstein's film *Battleship Potemkin*.

Hipgnosis produced this classic cover for Pink Floyd's *Dark Side of the Moon*, 1973.

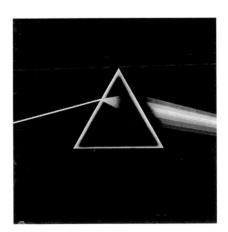

Hipgnosis British graphic-design partnership known for its record-cover designs. Founded in London in 1968 by Storm Thorgerson (b.1944) and Aubrey Powell (b.1946) with the third partner, photographer Peter Christopherson (b.1955), joining in 1974. A product of the Swinging Sixties, Hipgnosis was a major influence on the visual identity of the British music industry throughout the 1970s. Working in association with many famous rock musicians, Hipgnosis used SURREALISM, PSYCHEDELIA, COLLAGE, PHOTOMONTAGE and overt sexual imagery to shock and amuse a visually sophisticated record-buying public. In addition to working for groups like Pink Floyd, 10cc, Genesis and The Police, Hipgnosis also designed advertising and promotional material for a range of commercial clients in the music industry.

Hlavsa, Oldrich (b.1909) Czech book designer and typographer. Trained as a compositor and spent fifteen years running a typesetting workshop. Became editor and art director of the Prague journal *Typographia* in 1937. From 1955 he practised as a book designer, his work characterized by wit and elegance in the integration of typography and illustration. Co-author of *Typografická pisma latinková* (1957), *A book of type and design* (1960) and *Typographia,* vols 1 and 2 (1977,1981).

Hlavsa's proposal for the cover of an edition of George Bernard Shaw's *Pygmalion*.

Hoefler, Jonathan (b.1970)NewYork–based TYPE-FACE designer and principal of the Hoefler Type Foundry. A self-taught designer, Hoefler's extensive knowledge of historical typographic models informs many of his digitized type designs. His elegant type-faces combine historicism and the contemporary. He has created customized award-winning digital type families for such publications as *Rolling Stone, Harper's Bazaar, The New York Times* and *Esquire*. Other clients include the publisher Alfred A. Knopf and the Solomon R Guggenheim Museum. He designed Hoefler Text (1993) for Apple Computers, which became a standard feature in the APPLE MACINTOSH operating system. Recipient of numerous awards from the AMERICAN INSTITUTE OF GRAPHIC ARTS and the Type Directors Club of New York.

Hoffmann, Josef (1870–1956) Architect born in Moravia, at that time part of Austria. An early and influential member of the VIENNA SECESSION, he designed the Ver Sacrum room for its first exhibition in 1898. Inspired by Charles Rennie MACKINTOSH, his architecture emphasized strong graphic values, and his commitment to geometric simplicity contributed to many aspects of MODERNISM in the early decades of the 20th c. In 1903, along with Koloman MOSER, he founded the WIENER WERKSTÄTTE with the intention of controlling production in order to manufacture 'good, simple domestic requisites'. His versatility enabled him to make a distinctive contribution to graphic design, leatherwork, jewelry, metalwork and textiles. His greatest architectural achievement was the Palais Stoclet, Brussels (1905–11) for Belgian industrialist Adolphe Stoclet. Designed the Austrian pavilion at numerous international exhibitions throughout the 1920s and 30s.

Hofmann, Armin (b.1920) Swiss graphic designer and educator. After an apprenticeship in LITHOGRAPHY and studies at the Kunstgewerbeschule, Zurich, Hofmann and his wife established a design studio in Basle. At the same time he started teaching at the Kunstgewerbeschule, Basle, becoming head of the graphic-design department in 1973. His contribution to post-war SWISS STYLE graphic design was to demon-strate the importance of a graphic language based on consistent, rational principles. This visual discipline is apparent in Hofmann's posters, advertising, LOGOTYPE designs and environmental graphics. Influential as an educator in the US, he has taught at Philadelphia Museum School of Art and Yale and attracted many American students to his courses in Switzerland. His

Josef **Hoffmann** designed this Wiener Werkstätte exhibition poster in 1905; the lettering and lower rectangles were printed by lithography, with the geometric background pattern hand-stencilled.

work appeared in the '8 Swiss Graphic Designers' exhibition that toured the US 1957–58 and in many subsequent one-man exhibitions. Hofmann's *Graphic Design Manual* (1965) identified the fundamental requirements for a basic course in graphic design.

Hohlwein, Ludwig (1874–1949) Major German poster artist whose career spanned both World Wars, his style evolving in response to dramatic political and cultural pressures. Born in Wiesbaden, he studied architecture in Munich, turning to graphic design in 1906. Early work for restaurants, cafés and the clothing industry, including a striking series of posters for the men's clothier Hermann Sherrer, reveals a stylistic debt to the BEGGARSTAFF BROTHERS. However, his economy of execution was offset by a greater realism and a powerful compositional balance. During the First World War he produced emotive posters for fundraising and propaganda purposes, the impact of which was heightened by increasingly naturalistic imagery and a more painterly style. After 1918 he concentrated on commercial design, producing travel posters for Lufthansa and making greater use of photographic and AIRBRUSH techniques. Throughout the 1930s he created political posters for the Nazis, his style becoming increasingly severe and militaristic, culminating in the 1940s German army recruiting poster entitled *Und Du?*

hot metal composition Typesetting produced by a hot-metal casting system such as MONOTYPE or LINOTYPE. Although now largely replaced by 'cold' typesetting systems based on film and computers, many of today's typographic terms still relate to the conventions of hot metal setting.

house style Term used to describe a set of rules that organizations may adopt to create and maintain a visual consistency in their diverse activities. Now largely replaced by the more comprehensive term CORPORATE IDENTITY. Also used to describe a typographic set of composition rules, e.g. HART'S RULES.

Huber, Max (b.1919) Swiss-born graphic, industrial and exhibition designer, based mainly in Milan. Trained at the Kunstgewerbeschule, Zurich 1935–38, becoming art director for Studio Boggeri, Milan in 1940. His strongly typographical designs are complex and distinctive visual arrangements, employing overlapping devices, bold colours and photography. The war forced his return to Switzerland, where he worked for the Artemis publishing house in Zurich and

Poster for the Civic Theatre, Basle 1963–64 season, by Armin **Hofmann**.

Hohlwein's First World War poster demanding *People's Charity for Prisoners of War*.

collaborated on exhibition designs with Max BILL and the photographer Werner Bischof. Returned to Milan in 1946, the following year contributing to the design of the Milan Triennale, at which he won a gold medal. Huber's clients included La Rinascente stores, Olivetti, the Automobile Club of Italy, Monza cars and the De Agostini Geographical Institute in Novara. His work has been exhibited at one-man shows in Milan, Tokyo, Chiasso and Zurich.

Poster advertising motor racing at Monza in 1948, by **Huber**.

Huszar's 1926 poster for Miss Blanche Egyptian Cigarettes.

Hurlburt, Allen (1910–83) American art director renowned for publication design during the 1950s and 60s. After graduating in economics from the University of Pennsylvania in 1932, pursued a career as a cartoonist and later as a magazine art director. After the war he worked for National Broadcasting Company, New York, and from 1951 for Paul RAND at the Weintraub Advertising Agency. In 1953 he joined *Look* magazine in New York, establishing a reputation over the next fifteen years for innovative layout, typography and photography. He later moved to London. His interest in design education is reflected in his writings and books, including *Publication Design* (1971), *Layout: The Design of the Printed Page* (1977) and *The Grid* (1978).

Huszar, Vilmos (1884–1960) Painter and graphic artist, leading participant in the DE STIJL movement. Studied in Munich and his native Budapest where he entered the School of Applied Arts during the early 1900s. Settled in Holland in 1905. Designed the cover for the first issue of Theo van DOESBURG's *De Stijl* magazine (1917). His asymmetric designs were composed of tight squares and rectangles and the De Stijl colour range: black/white/grey and the primary colours. Favoured SANS SERIF varieties of TYPEFACE. Designed a furniture advertisement that was carried in the first six issues of *De Stijl* and worked with Piet ZWART and Bart van der LECK on exhibitions and interiors for the same furniture company. Contributed to *De Stijl* until 1923, after which he concentrated on figurative painting. Other design work of the 1920s included a powerful poster constructed from rectangles for Miss Blanche Egyptian Cigarettes (1926) and a typographic poster for the 'Exhibition of Contemporary Industrial Arts' (1929).

I

IBM (International Business Machines Corporation) International manufacturer of computerized information systems, renowned for the pursuit of excellence in all its visual manifestations – products, architecture, exhibitions, films. The IBM CORPORATE IDENTITY, created in 1956 by Paul RAND in collaboration with the architect and industrial designer Eliot Noyes, has been outstandingly successful in presenting the company's activities to the public. Rand's DESIGN MANUAL included variations of the famous IBM LOGOTYPE, the IBM alphabet (based on the TYPEFACE City Medium designed by Georg TRUMP), packaging and SIGNAGE systems.

ICOGRADA Acronym of International Council of Graphic Design Associations, which represents the national societies of professional designers and organizations concerned with the raising of graphic-design standards. ICOGRADA embraces over fifty design associations worldwide, representing nearly 30,000 designers. Founded in London in 1963, its activities include conferences, working groups, publications, education programmes and developments toward international standardization.

i-D British style magazine launched in London (1980) by Terry JONES. *i-D*'s 'winking eye' logotype has achieved iconic status. Innovative and irreverent, *i-D* has been highly significant in promoting the vitality and creativity of street culture. By connecting art, fashion, design, politics, literature, music and technology, the magazine has created an alternative voice to the conventions of mainstream publishing. *i-D*'s use of photography and its anarchic graphic style, promulgated by Jones, has had a marked influence on the subsequent generation of international style journals.

I.D. America's leading critical design journal. Special issues include the prestigious annual *Design Review* (published since 1954), which recognizes the best of American and international design across a range of disciplines: consumer products, furniture, equipment, environment, packaging, graphics, student projects and, since 1995, interactive media. The *I.D. Interactive Media Design Review*, published annually, features outstanding work in the field, and *I.D. Forty*, also an annual publication, celebrates forty leading designers renowned for their determination to challenge design boundaries.

Idea Japanese bi-monthly magazine illustrating the best in international advertising art. First published in 1953, it has been influential in introducing foreign designers to Japan and making Japanese designers better known throughout the world. *Idea* produces special issues featuring the work of selected countries, groups and individuals.

Front cover of *i-D* magazine, number 33, February 1986.

Front cover of the 2001 *Design Review* for *I.D.* magazine.

Masthead for *Idea* magazine.

ideogram/graph Character or graphic symbol designed to represent an idea or concept. An early ideogram, for example, was the symbol for the sun, which was used to represent daytime or the state of the weather.

Image, Selwyn (1849–1930) British designer and graphic artist associated with Arthur Heygate MACKMURDO and the establishment of the CENTURY GUILD in 1882. In 1884 Image designed the cover for the first issue of the Guild's journal *Hobby Horse*. His graphic work combined a passion for medieval imagery with a desire to create an appropriate visual aesthetic for the emerging ARTS AND CRAFTS MOVEMENT. Image's work embraced stained glass, TYPEFACE designs, illustrations, mosaics and embroidery.

Image produced this illustration for *Jesus Hominum Salvator* in c.1885.

imitation art paper Paper in which the surfacing material of china clay is mixed with the pulp during manufacture. The resulting surface is inferior to that of ART PAPER in which the surface coating is applied after the paper is made.

imposition Arrangement of individual pages of a book or brochure on a large sheet prior to printing, thus ensuring that the final printed pages appear in the correct sequence when folded, bound and trimmed. Common imposition schemes encompass 8, 16 and 32 pages.

imprint (a) Legal obligation that requires the name of the publisher, printer, date and place of printing to appear in any published work. The publisher's name normally appears on the title page, whilst the printing history is often shown on the reverse of the title page or at the end of the book. (b) ROMAN TYPEFACE cut for the British typographic and printing journal *The Imprint*, first published in 1913. The editorship of *The Imprint* was shared between F.E. Jackson, Edward JOHNSTON, John Henry MASON and G.T. Meynell. Modelled on CASLON OLD FACE, but with a larger X-HEIGHT, Imprint was the first OLD FACE design issued by the MONOTYPE Corporation.

Imprint, the typeface designed for the magazine of the same name.

ABCDEFGH
abcdefgh

Information Graphic Design Generic term applied to those graphic-design projects required to communicate complex data or information to a specific range of audiences. The detailed analysis of user needs that underpins successful information graphic design differs from the more subjective approach applied to projects aimed at selling a product. The presentation of major signage schemes, health and safety issues, public services and technical manuals are all examples of information graphic design.

ink-jet printer COMPUTER-linked printing device in which the image is created by high-speed jets of ink. Commonly used for reproduction in word processing and personal computing.

Kristall Book **inline** typeface.

inline Generic term for a TYPEFACE in which the vertical, diagonal and curved strokes are incised with a fine white line, which can either be centred or off-centre on the background stroke.

intaglio Generic term for printing processes in which the inked image on the printing plate is lower than the non-image area. The recessed image is created by etching or engraving. PHOTOGRAVURE is the most popular process to use this method of reproduction.

International Paper Sizes See A, B, C SYSTEM OF STANDARD PAPER SIZES

International Typeface Corporation (ITC) A New York–based organization founded in 1970 by Aaron BURNS, Herb LUBALIN and Edward Rondthaler to design and license forms of TYPEFACE for film and computerized typesetting systems. The master FONT of each different typeface is licensed to different manufacturers, with ITC providing copyright protection and royalties to the type designer. ITC's journal U&lc (Upper and lower case), which is distributed worldwide, is used to promote new typefaces. Art directed by Lubalin throughout the 1970s and early 80s, the journal has been influential in demonstrating the design potential of new typesetting systems.

International Typographic Style Rational typographic style, also known as Swiss Style, which developed in Switzerland after the Second World War. Building on innovations associated with CONSTRUCTIVISM, DE STIJL, the BAUHAUS and the NEW TYPOGRAPHY of the 1930s, the International Typographic Style sought to present complex information in a structured and unified manner. Ernst KELLER, Théo BALLMER, Max BILL and Max HUBER were major influences on the early evolution of the style. Characterized by a reliance on the typographic GRID, the style used SANS SERIF TYPEFACE designs (e.g. HELVETICA), narrow text columns with RANGED-LEFT setting, and photographs rather than hand-drawn illustrations. The international popularity of the style extended throughout the 1960s and 70s with major figures like Emil RUDER, Armin HOFMANN and Josef MÜLLER-BROCKMANN refining it to a new level of sophistication. The Kunstgewerbeschulen in Zurich and Basle have been significant in introducing succeeding generations of designers to an objective and systematic approach to problem solving. The publication of the Swiss journal NEW GRAPHIC DESIGN in 1959 provided an influential platform for leading exponents of the style to disseminate their philosophy. During the late 1970s the International Typographic Style became increasingly identified with a corporate style of design, particularly in the US. This visual predictability has since been strongly challenged by a number of Swiss and American designers, with Wolfgang WEINGART in Basle, ODERMATT & TISSI in Zurich, and April GREIMAN in California taking a lead. The vitality and freshness associated with these innovations of POST-MODERNISM suggest that modified and revised versions of the International Typographic Style will continue to be influential in the future.

Internet Global system of computer networks that evolved from ARPAnet, the US Department of Defence's Advanced Research Projects Agency network. This secure computer network was set up in 1972 to circulate secret information and represented the first opportunity for computers in different locations to be connected together, thus forming the basis of the ever-expanding information superhighway. In addition to facilitating new ways of shopping and conducting business, the Internet enables people to explore the World Wide Web (www) and to communicate via e-mail.

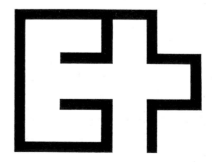

Symbol for the Swiss National Exhibition, 'Expo '64', an example of the **International Typographic Style**.

Ionic

Complete alphabet in an **Ionic** typeface.

ABCDEFGHIJKLMNOPQRSTUVWXYZ
abcdefghijklmnopqrstuvwxyz

Ishioka's 1984 poster *Tradition et Nouvelles Techniques*.

GEBURTEN UND STERBEFÄLLE IN WIEN

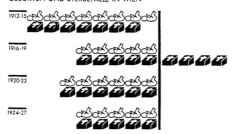

Example of the **Isotype** system, setting out the number of births and deaths in Vienna between 1912 and 1927: each baby represents 20,000 births, each coffin 20,000 deaths.

Ionic Popular TYPEFACE range designed for newspapers, originating in the 1830s and 40s. Similar in style to the EGYPTIAN family of typefaces. The bracketed SLAB SERIF, short ASCENDER and DESCENDER design assists legibility in the smaller sizes.

ISBN Publishing classification system used to identify all books published. The 'International Standard Book Number' uses ten digits to identify the country of origin, publisher and title.

Ishioka, Eiko Versatile Japanese designer and art director of advertising, exhibitions, film, theatre and fashion. After graduating in 1961 from the Tokyo National University of Fine Arts and Music, she joined the advertising department of Shiseido, Japan's largest cosmetics organization. Recipient of many awards including the prestigious Japan Advertising Artists Prize. Established Eiko Ishioka Design in 1970. During the 1970s she helped create the outstanding corporate image for Parco, the Japanese shopping complexes: Parco advertising did not focus on individual products, preferring to promote the concept of an innovative, forward-looking company. Ishioka helped dismantle conventions by using black models and featuring modern, liberated women. After a two-year spell in New York she returned to Japan in 1982. Her 1983 publication *Eiko by Eiko* reviews her work since 1970. In the area of film she designed posters for Francis Ford Coppola's *Apocalypse Now* (1979) and posters, sets and costumes for his 1984 production *Mishima*.

ISO Initials of the Swiss-based International Standards Organization. ISO has published many important standards including the A, B, C SYSTEM OF STANDARD PAPER SIZES, and the international recommendations for photographic film speed ratings.

Isotype (International System of Typographic Picture Education) Originally known as the Vienna Method, Isotype was devised by Otto Neurath (1882–1945) after the chaos of the First World War to assist public understanding of complex statistical information, particularly relating to health, housing and finance. Isotype is a pictorial method of presenting linked information – 'a world language without words'. The system uses pictographic symbols representing fixed quantities, with increasing quantities being suggested by a repetition of those symbols, rather than by changes of perspective or size. The information, compiled by statisticians, was converted into visual layouts by the Transformation Team, headed by Marie Reidemeister (1898–1986), who later married Otto Neurath. The German graphic artist Gerd Arntz then produced the finished format prior to printing. The Neuraths fled from Vienna to Holland in 1934, then to Britain in 1940, founding the Isotype Institute in Oxford, 1942. After Otto's death Marie led the work of the Institute, transferring it to London in 1948 where it continued until closure in 1972. Important amongst those who assisted the Neuraths was Rudolf Modley, who went to America in the 1930s and directed the work of Pictorial Statistics Inc. (later renamed the Pictographic Corporation) in New York; this organization represented the Isotype movement in North America. The Otto and Marie Neurath Isotype Collection was established at the University of Reading, England, 1971.

italic Cursive letterforms or alphabets that incline to the right. Originating in Italy in the 14th and 15th c., italic type was based on a fluid writing style known as chancery script. Normally used to highlight individual words or sections within a text set in a ROMAN TYPEFACE.

Itten, Johannes (1888–1967) Swiss painter and educator. After an early career as a teacher Itten decided to become a painter. His initial art studies in Geneva proving unsatisfactory, he then studied under Adolf Hölzel in Stuttgart, 1913–16, after which he moved to Vienna. After meeting Walter GROPIUS in 1919, Itten was engaged to teach at the newly established BAUHAUS, Weimar. Responsible for the preliminary 'basic' course from 1919–23, Itten's mystical ideas and search for fundamental visual principles eventually led to disagreements with Gropius; Itten's approach was seen as inappropriate to the needs of an institution searching for new ways of designing for the machine. László MOHOLY-NAGY succeeded Itten as head of the preliminary course. Itten then studied philosophy at Herrliberg, Zurich, before setting up his own design school in Berlin, 1926–34. He also became an influential administrator, directing the textile school in Krefeld, 1932–38. Fled to Amsterdam, then to Zurich, where he became director of the Museum and School of Applied Arts, 1938–54.

J

Jacobson, Egbert See CONTAINER CORPORATION OF AMERICA

Japanese graphic design The modern movement in Japanese graphic design evolved in the late 1940s during a period of rapid industrial expansion. There was a growing need to create a distinctive graphic language that combined traditional Japanese culture with the increasing post-war assimilation of Western ideas. Prior to this there had been relatively few examples of cultural exchange between Japan and the West. Japanese prints had influenced Western artists and designers from the middle of the 19th c., while during the 1920s and 30s a number of Japanese designers travelled to Europe to meet and work with leading practitioners in France and Germany. In the 1950s the move towards Western design standards was led by Masaru KATSUMIE, a critic and journalist. Yusaku KAMEKURA embraced the ideas of CONSTRUCTIVISM. He was instrumental in establishing the Japan Advertising Artists Club (JAAC) in 1951 that, up to its disbandment in 1970, provided a focus for debate. The publication of magazines like *IDEA* (1953), *Design* (1959) and *Graphic Design* (1959) – which was established by Katsumie – propagated international developments, with *Graphic Design* strongly supporting the INTERNATIONAL TYPOGRAPHIC STYLE. Japanese graphic design made an impact worldwide with Katsumie's visual co-ordination of the 1964 Tokyo Olympics, followed by his contribution to Expo '70 in Osaka and the 1972 Winter Olympics at Sapporo. Throughout the 1970s an emerging generation, including Ikko TANAKA, Shigeo FUKUDA, Kiyoshi AWAZU, Tadanori YOKOO and Eiko ISHIOKA, sought to establish a uniquely Japanese alternative to an imported internationalism. Increasingly, graphic designers worked alongside practitioners in architecture, films and fashion. During the 1980s a new wave of young designers (e.g. Takahisa Kamijyo, Takenobu Igarashi) followed a freer, more intuitive approach in marked contrast to the tradition of visual discipline established by Kamekura and his contemporaries. As in many European countries, the music and fashion industries continue to provide exciting graphic design opportunities. This richness and diversity suggest that graphic design in Japan will become increasingly influential within an international context.

Johnson Banks London-based design consultancy founded in 1992 by creative director Michael Johnson (b.1964) and Tom Banks (Banks left in 1994). Johnson studied design and marketing at Lancaster University and worked in corporate design at WOLFF OLINS in the mid-1980s. He then spent several years as a graphic designer and art director in Sydney, Melbourne and Tokyo before returning to London (1988). Renowned for its wit and style, the studio works with major corporate clients and on high-profile projects for the British Government, the Design Council, the Victoria & Albert Museum (London) and the British Council. Required to convey Britain's cultural diversity to an international audience, the studio successfully juxtaposed contradicting images in a set of posters for the British Council (1998). By contrast, they redesigned the seventy-six regional editions of *Yellow Pages*, Britain's business telephone directory. In addition to re-branding the covers they also created the new typeface Yellow, which needed less space and offered enhanced legibility (1999). Johnson Banks won four D&AD silver awards during the 1990s and an ART DIRECTORS CLUB OF NEW YORK gold award (1991). Johnson is a visiting lecturer at a number of UK art and design colleges.

Johnson Banks's poster for The British Council, 1998.

Johnston's Railway Type, designed in 1916.

ABCDEFGH
abcdefgh

Johnston, Edward (1872–1944) English master of calligraphy, TYPEFACE designer and influential teacher. Largely responsible for the modern resurgence of interest in penmanship. Abandoned medical studies at Edinburgh University in 1897, devoting himself to the practice and study of calligraphy. Taught at Central School of Arts and Crafts, London, 1899–1912 and the Royal College of Art, London, from 1901. His students included Eric GILL and the handwriting scholar, Alfred Fairbank. Between 1910 and 1930 designed type and initials for Count Kessler's CRANACH PRESS. His most significant contribution to type design was Railway, commissioned in 1916 by Frank PICK of London Underground. This early modern SANS SERIF face was of classical Roman proportions and remains in use today. After the war Johnston reworked the famous circle-and-bar SYMBOL from an earlier version of c.1907; this symbol and typeface are enduring elements in London Transport's renowned CORPORATE IDENTITY. Author of classic books including *Writing & Illuminating & Lettering* (1906) and *A Book of Sample Scripts* (1914).

Jones, Owen (1809–74) British architect, designer and printer. After early travels in Egypt, Turkey and Spain, Jones emerged as a major influence on Victorian taste through his writings on non-European ornament. His *Plans, Details and Sections of the Alhambra* introduced Moorish decoration to a Western audience. The book, which appeared in parts between 1836 and 1845, was a major production in CHROMOLITHOGRAPHY, printed by Jones himself. His design output thereafter covered tiles, interiors, book jackets, stamps and currency. Following his appointment as joint architect of the 1851 Great Exhibition in London, Jones began to formulate the ideas that led to the production of his most famous work, *Grammar of Ornament* (1856): this collection of ornamental styles from different periods and cultures became recognized internationally.

Design by Terry **Jones** for the jacket of *A Manual of Graphic Techniques* (1990).

Jugendstil book jacket for a 1905 edition of Edgar Allan Poe's *Curious Stories*.

Jones, Terry (b.1945) British designer and editorial art director who trained at the West of England College of Art. Worked on the magazine *Good Housekeeping*, then art directed British *VOGUE* 1972–79 where his unconventional approach produced adventurous cover designs. In 1980 he co-published, edited and art directed *I-D*, an alternative streetstyle magazine focusing on pop culture. During the 1980s he experimented endlessly at *I-D* with devices including polaroid photography, photocopier distortions, layering and mixing of type and image to create apparently random and chaotic 'instant design' solutions. *I-D* became an important springboard for many young designers and photographers. Jones has also worked in video and television graphics and for the fashion labels Fiorucci and Mexx. In 1990 he was appointed European art director for Esprit, the San Francisco fashion company. Editor and designer of *A Manual of Graphic Techniques: Instant Design* (1990), which reviews twenty years of his design.

Jugendstil Distinctively German equivalent of ART NOUVEAU. Jugendstil (Youth Style) emerged in 1896, taking its name from the popular arts weekly *Jugend* (1896–1914), published in Munich by Georg Hirth. Emanated from Munich – the home of the Munich Secession – and rapidly spread to Berlin and Darmstadt. In addition to the curvilinear naturalistic motifs of Art Nouveau, Jugendstil acknowledged the German printmaking tradition and medieval letterforms, producing a style that was less florid, more hard-edged. Important Jugendstil designers included Otto ECKMANN, Josef Sattler, Hans Christiansen and the influential Peter BEHRENS.

justified Typesetting format in which the letters and words of each line of text are spaced to ensure that the line fully occupies a specific column width. This entry is set in 8/10pt Gill Sans justified to a measure of 60 mm. *See* UNJUSTIFIED

Two **Jugendstil** typeface designs: Carmen, *c.* 1900 (top) and Eckmann-Schrift, 1896 (bottom).

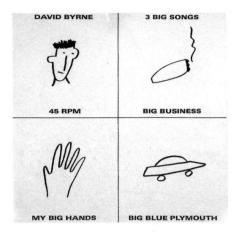

The cover of David Byrne's record *3 Big Songs*, designed in 1983 by Tibor and Maira **Kalman** and Carol Bokuniewicz.

Symbol for the Taiyo Machine Industry Co., designed by **Kamekura**.

K

Kalman, Tibor (1949–99) Graphic designer based in New York, principal of the innovative design collaborative M&Co, which he founded in 1979. Received no formal design training, having originally studied journalism. Kalman shuns conventional elegance in design, favouring quirky, witty solutions, often made possible by advanced technology; M&Co is renowned for its use of the vernacular visual elements (advertising signs, graffiti) found in American urban environments. An early client was David Byrne of the band Talking Heads, for whom M&Co has created album covers, posters, film titles and the experimental video *(Nothing But) Flowers* (1988). Other title sequences for films include those for Jonathan Demme's *Something Wild* (1986) and *Swimming to Cambodia* (1987). In 1987 he designed several issues of the New York journal *Artforum*. Kalman has also designed a range of witty wristwatches. Appointed creative director of the magazine *Interview* in 1990. Editor-in-chief of Benetton's promotional magazine *Colors* from 1991–95.

Kamekura, Yusaku (1915–97) Leading figure in post-war JAPANESE GRAPHIC DESIGN who contributed to its international standing. Studied at the Institute of New Architecture and Industrial Arts, Tokyo, 1935–37 where he was influenced by Russian CONSTRUCTIVISM, the BAUHAUS and the posters of A.M. CASSANDRE. Worked for Nippon Kobo (later called International Industrial Arts Information Company) 1937–60. Magazine art director of *Nippon* from 1937, of *Commerce Japan* from 1949, and editor of *Kaupapu* from 1939. Established the influential Japan Advertising Artists Club in 1951 and was co-founder and managing director of the Nippon Design Centre, Tokyo, 1960–62. His SYMBOL for the 1964 Tokyo Olympic Games received the grand prize from the Japanese Ministry of Education, and his popular PICTOGRAM designs and posters for the Games were an integral part of the complete graphic programme directed by Masura KATSUMIE. From 1962 his growing reputation enabled him to establish a successful freelance practice. An admirer of the INTERNATIONAL TYPOGRAPHIC STYLE, he designed posters for Expo '70 in Osaka, the 1972 Winter Olympics at Sapporo and Expo '89 in Nagoya, which illustrate his ability to build upon a Japanese aesthetic in order to communicate effectively with an international audience. His design output has embraced advertising, trademarks, book

Katsumie was design director of the 1964 Tokyo Olympics, for which Yoshiro Yamashita devised these symbols.

design and packaging. Characteristics of his work are his strong sense of linear and geometric form – as seen in work for the Nikon Camera Company – and dramatic photography, as in his posters for Kokudokeikaju ski resort. In 1978 he was elected president of the newly founded Japan Graphic Designers Association. A prolific writer on design, *The Works* of *Yusaku Kamekura* (1983) is a survey of his career.

Katsumie, Masaru (1909–83) Japanese design critic and journalist. After writing for *Industrial Art News* 1948–49, he became an energetic promoter of European design and a catalyst in the organization of the design profession in Japan. His enthusiasm contributed to the establishment of a number of important Japanese design schools during the early 1950s. In 1954 founded the Society for the Science of Design and organized the exhibition 'Gropius and the Bauhaus' at the National Museum of Modern Art in Tokyo. Katsumie's commitment to increasing Japanese understanding of modern design is evidenced by his 1957 translation of Herbert Read's *Art & Industry* and the publication of his own book *Good Design* (1959). In 1959 he launched and edited the journal *Graphic Design,* which promoted the work of European masters. His stature within JAPANESE GRAPHIC DESIGN is confirmed by his responsibility for the visual design programmes of the 1964 Tokyo Olympics (see Yusaku KAMEKURA), Expo '70 in Osaka and the 1972 Winter Olympics in Sapporo. See Shigeo FUKUDA

Kauffer, Edward McKnight (1890–1954)
American graphic designer and poster artist. Born in Great Falls, Montana, he became a major figure in British advertising art between the wars. Attended evening classes in painting at the Mark Hopkins Institute, San Francisco 1911–13, and spent six months at the Chicago Art Institute (1913). While in Chicago he saw the controversial 'Armory Show' (1913), which introduced modern European art to a sceptical US public. Sponsored by Professor McKnight of Utah University to study painting in Paris; Kauffer took his name in gratitude. Moved to London at the outbreak of war and in 1915 received his first poster commission, from Frank PICK of London Underground. His early commitment to painting and his familiarity with modern art were profoundly to influence his design. CUBISM, FUTURISM, ART DECO and SURREALISM all found expression in his posters. His famous *Flight of Birds,* a striking image

Soaring to Success !

DAILY HERALD

— the Early Bird.

Kauffer's *Flight of Birds* image, employed as a poster for the *Daily Herald*, 1919.

Annual report cover by **Keaney** (with Karen Wilks) for Apicorp (1988).

inspired by VORTICISM, was used as a *Daily Herald* poster in 1919. Designed 141 posters for London Underground and many others for such clients as Shell, British Petroleum and Eastman & Sons. His book jacket for Lytton Strachey's *Eminent Victorians* (1921) was the beginning of his series of designs and illustrations for Nonesuch Press, founded by Sir Francis MEYNELL, and Faber and Gwyer. Kauffer's own book *The Art of the Poster* was published in 1924. In 1930 he became art director of the publishing house Lund Humphries. He also designed textiles and carpets; in 1929 he exhibited those rugs alongside those designed by Marion Dorn, his future wife. Kauffer reached the zenith of his success in the 1930s with his posters bringing the language of modern painting to a large public. In 1937 the Museum of Modern Art, New York, held a one-man show of his work. Returned to the US in 1940 where he produced several posters for Greek war relief and the US Treasury. Post-war he designed for American Airlines (1947–48), the New York Subway Advertising Co. Inc. (1949) and the publisher Alfred A. Knopf.

Keaney, Siobhan (b. 1959) British graphic designer. Studied at the London College of Printing, graduating in 1982. Worked briefly with three London design consultancies (Smith & Milton, Robinson Lambie-Nairn, and David Davies Associates) before becoming an independent designer, 1985. Her design solutions are characterized by meticulous typographic detail combined with an ability to create subtle, multilayered photographic illustrations. Keaney's adventurous approach to information design has been recognized by a number of prestigious awards: in 1990 she received the DESIGNERS AND ART DIRECTORS

ASSOCIATION silver award for the Most Outstanding Brochure (for Seymour Powell) and for the Most Outstanding Annual Report (for Apicorp). Her colourful typographic/photographic compositions were featured in TDK posters and press advertisements, 1991. Designed set of four Science Fiction stamps for Royal Mail, 1995.

Keedy, Jeffery (b.1958) American educator, graphic designer and creator of experimental, digitized typefaces. Studied graphic design and photography at Western Michigan University, US, before working for CBS television, Boston (1981), as a designer of advertising and promotional material. In 1982 he joined Clarence Lee Design and Associates, Honolulu, producing corporate identity and signage. From 1983, attended the influential graphic-design programme at Cranbrook Academy of Art, Michigan, where he explored POST-MODERN approaches to graphic design. Moved to Los Angeles to take up an appointment at the California Institute of the Arts, later to become director of the CalArts graphic-design programme (1991–95). Keedy has worked for numerous cultural organizations, designing posters and catalogues for the Museum of Contemporary Art in Los Angeles, the San Francisco Artspace and the Santa Monica Museum of Art. He also created a series of calendars for LACE (Los Angeles Contemporary Exhibitions, 1988–90). Designed the TYPEFACE Skelter for the catalogue to accompany the exhibition 'Helter Skelter: LA Art in the 1990s' (1992), in which incisions across the text serve as a metaphor for the social breakdown suggested by the art. Keedy's typeface designs include Hard Times (1990), Menu Sans (1990), Keedy Sans (1991), Jot (1993) and LushUS, *Fuse* magazine's typeface. In 1996 launched his type company Cipher.

Keller, Ernst (1891–1968) Swiss graphic designer and educator, a key figure in the evolution of Swiss graphic design and the INTERNATIONAL TYPOGRAPHIC STYLE. After early training as a draughtsman in LITHOGRAPHY, he studied typography in Leipzig 1912–14. In 1918 he joined the Kunstgewerbeschule, Zurich to teach on the advertising course. From then until his retirement in 1956 he developed an internationally acclaimed training programme for student designers and typographers. His influence can be traced to this programme and the particular emphasis he placed on legibility and simplicity. His poster designs reveal a strong typographic discipline that is apparent in both the early asymmetric layouts and later symmetric solutions.

Type specimen of Glide by **Keedy**, originally developed for Condé Nast Publications in 1997.

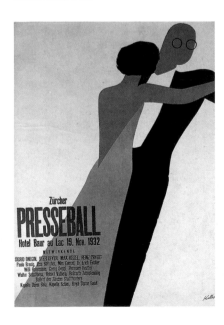

Lithograph advertisement by **Keller** for the Zurich Press Ball, November 1932.

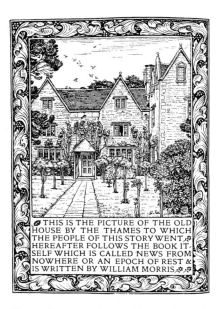

Woodcut frontispiece, depicting Kelmscott Manor, from *News from Nowhere*, printed by the **Kelmscott Press** in 1892.

Catalogue cover designed by **Kepes** for the exhibition 'What is Modern Painting?' held at the Museum of Modern Art, New York, 1952.

Kelmscott Press (1891–98) Printing press established by William MORRIS at Kelmscott Manor, Hammersmith, London as a reaction to mediocre standards of contemporary book production. Morris used the press to create luxurious volumes, printed on hand-made paper and vellum, for wealthy collectors. He employed his own TYPEFACE designs: Golden (1889), inspired by Jenson's 15th-c. Venetian ROMAN face; and the BLACKLETTER Troy (1891) and its smaller version Chaucer (1892), both based on 14th-c. German manuscript letterforms. By the time of its closure the Kelmscott had published fifty-three titles and provided a stimulus to designers in Europe and America to participate in the emerging PRIVATE PRESS MOVEMENT. Volumes such as *The Works of Geoffrey Chaucer* (1896), with WOODCUT illustrations by Edward BURNE-JONES, and *The Canterbury Tales* (1896) attempted to recreate the production standards of the 15th c. These outstanding examples of book art subsequently inspired commercial book design.

Kepes, Gyorgy (b. 1906) Hungarian-born designer recognized for his graphic and exhibition design and for his contribution to design education. Trained at the Royal Academy of Arts, Budapest, as a painter and film maker 1924–28. Influenced by Walter GROPIUS and fellow Hungarian László MOHOLY-NAGY whom he met during the early 1930s in Berlin, where Kepes was working as an exhibition and graphic designer. Moholy-Nagy and Kepes worked together in London (1936) before both emigrating to the US in 1937. Invited by Moholy-Nagy to run the Color and Light Department at the New Bauhaus, Chicago, 1938–43. Wrote his influential *Language of Vision* in 1944, a student text that articulated BAUHAUS principles. From 1946 until 1974 Kepes taught at the Massachusetts Institute of Technology where, in 1967, he established the Center for Advanced Visual Studies. Throughout his teaching career he practised as a designer, producing outstanding work for CONTAINER CORPORATION OF AMERICA 1938–44 and *FORTUNE* magazine.

kern Term used in HOT METAL COMPOSITION to describe those parts of a letter that extend over the edge of the metal body. These projecting parts overlap on to the adjacent letters, thus improving spacing. Letters with kerns are particularly common in ITALIC alphabets.

kerning Term used when the spacing between certain type characters is adjusted to achieve an even and consistent letter spacing. Kerning would normally be necessary in letter combinations such as To and VA,

Advance direction sign for a complex junction, designed by **Kinneir**, who placed white lettering and yellow route numbers on a dark-green background.

Kitching's 'Imagine' advertisement for Scheufelen Papers, 2000.

where the excessive space between the two characters is adjusted to create an overlap and produce a better fit. Letter spacing programmes, including a kerning facility, are available in most FILMSETTING and COMPUTERIZED TYPESETTING systems.

Kinneir, Jock (1917–94) Graphic designer and typographer, born in Hampshire, England. Trained at Chelsea School of Art 1935–39, specializing in engraving. After the war worked as an exhibition designer at the Central Office of Information, London, then moved to DESIGN RESEARCH UNIT before setting up his own practice in the early 1950s. First major commission, originating in the mid-50s, was the SIGNAGE scheme for Gatwick Airport, London, then being developed by architects Yorke, Rosenberg & Mardall. This project profoundly influenced the future direction of his career: working with Margaret Calvert, he dominated the design of public signage in Britain for the next two decades. Starting with motorway signage for the Ministry of Transport, he progressed to his most demanding project, designing the signs for all British roads (1964). Other schemes followed for British Rail, the armed forces, airports and hospitals. Often using specially drawn SANS SERIF alphabets, his work established new standards of consistency and clarity for signage systems, with many of his solutions being adopted worldwide. Kinneir was head of the department of graphic design at the Royal College of Art, London in the early 1960s. In 1980 he wrote *Words and Buildings,* a valuable text on public signage.

Kitching, Alan (b.1940) British typographer and graphic designer whose designs for contemporary letterpress printing have helped to distance the art from the nostalgia of its past traditions. Began his career at the age of fourteen, with a six-year apprenticeship as a compositor. Highly influenced by the modernist typographer, printer and teacher Anthony FROSHAUG whom he met in 1964, thereafter becoming his assistant at the Experimental Typography Workshop at the School of Art, Watford College of Technology, UK. In 1970 Kitching produced the *Typography Manual,* his response to Froshaug's significant *Typography Norms* (1964). Freelance designer (1970–78), before joining Derek BIRDSALL and Martin Lee at Omnific Studios (1978), working on corporate identities, exhibition design and publishing design for such clients as Mobil and IBM. Established his own studio in Clerkenwell, London (1989). An influential tutor at the Royal College of Art, London, designing the college's new marque in 1997.

Klein, Lou (b.1932) American art director, born in Czechoslovakia. Studied at Cooper Union School, New York, and Yale University School of Art, New Haven. After graduating in 1959 he worked as art director for the magazines *Interiors* and *Time,* and briefly for the Charles Hobson advertising agency, London. In 1962 he returned to New York to form the Gips and Klein group, moving back to London as creative director of Charles Hobson & Grey in 1964. Established his own practice in London (1966), subse-

Klimowski's poster for the Buñuel film *Phantom of Liberty*, 1981.

Klimt produced this controversial colour lithograph to advertise the first Vienna Secession exhibition, 1898.

quently forming a partnership with Michael PETERS. Head of graphic design at the Royal College of Art, 1972–78. Design director of Time-Life Books International, he was based in London from 1976–82, thereafter relocating to Washington. Klein's experience of working on both sides of the Atlantic has produced a graphic style displaying sharp wit and clarity of thought. Member of AGI.

Klimowski, Andrzej (b.1949) British designer and poster artist of Polish descent. Trained at St Martin's School of Art, London, originally in painting (1968–72) and then graphics (1972–73). Travelled to Poland to study with Henryk TOMASZEWSKI at the Warsaw Academy of Fine Arts, where he remained until 1980, producing numerous theatre and cinema posters, television graphics and the animated film *Dead Shadow*. His work received widespread acclaim through one-man shows and his submissions to the Poster Biennale in Warsaw. Since his return to London, his clients have included the Royal Shakespeare Company and *The Guardian* newspaper. His disturbing illustrations and coloured photographic COLLAGE designs are a continuation of the great post-war Polish poster tradition.

Klimt, Gustav (1862–1918) Austrian JUGENDSTIL painter and designer. Leader of the group of artists and designers who founded the VIENNA SECESSION. He produced many designs and posters for the group's journal, *Ver Sacrum*. His poster for the first Vienna Secession exhibition in 1898 created a storm of controversy, with an additional overprinting of trees being required to make the male nude acceptable. His graphic work acknowledged the growing influence of Charles Rennie MACKINTOSH and the Glasgow School, particularly in its strong sense of order, integrated typography and delicate interplay of geometric patterns. His later exotic and richly textured paintings of the female form achieved widespread acclaim.

Klinger, Julius (1876–1942) Austrian poster artist, type designer and painter who trained at the Vienna Technologischen Gewerbemuseum (Museum of Technology and Industry) before working as a magazine illustrator in Vienna, Munich and Berlin. Closely associated with the VIENNA SECESSION. His early work for the Berlin printing firm of Hollerbaum und Schmidt reveals the influence of ART NOUVEAU and the BEGGARSTAFF BROTHERS. Refined and reduced his imagery to symbolic forms, favouring dramatic, restricted colours and precisely integrated lettering.

Klinger's *8 Kriegsanleihe* (Eighth War Loan) poster, 1918.

One of **Kneebone**'s illustrations for the Davey and McDonnell book *How to Interview* (1975), which appeared with the caption: 'Do show interest: Your facial expression can do a great deal to encourage (or discourage) the candidate. If you acknowledge what he says with a smile and a nod of interest he is more likely to continue doing it than if you appear to be ignoring what he says, or to be bored by it.'

Returned to Vienna in 1915, where he worked for the Austrian war archives. One of his most powerful posters is *8 Kriegsanleihe,* for the eighth Austrian war-loan campaign in 1918. After the war he opened a studio in Vienna, continuing to design advertising posters and producing books including *12 Klinger-Plakate (12 Klinger Posters,* 1923). TYPEFACE designs include Klinger-Antiqua and Klinger-Kursiv.

Kneebone, Peter (1923–90) British designer, illustrator and teacher, educated at Oxford University. After the war he became assistant director of exhibitions for the 1951 FESTIVAL OF BRITAIN. Throughout the 1950s and 60s he established a reputation as an illustrator for numerous publications and books, specializing in finding visual expressions of complex concepts. As an educator he was co-ordinator of MA studies at the Central School of Art and Design, London. Moved to France in 1974. He was a major force in the establishment of ICOGRADA, becoming secretary 1963, secretary-general 1977–79 and president 1979-81.

Kner, Albert (1899–1976) Hungarian designer who emigrated to America in 1940, settling in Chicago. Appointed by CONTAINER CORPORATION OF AMERICA's Walter Paepcke as the first staff packaging designer. Kner led CCA's Design and Market Research Laboratory for over twenty years. This pioneering laboratory was concerned with the research and development of packaging, along with the scientific evaluation of its market effectiveness.

Koch, Rudolf (1876-1934) German type designer, calligrapher and teacher of lettering. Born in Nuremberg, the son of a sculptor and museum curator, he became an apprentice metal-worker in Hanau, near Offenbach, studying part-time at a local art school. After further studies at Nuremberg he moved to Munich and, in 1898, to Leipzig. Until 1902 he was employed by a lithographic printer and a firm of bookbinders, producing JUGENDSTIL designs. Freelanced before joining the Klingspor foundry, Offenbach (1906), where he spent the remainder of his career. Apart from the Deutsche Anzeigenschrift family (1923–34), created for Stempel, all his TYPEFACE designs were for Klingspor. Many are based on calligraphic and hand-drawn letterforms. Amongst his most successful BLACKLETTER and ROMAN faces are Deutsche Schrift (1906–21), Wilhelm-Klingspor-Schrift (1920–26), Koch-Antiqua (1922–29), Peter Jessen Schrift (1924–30) and Claudius (1931–38), which was cut by Koch's son after his death. Popular SANS SERIF faces include the unusual Neuland (1923), which evokes WOODCUT printing and, by contrast, the elegant and refined Kabel (1926–29) with its companion faces Zeppelin (1929) and Prisma (1931). Koch taught at the Offenbach Technical Institute, where in 1921 he established an important lettering workshop.

DENN EINE JEGLICHE KUNST ODER WERK WIE KLEIN SIE SEIEN DAS SIND ALLE SAMT GNADEN UND WIR KET SIE ALLESAMT DER HEI+ LIGE GEIST ZU NUTZ UND ZU FRUCHT DER MENSCHEN +WÄRE ICH NICHT EIN PRIE STER UND WÄRE UNTER EINER VERSAMMLUNG+ICH NÄHME ES FÜR EIN GROSSES DING DASS ICH SCHUHE MA CHEN KÖNNTE UND ICH WOLLTE AUCH GERNE MEIN BROT MIT MEINEN HÄN DEN VERDIENEN KINDER DER FUSS NOCH DIE HAND DIE SOLLEN NICHT DAS AUGE SEIN WOLLEN EIN JEGLI CHER SOLL SEIN AMT TUN DAS IHM GOTT ZUGEFÜGT.

Specimen setting of **Koch**'s Neuland typeface (1923).

Advertisement by **Kurlansky** for the Graphic Design Workshop in Cambridge, England, July 1983.

Krimpen, Jan van (1892–1958) Dutch TYPEFACE designer, calligrapher, letterer and book designer. Spent much of his career as house designer at the renowned Haarlem printing house of Joh.Enschedé en Zonen. Influenced by the work and writings of Edward JOHNSTON. Van Krimpen created restrained and elegant ROMAN types including Lutetia (1925), Romanée (1928) – to accompany a Dutch 17th-c. ITALIC by Christoffel van Dijck – Romulus (1931) and his most successful Spectrum (1952). The handsome volumes he designed at Enschedé demonstrate finely proportioned classical typography. In 1929 he created decorated capitals for the Curwen Press (see Harold CURWEN) and was later responsible for the headline for Oliver SIMON's *Signature* journal (1947).

Van **Krimpen**'s 1929 initials for the Curwen Press (below) and 1947 headline for *Signature* (bottom).

ABC

SIGNATURE

Kurlansky, Mervyn (b.1936) London-based graphic designer who in 1972 was a founding partner of PENTA-GRAM. Born in South Africa, he emigrated to Britain in 1958. Trained at the Central School of Art and Design, London 1959–61. Worked freelance before becoming graphics director of Planning Unit, the design consultancy service of Knoll International, 1962–67. During two decades at Pentagram he has designed CORPORATE IDENTITY schemes, annual reports, book jackets, posters and packaging for clients such as Reuters, Roche, Olivetti, Shiseido and Penguin Books. Holder of several major awards, including three silver awards from the British DESIGN-ERS AND ART DIRECTORS ASSOCIATION and a gold award from Japan's Ministry of Trade and Industry (1978). Active in design education, he has taught Syracuse University students visiting London and directed Pentagram/Kent State University Graphics Work-shops for US designers and teachers. Since 1993 he has worked with Image Bank, which supplies still and moving images to the design world, evolving the company's corporate identity. Member of AGI.

L

laid paper Uncoated printing and writing paper identified by the faint impression of ribbed lines on the surface. A barely visible vertical pattern of lines is intersected at regular intervals by a thicker, more widely spaced series of horizontal lines. The lines are created by the wires of the dandy roller leaving an impression during manufacture.

Lambie-Nairn, Martin (b.1945) Graphic designer for television and print. Studied at Canterbury College of Art & Design 1960–65 before joining the BBC graphic design department, London. From 1966 he gained further experience with Rediffusion Television, Conran Associates and Independent Television News. Joined London Weekend Television as a designer, 1970, working on light entertainment, drama and current affairs programmes. In 1976 he formed Robinson Lambie-Nairn Ltd, a design partnership in London. In 1990 the company was renamed Lambie-Nairn & Co with Lambie-Nairn as creative director designing specifically for television. The dominant British influence in the field of brand identity for television companies, their work included the famous animated LOGOTYPE for Channel 4 Television (1982), Scottish Television corporate identity (1985), BBC 9 O'Clock News titles (1988), TF1 corporate identity, Paris (1989) and the channel identities for BBC1 and BBC2 (1991), as well as many television commercials. In 1997 Lambie-Nairn & Co merged with brand identity specialists Tutssels to form Lambie-Nairn@The Brand Union. Lambie-Nairn developed the original idea for the acclaimed satirical television programme *Spitting Image*. A consistent award winner at international animation and advertising festivals. Appointed RDI in 1987. Elected President of the DESIGNERS AND ART DIRECTORS ASSOCIATION, London, 1990. In 1993 helped to establish Tutssel, St John, Lambie-Nairn, a design consultancy in London. Honoured with the Queen's Award for Export Achievement in 1995 and the 1999 Prince Philip Designer's Prize.

lamination Process of covering paper or card with a strong, transparent plastic film. The film, which is applied using heat or pressure, provides long-term protection for documents and brochures in constant use.

Landor, Walter (1913–95) Industrial and graphic designer, born in Munich. Studied at university in Munich and London. Along with Milner GRAY and Misha Black established Industrial Design Partnership, London 1935–39. After working on the British Pavilion for the New York World's Fair of 1939 Landor emigrated to the US in 1940, where he formed Landor Associates, San Francisco, in 1941. The practice has become one of the leading visual communication companies in the world with offices in Europe, the Far East, Africa and Latin America. Renowned for its analytical, research-based design solutions it has produced CORPORATE IDENTITY programmes for many major organizations including Coca Cola, Levi Strauss, 3M, H.J. Heinz and General Electric.

Lane, Sir Allen (1903–70) British publisher who founded Penguin Books in 1935. Insisted that his paperbacks should be cheap, well-designed editions of acclaimed contemporary and historical literature. Penguin proved that excellent standards of typography and illustration were appropriate for a mass market. Following an invitation from Lane, Jan TSCHICHOLD established the Penguin Composition Rules for typographic design (1947). Designers who have worked for Penguin include Edward Young (designer of the original Penguin SYMBOL in 1935), Hans SCHMOLLER, David GENTLEMAN, Abram GAMES, Germano FACETTI Alan ALDRIDGE and Derek BIRDSALL.

laser printer A COMPUTER-linked printing device in which digitally controlled beams of laser light activate a photoconductive powder material. The precision of the laser beams create a powder image that is then transferred electrostatically to the paper. The image is fused to the paper by heat. Laser printers are common in DESKTOP PUBLISHING systems.

Latin (a) Broad category of TYPEFACE embracing those designs whose antecedents can be traced back to the rich vocabulary of Western European letterforms. (b) Family of bold, modern ROMAN typefaces with distinctive triangular SERIF forms.

layout Design draft/sketch of book, advertisement, title page, etc. produced by designer to establish the overall appearance and relationship between such elements as illustrations, photographs and typography. Alternate layouts exploring colour and scale are prepared before selecting the final design for production.

Leck, Bart van der (1876–1958) Dutch painter and designer. Trained at the State School for Decorative Arts, Utrecht, and the Academy in Amsterdam. In 1917 he joined Théo van DOESBURG in forming the DE STIJL movement and journal. The graphic design language favoured by De Stijl, with its emphasis on flat shapes, heavy black lines and severe geometry, pays due homage to the geometric abstract paintings produced by van der Leck prior to 1917. His 1915/16 poster for the Batavier Line, Rotterdam-London shipping service, with its strong horizontal emphasis, black rules and SANS SERIF lettering is a precursor of De Stijl values. In retaining some degree of illustrative representation in his design output, he never quite achieved De Stijl's declared aim of an abstract, universal visual language.

Leete, Alfred (1882–1933) British illustrator and poster designer famous for his First World War recruitment poster depicting the Secretary of War, Lord Kitchener, confronting the spectator with an accusing finger and the slogan 'YOUR COUNTRY NEEDS YOU'. This image appeared first in 1914 as a cover design for the weekly Magazine *London Opinion*. The poster was printed in several versions, carrying different texts. It spawned numerous imitations, the most famous being James Montgomery FLAGG's 1917 poster of Uncle Sam, *I want YOU for US Army*. Leete also designed posters for the London Underground Electric Railways and contributed humorous cartoons and illustrations to books and magazines.

Advertising poster for the Müller shipping line (1915) by van der **Leck**.

Lenica's poster for the opera *Wozzeck*, 1964.

Lenica, Jan (b.1928) Poster artist, illustrator, film animator and teacher. Born in Poland, he studied architecture at Warsaw Polytechnic 1947–52. From 1945 to the early 1950s contributed cartoons to newspapers and magazines, including the satirical weekly *Szpilki*. A prolific poster designer throughout the 1950s and 60s, he was awarded the Toulouse-Lautrec award for film posters (1961) and first prize at the International Poster Biennale in Warsaw (1966); also designed posters for the 1972 Munich Olympic

Leete's famous recruitment poster (1914).

Games. Influenced by the teaching of Henryk TOMASZEWSKI, he uses political and cultural themes to explore the complex relationship between the individual and the state. Began making experimental animated films and designing stage sets in the late 1950s. Moved to Paris in 1963 where his films achieved international acclaim: of particular note is *Adam 2* (1969), written, designed and animated by Lenica using a dazzling range of COLLAGE techniques. His surreal illustrations often employ dramatic colour contrasts and a flowing linear technique to produce powerful, haunting images. His vast output of cartoons, illustrations, posters, stage designs and animation has been featured in exhibitions throughout the US and Europe.

Letraset Dry transfer process providing the graphic designer with instant headline lettering. When first released in the UK in 1960, it was a wet process exploiting the principle of the child's wafer 'slide transfer'. Since then Letraset has expanded rapidly and offers a comprehensive range of TYPEFACE designs and graphic products. The ever-increasing range of alphabets available worldwide both reflects and influences changing typographic trends. Letraset faces are also available to the designer working with the new technologies, through software developments such as Letra Studio and Letrafonts for use with the APPLE MACINTOSH.

letterpress Traditional relief printing process in which the type and images to be printed are raised above the non-image areas. The raised surfaces are inked and an impression obtained when the paper and inked surface come into contact. Largely supplanted by LITHOGRAPHY, letterpress is still used in the production of high-quality, limited-run publications.

LettError Typographic partnership set up in 1989 between Dutch font designers Just van Rossum (b.1966) and Erik van Blokland (b.1967) who work from their respective homes in The Hague, the Netherlands. Trained together as typographic designers at The Royal Academy for Fine and Applied Arts (KABK), The Hague before working for Erik SPIEKER-MANN at MetaDesign in Berlin. Designed the TYPEFACE Beowolf (1990), the rough and ragged characteristics of which change with every keystroke to suggest the irregular forms of handwriting. In 1991 they scanned in their own handwriting to produce the digitized fonts JustLeftHand and ErikRightHand. Other popular fonts include Trixie (1991) that emulates the letters of a battered typewriter, and Kosmik (1993)

another quasi-random typeface. The studio also creates animations and music and designs websites. Clients include MTV, FontShop International and the Dutch PTT. *LettError* (2000), which explores the relationship between programming and design, received the 2000 Charles Nypels award and was selected as one of the Best Dutch Book Designs.

Leu, Olaf (b.1936) German art director and designer. Having trained as a compositor at Ulm 1951–54, worked as a type director with the Bauer foundry in Frankfurt 1954–57 and assistant art director of a Frankfurt advertising agency 1957–59, prior to becoming a freelance designer. His practice flourished, culminating in the establishment of Olaf Leu Design + Partner (Fritz Hofrichter) in Frankfurt, 1971. Leu's wit and originality is visible in packaging, advertising and symbols, while his lavish calendar designs for international clients, including the Zanders paper company, have attracted widespread acclaim over the past decade. Collaborates regularly with leading US and European designers, including Milton GLASER and the photographer Sam Haskins, his powerful concepts communicating effectively in an international marketing context. Influential in bringing exhibitions of American and Japanese graphic design to the attention of the German design profession. A regular award-winner in international design competitions, he has exhibited in one-man shows in Europe and the US. *Olaf Leu: Graphic Design Direction 1955–1990* (1990) reviews his design achievements.

Packaging designs by **Leu**, part of his corporate design scheme for Brandes & Partner Film & Television Productions, 1967.

Advertising poster for a printer in Lausanne, designed by **Leupin** in 1959.

Lewitt-Him's advertisement for an industrial oil company, 1934.

Leupin, Herbert (b.1916) Swiss poster and advertising designer, illustrator and painter. Studied in Basle at the Allgemeine Gewerbeschule 1932–35 and with Paul COLIN in Paris 1936–37. Since the establishment of his studio (1939) Leupin has enjoyed great acclaim, winning many awards in the annual 'Best Swiss Posters' competition. Developing a highly original style of illustration that relies upon a naive flatness of form, humour, and a disarming directness, he has designed posters for cultural and commercial clients throughout Europe and America. Perhaps his best-known images are for the Swiss Circus Knie. One-man exhibitions in Offenbach (1957), Toronto (1958), Basle (1969) and Essen (1972). Member of AGI. Has worked as a painter since 1970.

Lewis, Wyndham See VORTICISM

LeWitt-Him Design partnership formed by the Polish-born graphic designers Jan Le Witt (1907–91) and George Him (1900–82) who began their association in Warsaw in 1933, moving to London in 1937. They achieved great distinction during the war with work produced for the British Ministry of Information, the Home Office and the Post Office. Post-war, their originality and wry humour were applied to posters and book illustrations. They designed murals and the Guinness clock for the FESTIVAL OF BRITAIN (1951). The partnership was dissolved in 1954, with Le Witt abandoning graphic design to become a painter and poet, and Him continuing as a freelance advertising designer and illustrator. During the 1950s and 60s Him collaborated with Stephen Potter on a famous series of advertisements for Schweppes drinks featuring the imaginary English county of 'Schweppshire'. He was elected RDI in 1977.

Leyendecker, Joseph Christian (1874–1951) Illustrator and advertising artist who enjoyed huge popularity in America between the wars. Born in Montabour, Germany, he emigrated to Chicago in 1882. Beginning with his first cover for the *Saturday Evening Post* in 1901, he went on to design 321 covers for the magazine. Studied at the Art Institute of Chicago and in Paris at the Académie Julian. He designed painterly posters for government agencies, many commissioned through the US Division of Pictorial Publicity. Along with his brother Frank X. Leyendecker, he worked for the Navy, the first US government agency to use posters. Originated the famous Arrow Collar Man for Arrow Shirts and Collars, producing numerous advertisements for this company throughout the 1920s. Increasingly ART DECO in feel, his advertising images encapsulated contemporary values in their portrayal of sophisticated young Americans.

Liberman, Alexander (1912–99) Magazine art director with Condé Nast publications. Born in Kiev, Russia, his formative years were spent in Paris where he studied at the École des Beaux Arts during the early 1930s. Worked briefly for A.M. CASSANDRE before joining the French picture weekly *Vu*, initially as a lay-out artist, becoming art director in 1933. Awarded a gold medal for an exhibition design in the 1937 Paris World's Fair. In 1940 he fled to America, where he joined the Condé Nast art department, creating lay-outs for *VOGUE*. Succeeded Mehemed Fehmy AGHA as art director of *Vogue* 1943. Liberman was concerned that style should not take precedence over effective communication. Through the photographs of Irving Penn, Cecil Beaton and Lee Miller he brought contemporary images to the magazine. Miller's harrowing pictures of the Buchenwald gas chambers were first published in *Vogue*. In 1947 he boldly changed the LOGOTYPE of *Vogue* to FRANKLIN GOTHIC, a newspaper face. He was appointed editorial director of all Condé Nast publications worldwide in 1961, a position he held over the next three decades.

Licko, Zuzana (b.1961) Slovakian typeface designer who emigrated to the US in 1968. Studied graphic communication at University College Berkeley, graduating in 1984. Lives in Berkeley, California, where, with husband Rudy VANDERLANS, she created the influential graphic-design and typography magazine EMIGRE (1988), which spawned a design studio and a digital type foundry. As Licko's career coincided with the emergence of the APPLE MACINTOSH she has embraced the possibilities created by the computer for typeface design. She is the principal designer of customized digital fonts for *Emigre* and its publishing arm Emigre Fonts. Licko's acclaimed typefaces include Modula (1985), Matrix (1986), Citizen (1986), Variex (with VanderLans, 1988), Triplex Roman (1989), Journal (1990), Dogma (1994), Hynopaedia (1997), Tarzana (1998) and Solex (2000). She has also designed revival typefaces that are interpretations of historic models, for example, Mrs Eaves (1996) inspired by BASKERVILLE, and Filosofia (1996) with its origins in BODONI. Licko's typeface design is showcased in *Emigre (The Book): Graphic Design into the Digital Realm* (1993).

Lienemeyer, Gerhard
See RAMBOW/LIENE-MEYER/VAN DE SAND

First World War poster to raise money for the American war effort, by **Leyendecker**.

Licko's typeface Mrs Eaves.

Æ AARDVARK

Theorists find energy sticky

ligature Typographic term for the connecting link that joins two or three type characters together. By joining the characters space is saved and KERNING simplified. Ligatures are commonly used to join fi, ffi, ffl, fl, ff, tt and ct.

fi ffi ffl fl ff

Ligatures in lower-case letters from the Garamond typeface.

Capital letters and **lining numerals** from the Bembo typeface.

XYZ 1234567890

lining numerals/figures Also known as Modern Figures. Set of numerals that align with the top and bottom of the matching capitals in a TYPEFACE. This modern convention is in contrast to OLD STYLE NUMERALS/FIGURES.

linocut Traditional printmaking technique in which a knife or engraving tool is used to cut an image into the surface of a thick slab of linoleum. As in RELIEF PRINTING, lines, patterns and areas that are not cut away are inked prior to printing. A separate slab of linoleum is normally used for each colour required. The potential of the medium is well illustrated in the work of Edward BAWDEN.

Linotype Hot-metal type-composing machine controlled by skilled keyboard operator. The system produces separate lines of lead typesetting, known as 'slugs'. The raised letters and words on the slug are formed when circulating matrices are positioned and filled with molten lead. No longer in common usage, the Linotype system was used extensively in the LETTERPRESS printing of newspapers and books. Invented in America by Ottmar Mergenthaler (1854–99) in 1886, a year before the invention of the MONOTYPE machine.

Lionni, Leo (1910–99) American graphic designer, art director, painter and illustrator. Born in Amsterdam, he trained as an economist in Italy 1931–35. Became involved with the Italian Futurist Filippo MARINETTI, under whose influence he produced abstract paintings. Lionni began his career as an art

Second World War photomontage poster, designed by **Lionni**.

director and designer with Motta, an Italian food supplier 1933–35. Produced BAUHAUS-influenced advertisements for magazines like *Domus* and *Casabella*. Emigrated in 1939 to the US, becoming art director at the Philadelphia advertising agency N.W. AYER 1939–47, which was responsible for CONTAINER CORPORATION OF AMERICA advertising. During the war he exploited PHOTOMONTAGE in work for CCA and in powerful, economic posters for the war effort. He moved to New York and succeeded Will BURTIN as art director of the innovative FORTUNE magazine, 1949. Lionni freed *Fortune* from the constraints of SANS SERIF type and the Bauhaus GRID, achieving a distinctive visual identity through his use of photography and illustration. In addition to his work at *Fortune*, he was Olivetti's design director in America, responsible for CORPORATE IDENTITY, including showroom interiors, 1950–57. Co-editor of the New York *Print* magazine 1955–59. In 1961 he retired from *Fortune* to concentrate on writing and illustrating children's books, and painting. He published his autobiography *Imagination and Wisdom: Between Worlds* in 1997.

Lissitzky, Lazar El (1890–1941) Russian designer, painter, architect and photographer, born in Smolensk province. Studied architecture at Darmstadt Technische Hochschule, Germany, 1909–14, returning to Moscow in 1914 to pursue a career in architecture. In 1919 Marc Chagall, the principal of the Vitebsk School of Fine Arts, appointed Lissitzky to teach architecture and graphic arts. Whilst there he met the painter Kasimir Malevich, creator of SUPREMATISM. A passionate supporter of the Russian Revolution, Lissitzky brought the philosophy of CONSTRUCTIVISM to industrial and graphic design. Along with contemporaries like Alexander RODCHENKO and Vladimir Tatlin, he aspired to an accessible art for the proletariat. His graphic design uncompromisingly challenged typographic convention, with dynamic ASYMMETRIC layouts, changes of scale, and white space used as a positive formal element. In 1919 he designed the famous Soviet propaganda poster *Beat the Whites with the Red Wedge* and also created his first 'Proun', a series of Constructivist images that combined architectural concepts with painting; the term was taken from the Russian words meaning Project for Affirmation of the New. Moving to Berlin in 1921, he exploited the design opportunities presented by excellent printing facilities. Following contact with László MOHOLY-NAGY and Théo van DOESBURG, his work appeared in DE STIJL magazine. Committed to the

Leaflet designed by **Lissitzky** to advertise a Berlin exhibition of his work (1923): his own name was printed in red.

Lissitzky's advertisement for Gunther Wagner's Pelikan carbon paper, 1924.

propagation of his ideals, he organized the Constructivist Congress in 1922. In the same year he completed *Of Two Squares*, a children's book, and with Ilya Ehrenburg created the Soviet government periodical *Veshch* (*Object*). In 1923 he designed *For the Voice*, a book of poems by Mayakovsky. A victim of tuberculosis, Lissitzky moved to Switzerland in 1924. Jointly designed and edited a double issue of MERZ with Kurt SCHWITTERS (1924). In 1925, along with Hans Arp, he edited and designed *The Isms of Art 1914–1924*, an influential typographic achievement. In his work as a consultant designer, Lissitzky's relationship with the Pelikan ink company throughout the 1920s illustrates his ability to produce innovation within the constraints of a commercial brief. In 1925 he returned to Moscow to teach interior and furniture design at the Vhkutemas, the Russian BAUHAUS. Lissitzky's work provides a key link between contemporary graphic design and its roots in MODERNISM. His pivotal role in typographic theory is generously acknowledged by Jan TSCHICHOLD in his seminal text *Die neue Typographie* (1928). A much-travelled designer, he was a catalyst in establishing links between kindred spirits in Russia, Germany, Holland and Switzerland.

literals Minor typesetting mistakes (spelling, punctuation, etc.) requiring correction before printing. *See* AUTHOR'S CORRECTIONS, PROOF CORRECTION MARKS

lithography Planographic printing process in which the image and non-image areas are not differentiated in level and appear together on a completely flat plate or stone. The process is based on the principle that oil and water do not mix. The image to be printed is treated to make it water-resistant but attractive to oil or grease (the printing ink); the non-image area is treated to make it water-attractive but grease-resistant. In commercial printing demanding large runs, lithographic printing plates are made of thin sheets of aluminium. These are attached to the cylinders of a printing machine, with separate rollers applying the ink for the image area and the water for the non-image area. Normally the image to be printed is then transferred on to another cylinder covered with a smooth rubber blanket from which it is 'offset' on to the paper. Lithography is a popular and versatile process used to print books, packaging, magazines, etc. Also known as litho, offset litho and photolithography.

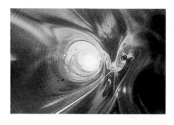

Frame from Version 4 of the title sequence for the BBC television series *Dr Who* (1973), designed by **Lodge**.

Geschichte als Argument (History as Argument), **Loesch**'s poster for the Deutscher Historikerstag München, 1996.

Lodge, Bernard (b.1933) British designer who was an early and influential practitioner in television graphics. After studying graphic design at the Royal College of Art, London, 1956–59, he joined the BBC in London. From 1960 until 1977 he produced numerous titles, including the award-winning title sequence for the *Dr Who* series. Lodge's work is characterized by an ability to exploit new opportunities for image generation presented by technological developments. His period at the BBC was briefly interrupted when he was a designer/director with Streich, Fletcher, Perkins 1967–69. From 1977 until 1979 he freelanced, before forming a partnership with the designer Colin Cheeseman. Up to its disbandment in 1986 this association produced outstanding television titles and commercials. Lodge now works as a freelance consultant. Elected RDI in 1982.

Loesch, Uwe (b.1943) German graphic designer and poster artist. Born in Dresden during a period of momentous political, cultural and social upheaval. Loesch's work is distinguished by a strong conviction that designers should integrate their moral and social beliefs into design practice. Studied graphic design at the Peter Behrens Academy, Düsseldorf (1964–68), where in 1980 he returned to teach. In 1970 he founded the Uwe Loesch Group for Visual and Verbal Communication, Düsseldorf, working on corporate communications, editorial and exhibition design. Loesch's most significant contribution is in the field of poster design. Often working for non-commercial organizations, including museums, social services and a small theatre company called Das Kom(m)odchen, he has developed a sparse and direct style, rich in wordplay and clever visual puns, communicating each message with powerful effect. Loesch's approach is exemplified in his famous poster Punctum (1982), composed of minimal elements and overlaid with a multiplicity of meanings. The poster was awarded first prize at the Lahti poster Biennale (1983). Since 1990 he has held a professorship for communication design at the University of Wuppertal, succeeding Willy FLECKHAUS. A winner of numerous international awards throughout the 1980s and 90s, Loesch is a member of AGI and the Art Directors Club of Germany. His posters feature in the permanent collection of the Museum of Modern Art, New York.

Loewy, Raymond (1893–1986) French-born industrial designer. Moved to US after studying as an electrical engineer in Paris (1910–14, 1918) and serving in the First World War. Loewy's highly successful career spanned half a century, with his practice, Raymond Loewy Associates, operating in New York, California, Paris and London. The first designer to appear on the cover of *TIME* magazine (1949), he designed products, interiors, textiles, furniture and graphics and was renowned for the streamlining styling that he introduced to numerous American cars, trains and machines; his influence extended to projects for the NASA Skylab 1967–73. His most famous graphic design achievement is the Lucky Strike cigarette pack of 1940. Major LOGOTYPE designs include those for Shell, BP and Exxon.

logotype Letters or word formed into distinctive and unified form. Can often provide the basis for a company TRADEMARK, brand or CORPORATE IDENTITY. Often abbreviated to 'logo'.

Lois, George (b.1931) American advertising art director. Educated at the High School of Music & Art 1945–49 and at the Pratt Institute, New York 1949–50. Worked with William GOLDEN at CBS 1954–56 and during the late 50s with Bill Bernbach, the creative director of DOYLE DANE BERNBACH, New York. Left DDB in 1960 to form the agency Papert Koenig Lois, New York. His reputation as the *enfant terrible* of the American communications industry was gained through an ability to produce irreverent, unpredictable but effective advertising. In 1962 his persuasive skills were utilized to save the financially troubled magazine *Esquire*. Over the next decade he

May 1969 cover of *Esquire* magazine, designed by **Lois**.

art directed ninety-two covers, many in collaboration with the photographer Carl Fischer. These powerful images, including anti-Vietnam War covers, helped the magazine regain stability. Named Art Director of the Year by the ART DIRECTORS CLUB OF NEW YORK in 1963. After leaving Papert Koenig Lois in 1967, he went on to set up a number of other agencies. Author of *The Art of Advertising: George Lois on Mass Communications* (1977), along with Bill Pitts.

loose-leaf binding See BINDING METHODS

lower case Typographic term for the small letters (a, b, c, d, etc.) in an ALPHABET or FONT of type. See UPPER CASE

a b c d e f g h i j k l m
n o p q r s t u v w x y z

Lower case letters from the Bembo typeface.

Lubalin, Herb (1918–81) American, graphic designer and typographer. Born in New York, graduated from Cooper Union School, New York in 1939. Appointed art director at Sudler & Hennessey, New York in 1945, becoming vice-president in 1955. Left to set up his own design consultancy, Herb Lubalin Inc. in 1964. From 1969 took the creative lead in a number of partnerships and associations, including those with Tom Carnase and Tony DISPIGNA. He was an innovative

Lubalin's design for the cover of *Avant Garde* magazine, January 1968.

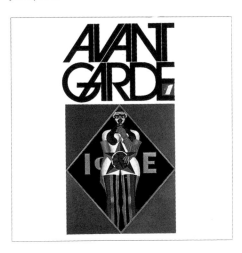

typographer who rejected the functionalist philosophy espoused by his European counterparts in favour of an exuberant, eclectic style. A gifted communicator, he combined words and images to express his ideas with maximum impact. His manipulation of type reflected a desire to break with tradition and exploit the typographic possibilities offered by the new systems of PHOTOCOMPOSITION. Lubalin's output embraced advertising, packaging, editorial design, SIGNAGE, TYPEFACE design, postage stamps, etc. As an editorial designer he was responsible for the *Saturday Evening Post*, and the magazines *Eros* (1962), *Fact* (1967) and *Avant Garde* (1968). These magazines provided Lubalin with a regular platform for his creative ideas. The typeface Avant Garde, which he first designed for the masthead of the magazine, became available commercially in 1970. He also designed the typeface Serif Gothic (1974) in association with DiSpigna. In 1970, formed INTERNATIONAL TYPEFACE CORPORATION in partnership with Aaron BURNS and Edward Rondthaler. ITC's promotional journal *U&lc* (Upper and lower case), with Lubalin as editorial design director, was a major influence on the typographic industry worldwide throughout the 1970s and 80s. Shortly before his death he formed a partnership with Seymour CHWAST and Alan PECKOLICK. Lubalin's work featured in many exhibitions and received numerous international awards. Elected to the ART DIRECTORS CLUB OF NEW YORK Hall of Fame (1977) and awarded the AIGA medal (1981).

Ludlow Type Composing Machine *See* MIDDLETON, ROBERT HUNTER

Lupton, Ellen (b. 1963) New York–based exhibition curator, graphic designer and educator. Studied graphic design, painting and sculpture at the Cooper Union School of Art, New York, graduating in 1985. Cofounded the multidisciplinary design studio Design Writing Research with J. Abbott MILLER (1985). Appointed curator of the Herb LUBALIN Study Centre in New York (1985–92), where she created exhibitions that have developed people's understanding of the theory and practice of graphic design. In 1992 she became curator of contemporary design at the Cooper-Hewitt, National Design Museum at the Smithsonian Institute, New York. As a scholar and designer, she is involved in curating and designing exhibitions, as well as writing and designing catalogues and other related material. Landmark exhibitions generated by Lupton through the Cooper-Hewitt include 'Mixing Messages: Graphic Design in

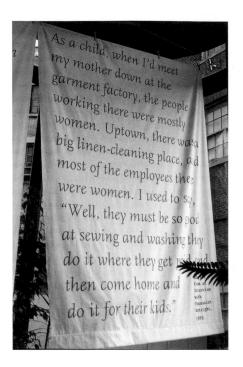

'Mechanical Brides' exhibition at the Cooper-Hewitt, designed by **Lupton**, 1993.

Lustig used a montage of five photographs for this cover of *3 Tragedies* by Federico Garcia Lorca, 1949.

Contemporary Culture' (1996) and 'Graphic Design in the Mechanical Age' (1998). Chair of the graphic-design department at the Maryland Institute College of Art in Baltimore. She and Miller were awarded the Chrysler Award for Innovation in Design (1994).

Lustig, Alvin (1915–55) American graphic and interior designer and educator who adapted the visual precedents of modern art to design. Trained at the Art Center School of Design, Los Angeles 1934–35, where he later taught Louis DANZIGER. Briefly studied architecture under Frank Lloyd Wright (1935) before opening a design studio and printing shop in Los Angeles 1936–40. His career alternated between New York and Los Angeles: during 1945 and 1946 he worked as visual design director of *Look* magazine in New York. Amongst his most distinguished work were book jackets for New Directions, New York, and Noonday Press and editorial designs for the magazines *Art Digest* and *Industrial Design*. His design approach utilized abstract shapes and symbols to express the essence of a product whether it be a book, record sleeve or CORPORATE IDENTITY programme. Lustig was a major contributor to the graphic design programme established at Yale University, New Haven in 1951. The Museum of Modern Art, New York staged an exhibition of his work in 1953. His career was tragically cut short by progressive illness and his premature death at the age of forty.

M

McConnell, John (b.1939) British graphic designer and art director. Trained at Maidstone College of Art, Kent. From 1963 until 1974 he had a practice in London serving a wide range of clients including Biba, the archetypal London fashion boutique of the 'Swinging Sixties'. In 1967 he co-founded Face Photosetting, London, producing a series of acclaimed calendars that illustrate his sharp humour. Joining PENTAGRAM in 1974, he developed a special working relationship throughout the 1980s with three major UK clients: Clarks Shoes, the publishers Faber & Faber and Boots the pharmaceutical company. He was invited to join each company at board level, thus determining design policy from within. His abilities range from elegant, one-off solutions for small projects through to managing the corporate design requirements of international organizations. Member of the Post Office Stamp Advisory Committee for British

pictorial and commemorative postage stamps. He received the DESIGNERS AND ART DIRECTORS ASSOCIATION President's Award in 1985 for his outstanding contribution to design. Elected RDI in 1987. Member of AGI.

McCoy, Katherine (b.1945) and **Michael** (b.1944) American graphic, product and interior designers and influential educators. Graduates of Michigan State University, with Michael receiving an MA from Wayne State University, Detroit (1968). They pursued separate early careers; Katherine worked for Unimark International, Chrysler Corporation and Omnigraphics Inc.; Michael developed projects for San Francisco's Bay Area Rapid Transit Vehicle and Lockheed International. Appointed co-chairmen of the post-graduate design department, Cranbrook Academy of Art, Michigan (1971–95). Moved to Illinois Institute of Technology in 1995. Internationally respected teachers, they received the Society of Typographic Arts Educator Award (1987). They share an interdisciplinary approach to design, demonstrated in the range of work undertaken by their consultancy, McCoy & McCoy, founded in 1971. Projects include packaging, posters, SIGNAGE, exhibitions, furniture, interiors and a television documentary on Japanese design. Katherine McCoy has lectured on graphic design education and practice at numerous international conferences. Her *Design Discourse – Cranbrook Design in the 80's* was published in 1990. She is a member of AGI, a past president of the Industrial Designers Society of America (1983–85) and vice-president of AIGA (1990). Michael McCoy is co-author of *Problem Solving in the Man-made Environment* (1975), one of the first design education programmes for children.

McDonald's logotype for the 1986 Holland Festival.

McDonald, Edward (b.1960) Graphic designer. Born in Toronto, he trained originally at Ontario College of Art 1979–83 and then at Cranbrook Academy of Art, Michigan, graduating in 1985. Worked for a year in Holland with Studio DUMBAR where he designed the LOGOTYPE and publicity for the 1986 Holland Festival. Returned to Michigan to establish his consultancy, Signa (1986–88), which specialized in print and video production. Since 1989 McDonald has been assistant professor with the School of the Art Institute of Chicago, and principal designer with The Siren, a design collaborative. He demonstrates an ability to assimilate the best of contemporary European design, infuse it with a hard-edged elegance and apply it successfully to an increasing range of design problems. His commitment to a transatlantic cross-fertilization of ideas is reflected in his co-direction of an annual travel study programme that enables American students to study with leading designers in Holland.

McKnight Kauffer See KAUFFER, E. MCKNIGHT

Machado, Joao (b.1942) Portuguese graphic designer. Born in Coimbra, he was educated at the School of Fine Arts, Porto, graduating in sculpture (1968). Returned in 1976 to lecture on the graphic arts. Established a studio in 1982 specializing in poster design, illustration and packaging. His posters are characterized by joyous colours, a playful arrangement of sharply defined geometric elements and bold contrasts between flat surface and textured pattern. Providing a focus for the development of graphic design in Portugal, his work has been featured in a number of poster biennali including Warsaw, Lahti, Brno and Colorado.

machine-coated paper Paper coated during the manufacturing process, using rollers that carry a mixture of adhesive and minerals. The finished surface quality can emulate some of the cheaper ART PAPERS. See CAST-COATED PAPER, COATED PAPER

machine-finished paper Often abbreviated to MF paper. Range of uncoated papers that are finished on both sides between the mechanical rollers of a calender. The surface texture is smooth but not glossy. Machine-finished papers can vary considerably according to the individual requirements of the paper maker and/or printer.

machine-glazed paper Often abbreviated to MG paper. Uncoated paper, often used for posters, which is rough on one side and machine-glazed (polished) on the other.

Macintosh (Computer) See APPLE MACINTOSH

Mackintosh, Charles Rennie (1868–1928) Scottish architect and applied artist. Designer of furniture, stained glass, ironwork, jewelry, lettering, textiles and posters. Mackintosh's individual interpretation of ART NOUVEAU emphasizes symmetrical elongated verticals in strong rectilinear compositions. Influenced by Lethaby's *Architecture, Mysticism and Myth* (1892) and by reproductions of work by Aubrey BEARDSLEY and Jan TOOROP in *The STUDIO*. Joined the Glasgow architectural practice of Honeyman & Keppie in 1889. Leader of the Glasgow Four (the Four

Mackintosh designed this radical poster for the magazine *The Scottish Musical Review* in 1896.

Macs), including the architect/furniture designer J. Herbert McNair and the Macdonald sisters, Frances (1874–1921) and Margaret (1865–1933); Margaret married Mackintosh in 1900. The Four exhibited in the 1896 show staged by the ARTS AND CRAFTS EXHIBITION SOCIETY, London, but in spite of a supportive article in *The Studio* (1897) their work was too advanced for British taste. Inclusion in Alexander Koch's journal *Dekorative Kunst* (1898) and designs for the Scottish sections of the VIENNA SECESSION Exhibition (1900) and the Turin Exhibition (1902) established their reputations abroad, particularly in Vienna. Mackintosh's architectural masterpiece was the 1897 Glasgow School of Art (library extension 1909). He created interiors and furniture for Mrs Cranston's tea-rooms (1897-1904) and designed his first important house, Windyhill, in 1900. Hill House, Helensburgh, for the publisher W.W. Blackie, was designed in 1902. He produced a small number of outstanding examples of graphic design, including posters for the Glasgow Institute of the Fine Arts and the *Scottish Musical Review*. Mackintosh left Glasgow in 1914 and three years later designed graphic displays for W.J. Bassett-Lowke in London. He finally departed England for France in 1923 where he painted until his death.

Mackmurdo, Arthur Heygate (1851–1942)
English architect and designer of furniture graphics, fabrics, wallpapers, metalwork, etc. A founder of the CENTURY GUILD, his TRADEMARK for the Guild (1884), with its fluid, compressed initials and floral motif, offered a stylistic foretaste of ART NOUVEAU. Similarly the undulating forms illustrating his book *Wren's City Churches* (1883), along with designs he created for *Hobby Horse*, the Guild's journal, anticipated the movement by several years. An associate of both John Ruskin and William MORRIS, he is reputed to have advised Morris on the setting up of the KELMSCOTT PRESS. After 1906 he concentrated on social politics, publishing *The Human Hive* (1926) and *A People's Charter* (1933).

Maeda, John (b.1967)
American graphic and interactive designer and educator who combines skills as a computer scientist and graphic artist to innovate visual languages in screen-based design. Studied electrical engineering and computer science at Massachusetts Institute of Technology. Moved in 1990 to Japan to study graphic design on the modernist-inspired programme at the University of Tsukuba Institute of Art and Design, Tokyo, where he was

Cover design for *Wren's City Churches* (1883) by **Mackmurdo**.

The Reactive Square by **Maeda** reconciles print media with digital media, 1995.

awarded a PhD. Returned to MIT in 1996 to succeed Muriel COOPER as professor of design. He is associate director of the MIT Media Laboratory, where he is also Sony Career Development Professor of Media Arts and Sciences and director of the 'Aesthetics and Computation Group (an experimental research studio founded in 1996). Alongside his work at MIT, Maeda runs MaedaStudio in Lexington, Massachusetts, with his wife Kris Maeda. He believes that the computer is a design medium in itself and not simply a tool for re-creating traditional design models. Maeda has produced a series of interactive publications called *Reactive Books*. Among the expressive graphic elements he has pioneered is The Reactive Square (1995), a black voice-activated square whose shape responds in different ways to voice commands. Also responsible for TimePaint (1995), in which colour splashes across the screen. Maeda acknowledges the influence of American designer Paul RAND in his work. A key characteristic of his approach to design is the complexity generated by the repetition of simple elements. Clients include Sony, Shiseido and Absolut Vodka. Winner of numerous awards, Maeda has published *Design Machines* (an introductory text to encourage greater design experimentation, 1994), *Maeda@Media* (which is both manifesto and autobiography, 2000) and *Design By Numbers* (1999).

Majo, Willy Maks de (1917–93) Graphic designer, largely self-taught. Born in Vienna, he set up his first studio in Belgrade 1936–39. Emigrated to England in 1939, serving with the Royal Yugoslav Air Force and the Royal Air Force throughout the Second World War. After demobilization, established an exhibition and graphic design practice in London. His work is strongly typographic and stylistically varied, indicating his businesslike approach to design problems. A gifted communicator, he was highly influential in establishing ICOGRADA in 1963; as its first president (1963–65), he sought to improve communication between designers throughout the world. Awarded the Design Medal of the Society of Industrial Artists and Designers, London (now the CHARTERED SOCIETY OF DESIGNERS) in 1969.

majuscules Alternative term for UPPER CASE.

Makela, P. Scott (1960–99) American graphic designer, typographer, educator and writer on design for the digital environment. Studied political science at the University of Minnesota (1978–82) before attending Minneapolis College of Art and Design (1982–84). Ironically, his training reflected the modernist tradition of the INTERNATIONAL TYPOGRAPHIC STYLE. Taught graphic design at the California Institute of the Arts (1984–88), where he was influenced by April GREIMAN. Makela enrolled as a graduate student at Cranbrook Academy of Art, Michigan (1989–91), developing a complex, densely layered aesthetic that embraced technology and exploited the visual possibilities of the computer. His seminal promotional poster for *Cranbrook Design: The New Discourse* (1990), with its dissolving typography swirling around a human brain, marked a shift in his design vocabulary. The prospectus for the Minneapolis College of Art and Design (1991–93) demonstrates Makela's early digitally created design. In 1992 Makela and his wife, designer Laurie Haycock Makela, formed the studio Words + Pictures for Business + Culture, Minneapolis, creating design for print, video and multimedia for such clients as Warner Bros., Virgin Records, Nike and Apple. He has also worked on music videos for Miles Davis and the ScreaM! video for Michael and Janet Jackson. Makela collaborated with director Jeffrey Plansker to make commercials for a Canadian television station to promote Vans shoes and also the award-winning title sequences for the David Fincher film *The Game* (1997). In 1996 Makela and Laurie Haycock Makela succeeded Katherine and Michael McCoy as co-chairs of 2-Dimensional design at Cranbrook Academy of Art. Collaborated with Laurie Haycock Makela and Lewis Blackwell on the book *Whereishere* (1998), which reflects on contemporary design issues and its launch was accompanied by an exhibition at Cranbrook Academy of Art.

Man Ray See RAY, MAN

Manwaring, Michael (b. 1942) American graphic designer. Studied at the San Francisco Art Institute 1961–64, since when he has practised in San Francisco. Worked for an exhibition design studio

Combined logotype and symbol for diary publishers Charles Letts & Co., designed in 1966 by de **Majo**.

DE
DIVINA
PROPORTIONE
DI
LUCA PACIOLI

MILANO · MCMLVI

Title page of Pacioli's *De divina proportione* (Officina Bodoni edition), designed in 1956 by **Mardersteig**.

Marinetti's Futurist book jacket for *Zang Tumb Tumb*, 1912.

(1964), before joining the Robertson/Montgomery graphic design practice 1964–68. Thereafter became a principal in the Reis/Manwaring partnership 1968–76 before establishing the Office of Michael Manwaring in 1976. Noted for rich surface textures, subtle colour combinations, inventive typography and multilayered compositions, his work represents an assimilation of the cultural milieu of California. Expert at manipulating surface planes; his posters, SIGNAGE programmes and environmental graphics engage the viewer through an elegant mixture of illusion and ambiguity. His involvement in environmental projects has increased since 1987 when he established EI (Environmental Image) in collaboration with urban designer David Meckel. In 1994 he designed the environmental graphics for the San Jose Arena, a sports stadium in California. Teacher at California College of Arts and Crafts from 1976. Received gold medal of ART DIRECTORS CLUB OF NEW YORK in 1980.

Mardersteig, Giovanni (Hans) (1892–1977)
Typographic scholar, printer, TYPEFACE and book designer. Born in Weimar, Germany. After studying law he joined the Leipzig publishing firm of Kurt Wolff. Along with two friends he founded a short-lived arts biannual, *Genius* (1919), which became the starting point for a life-long passion for fine printing and the PRIVATE PRESS MOVEMENT. Moving to Switzerland for health reasons, he established his own press, Officina Bodoni, near Lugano in 1922. The press was so named because the Italian government had granted him the exclusive privilege of using types cast from the original matrices by Giambattista BODONI. Starting to publish in 1923, Mardersteig established contact with Stanley MORISON, and co-operated with him on an early series of books on Renaissance calligraphy. In 1927 he moved Officina Bodoni to Verona, from where he developed it into one of the most distinguished presses of the 20th c. Mardersteig changed his Christian name to Giovanni and became a naturalized Italian. As a type designer, working closely with the French punch-cutter Charles Malin, he produced a number of ROMAN faces, including Zeno (1936) and Dante (1946–52).

Marinetti, Filippo Tommaso (1876–1944) Italian poet, writer, critic. Founder of FUTURISM. Studied law at the Sorbonne, Paris, during the mid-1890s. In 1905 he founded the literary magazine *Poesia* in Milan, using it as a vehicle to establish literary and artistic contacts throughout Europe. A gifted self-publicist, he exploited these links in canvassing support for *The Foundation* and *Manifesto of Futurism* (1909). Marinetti's publications rejected traditional concepts of literary and typographic order, favouring an unstructured arrangement of words and the random placement of individual letters. This emphasis on experimentation was influenced by the collages of CUBISM and reflected Futurism's support for chaos and revolution. Futurist typography provided stimuli for the later innovations associated with CONSTRUCTIVISM and the NEW TYPOGRAPHY of the 1920s.

Mariscal, Javier (b.1950) Prolific and versatile Spanish designer of graphics, interiors, furniture, lighting, fashion and textiles, all revealing the influence of POST-MODERNISM. He studied philosophy in Valencia 1967–70, then trained as a graphic designer at Barcelona's Escuela de Grafismo Elisava 1971–73. Began his freelance career in Barcelona during 1976. Intuitive creator of exuberant, unconventional and witty work. Designer for the Marieta textile collection between 1978 and 1983. Designed many famous bars and nightclubs, including Bar Duplex in Valencia (1980) and, along with architect Alfredo Arribas, the Torres de Avila nightclub in Barcelona (1990). Collaboration with industrial designer Pepe Cortes resulted in the Duplex bar stool (1980), with its zig-zag leg, and startlingly original furniture and lighting, including the Arana lamp and the Valencia lamp (1983). Artist responsible for 'Los Garriris' comic strip in *El Vibora* magazine (Barcelona, 1980–82). Established Estudio Mariscal in 1989. Achievements include the Bar-Cel-Ona pictographic poster (1980) and carnival posters for Barcelona (1982) and Tenerife's Santa Cruz festival (1989). In 1997, developed the identity for Lighthouse (the Scottish Design and Architecture Centre) in Glasgow, a building originally designed by Charles Rennie MACKINTOSH in 1893. Creator of the cartoon character 'Cobi', the official mascot of the 1992 Barcelona Olympic Games. Designed the Swatch clock tower for the 1996 Olympics, Atlanta. Founded Muviscal, an audiovisual production company (1998). At the end of the millennium created Colors, a multimedia theatre experience, which explores the power of the image throughout the 20th c.

Mariscal publicized the 1989 Santa Cruz festival with this poster.

Container Corporation of America produced this 1966 poster, designed by John Riebeu under the artistic direction of **Massey**.

is the first letter of the alphabet
there are twenty-five more
the chicago public library has all of them
in some very interesting combinations

Mason, John Henry (1875-1951) British printer, typographer and teacher. A leading figure in the development of fine printing and the PRIVATE PRESS MOVEMENT in England and abroad. Major creative influence on the Doves Press, which he joined in 1900 when it was founded by Emery WALKER and T.J. Cobden-Sanderson. Taught printing and typography at the Central School of Arts and Crafts, London, 1905–40, where he was a contemporary of Edward JOHNSTON. Advised on the setting up of the CRANACH PRESS, Weimar. Along with Edward Johnston, Ernest Jackson and Gerald Meynell he was a co-founder and editor of *The Imprint*, a short-lived but important printing journal published in January 1913. Consultant to the Lanston Monotype Company (see MONOTYPE) on cutting of the IMPRINT typeface in 1913. Elected RDI, 1936.

Massey, John (b.1931) American art director, designer, painter and printmaker. Born in Chicago, Illinois, he trained as an advertising designer at the University of Illinois 1950–54, later becoming art director of the University Press. He made a major contribution to CONTAINER CORPORATION OF AMERICA, which he joined in 1957, becoming advertising and design manager (1961) and director of design, advertising and public relations 1964–83. Concerned with clarity of communication, he adopts the rational principles of the INTERNATIONAL TYPOGRAPHIC STYLE. In 1967 he founded and directed the Center for Advanced Research in Design, a CCA subsidiary that developed CORPORATE IDENTITY schemes for clients including the Atlantic Richfield Co. and the US Department of Labor. Both as a designer and a painter he explores geometric patterns and volumes, as is evident in the civic and cultural posters and banners he has created for the cities of New York, Chicago and San Francisco. Founded John Massey Inc., Chicago in 1983. He teaches design at the Illinois Institute of Technology. Awarded a gold medal by the ART DIRECTORS CLUB OF NEW YORK in 1979.

Massin, Robert (b.1925) Art director and typographer. Born in Boisvillette, Eure-et-Loir, France. No formal design education having worked with his father, a sculptor and letter-cutter, before training with the typographer Pierre Faucheux. Massin's career has been spent in Paris, working in the French publishing industry. Beginning with the Club Française du Livre 1948–52, he moved to Club du Meilleur Livre 1952–58. His appointment to the publishers Gallimard in 1958 was the beginning of two decades of distinguished book design. He transformed Gallimard's traditional image and produced a series of books on poetry and drama, which received great acclaim for their unconventional typographic approach. Word and image were integrated in a dynamic visual form in order to improve the understanding of the text. Designs of note include those for *Exercises de Style* by Raymond Queneau (1964), and two works by Eugène Ionesco, *La Cantatrice Chauve* (1964) and *Delire à Deux* (1966). During the late 1970s Massin was a director of Hachette-Réalités before becoming editor of Editions Denoel in 1981. Published *Letter and Image*, a perceptive summary of lettering and alphabet design (1970). Massin also writes under the pseudonym Claude Menuet. Awarded the Prix des Graphistes, Paris, 1970.

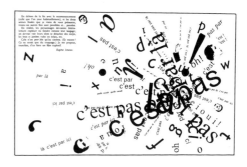

Two double-page spreads from Ionesco's *La Cantatrice Chauve* (The Bald Primadonna), designed by **Massin** in 1964.

Matter

Matter's 1936 poster for the Swiss Tourist Office.

Poster by **Matthies** for a production of a play by
Albert Camus at the Kiel theatre.

Matter, Herbert (1907–84) Swiss designer, poster
artist and photographer. Studied painting at the École
des Beaux Arts, Geneva, 1925–27, and at the
Académie Moderne, Paris, under Fernand Léger
1928–29. In Paris he worked with A.M. CASSANDRE, the
architect Le Corbusier and at DEBERNY & PEIGNOT.
Returning to Switzerland (1932) he designed the
famous series of dynamic posters for the Swiss
National Tourist Office in Zurich: each poster presented a particular aspect of the Swiss tourist industry, brilliantly illustrated by his startling use of
PHOTOMONTAGE and dramatic exploitation of scale and
space. Throughout his career he promoted photography as an integral element of successful visual communication. In 1936 he moved to New York, working
as a photographer for HARPER'S BAZAAR, VOGUE and other
magazines. From the 1940s he became a regular contributor to the celebrated advertising campaigns
devised by the CONTAINER CORPORATION OF AMERICA. He
produced some of his most innovative advertising
work as graphic design consultant for Knoll
International, the furniture manufacturer, 1946–66.
His versatility and virtuosity are well illustrated by the
range of activities he undertook during this period.
He produced a colour film on the work of the sculptor Alexander Calder (1949); was a photographer for
Condé Nast publications 1946-57; and designed a
comprehensive but short-lived CORPORATE IDENTITY
scheme for the New Haven Railroad (1954). From
1958–68 Matter was design consultant to the
Guggenheim Museum, New York and the Museum of
Fine Arts, Houston. As a committed educator, he
became a much respected professor of photography
at Yale University, New Haven, Connecticut between
1952 and 1976. Many international exhibitions have
acknowledged the importance of his work, and he
was accepted into the ART DIRECTORS CLUB OF NEW YORK
Hall of Fame in 1977.

Matthies, Holger (b.1940) German posterist and
designer/photographer working in album covers,
book jackets, calendars and CORPORATE IDENTITY.
Served an apprenticeship in colour LITHOGRAPHY, continuing his training at the Werkkunstschule, Hamburg
(1961) and the Hochschule für bildende Kunste,
Hamburg (1962), under Erwin Krubeck and Hans
Michel. Freelance practice in Hamburg since 1965.
Creator of numerous posters for concerts, exhibitions and, particularly, the theatre. His thoughtful,
provocative images combine photography, PHO-
TOMONTAGE and COLLAGE, manipulating disparate elements to create surreal effects. Designer of album

covers for clients including Polydor International, Philips and RCA. In 1983 he was appointed Professor of Communication Design at Fachhochschule für Gestaltung, Hamburg. Since 1994 he has been professor of visual communication at the University of Fine Arts in Berlin. Numerous exhibitions in Germany, Japan and the US since 1968. Awards include the Toulouse-Lautrec medal, Essen, 1984, and the ART DIRECTORS CLUB OF NEW YORK Merit Award, 1987.

Mau, Bruce (b.1959) Canadian graphic designer. Mau's contribution to book design reflects his conviction that the designer also has an authorial role in developing the content and meaning of a text. Educated at Ontario College of Art and Design (1978–80), Mau worked for Fifty Fingers Inc., Toronto (1980–82) before joining PENTAGRAM, London (1982–83). Co-founded Public Good Design and Communications (1983–85), a consultancy that specialized in design for public and non-profit-making organizations. Appointed creative director of *I.D.* magazine, New York (1991–93). Established Bruce Mau Design (BMD) in 1985; clients include Zone Books in New York for whom he designed an influential series dealing with such subjects as philosophy, the contemporary city and the history of the body. Mau worked with Dutch architect Rem Koolhaas on a 1345-page volume, *S,M,L,XL* (1996), which adopts formal innovation to explore the history of Koolhaas's architectural practice. Mau has designed numerous visual identities for such corporations as The Netherlands Architecture Institute, Vitra, The Andy Warhol Museum in Pittsburgh and The Art Gallery of Ontario. Through a number of important collaborative projects, Mau's work has reached into areas beyond graphic design; for example, with Koolhaas, Toronto's Oleson Worland Architects and Petra Blaisse of Inside/Outside, he created the winning landscape design for the Downsview Park, Toronto (2000). *Life Style* (eds. Kyo Maclear and Bart Testa, 2000) reveals the process and philosophy of Mau's practice. Received the Chrysler Award for Design Innovation (1998) and the Toronto Arts Award for Architecture and Design (1999).

M&Co *See* KALMAN, TIBOR

Me Company London-based, multidisciplinary design consultancy established by Paul White in 1985 and renowned for its complex, hyper-real imagery applied to brand creation and identity development. The designers' unsettling vision of modernity and

technology, combined with subtle twists in narrative and mood, has attracted commissions from the international music and leisure industries. They have worked on record sleeves and videos for the Icelandic singer Bjork (1998), a print campaign for Nike to promote football boots in the Netherlands (1996) and graphics for Laforet Harajuku's grand bazaar, Japan (1998).

measure Width to which a piece of typesetting is set, traditionally measured in 12pt (PICA) EMS.

mechanical American term for ARTWORK.

Mechano-Faktura (Theory of)

See BERLEWI, HENRYK

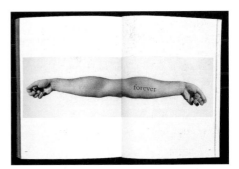

Spread from **Mau**'s design for the book to accompany the 'Douglas Gordon • Black Spot' exhibition, 2000.

Soundtrack cover by **Me Company** for Bjork's album *Dancer in the Dark*, 2000.

Mendell & Oberer Munich design studio established in 1961 by Pierre Mendell (b.1929, Essen) and Klaus Oberer (b.1937, Basle). The two designers studied under Armin HOFMANN at the Kunstgewerbeschule in Basle during the late 1950s. Both worked with Michael Engelmann in Munich in 1960. Their designs for advertising, posters, book jackets, CORPORATE IDENTITY and packaging reflect a Swiss discipline applied to strong graphic concepts. Concerned with clarity of communication, their work is always elegant and simple, as in the 1986 poster for the Kieler Woche sailing regatta. Designers of outdoor sculpture for public places; Mendell has exhibited sculpture at the Museum für Moderne Kunst, Munich. He received a gold medal from the ART DIRECTORS CLUB OF NEW YORK, 1973.

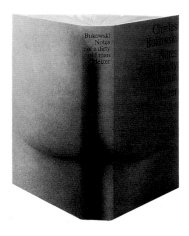

Mendell & Oberer's book jacket for Charles Bukowski's *Notes of a Dirty Old Man*, c. 1979.

Spread from *IF/THEN* by **Mevis + van Deursen**, 1999.

Merz (periodical) See SCHWITTERS, KURT

Mevis + van Deursen Dutch graphic-design studio founded in Amsterdam (1986) by Linda van Deursen (b.1961) and Armand Mevis (b.1963). Van Deursen trained at the Academy of Fine Arts in Tilburg (1981–82), then at the Gerrit Rietveld Academy in Amsterdam (1982–86). Mevis studied at St. Joost Academy in Breda (1981–82) before joining van Deursen at the Gerrit Rietveld Academy (1982–86). Both worked briefly for Studio Dumbar (1985). Much of their work emerges from their close associations with the world of fine art. Powerful poster and publication designs reveal a rawness and vitality that is a marked departure from the traditions of modernist Dutch design. Their design of *IF/THEN* (1999), for the Netherlands Design Institute, was awarded a distinction in the *I.D.* Annual Design Review (1999). They have exhibited and lectured in Europe, Japan and the US.

Meynell, Sir Francis (1891–1975) Publisher, typographer and book designer. Born in London, he was educated at Trinity College, Dublin, 1909–11. Designer at Burns and Oates, the Catholic publishers 1911–16, where in 1913 Stanley MORISON became his assistant. He founded the Pelican Press, London, directing it from 1916 until 1919 and again 1921–22. Moved into the newspaper industry, in 1919 becoming assistant editor of the *Herald* and editing the *Communist* in 1921. He founded the Nonesuch Press, London (1923) with the intention of producing books that combined 'significance of subject, beauty of format, and moderation of price'. This last objective he achieved by abandoning the hand-press production methods of the PRIVATE PRESS MOVEMENT; nearly all books published by the Press were machine-set by various printers. Meynell's choice of exquisite paper, TYPEFACE, illustration and BINDING METHODS created volumes of real distinction. George GROSZ, McKnight KAUFFER, Rudolf KOCH, and Reynolds STONE were among those who contributed to Nonesuch books. The publication of the first one hundred books was celebrated in *The Nonesuch Century* (1936). The Limited Editions Club, New York, took over the Press 1935–51, with Meynell reviving it again from 1951 until 1972. In addition to his publishing activities he practised as a successful freelance advertising designer. A founding member of the DOUBLE CROWN CLUB in 1924. Elected RDI (1945), Meynell was appointed typographic adviser to His Majesty's Stationery Office (HMSO), London, after the war. Received knighthood in 1946.

M F paper *See* MACHINE-FINISHED PAPER

M G paper *See* MACHINE-GLAZED PAPER

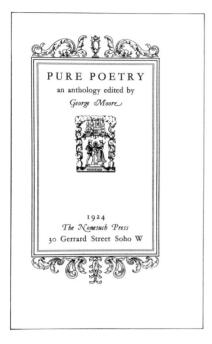

Meynell designed this title page for an anthology of George Moore's poems printed by The Nonesuch Press, 1924.

ABCDEFGH

Microgramma typeface, designed in 1952.

ABCDEFGH
abcdefgh

Record Gothic, one of the numerous typefaces designed by **Middleton**.

MICR Initials of Magnetic Ink Character Recognition, a security system that uses machines to recognize and read specially designed characters applied to cheques etc., using magnetic ink.

Microgramma SANS SERIF TYPEFACE designed in Italy in 1952 by A. Butti and Aldo NOVARESE. The letters are block-like with rounded corners. UPPER CASE only, no LOWER CASE available. There are a number of BOLD, CONDENSED and extended versions. Much favoured by architects for technical drawing details and exterior SIGNAGE. In 1962 Novarese designed a complementary lower case and thereafter the face was known as Eurostile.

Middleton, Robert Hunter (1898–1985) Type designer. Born near Glasgow, Scotland, emigrating with his parents to the US in 1908. Trained at the Chicago Art Institute, specializing in printing arts under Ernst F. Detterer, an inspirational teacher who had studied with Edward JOHNSTON. Middleton's entire professional career was spent with the Ludlow Typographic Company, Chicago, 1923–71. The Ludlow type-composing machine was largely used by the newspaper industry for headlines and DISPLAY setting. Now obsolete, it cast high-quality solid lines (slugs) of metal typesetting from hand-set matrices. The machine was not designed to compete with the volume text-setting produced by the LINOTYPE or MONOTYPE systems. Middleton designed nearly a hundred faces for Ludlow. In addition to a number of SCRIPTS, e.g. Coronet (1937) and Admiral (1953), faces of particular note include the SANS SERIF designs Record Gothic (started 1927, concluded 1956–61) and Tempo (1930).

Miller, J. Abbott (b. 1963) American graphic and exhibition designer, educator and writer, studied at the Cooper Union School of Art, New York (1981–85). In 1985 he co-founded Design Writing Research, a multidisciplinary design studio in New York, with his wife Ellen LUPTON. Committed to the idea of the 'designer as author', Miller is a perceptive commentator on the link between POST-MODERN graphic design, typography and post-structuralist philosophy. His challenging approach to design issues is demonstrated by his work for visual culture journal *2wice* and *Dimensional Typography* (1996), an exploration of typographic elements in time and space. In 1995, Miller and Lupton established Kiosk, an imprint concerned with research into design fields other than architecture. He is a contributing editor to *EYE* magazine and has coauthored four books, including *Design Writing Research: Writing on Graphic Design* (1996). Teaches in the graphic-design department of the Maryland Institute College of Art in Baltimore. He and Lupton were awarded the Chrysler Award for Innovation in Design (1994). Member of ALLIANCE GRAPHIQUE INTERNATIONALE (AGI). Joined PENTAGRAM, New York, as a partner in 1999.

J. Abbott **Miller**'s brick books, 1997.

A CD cover by **Mills** for *Russell Mills: Undark – Pearl + Umbra* Bella Union Records, 1999.

Mills, Russell (b.1952) British illustrator and multi-media artist whose work challenges the traditional divisions between art, design and illustration. Trained in England, initially as a graphic designer at Canterbury College of Art (1970–71) and Maidstone College of Art (1971–74), before studying illustration at the Royal College of Art, London (1974–77). Influenced by Dada and Surrealism, particularly the work of Marcel Duchamp (1887–1968) and Kurt Schwitters (1887–1948), and also by such contemporary artists as Antonio Tàpies and Anselm Kiefer. From early illustrations inspired by Brian Eno songs, Mills has continued to find motivation for his work in music and literature. He has designed numerous album and CD covers for such performers as David Sylvian, Roger Eno, Peter Gabriel and the Cocteau Twins. Mills's mature graphic style is characterized by richly textured surfaces, often using collage and obscure, near-abstract imagery. He has worked for publishers, such as Penguin, Picador and Faber & Faber, illustrating book jackets for numerous authors, including Samuel Beckett, Milan Kundera and Ian McEwan. He collaborated with Sylvian on *Ember Glance: The Permanence of Memory* (1990), which accompanied an art installation focusing on sound, sculpture, objects and light, shown at F-GO SOKO, Tokyo and marked the beginning of subsequent collaborative installations, often with Ian Walton. Mills has lectured in art colleges and universities in the UK, the US and Japan.

Minale, Tattersfield & Partners Multidisciplinary design consultancy founded in London in 1964 by Marcello Minale (1938–2001, born Tripoli, Libya) and Brian Tattersfield (b.1936, Yorkshire). A major contributor to the British design boom of the 1970s and 80s, the company works in a range of design disciplines including CORPORATE IDENTITY, packaging, industrial design, architectural graphics, furniture design and interiors. One of the largest consultancies in the world, they have design studios in London, Paris and Brisbane, as well as marketing offices in other major cities. Minale studied at the Istituto Tecnico, Naples, before working in Scandinavia as a designer and art director. He moved to London in 1962 to join the advertising agency Young & Rubicam as a designer. At this time he was also designing children's books. At Young & Rubicam Minale met Tattersfield who studied graphic design at the Royal College of Art, London 1959–62, worked briefly in Switzerland, and became art director for Young & Rubicam before forming a partnership with Minale. The consultancy avoids a recognizable house style by utilizing an advertising-

American in Paris: a poster designed in 1962 by Brian Tattersfield, of **Minale, Tattersfield & Partners**.

Minale designed this poster for the 1979 exhibition 'British Airports at the Design Centre'.

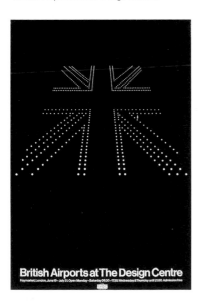

based 'solution within the problem' approach. Their distinctive 'scribble' SYMBOL has remained unchanged for thirty-eight years. Their output ranges from a LOGOTYPE for an arts foundation through to major projects for the Milton Keynes new city, the Heathrow Express Rail link and for London stores like Heals and Harrods.

minuscules Alternative typographic term for LOWER CASE characters.

Mlodozeniec, Jan (b.1929) Polish illustrator and poster artist. Studied poster design at the Warsaw Academy of Fine Arts, under Professor Henryk TOMASZEWSKI, graduating in 1955. Since 1952 he has produced book jackets and illustrations for a number of Polish publishers. Mlodozeniec's bold and free-flowing illustrations appear in Poland's leading periodicals and have been applied to the promotion of many cultural events. Designer of some three hundred posters, he has made a substantial contribution to Poland's strong creative tradition in this field. The range and vitality of his work have been recognized by the award of many prizes, including silver medals at the Leipzig Book Fair 1965 and 1971, a gold medal at the International Poster Biennale, Warsaw, 1980, and first prize at the Poster Biennale, Lahti, Finland, 1983. Winner of the 'Best Poster of the Year' award in Warsaw eleven times 1965–89. Over twenty one-man exhibitions of his work have been held throughout the world. Member of AGI.

Drawing for *Film* magazine, issue 10 (1974) by **Mlodozeniec**.

M/M French graphic-design practice founded in Paris in 1991 by Michael Amzalag (b.1968) and Mathias Augustyniak (b.1967). Amzalag trained at the Ecole Nationale Superieure des Arts Decoratifs, Paris, and Augustyniak studied graphic design at the Royal College of Art, London, graduating in 1991. They first met in 1989 when Amzalag (who is also a DJ) was art director of the French rock and cultural magazine *Les Inrockuptibles*. During the early years of M/M, Amzalag and Augustyniak developed a strong creative relationship with the French music industry. Their work endeavours to challenge the traditional demarcation between the practice of graphic design and fine art. Determined not to adopt a consistent style, M/M's approach is often surprising and provocative. Now more broadly based, Amzalag and Augustyniak work in fashion (APC, Jil Sander, Yohji Yamamoto and Martine Siborn), music (Björk) and for a range of European art and cultural institutions and events (the catalogue for the first Berlin Biennale in 1998).

M/M's design for Balenciaga's Fall/Winter invitation card, 2001.

Bodoni, a **Modern Face**.

ABC

Modern Face Term for any ROMAN TYPEFACE, originating in the late 18th c., that can be identified by a vertical STRESS, unbracketed SERIF form, and a sharp contrast between the weight of the thin and thick strokes.

modern figures
Alternative term for LINING NUMERALS/FIGURES.

Modernism/Modern Movement Term used to embrace a diverse range of art movements and ideas that emerged during the first half of the 20th c. and profoundly influenced the subsequent development of art, architecture and design. Reacting particularly to the declining standards of craftsmanship in the late 19th c. and to the decorative excesses of ART NOUVEAU, many practitioners and critics recognized the need for a new approach that would enable the production of well-made artefacts for mass consumption. There was also a widespread utopian belief that mechanization and technology, if properly channelled, could produce a better, less divided society. Louis Sullivan, the American architect renowned for his Chicago skyscrapers, declared that 'Form follows function' (1885); this became a credo for those progressive designers endeavouring to combine functionalism and rationalism. The art and design movements central to Modernism – CUBISM, FUTURISM, CONSTRUCTIVISM, DE STIJL and DADA – had a profound influence on the practice of graphic design, typography and photography. Collectively, these movements advocated a stronger link between art and industrial production and encouraged the move towards bold geometric forms, the elimination of decoration and the use of ASYMMETRIC layouts. During the 1920s and 30s leading practitioners, such as László MOHOLY-NAGY, El LISSITZKY and Théo van DOESBURG were active in many creative fields, refusing to acknowledge boundaries that restricted interaction between art and design. The BAUHAUS was a high point in Modernist thinking, with a number of its staff strongly identified with contemporary art movements. Graphic design at the Bauhaus was primarily the responsibility of Moholy-Nagy and Herbert BAYER, with both extending their considerable influence to the US after the demise of the Bauhaus. The legacy of early Modernist debates is apparent in the rationalism associated with the INTERNATIONAL TYPOGRAPHIC STYLE of post-war Switzerland. Also, the disciplined application of disparate design elements within the CORPORATE IDENTITY of international organizations, particularly in America in the 1950s and 60s, can be traced to earlier debates on standardization and the search for a universal visual language. Modernism's decline into the superficiality of style, with an inherent inability to respond quickly to changing consumer needs, inevitably produced a critical reaction from a new generation of designers. From the early 1950s artists, architects and designers sought to challenge the constraints imposed by modernist ideology. In graphic design terms, innovations of POST-MODERNISM in America and Switzerland gave a new respectability to decoration and spontaneity.

Modley, Rudolf See ISOTYPE

Moholy-Nagy, László (1895–1946) Film maker, designer, painter, writer, educator and photographer. Born in Hungary, he studied law in Budapest, but his education was interrupted by war. Joined the Hungarian army in 1915, wounded in action during 1917. Pursued his interest in art during a period of recuperation. Awareness of avant-garde art movements, including CONSTRUCTIVISM, DE STIJL and DADA, took him to Vienna (1919) and then to Berlin (1921). His studio in Berlin was a popular meeting point for Kurt SCHWITTERS, Hans Arp, El LISSITZKY, Théo van DOESBURG and the sculptor Naum Gabo. In 1923 Walter GROPIUS invited Moholy-Nagy to teach at the BAUHAUS in Weimar. Initially responsible for the metal workshop, he was soon placed in joint charge of the preliminary course, previously run by Johannes ITTEN. Moholy-Nagy flourished at the Bauhaus, working in numerous disciplines and experimenting with new materials and techniques. In 1925 the Bauhaus moved to Dessau, where Gropius and Moholy-Nagy remained until their resignation in 1928. Moholy-Nagy's commitment to typography and photography ensured that graphic design became accepted within the curriculum. As a photographer he believed that his 'Photoplastics' (photographic COLLAGE pictures) and Photograms (the recording of objects by placing them on light-sensitive paper) were objectively superior to painting. His typographic achievement included designing the Bauhaus prospectus and a number of the fourteen books published by the school after 1925. Moving to Berlin in 1928, he established himself as a typographer, set designer and film maker. About this time he developed a close working relationship with Gyorgy KEPES, later to be an influential colleague at the Institute of Design in Chicago. Moholy-Nagy's classic text on the Bauhaus preliminary course, *The New Vision*, appeared in German in 1929, with an English version published in America in 1932. Fearing the rise of Hitler, he left Berlin for Amsterdam (1934) and in the following year moved to London, where he designed for the *Architectural Review* and again

worked with Gropius. Following a recommendation from Gropius, he was appointed Director of the New Bauhaus, Chicago in 1937. This ambitious undertaking failed after only one year due to the financial difficulties of its main sponsor, the Association of Arts and Industries. It reopened in 1939 as the School of Design, using Moholy-Nagy's own finances with support from Walter Paepcke, founder of CONTAINER CORPORATION OF AMERICA. (Renamed the Institute of Design in 1944, it became part of the Illinois Institute of Technology.) As an educator, Moholy-Nagy played a major part in determining the future direction of American design education. His Constructivist roots ensured that student designers embraced the functionalist ethos of the Bauhaus and also recognized the opportunity to bridge the divide between art, science and technology. This philosophy was outlined in his *Vision in Motion*, which was published posthumously in 1947. Moholy-Nagy also practised as an industrial and graphic designer in America, working for, amongst others, FORTUNE magazine, the Container Corporation of America, and the Parker Pen company, for which he designed the Parker 51 fountain pen (1941). Following his premature death from leukaemia, his post as director of the Institute of Design in Chicago was taken by the architect and designer Serge Chermayeff.

Title page of a Bauhaus prospectus, 1924, by **Moholy-Nagy**.

Monguzzi, Bruno (b.1941) Swiss graphic and exhibition designer. Studied at the École des Arts Décoratifs, Geneva 1956–60, winning a travel scholarship to study in London 1960–61. Worked with Studio Boggeri, Milan 1961–63, after which he practised as a freelance designer in Milan and London 1963–65. Moved to Montreal in 1965, designing nine pavilions for Expo '67. Returned to Milan in 1968 to establish a freelance practice. Since 1972 he has collaborated with Roberto Sambonet on exhibition projects. His travels to England, Italy and America in the 1960s enabled him to assimilate new influences and encouraged a reassessment of the fundamental terms of SWISS GRAPHIC DESIGN. Building upon the disciplines of his original training, his work displays a rare combination of rationalism and lyricism. An intuitive sense of order underpins many of his elegant and powerfully effective solutions. *Bruno Monguzzi: A Designer's Perspective* celebrates his work and design philosophy. His work has featured in many exhibitions in Europe and America. Awarded the Bodoni Prize in 1971. Member of AGI.

Monguzzi's poster promoting the opening of the Musée d'Orsay, Paris (1986).

ABCDEFGH
abcdefgh

Cable Medium, a **Monoline** typeface.

Morison's visiting card, used during his time at the Pelican Press (1919–21).

STANLEY MORISON
THE PELICAN PRESS
No. 2
CARMELITE STREET, E.C.
LONDON

Monoline Any TYPEFACE design constructed from letter strokes that are of equal weight or thickness. On closer examination some so-called monoline typefaces may reveal a subtle variation in line weight.

Monotype Trade name for a HOT METAL COMPOSITION system that uses a composition keyboard and a metal caster to cast individual, movable, type characters in metal. Following its invention by the American Tolbert Lanston in 1887, the system was in limited production by 1894. Shortly after, British owners took charge of the Lanston Monotype Company, with production transferring to England in 1900. In 1923 Stanley MORISON was appointed typographical adviser to Monotype, with responsibility for the company's influential type-development programme. Beatrice WARDE, the typographic and printing historian, was appointed editor of the company's prestigious periodical *Monotype Recorder* in 1927. In 1931 the company was renamed the Monotype Corporation, by which name it is still known. Typographically superior to the LINOTYPE system, Monotype was in widespread usage for LETTERPRESS printing throughout the world up to the mid-1970s. It is now largely replaced by high-speed PHOTOCOMPOSITION systems (e.g. Monophoto) and COMPUTERIZED COMPOSITION systems.

Morison, Stanley Arthur (1889–1967) Typographer and typographical historian. Born in Wanstead, Essex, he had no formal education in design. After an early career as a clerk, he joined the staff of the printing journal *The IMPRINT* in 1913. Moved to Burns and Oates, the Catholic publishers in 1913 as an assistant to Francis MEYNELL. His career was interrupted by his stance as a conscientious objector during the war. In 1919 moved to the Pelican Press, London (established by Francis Meynell) where he wrote his first book on typography, *The Craft of Printing* (1921). From 1921 he worked for the short-lived Cloister Press, Manchester, before joining with Oliver SIMON and others to launch the outstanding typographic journal *The FLEURON* (1922), which he edited 1926–30. In the seventh and last issue in 1930, Morison published a revised version of his classic text

First Principles of Typography, which first appeared in the *Encyclopaedia Britannica* of 1929. Appointed typographical adviser to MONOTYPE 1922–67, and to Cambridge University Press 1925–44, 1947–59. Exploited his collection with the University Press and other publishers to generate interest and custom for the prolific TYPEFACE development programme at Monotype. This major initiative produced some of the most popular text faces of the 20th c. and established Monotype at the forefront of the move from traditional hand-setting methods to mechanized typesetting for LETTERPRESS printing. Under Morison's direction a range of classic typeface 'revivals' were produced, including BASKERVILLE (1923), Fournier (1924), BEMBO (1928) and Walbaum (1933). His support for Eric GILL enabled PERPETUA (1925) and Gill Sans (1928) to become realities. Morison met his long-term colleague Beatrice WARDE in 1924 and in the same year became an original member of the DOUBLE CROWN CLUB, established by Oliver Simon. For three decades from 1929 Morison was typographic consultant to *The Times*, London, redesigning the newspaper and creating a highly successful text typeface: TIMES NEW ROMAN was designed in 1931/32, with the help of

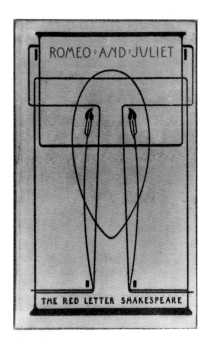

Cover design by Talwin **Morris** for the Blackie & Sons 1904 edition of Shakespeare's *Romeo and Juliet*.

Victor Lardent, an artist in the newspaper's publicity department. As a writer on typographic history Morison's contribution is of major significance, with over fifty books to his credit. The following are of particular note: *Four Centuries of Fine Printing* (1924), *The Typographic Arts, Past, Present and Future* (1944), *Printing The Times since 1785* (1953), and *A Tally of Types* (1953). Although conservative in his typographic approach, Morison produced designs for the London publisher Victor Gollancz that stand out as a remarkable exception. Responsible for design and production at Gollancz for a decade from 1928, Morison's 'yellow' book jackets from 1929 onwards use brash colours and bold display faces (including Gill Sans) in a radical and effective manner. A leading influence on gothic typographic design, his reputation rests on his supervision of the Monotype type-cutting programme and on his scholarly typographic researches, which established the need to recognize the links between past and current practice. Awarded a gold medal by AIGA in 1946. Elected RDI in 1960.

Morris, Talwin (1865–1911) Art director, born in Winchester, England. Initially trained as an architect before becoming a designer with *Black and White* magazine in London. In 1893 he joined the publishers Blackie & Sons, Glasgow, as art director. In this role he was instrumental in introducing the emerging ART NOUVEAU style to a wider public. His covers, bindings, page layouts and typography often reflected the spatial discipline and organic shapes favoured by the Glasgow School, led by Charles Rennie MACKINTOSH.

Morris, William (1834–96) Designer, Socialist writer, painter and member of the Pre-Raphaelite Brotherhood. Leader of the British ARTS AND CRAFTS MOVEMENT. Influenced by the philosophy of the art critic John Ruskin, Morris was a medievalist, dedicated to rediscovering the traditional standards of craftsmanship, materials and design that existed prior to a degradation during the Industrial Revolution. The son of a wealthy businessman, he was educated at Exeter College, Oxford, becoming friends with Edward BURNE-JONES. Both intended to enter the Church but, after holidaying together in France during 1855, Morris decided upon architecture and Burne-Jones upon painting. In 1856 Morris briefly entered the Oxford practice of G.E. Street as a junior to the architect Philip Webb. He soon abandoned architecture and, under the influence of Dante Gabriel ROSSETTI, turned to painting. Webb designed Morris' home, the Red House, near London

(1859/60), during the furbishment of which Morris's interest in the design of furniture and decoration came to the fore. In 1861 he joined six friends to found Morris, Marshall, Faulkner & Co. designing stained glass, wallpapers, textiles, furniture, carpets and tapestries. He was a conservative in design. His dense and lavish decoration of all available space was often inspired by the natural world of flora and fauna. In 1875 he became sole proprietor of the business, renamed Morris & Co. Enthused by a lecture from Emery WALKER on medieval manuscripts and letterforms (1888), Morris turned to TYPEFACE design and fine book production. He established the KELMSCOTT PRESS in 1891, which produced fifty-three titles of superb quality and refinement, including *The Story of the Glittering Plain* (1894). Although a Socialist reformer, his design output was exclusively for a few rich clients. His significance extends beyond his personal design contribution to the interest he provoked in quality printing and the stimulus thus provided for the PRIVATE PRESS MOVEMENT, which in turn raised standards in commercial printing and publishing. His concern with craftsmanship and truth to materials became important precepts adopted by the BAUHAUS and the MODERN MOVEMENT.

Page from *The Story of the Glittering Plain*, produced by William **Morris**'s Kelmscott Press (1894).

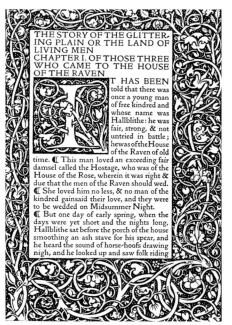

Moser, Koloman (1868–1918) Painter, designer and craftsman. Born and educated in Vienna, he was based there throughout his career. He entered the Academie (1888) to study painting, then transferred to the Kunstgewerbeschule (1892) to study design. Along with Gustav KLIMT, he was a founding member of the VIENNA SECESSION and designed the publicity for a number of Secession exhibitions. He was also a major influence on the experimental covers and page layouts of *Ver Sacrum*, the Secession's magazine. In 1900 he became a professor at the Kunstgewerbeschule, a post he held until his death. A versatile designer of furniture, glass and textiles, a range of his furniture designs was shown at the Secession exhibition in 1900. In 1903 Josef HOFFMANN, Moser and Fritz Wärndorfer founded the WIENER WERKSTÄTTE. From then until 1907 Moser designed many items for the Werkstätte, passionately supporting its aim of improving the artistic quality of everyday objects; he is believed to have designed the famous Werkstätte LOGOTYPE. In 1908 he produced a set of postage stamps for the jubilee of the Emperor Franz Josef. Thereafter most of his time was dedicated to his work as a painter.

Mouron, Adolphe Jean-Marie See CASSANDRE, A.M.

mouse Device used with graphics-based software approximately 2 x 3in (5 x 7.6cm), with a small rubber ball embedded in its base and control buttons on the top. When the mouse is moved over a flat surface the ball is rotated and the direction of rotation transmitted to a COMPUTER, which responds by moving a small mobile image, usually called a cursor, in the corresponding direction on the screen. The operator can select items on the screen by pointing to them with the cursor and pressing the appropriate mouse button.

Mucha, Alphonse (1860–1939) Poster artist, illustrator and designer. Born in Moravia, Czechoslovakia. From 1879 he worked as a theatrical scene painter in Vienna where a benefactor recognized his talent and financed his studies in Munich 1884–87 and in Paris 1888. Remaining in Paris, he designed his first stamps (1889) and numerous posters throughout the early 1890s. In 1894 he brilliantly exploited an opportunity to design a life-size poster for Sarah Bernhardt as *Gismonda*. This richly textured poster was a sensation, leading to a six-year contract from Bernhardt and providing the basis for his subsequent success as the archetypal ART NOUVEAU designer. For the next decade

Poster for XIII Vienna Secession exhibition, designed by
Moser in 1903.

his prolific output – embracing posters, magazines, books, calendars, packaging, textiles and jewelry – provided some of the best examples of the Art Nouveau style. His beautiful women, centrally located within the poster frame and surrounded by elaborate plants and flowing organic forms, became icons of a glamorous era. Although acknowledging the earlier achievements of Jules CHÉRET and Eugène GRASSET, *le style Mucha* was richer in decoration and more obviously stylized. An exhibition of his CHROMOLITHOGRAPHY posters, first held in Paris in 1897, travelled to other European cities and then to New York. Posters of note thereafter include those for Job cigarette papers (1898) and Moët & Chandon (1899). In the early years of the 20th c. Mucha's success enabled him to travel and work in Paris, America and his native Czechoslovakia. About 1910 he returned permanently to Czechoslovakia, where he produced a major set of twenty murals, *Slav Epic*, which outlined the history of his nation. In 1918 he designed the stamps celebrating Czechoslovakia's new-found freedom of 1917. He died in 1939, some months after being interrogated by the Nazis, following their occupation and partitioning of Czechoslovakia.

Salon des Cent exhibition poster designed by
Mucha in 1896.

Müller, Rolf (b.1940) Graphic designer. Born in Dortmund, studied visual communication at the ULM HOCHSCHULE FÜR GESTALTUNG during the early 1960s. Returned for post-graduate study after working for one year with Josef MÜLLER-BROCKMANN in Zurich. Freelance designer in Ulm for two years, before collaborating with Otl AICHER on a series of projects 1967–72. In 1972 he was deputy designer of the Munich Olympic Games, working within Aicher's overall visual co-ordination. Müller's crisp, geometric style has been applied successfully to major public institutions: of particular note is his development of a visual image to convey the civic pride of the city of Leverkusen from 1970, and his work for the Bavarian Tourist Board. The importance he attaches to the clear, objective presentation of information has enabled him to tackle complex directional and display systems for exhibitions and architectural environments, including the municipality of Bonn and the Medical Academy of Bundeswehr. Work featured in numerous European exhibitions and publications. Member of AGI.

Müller-Brockmann, Josef (1914–96) Swiss graphic designer, typographer and teacher. Born Josef Mario Müller, he changed his name to Müller-Brockmann in 1942 and again to Müller-Yoshikawa in 1967. Influential practitioner and writer on the INTERNATIONAL TYPOGRAPHIC STYLE. Studied architecture, design and history of art at both the University and Kunstgewerbeschule in Zurich. Apprenticed to the designer and advertising consultant Walter Diggelmann, Zurich 1934–36. In 1936 he established a studio in Zurich, specializing in graphics, exhibitions and photography. He designed exhibitions for the 1939 Swiss National Exhibition in Zurich. From 1951, designer of celebrated concert posters for the Tonhalle- Gesellschaft, Zurich. These works, inspired by CONSTRUCTIVISM, achieve a mathematical harmony of formal elements that equates with music. An advocate of socially responsible design, he has created powerful public health and safety posters, often employing a PHOTOMONTAGE technique. In 1958 he became a founder and co-editor of NEW GRAPHIC DESIGN (Neue Grafik), a trilingual journal that spread the Swiss design ethic internationally. Appointed professor of graphic design at the Kunstgewerbeschule, Zurich 1957–60, he has also lectured at the ULM HOCHSCHULE FÜR GESTALTUNG, 1963, and at universities in Japan and America. In 1966 he was appointed European design consultant for IBM. Responsible for the SIGNAGE system for Zurich airport and, during the late 1970s, the corporate image for Swiss Federal Railways (SBB). Müller-Brockmann has also created theatre sets in Zurich, Copenhagen and Munich 1942–58. Author of the classic text History of Visual Communication (1971), History of the Poster (1971) with Shizuko Müller-Yoshikawa and Fotoplakate (1989) with Karl Wobmann. One-man exhibitions in Europe, America and Japan. Member of AGI.

Munari, Bruno (1907–98) Italian artist, designer, photographer and writer. Briefly studied at the Technical Institute, Naples; primarily self-taught as an artist and designer. Munari's prolific and varied career developed from the late 1920s, through his involvement with FUTURISM in Milan and Rome. Practising as a graphic designer and photographer from c. 1930 he worked for clients such as Pirelli, Olivetti, Cinzano and IBM. A pioneer of animation techniques in Italian advertising films, his restless nature also embraced illustration, PHOTOMONTAGE and magazine design. The visual dynamics of Futurism are evident in his early designs, particularly those featuring human forms. After the Second World War he practised increasingly as an industrial designer, producing furniture, interior designs, toys and domestic products. In an attempt to erode the barriers between art, design and architecture he established the Movimento Arte Concreta (along with Gillo Dorfles and Gianni

Müller-Brockmann's poster *Schützt das Kind!* (Protect that Child!) for the Swiss Automobile Club, 1955.

Monnet) in 1948. Influential as a design critic and researcher, his books sought to analyse the form and function of the natural world, machines and visual communication; of particular note is *Arte come mestiere* (1966), published in London as *Design as Art* (1971). Still active as a designer in his seventies, he produced a series of posters for Campari (1984). Received the Compasso d'Oro Award, Milan, 1954, 1955, 1979.

Muybridge, Eadweard (1830–1904) British-born photographer who settled in America, initially working for the US government recording expeditions to the unexplored West. Muybridge sought the financial assistance of the entrepreneur Leland Stanford, to prove that all four legs of a horse were simultaneously off the ground during a trot or gallop. He proved his case by a clever use of multiple exposures, activated by the trotting horse breaking threads attached to the shutters of a series of cameras. The experiments took place in California 1877–78, with the results attracting great interest internationally following their publication in periodicals. Muybridge travelled widely, giving numerous illustrated lectures. Influential thereafter on how artists portrayed movement, his studies of humans and animals in motion were a portent of later experiments with the moving image.

N

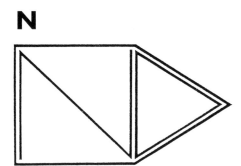

Symbol for Nippon Design Centre, Tokyo, by **Nagai** (*c.* 1965).

Nagai, Kazumasa (b. 1929) Japanese graphic designer, printmaker and sculptor. Trained at Tokyo University of Art as a sculptor 1949–51, before becoming a graphic designer at the Daiwa Spinning Co., Osaka, 1951–60. In 1960 he joined the newly established Nippon Design Centre, Tokyo, a large multidisciplinary design organization funded by eight investor companies. Nagai was president 1975–86, becoming a director thereafter. Renowned for his vibrantly coloured posters, he transforms the two-dimensional pictorial plane into a three-dimensional 'cosmic' space, often making reference to space technology. Recurring motifs, including the planets, clouds and particularly the rising sun, are reduced to abstract geometric forms. He has designed posters for Asahi Breweries (1965), *Space Design* magazine (1968), *GQ* magazine (1974), Adonis advertising agency (1976–78), The Museum of Modern Art, Toyama (1981–83) and World Design Expo '89. SYMBOL designs include those for the 1972 Winter Olympic Games at Sapporo and Expo '75, Okinawa. Regular exhibitions, beginning with a one-man show at the Museum of Modern Art, Warsaw (1968). Awarded a gold medal at the first Warsaw Poster Biennale (1966). His poster 'Save Nature' was awarded the Grand Prize at the Helsinki International Poster Biennale (1997).

Nash, Paul (1889–1946) British artist, book illustrator and theatre designer. Trained at Slade School of Art, London (1910–11). Served in the army before he was invalided from France in 1917. Appointed official war artist in both World Wars. His powerful paintings and lithographs illustrating the desolation caused by the First World War were followed by a prolific period as a book illustrator. From 1918–32 Nash's black-and-white illustrations acknowledged the dynamics of the diagonal and the harsh contrasts associated

One of **Nash**'s classic ilustrations for *Urne Buriall and the Garden of Cyrus* (1932).

with VORTICISM. His bold use of WOOD ENGRAVING in *Places* (1922/3), *Genesis* (1924), *Abd-er-Rhaman* (1928) and hand-coloured COLLOTYPE illustrations for his masterpiece *Urne Buriall and the Garden of Cyrus* (1932) are of particular note. In 1935 he compiled the *Dorset Shell Guide*. During the 1930s achieved great success as an artist: in 1933 he founded Unit One, a group of progressive British painters, sculptors and architects committed to the ideals of European MODERNISM. Participated in the International Surrealist Exhibition, London, 1936. Nash's photographs reveal an eye for the unexpected, notably in haunting images for his essay on two fallen trees, *Monster Field* (1946). During the Second World War produced three lithographic posters for the Ministry of Information in London, with *The Battle of Britain* (1941) attracting widespread acclaim.

Neuburg, Hans (1904–83) Graphic, exhibition and industrial designer. Born in Czechoslovakia, he emigrated to Switzerland in 1910. Studied at the Art Institut Orell Füssli, Zurich, 1919–22. From 1928 he practised in Basle and Zurich, employing his copywriting and design skills in advertising and graphic design. During this period he established contact with Max BILL, Herbert MATTER and Anton STANKOWSKI. In 1936 he founded a studio in Zurich, specializing in advertising and exhibition design. Committed to the INTERNATIONAL TYPOGRAPHIC STYLE, his belief in the clear presentation of information was apparent in his exhibition designs for the 1939 Swiss National Exhibition in Zurich and for the Swiss exhibit at the World Fairs in Prague (1945) and Brussels (1958). A co-founder and joint editor of *NEW GRAPHIC DESIGN*, Neuburg designed and wrote many of the journal's influential articles. From the early 1930s, he was an energetic promoter of the SWISS STYLE through his journalistic contributions on developments in art, design and photography.

Neuburg produced this symbol for 'Hyspa', a Swiss exhibition of sport and hygiene, 1961.

Neue Grafik (journal) *See NEW GRAPHIC DESIGN*. Not to be confused with *Die Neue Grafik (The New Graphic Art)*, an influential book, published in Switzerland in 1959 and written by Karl GERSTNER and Markus Kutter.

Neurath, Otto *See ISOTYPE*

New Graphic Design (1958-65) Progressive graphic design journal, published in Switzerland. Edited by four Zurich-based designers, Richard P. Lohse (b.1902), Josef MÜLLER-BROCKMANN, Hans NEUBURG, and Carlo L. VIVARELLI. Featuring articles on SYMBOL design, posters, exhibitions and typography, the journal was instrumental in formulating and disseminating the principles of the INTERNATIONAL TYPOGRAPHIC STYLE. Designed on a flexible four-column GRID and printed in three languages, it was a classic demonstration of its own visual ethos.

New Haas Grotesque *See HELVETICA*

New Typography Revolutionary approach to typographic design, which developed in Europe throughout the 1920s and early 30s. A highly visible component of MODERNISM in graphic design, the new typography combined elements of the work and writings of William MORRIS (his respect for materials and good workmanship) with aspects of contemporary art movements like CUBISM, FUTURISM, DADA, DE STIJL and CONSTRUCTIVISM. Originating in Russia and Germany, it attracted followers in Holland (see Paul SCHUITEMA, Hendrik WERKMAN and Piet ZWART), Czechoslovakia (see Ladislav SUTNAR) and Poland (see Henryk BERLEWI). Key figures in the development of the movement were El LISSITZKY, László MOHOLY-NAGY, and Jan TSCHICHOLD. Lissitzky rejected decoration and was an early advocate of dynamic ASYMMETRIC layouts that used geometric forms and SANS SERIF lettering. Primarily through Moholy-Nagy's influence, Lissitzky's ideas were adopted by the BAUHAUS and promoted as a typography that would meet the needs of an emerging technological era. In the search for the objective presentation of information, Bauhaus teaching aimed to develop rational principles to determine the organization of type, rules, white space, colours, etc. In 1928 Tschichold, a German designer not associated with the school, wrote *Die neue Typographie*. This influential book developed many of the ideas evolved by the Constructivists and teachers at the Bauhaus. In establishing a new utilitarian order and simplicity, Tschichold unintentionally undermined the style by creating an alternative set of conventions; furthermore, his subsequent rejection of New Typography highlighted the inherent limitations imposed by its denial of past typographic achievements. After the Second World War the principles were pursued in America (by ex-Bauhaus staff including Moholy-Nagy and Herbert BAYER) and in Switzerland with the evolution of the INTERNATIONAL TYPOGRAPHIC STYLE.

New Wave *See* POST-MODERNISM

New York Art Directors Club *See* ART DIRECTORS CLUB OF NEW YORK

New York School Term applied to New York–based designers who from the 1940s onwards developed a distinctly American graphic language. Although absorbing the formal vocabulary of European MODERNISM they increasingly reflected the competitive values, cultural and ethnic diversity of the US. The most influential practitioners include Paul RAND, Alvin LUSTIG, Bradbury THOMPSON, George TSCHERNY, Alexey BRODOVITCH, Herb LUBALIN, George LOIS and the advertising agency DOYLE DANE BERNBACH.

Newbould, Frank (1887-1951) English poster artist and illustrator. Studied at Bradford College of Art in Yorkshire. Stylistically indebted to the BEGGARSTAFF BROTHERS, he was renowned for brightly coloured inter-war posters that promoted the travel opportunities available to users of the Great Western Railway, the London and North Eastern Railway and London Transport. He also produced work for Belgian Railways and Orient Line Cruises. His ability to evoke a nostalgic view of the British countryside was used to bolster morale during the Second World War: employed as an assistant to Abram GAMES at the War Office in 1942, he produced eleven posters, including the cleverly understated series, *Your Britain: Fight for it Now*.

Newdigate, Bernard (1869–1944) Typographer and printer. Along with Stanley MORISON, Francis MEYNELL and Oliver SIMON, he was a leading influence on the typographic revival in Britain before and after the First World War. The son of a printer in Leamington, Warwickshire, he worked in his father's firm from 1890, renaming it the Arden Press; it was taken over by the newsagents W.H. Smith in 1907. From 1905 he worked as a typographic designer with Burns and Oates, the Catholic publishers, collaborating with Morison. A traditionalist with a particular penchant for CASLON OLD FACE, he moved to the Shakespeare Head Press in 1920 as master printer, subsequently producing books of great distinction. Founder member of the DOUBLE CROWN CLUB.

Nicholson, Sir William (1872–1949) British poster artist and painter. Born in Newark-on-Trent, he studied art at Bushey, Hertfordshire under Sir Hubert van Herkomer 1888–89 and then in Paris 1889–90. Married Mabel Pryde, sister of the Scottish painter James Pryde in 1893. Using the pseudonym the BEGGARSTAFF BROTHERS he formed a five-year poster-designing partnership with Pryde (1894). He then produced WOODCUT designs of archetypal Victorian characters, many for the publisher Heinemann. He also became a successful painter of still-lifes, landscapes and portraits. Father of the abstract painter Ben Nicholson.

Your Britain: Fight for it Now ('The South Downs'), one of a series of posters by **Newbould** (1942).

Woodcut illustration by **Nicholson** for *An Alphabet* (1897).

Nonesuch Press *See* MEYNELL, SIR FRANCIS

non-lining numerals/figures
See OLD STYLE NUMERALS/FIGURES

Noorda, Bob (b.1927) Dutch graphic and exhibition designer. Trained at the Amsterdam Institute of Design 1944–47 before travelling to Indonesia to design military publications for the Dutch government. Freelanced in Amsterdam, then moved to Milan in 1952 where he established a successful practice with major clients like Philips, Alfa Romeo, Pirelli and Montecatini. Became art director of Pirelli in 1961, contributing to this company's excellent reputation for design through his many memorable advertisements, posters and exhibitions. In 1965 he became co-founder (along with Massimo VIGNELLI) of Unimark International, a consortium working in the areas of design and marketing. Noorda's design displays clarity of thought and precision of execution, evident in his SIGNAGE systems, CORPORATE IDENTITY programmes, packaging and major exhibition projects. During the early 1960s his award-winning work for the subway system in Milan, covering posters, maps, signs, timetables, clocks, etc. led to similar commissions for subways in New York and São Paulo.

Novarese, Aldo (1920–95) Italian TYPEFACE designer. Studied at the GB Paravia School of Graphic Arts in Turin. His long career with the Società Nebiolo Typefoundry, Turin, began in 1936, becoming art director in 1952. His prolific and varied output

ABCDEFGH abcdefgh

Fenice (1980), a typeface by **Novarese**.

Elements of the corporate identity and signage devised for the Milan subway system by **Noorda** (1962–63).

includes the script Cigno (1954), an inclined SANS SERIF, Ritmo (1955) and the elegant ROMAN faces Fenice (1980) and Novarese (1980). During the 1940s and 50s he collaborated with Alessandro Butti (1893–1959) on a number of faces including a FAT FACE roman, Normandia (1946), the inscriptional roman capitals, Augustea (1951) and MICROGRAMMA (1952), retitled Eurostile in 1962.

Novum Gebrauchsgraphik (journal)
See GEBRAUCHSGRAPHIK

O

Oberer, Klaus *See* MENDELL & OBERER

OBR Abbreviation for Optical Bar(code) Recognition. *See* BAR CODE

OCR Abbreviation for Optical Character Recognition. OCR readers are devices, often hand-held, that decipher specially printed data in the form of alphabetic and numeric characters. The characters are usually in a FONT that is easy for a machine to identify and also reasonably legible to the human eye. OCR readers are mainly used at point-of-sale terminals to scan data on labels attached to merchandise. *See* BAR CODE

Octavo *See* 8vo, preceding letter A.

Odermatt & Tissi Zurich design practice founded in 1968 by Siegfried Odermatt (b.1926) and Rosmarie Tissi (b.1937). Odermatt is self-taught. Worked in Zurich with the industrial designer Georg Vetter 1944–45 and with the designer/painter Hans Falk 1945–48 before spending three years with the Paul Zurrer advertising agency. Photography became an important design element in his work when he established his own studio in Zurich (1950). Tissi was

trained at the Kunstgewerbeschule, Zurich 1954–58, after which she served four years as an apprentice designer. Specializing in CORPORATE IDENTITY, advertising, posters and book design, their work has evolved from the rigorous formality of the INTERNATIONAL TYPOGRAPHIC STYLE to embrace a more playful and intuitive approach inspired by POST-MODERNISM. Unexpected typographic arrangements are held in taut ASYMMETRIC balance by subtle variations in type weight and colour contrasts. Odermatt has designed a number of typefaces, including Antiqua Classica (1971), Marabu (1972), Sonora (1972) and Mindanao (1975). Recipients of many international awards, they have exhibited together in New York (1966), Germany (1967, '68, '72, '84) and Warsaw (1988). *Odermatt & Tissi: Graphic Design* (1995) reveals the collaborative process that has produced their striking body of work. Both members of AGI.

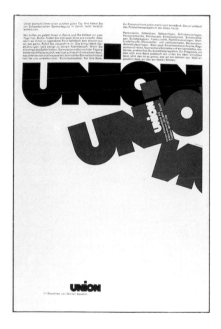

Advertising poster for the Union safe manufacturer, 1968, by **Odermatt**.

ABCDEFGH
abcdefgh

Odgers, Jayme (b.1939) American NEW WAVE designer and photographer. Studied graphic design at the Art Center School, Los Angeles 1958–62 before serving a two-year apprenticeship with Paul RAND. Odgers uses photography and computers to explore kinetic qualities of design. Manipulating, layering and overlapping formal elements, he propels objects into an illusionary space. Collaboration with the designer April GREIMAN resulted in acclaimed experimental posters and promotional material for the California Institute of the Arts during the late 1970s. One of fifteen artists commissioned to design posters for the 1984 Los Angeles Olympic Games.

Officina Bodoni *See* MARDERSTEIG, GIOVANNI (HANS)

offset litho/offset photolithography
Popular commercial method of printing, based on LITHOGRAPHY. The image to be printed is transferred (offset) first from the cylindrical metal plate on to a rubber-covered cylinder and then from this cylinder on to the paper surface. The popularity of this versatile process, which is capable of printing on various paper surfaces, has been aided by the availability of a wide range of offset printing presses. 'Small Offset' presses provide the in-house printing facility in many commercial organizations. Capable of high-quality, four-colour work, they are normally restricted to a maximum sheet size of 297 x 420 mm (A3, c.11½ x 16½ in). 'Sheet Fed Offset' presses are manufactured in many sizes and print on separate sheets of paper. Their great flexibility is much favoured by the professional printer. They can print on both sides of the sheet (perfecting) and can also print a number of colours simultaneously. 'Web Offset' presses print on continuous reels (webs) of paper. Capable of great speeds, they are normally used for long-run magazines and catalogues. The web can be printed on both sides at the same time (perfecting) and, if required, trimmed and folded to the finished size.

old face/old style Category of ROMAN typefaces originating in France in the 16th c. Popular in book designs they are characterized by their oblique STRESS and oblique top-SERIF form. The lack of contrast between the thick and thin strokes of old faces makes them 'light' in overall colour. Popular old faces include BEMBO, CASLON and GARAMOND. The term old style has widespread usage in the US, whilst in Britain it is occasionally used to describe a 19th-c. revival of old face.

Janson **old face**.

old style numerals/figures Set of numerals with certain characters projecting below the baseline. Also known as hanging or non-lining numerals. *See* LINING NUMERALS/FIGURES

1234567890

Garamond **old style numerals**.

Oliver's record sleeve for the Pixie's Doolittle, 1989.

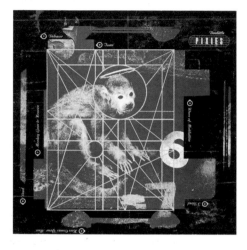

SPACING
unadjusted

SPACING
optically letterspaced

Examples of **optical spacing** (above).

The **Optima** typeface.

ABCDEFGH
abcdefgh

Olins, Wally *See* WOLFF OLINS

Oliver, Vaughan (b.1957) British designer, art director, illustrator and typographer. Studied graphic design at Newcastle Polytechnic, England 1976–79. Moved to London, working as a designer with Benchmark and then with the Michael PETERS group. From 1981 he worked on freelance projects for 4AD, a progressive, independent record label in London. Left the Michael Peters company in 1983 to work full-time for 4AD. Collaborating with 4AD's founder Ivo Watts-Russell, he has created some of the most innovative promotional images in contemporary music. His early record sleeves for 4AD display a distinctive and eclectic illustrative approach, with many of the images produced in association with the photographer Nigel Grierson. Oliver and Grierson signed their projects '23 Envelope'. After the demise of '23 Envelope' in 1988, Oliver established v23, working with Christopher Bigg. With his inventive use of multi-layered imagery, Oliver displays an intuitive ability to mix random visual fragments. An admirer of earlier typographic styles, particularly the NEW TYPOGRAPHY of the 1920s and 30s, his typography is varied and idiosyncratic. In 1987 he created a *tour-de-force* for the compilation record *Lonely is an Eyesore*. Featuring eight bands, the limited-edition version of the album was presented in a wooden box with specially commissioned prints and videos. Increasingly interested in the capabilities of the Quantel PAINTBOX Oliver has also produced book jackets, posters and television titles for clients other than 4AD. Exhibitions of his work have been held in Nantes, 1990, Paris, 1991 and Los Angeles, 1994. Oliver and Bigg left 4AD in 1998 to set up v23, where they work with a diverse range of clients. *Vaughan Oliver Visual Pleasures* by Rick Poyner (2000) assesses the significance of his work to date.

optical spacing/optically even spacing
Term used to describe arrangement of letters (normally UPPER CASE) to avoid the appearance of uneven gaps and give the impression of consistent, even spacing between each letter. Also known as optical letter spacing.

Optima Elegant SANS SERIF TYPEFACE designed by Hermann ZAPF in 1958. Used as a DISPLAY or text face, Optima is characterized by strokes that widen slightly towards the end. Described by Zapf as a 'seriffless ROMAN'.

Poster for La Maison Moderne (c. 1905) by **Orazi**.

Open Roman capitals, examples of **outline letter**s.

O P Q

Cover for the April-May 1895 issue of **Pan** magazine.

Orazi, Emmanuel (1860–1934) ART NOUVEAU poster artist, active between 1880 and 1905. Working in Paris, he created theatre posters for Sarah Bernhardt (1884) and Loïe Fuller (1900). Influenced by Alphonse MUCHA and Eugène GRASSET, his most acclaimed poster was for the elegant Parisian shop La Maison Moderne (c. 1905), depicting a sophisticated lady in silhouette, bedecked with fashionable accessories. The subtle balance between lettering and image and the strong horizontal composition elevate this poster to a high point in Art Nouveau style. Orazi also designed jewelry for the same shop, which was owned by Julius Meier-Graefe, founder of the magazine *Dekorative Kunst*.

ornament See PRINTER'S ORNAMENT

outline letter Those letters defined by an outer contour line, with the inner part remaining unfilled. Also known as open letter.

P

Paintbox COMPUTER system that allows a user to produce an image on a visual display by providing tools to fill in and colour pixels (points on the screen). Paintbox systems vary dramatically in their capabilities and cost. Some produce low-resolution images with a limited range of colours, whilst others produce high-resolution images with millions of colours. Many standard computers/workstations offer paintbox software that transforms the machine into the hub of a paintbox system. A full paintbox system has many peripheral devices for inputting and outputting colour images to and from the computer. The final image is output to a film recorder (for 35mm slides), colour printer or a professional video recorder.

Pan (1895–1900) Cultural magazine published in Berlin, which promoted the emergent German ART NOUVEAU style (JUGENDSTIL). Its first co-editors, the art historian Julius Meier-Graefe and the poet Otto Julius Bierbaum, resigned after three issues amidst controversy surrounding their attempts to publish a poster by Henri de TOULOUSE-LAUTREC. Jungendstil designers who contributed included Josef Sattler, Otto ECKMANN and Peter BEHRENS. It ran for twenty-one issues and featured articles on Aubrey BEARDSLEY and Henry van de VELDE, amongst others. The magazine's emblem, showing a head of the god Pan, was by the painter/ illustrator Franz von Stuck.

Pantone System Colour system that enables designers to specify consistent colour-matching across printing inks, pens and papers. Each Pantone colour specified for printing has a colour swatch and associated reference number. (Pantone is a registered trade name.)

paper sizes In contrast to the mathematical logic of the A, B, C SYSTEM OF STANDARD PAPER SIZES, traditional 'Imperial' paper sizes in the UK evolved over a long period and consequently lack any rational coherence. The following are some of the most common Imperial sizes, indicated in inches. (The metric equivalent of these sizes may vary from one supplier to another.)

Foolscap	13½ x 17
Double Foolscap	17 x 27
Large Post	16½ x 21
Double Large Post	21 x 33
Demy	17½ x 22½
Double Demy	22½ x 35
Medium	18 x 23
Double Medium	23 x 36
Royal	20 x 25
Double Royal	25 x 40
Imperial	22 x 30
Double Elephant	27 x 40
Crown	15 x 20
Double Crown	20 x 30
Quad Crown	30 x 40

A similar diversity exists in the US, the most popular sizes being:

Untrimmed	23 x 35
	25 x 38
	26 x 40
	28 x 44
	36 x 48
Trimmed	6 x 9
	7 x 10
	8½ x 11
	9 x 12
	11 x 13

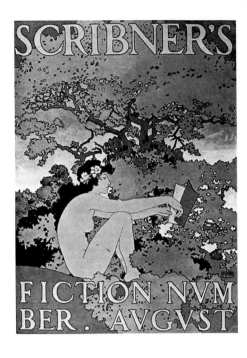

Poster for *Scribner's* magazine, 1897, by **Parrish**.

Thrislington Cubicle's 'Now Wash Your Hands of the 20th Century' soap calendar by The **Partners**, 2000.

Parrish, Maxfield (1870–1966) American book and magazine illustrator, poster and advertising artist, and painter. Active from 1895 when he received his first cover design commission from HARPER'S BAZAAR. The various romantic worlds he meticulously illustrated include idealized, ethereal landscapes and the comic fantasy land of his children's stories. Hugely popular, he illustrated all the major American magazines. *Collier's Weekly* offered him an exclusive contract in 1903 and during the ensuing seven years he produced some of his finest illustrations. His contribution to advertising includes the 'Dutch boy', which became synonymous with Colgate products. Other clients included Cranes' Chocolates and Fisk Tires. Between 1918 and 1934 he created calendars for Edison Mazda: printed annually in vast runs, they ensured his fame across America. In later years he turned to painting landscapes for reproduction. He produced a landscape annually for the calendar and greeting card publishers Brown & Bigelow, which was reproduced in their calendar 1936–62.

The Partners London-based graphic-design company formed in 1983 by David Stuart (b.1946) and Aziz Cami (b.1950). Three other founding partners, Keren House, Malcolm Swatridge and Nick Wurr (1950–94), have since left the practice. Their approach, which combines originality and wit, is demonstrated in the calendars for toilet cubicle manufacturers Thrislington (from 1993). The studio's inventive, word-based design solutions have been highly successful in a wide range of competitions. Increasingly involved in identity and branding projects for international companies, e.g., KLM's budget airline Buzz, Granada Media and Wedgwood. Aziz Cami was president of British Design & Art Direction (D&AD) in 1992. David Stuart is coauthor, with Beryl McAlhone, of *A Smile in the Mind* (1996), a book exploring the relationship between creativity and wit. Stuart became creative director of The Partners in 1997 and was president of D&AD in 2001.

Paul, Arthur (b.1925) American designer, illustrator and art director, associated with *Playboy* magazine for three decades. Born in Chicago, Illinois, he trained in his home town at the Art Institute 1940–43 and the Institute of Design 1946–50. Working as a freelance designer and illustrator he designed the first issue of *Playboy* (1953) and created the famous 'Bunny' LOGOTYPE. Joining the magazine as its first art director in 1954, he orchestrated an experimental approach to editorial design that complemented the *Playboy* reputation for risk-taking. He organized two major touring exhibitions, 'Beyond Illustration: The Art of *Playboy*'(1971) and its updated version 'The Art of *Playboy* The First 25 Years' (1978). Retired from *Playboy* in 1982 to establish Art Paul Design, Chicago. He has also designed for television, creating film titles and acting as a visual consultant. Member of AGI. Awarded a gold medal from the ART DIRECTORS CLUB OF NEW YORK (1980) and inducted into their Hall of Fame (1986).

Paul's symbol for the Playboy Corporation, 1953.

PC (Personal Computer) Synonymous with a COMPUTER that can run the same software as IBM's Personal Computer series. The PC has become the most widely used type of computer in the world, with many thousands of software packages designed to run on compatible machines. Within the graphic design profession the PC is rivalled by the APPLE MACINTOSH, which was supplied with a graphics-based user interface (suitable for design applications) before such interfaces became widely used on PCs.

Peckolick, Alan (b.1940) New York designer and art director working in advertising, CORPORATE IDENTITY, packaging, typography, books and films. Graduated from Pratt Institute, New York, before working as art director with the agencies McCann-Erickson and Kenyon & Eckhardt. Assistant to Herb LUBALIN 1964–68 prior to opening his own New York studio. Like Lubalin, he explores the expressive qualities of letterforms. Collaborating with lettering artists including Tony DISPIGNA and Tom Carnase, he has produced outstanding typographic solutions and memorable LOGOTYPE designs. Joined Lubalin, Smith, Carnase in 1973, where he designed the gold medal for the ART DIRECTORS CLUB OF NEW YORK (1974), which was awarded to him shortly after. Creative director with Herb Lubalin Associates 1978–80 when he became President of Lubalin, Peckolick Associates. In 1981 he joined with Seymour CHWAST and Herb LUBALIN to form Pushpin, Lubalin, Peckolick. Peckolick & Partners was founded in 1986 and acquired by the London-based Addison Design in 1988. In 1991 Peckolick Inc. was created with offices in Atlanta, New York and Tokyo. Taught at Pratt Institute, New York 1978–79. Widely exhibited, including the *U&lc* design exhibition, which toured numerous countries during 1979. Member of AGI and AIGA.

Symbol for Star Channel, Cable Television, devised by **Peckolick**.

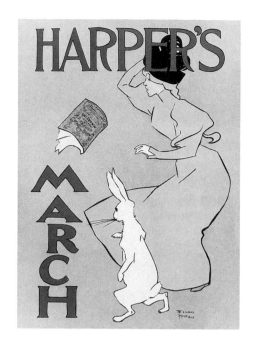

One of **Penfield**'s posters for *Harper's* magazine (1894).

Title page from Volume I of The **Penrose Annual**, 1895.

Penfield, Edward (1866–1925) Along with Will BRADLEY, a seminal figure in the development of the American art poster. Studied at the Art Students League, New York. Designer of highly successful posters for *Harper's* magazine, for whom he worked exclusively 1893–99. Influenced by French poster artists and Japanese prints, his monthly posters for the magazine illustrate a rapid evolution from naturalistic illustration to the fluid contours, broad flat colours and unusual viewpoint of his mature style. Eliminated background detail to concentrate the eye on lettering and subject – which was frequently the affluent *Harper's* consumer, depicted carrying or reading the magazine. Worked for other clients including publishing houses and bicycle manufacturers.

Penguin Books *See* LANE, SIR ALLEN

Penrose Annual, The (1895–1982) British publication that reviewed design for print and changes in printing technology, originally entitled *Process Work Yearbook – Penrose's Annual*. Under the first editor William Gamble, a director of the printing firm A.W. Penrose & Co., the magazine's objective was to promote interest in the new process engraving tech-

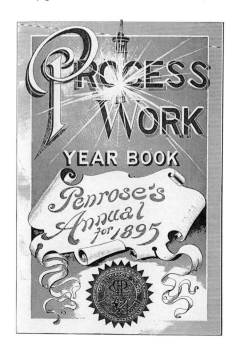

niques. Gamble was succeeded in 1933 by R.B. Fishenden, who attracted contributions from Paul NASH, Herbert Read, John Betjeman, Nikolaus Pevsner and László MOHOLY-NAGY. During the late 1930s Jan TSCHICHOLD and Francis MEYNELL were responsible for the design of individual volumes. Later editors of the magazine included Allan Delafons and Herbert SPENCER.

Pentagram Multidisciplinary design partnership specializing in graphic design, product design and architecture. Founded in London, 1972, now with offices in New York and San Francisco. The five founding principals were Alan FLETCHER (left 1992), Colin FORBES, Mervyn KURLANSKY (left 1993, moving to Denmark), architect Théo Crosby (1925–94) and industrial designer Kenneth Grange. The partnership includes graphic designers Michael BIERUT, April GREIMAN, Angus Hyland, David HILLMAN, Fernando Gutiérrez, John MCCONNELL, Woody PIRTLE, John Rushworth and Paula SCHER. Within the Pentagram structure partners work as individuals, managing their own creative teams and servicing a wide spectrum of prestigious clients. In 1993 a definitive statement of Pentagram's beliefs and achievements, *The Compendium*, was published.

Peret's illustration for an article on the Algerian civil war, 1996.

Peret (Pere Torrent) (b.1945) Spanish graphic designer producing posters, CORPORATE IDENTITIES, stamps and television graphics. From 1965 he worked as an illustrator and graphic designer, leaving Spain in 1970 for Paris where he became an advertising art director with French department store Prisunic and the advertising agency Delpire Advico and established himself as a freelance illustrator. Clients included Air France, Citroën and *L'Express* and *Marie Claire* magazines. Returned to Barcelona in 1977 to design cultural posters for the city council and the Generalitat, the regional government of Catalonia. He also created titles for the regional television station TV3. Contributor to the growth of POST-MODERNISM in Barcelona during the 1980s. From 1984–88 he produced a weekly illustration for the Barcelona newspaper *La Vanguardia*. Influenced by such art movements as CUBISM, CONSTRUCTIVISM and SURREALISM, Peret's stark and colourful design solutions have attracted international recognition. His La Biennal poster for Barcelona was awarded a gold medal by the International Illustration & Design Council (1987). He has worked for the Spanish Red Cross, Amnesty International, Japan Airlines, the Paris bicentennial committee and Cinzano. Peret was the designer of a set of brightly coloured stamps for the 1992 Barcelona Olympic Games, which reduce the sporting activities to simple geometric forms. His work has appeared in numerous shows, with solo exhibitions in Barcelona, Paris and Osaka. Winner of Spain's National Design Prize in 1998.

perfect binding *See* BINDING METHODS

Perpetua Elegant ROMAN TYPEFACE designed by Eric GILL for MONOTYPE between 1925 and 1930. The incised quality of Perpetua reflects Gill's background as a letter cutter in stone. Popular as a text face, it has sharp SERIF forms and a small X-HEIGHT with generous ASCENDER and DESCENDER elements. The capitals are shorter than the ascenders of the LOWER CASE. The related ITALIC, Felicity, was added later and is more of a sloped roman than a true calligraphic italic.

ABCDEFGH
abcdefgh

Letters from the **Perpetua** typeface.

Part of the packaging range designed by **Peters** for Winsor & Newton inks, 1972.

Peters, Michael (b.1941) British graphic designer. Trained at the London College of Printing and the School of Art and Architecture, Yale University, New Haven. He worked for CBS Television in New York, returning to London (1965) to establish the design department of the advertising agency Collett Dickenson Pearce. Thereafter he collaborated with Lou KLEIN, before founding Michael Peters & Partners (1970–90). Renowned for innovative packaging solutions for clients including Winsor & Newton inks, Seagram, Penhaligon's perfumery, British Petroleum and Elsenham Jams. Going 'public' in 1983 on the London Unlisted Securities Market (USM), the company acquired numerous international subsidiaries throughout the 1980s. Peters' achievement was to combine design excellence with outstanding business acumen. As a representative of a new breed of design entrepreneur with a distinguished record in international competitions, he worked in London as chairman of a smaller company, Michael Peters Limited (1990–92), before establishing Identica (renamed The Identica Partnership in 1995). Member of AGI.

Pfund, Roger (b.1943) Swiss illustrator and designer of posters, books, banknotes and murals. He studied at the Kunstgewerbeschule, Berne, 1963–66, after which he was awarded three successive federal scholarships in applied art. In 1971 he gained first prize in a Swiss National Bank competition to design bank notes. In the same year he moved to Geneva, where he continued a collaboration with Elizabeth Pfund that lasted until 1976, thereafter working with Jean-Pierre Blanchoud. The richly textured quality of his cultural posters results from a random layering of photography and illustration, combined with a hand-lettering technique that often resembles graffiti. Member of AGI.

photocomposition Generic term for typesetting systems that use photographic principles to produce DISPLAY and text setting on film or paper. Also known as phototypesetting. Recent systems use lasers to expose the type image on to the film or paper.

photoengraving Photomechanical etching process used to produce line or HALFTONE plates for LETTERPRESS printing.

photogram Photographic image that records the shadows of an object placed between a light source and light-sensitive photographic paper. Great subtlety can be achieved depending on the transparency or translucency of the selected object. No camera or film is involved in the production of a photogram.

photogravure Photomechanical INTAGLIO printing process, based on a principle whereby recessed dots (of varying depth) are engraved into a copper-plated steel cylinder, filled with ink, and then transferred directly to the printed surface. Before printing, any surplus ink is removed from the surface of the printing cylinder by means of a doctor-blade. A high-quality process, it is used for the production of long-run magazines and packaging.

Classe Enemie, a poster by **Pfund**, 1988.

Record cover by **Piatti**, *Lieder von Sonne, Mond und Sternen* (*Songs of the Sun, Moon and Stars*).

Pick commissioned this signage panel for London Underground, using Edward Johnston's Railway Type.

photolithography See OFFSET LITHO/OFFSET PHOTO-LITHOGRAPHY

Photo-Mechanical Transfer See PMT

photomontage Technique of combining or super-imposing photographic images from different sources to produce a new and surprising relationship between the individual components.

Photoshop Popular computer software program from ADOBE SYSTEMS used by designers and photographers to create and manipulate bitmapped imagery. Developed in 1989 from the BarneyScan slide scanner and BarneyScan XP, this powerful and versatile program revolutionized the design process. The technical sophistication of Photoshop facilitates the manipulation of scanned photographic imagery and allows for the introduction of an infinite range of visual effects.

Piatti, Celestino (b.1922) Swiss-born graphic designer, poster artist and illustrator. After studying graphic design at the Kunstgewerbeschule, Zurich, worked with Fritz Buhler in Basle 1944–48. Since then has operated a freelance practice embracing book design, advertising, posters, stamps, packaging and animation. His exuberant images with their bold, black outline have made a distinctive contribution to European illustration over the past four decades. Expert at applying his graphic skills to a wide range of design requirements, Piatti's expressionistic drawings and work in LITHOGRAPHY, WOODCUT and LINOCUT have appeared in children's books, magazines and many posters supporting political and humanitarian causes. His versatility is demonstrated by his long association with the German publisher Deutscher Taschenbuch-Verlag. Since 1961 he has controlled the visual identity of DTV, designing the typography and illustrations for thousands of paperbacks. The popularity of his work is confirmed by numerous one-man shows held throughout Europe since 1964. Member of AGI.

Pica, Pica em Traditional unit of typographic measurement based on 12 POINT, i.e. 4.216mm (c. 3/16in). Line lengths and spacing requirements are often specified in 12pt Pica ems.

Pick, Frank (1878–1941) Pioneering figure in British design management, committed to the union of good design and industry. Involved in the establishment of the DESIGN AND INDUSTRIES ASSOCIATION (1915), becoming president in 1931. Pick joined London

Underground in 1906, eventually rising to the post of vice-chairman of the London Passenger Transport Board, which was created in 1933. He commissioned poster designs from the finest artists and designers including Edward McKnight KAUFFER, Edward BAWDEN, Fred TAYLOR, Frank NEWBOULD, Graham Sutherland, Laura Knight and Frank Brangwyn. In 1916 he was responsible for commissioning Edward JOHNSTON to design the SANS SERIF alphabet Railway, which, along with Johnston's 'circle-and-bar' SYMBOL, became a key element in London Transport's CORPORATE IDENTITY. Pick's appointment of Christian Barman as publicity officer in 1935 helped to maintain London Transport's pre-eminent place in poster design.

pictogram/graph Pictorial sign that depicts a simplified representation of a particular object or activity.

pie graph/chart Diagram in which different components are visually represented as a proportional slice of a circular pie. The complete circle represents 100 per cent, with each slice allocated an appropriate percentage of the whole. Pie graphs/charts enable instant visual comparisons to be made of complex statistical information.

Pineles, Cipe (1910–91) Magazine art director, graphic designer and teacher. Born in Vienna, she emigrated to the US (1923) where she was awarded a scholarship to the Pratt Institute, New York 1927–31. Designer with Contempora, a New York industrial design practice 1931–33, before joining Condé Nast publications (1933) as Mehemed Fehmy AGHA's assistant. Transferred to *VOGUE* in London as associate editor and art director 1936–38. Art director of *Glamour,* New York 1938–45 and *Overseas Woman,* Paris 1945–46 where she worked alongside her first husband William GOLDEN. Pineles explored the progressive new devices of editorial design – SANS SERIF type, cropped photography, BLEED pages and exploitation of white space and margins. As art director of *Seventeen* 1947–50 she extended the visual vocabulary of the young readership by commissioning outstanding photographers, illustrators and painters like Ben SHAHN and Robert Gwathmey. Pineles continued as art director of *Charm* 1950–58 and *Mademoiselle* 1958–59. In 1959 she became a freelance designer in New York, mainly working for Will BURTIN, whom she married in 1961. Art director of the Lincoln Center for the Performing Arts 1965–72. Closely associated with Parson's School of Design, New York, becoming a teacher in 1963 and from 1970 responsible for

designing the school's printed and promotional material. Member of AGI and AIGA, she was the first woman elected to ART DIRECTORS CLUB OF NEW YORK Hall of Fame (1975).

Pintori, Giovanni (b.1912) Italian graphic, exhibition and industrial designer who during thirty-one years with Olivetti, Milan, made a major contribution to the company's reputation for consistent excellence in the design of publicity, products and buildings. He studied at the Istituto Superiore per le Industrie Artistiche, Monza (near Milan), 1930–36. Invited by Adriano Olivetti, son of the founder, to join the company in 1936. Creator of outstanding advertising materials, he was a master at visually communicating Olivetti's technologically advanced products. Favourite devices include the juxtaposition of a photograph with a schematic illustration or the playful exploitation of letterforms. Designed the Olivetti LOGOTYPE in 1947. He led the graphic-design department 1950–67 and during the 1960s collaborated with Walter BALLMER and Max HUBER on advertising campaigns. After his retirement from Olivetti he established a studio in Milan. Awarded Palme d'Oro, Milan, 1950 and the grand prize at the Triennale, Milan, 1957. Member of AGI.

Pira Acronym for Printing Industries Research Association – the British technical association that carries out testing and research into packaging, paper and board, and printing. Pira publishes research reports and training material for the benefit of members.

Pirtle, Woody (b.1944) American graphic designer working in advertising, editorial and corporate design. Initially studied architecture at the University of Arkansas, later transferring to the School of Fine Arts. He began his design career with Stan Richards at the Richards Group, Dallas 1969–78, with a brief interruption to establish a partnership in Houston. He founded Pirtle Design in Dallas in 1978. Influenced by Milton GLASER and Seymour CHWAST, his work is distinguished by strong graphic ideas and visual wit. He is known for projects for United Airlines, the Dallas Opera, Neimann and Marcus, and his award-winning Info-Works designs commissioned by the Dallas Market Center. In 1989 he moved to New York to become a partner in PENTAGRAM. His designs are included in the permanent collections of the Library of Congress, Washington, the Cooper Hewitt Museum, New York, and the Neue Sammlung Museum, Munich. Member of AGI and AIGA.

Olivetti Elettrosumma 22

Poster for Olivetti's Elettrosumma 22 calculating machine (1956) by **Pintori**.

Pirtle used this 'red pepper chair' illustration, *Hot Seat*, to advertise Knoll International Furniture, 1980.

Plakatstil Poster movement that emerged in Germany during the early 1890s and elevated the commercial advertising poster to an art form. The resulting Sachplakat (object poster) was characterized by a strong central image, bold but simple lettering and striking colour; its hallmarks were economy and clarity. Masters of Plakatstil included Ludwig HOHLWEIN, Lucian BERNHARD and Hans Rudi ERDT. The monthly Berlin magazine *Das Plakat* (1910–21) was an influential showcase for Plakatstil and featured the finest contemporary poster artists.

planographic Type of printing process that uses a smooth, even printing plate without any recessed (INTAGLIO) or raised (RELIEF) areas. LITHOGRAPHY, for example, is a planographic process.

Plantin Popular ROMAN TYPEFACE much used in book design. Created by F.H. Pierpont and issued by MONO-TYPE (1913), it is based on a 16th-c. type found in the Antwerp office of Christophe Plantin, a famous printer and publisher. A typeface with strong features, it is recognized for its large X-HEIGHT and narrow set, which make it very economical in use. A full range of weights is available. The fluid ITALIC is distinguished by rather short DESCENDER forms.

Plantin typeface, popular in book design.

ABCDEFGH
abcdefgh

PMT Abbreviation for photo-mechanical transfer. Method of producing high-quality duplicate photoprints from an original. The black and/or white copies, which can be the same size, or bigger or smaller than the original, are often used in the production of FIN-ISHED ARTWORK. The term PMT is derived from the Kodak paper used during the process.

point Standard unit of typographic measurement. The Anglo/American point is 0.351mm (0.01383in); 12 points make 1 PICA EM. There are 72 points in one inch. The European DIDOT point is 0.375mm (0.0148in). Standard point sizes used in type measurement are 6, 7, 8, 9, 10, 12, 14, 18, 20, 24, 30, 36, 42, 48, 60 and 72.

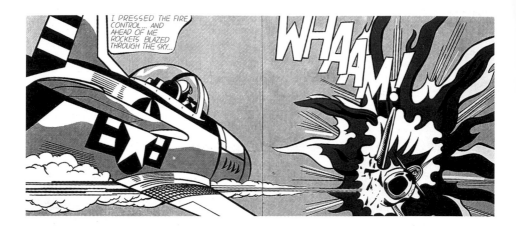

Pop Art Art movement that elevated the imagery of popular advertising (packaging, comic strips, etc.) to fine art. Often working on a large scale, Pop artists highlighted the powerful relationship between the consumer and the artefacts of consumerism. The combination of flat, brash colours with super-enlargements of HALFTONE screen dots established a rich new vein for graphic designers and illustrators. Emerging in the late 1950s in Britain and the early 60s in the US, Pop Art challenged the dominance of Abstract Expressionism. Building upon some aspects of SURREALISM and the 'ready-made' objects of DADA, it exploited the random imagery generated by television and popular films. The first significant Pop Art image was a COLLAGE by Richard Hamilton, entitled *Just What Is It That Makes Today's Home So Different, So Appealing?,* which was exhibited at an Independent Group exhibition at the Institute of Contemporary Arts, London (1956). Ephemeral images were recycled until they took on the status of contemporary icons (e.g. Warhol's ubiquitous images of Marilyn Monroe and Campbell's soup cans). Major practitioners in the UK were Richard Hamilton, Eduardo Paolozzi, Allen Jones and Peter Blake; in the US, Andy Warhol, Roy Lichtenstein, James Rosenquist and Tom Wesselmann built upon earlier foundations laid by Jasper Johns and Robert Rauschenberg.

Poster, The (1898–1901) Published in London, this short-lived magazine reviewed the best of international poster design, including work by Alphonse MUCHA, Will BRADLEY and John HASSALL. Emerging as the English vogue for collecting posters peaked, it was absorbed by *The Art Collector.*

Roy Lichtenstein's classic **Pop Art** painting, *Whaam!* (1963).

Cover design for the first issue of **The Poster** by 'M. Yendis' (Sidney Ransom), June 1898.

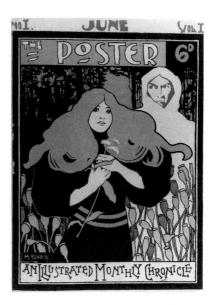

post-modernism Design movement that evolved in the mid-1960s as a critical response to the dominance, and perceived sterility of MODERNISM. Embracing art, architecture and the applied arts, it re-established interest in ornament, symbolism and visual wit. Unconstrained by dogma, post-modern designers rejected modernism's obsession with progress and challenged the fundamental tenets of order and discipline espoused by the BAUHAUS and its followers. Underpinning the rational INTERNATIONAL TYPOGRAPHIC STYLE in Switzerland was the belief that form follows function, but by the late 1960s a new generation of Swiss graphic designers sought to challenge the limitations of this increasingly predictable style. At the forefront were ODERMATT & TISSI in Zurich and Wolfgang WEINGART in Basle. From the early 1970s Weingart's influence as a teacher spread to the US, with his rejection of 'dogmatic' typographers like TSCHICHOLD, RUDER and GERSTNER attracting acclaim and controversy in equal measure. His eclectic, anarchic approach – also known as New Wave – with legibility often sacrificed to expression, was promulgated in the US by ex-Basle students like Daniel FRIEDMAN, April GREIMAN and Inge DRUCKREY. The new-found emphasis on intuition and the potency of typography was pursued in Britain by Neville BRODY, in Holland by Studio DUMBAR and in Spain by Javier MARISCAL and PERET. Although latterly applied more as a 'style' than an alternative to mainstream practice, post-modernism provides a pointer to future graphic-design developments. By extending the range of historical source material available to designers and through its embrace of the new technologies, its influence has been liberating and positive.

prelims Abbreviation for the preliminary pages/matter preceding the main contents of a book. Prelims vary according to the book but normally include half-title, frontispiece, title page, list of contents/illustrations and preface/foreword. See FRONT-MATTER

printer's flowers Decorative (traditionally in metal) type ornaments composed of motifs using floral or abstract organic shapes. Often used as background patterns or repeated to form typographic borders.

printer's ornament Traditional, decorative type elements such as PRINTER'S FLOWERS, borders and arabesques used for visual effect in type matter, e.g. title pages and chapter headings.

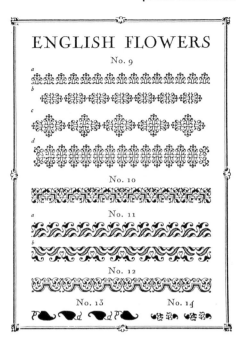

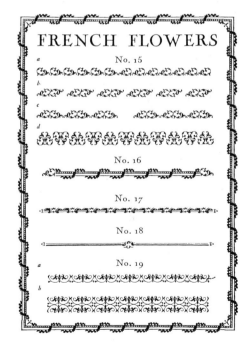

English and French **printer's flowers** from the Pelican Press Specimen Sheet, 1921.

Private Press Movement Craft movement that pursued the high-quality presswork, materials and typography in book production that had existed prior to industrial mechanization. Strongly influenced by the ideals of the ARTS AND CRAFTS MOVEMENT and in particular the KELMSCOTT PRESS. In England, exquisite limited-edition volumes were produced by the Doves Press (see Emery WALKER), Vale Press (see Charles RICKETTS), ASHENDENE PRESS, ERAGNY PRESS, Curwen Press (see Harold CURWEN) and the Nonesuch Press (see Sir Francis MEYNELL). Essentially medievalist, the presses inspired many OLD STYLE TYPEFACE revivals, particularly from 15th-c. Italy. In America the mantle of Kelmscott was taken up by three great typographers, Frederic W. GOUDY, Daniel Berkeley UPDIKE of the Merrymount Press and Bruce ROGERS of the Riverside Press. The movement was of enormous influence in Germany where in 1913 Count Harry von Kessler founded the CRANACH PRESS, Weimar. The ideals of truth to materials and fitness for purpose espoused by private press printers were to become fundamental precepts at the BAUHAUS. Influential as a movement up to the Second World War, its legacy was a major improvement in the production standards of commercial printing and publishing houses.

Psychedelia produced this classic poster by Peter Max, *Love* (c. 1967).

proof correction marks Standard set of signs used by typographers, editors and proofreaders in the preparation and correction of copy for printing. There are significant differences between the proof correction marks used in Britain and the US.

Pryde, James *See* BEGGARSTAFF BROTHERS, THE

Psychedelia Alternative art and design movement that emerged on the West Coast of America during the social unrest of the mid-1960s. Associated with rock music and alternative 'hippy' lifestyles, psychedelic images endeavoured to recreate the visual sensations associated with mind-expanding drugs, such as LSD. Distorted imagery and illegible lettering, often reproduced in garish colours, were applied to posters, magazines and record covers. Some of the stylistic devices associated with ART NOUVEAU, Op Art and POP ART were ruthlessly plundered. By the early 1970s psychedelia was an important visual component of youth culture throughout the US and Europe. Many of the original designers of the movement were self-taught, with the Americans Wes Wilson, Victor Moscoso and Peter Max being of particular note.

Punk Subversive street culture movement that originated in London in the mid-1970s. Embracing art, music and fashion, followers of Punk were recognizable by their aggressive visual appearance and anarchic behaviour. Anti-establishment in all its manifestations, it achieved notoriety through the Sex Pistols music group managed by Malcolm McLaren and dressed by Vivienne Westwood; the group's visual identity on record covers, posters and T- shirts was controlled by the influential Jamie REID. Punk s graphic style was characterized by a throwaway COLLAGE technique with chaotic typography and shocking slogans. Record companies like Stiff and Factory encouraged emerging talents like Neville BRODY, Barney BUBBLES, Peter SAVILLE and Malcolm GARRETT. The early issues of i-D magazine, first published in 1980 and designed by Terry JONES, reflected Punk and pointed the way for the glossy 'style' magazines of the mid-1980s. About 1980, following the lead of London, Punk emerged in a modified form in the US and Europe. Running out of steam in the early 1980s, the style innovations of Punk were quickly assimilated into the graphic imagery of POST-MODERNISM in the mid-80s.

Purvis, Tom (1888–1959) English graphic designer and poster artist. Studied painting at Camberwell

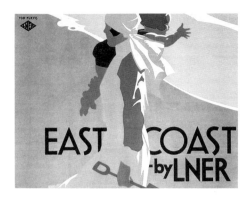

Poster promoting travel to Britain's east coast on the London and North Eastern Railway, by **Purvis**, 1935.

Cover of the **Push Pin Studio** magazine, *Push Pin Graphic*, by Seymour Chwast (December 1976), entitled *Mothers*.

School of Art, London, and with Degas and Sickert. Designer with the advertising agency Mather and Crowther, London, for six years before establishing a freelance practice. Designed posters during both wars, also serving with the Artists Rifles in France in the First World War, until wounded. From 1940–45 he was a war artist for the Ministry of Supply, London. An innovative designer, his bold use of lettering and flat colour moved British poster design away from its reliance on traditional imagery to a symbolism influenced by European designers like Ludwig HOHLWEIN. He produced many classic posters for London Underground, LNER, Austin Reed, Shell and Pilkington. Elected as one of the first eleven ROYAL DESIGNERS FOR INDUSTRY (1936), becoming Master of Faculty in 1940. Post-war, he concentrated on painting portraits and, in his last years, religious subjects.

Push Pin Studio New York graphic-design group founded in 1954 by Seymour CHWAST, Milton GLASER and illustrators Reynold Ruffins and Edward Sorel. During the 1960s they challenged the orthodoxy of the dominant INTERNATIONAL TYPOGRAPHIC STYLE, offering a witty, eclectic alternative with immediate consumer appeal. The studio drew endless inspiration from diverse art historical sources, such as Italian Renaissance painting, Victorian letterforms, comic books and primitive WOODCUT illustrations. The Push Pin style was characterized by brightly coloured narrative illustration, with forms exaggerated, flattened and unexpectedly juxtaposed to humorous effect. The group specialized in book jackets, record covers, posters and magazine illustrations. Prior to the establishment of the studio, the designers had collaborated on the bi-monthly *Push Pin Almanac*, featuring illustrations alongside editorial material pillaged from old almanacs. The journal evolved into the acclaimed *Push Pin Graphic*, which promoted the work of the studio. Young designers/illustrators launched at Push Pin include Paul DAVIS and Barry Zaid. In 1970 it became the first American design group honoured by an exhibition at the Musée des Arts Décoratifs, Paris, a show that subsequently travelled to other cities in Europe and Japan. The exhibition 'Push Pin and Beyond' was shown in Japan at the Suntory Design Museum (1997).

Pyle, Howard (1853–1911) Prolific American illustrator, writer and inspirational teacher, regarded as the father of American illustration. The leading representative of a school of illustration that came to be known as the Brandywine School. His romantic rep-

Illustration by **Pyle** for *The Merry Adventures of Robin Hood* (1883).

Poster for an international puppet show festival, 1987, by Le **Quernec**.

resentations of European and African legend and American colonial life were a major influence on a younger generation of illustrators, many of whom studied at his private art college, founded in Wilmington, Delaware (1900). He produced thousands of illustrations for periodicals like *Scribner's Monthly, St Nicholas, Harper's Weekly, Harper's Monthly* and HARPER'S BAZAAR. In addition he illustrated over a hundred books and wrote and illustrated some twenty-four of his own stories, many for children. Some of his books, including the first, *The Merry Adventures of Robin Hood* (1883), remained in print for over a century.

Q

quad Paper size four times the basic, uncut broadsheet size, e.g. Crown 15 x 20 in (38 x 51 cm), Quad Crown 30 x 40 in (76 x 101.6 cm). See PAPER SIZES

quad/quadrat Traditional term for typographic spacing units, used to fill out gaps and short lines in a piece of text setting. Available in a range of sizes, all fractions of EM body size, e.g. EN (half of em), 2ems, 3ems, etc.

QuarkXPress Professional design software created in 1987 and used to assemble text and image on a page layout. The package offers near infinite ways to handle and combine type families, colour and graphic elements. By facilitating new opportunities in the layering of information programs, QuarkXPress has contributed to the creation of a new visual language.

quarto, 4to Resulting paper size when basic broadsheet is cut or folded into four. See PAPER SIZES

Quernec, Alain Le (b.1944) French designer and teacher, creator of dramatic and witty public information, political and cultural posters. Following art training at the Lycée Claude Bernard, Paris 1961–64, was awarded a scholarship to study under Henryk TOMASZEWSKI at the Warsaw Academy of Fine Art (1972), since which time he has freelanced and taught in Quimper, Brittany. Specializes in poster, catalogue and LOGOTYPE design. Indebted to the Polish poster tradition, his powerful graphic ideas are given urgency through an original style of illustration, inventive COLLAGE and an ability to exploit the expressive potential of TYPOGRAPHY and hand-drawn letterforms. His awards include the ICOGRADA prize at the Warsaw Poster Biennale (1988) and first prize at the Zanders Z-Sculpture competition (1994).

quire Quantity of paper, ½₀th of a REAM, normally 24 or 25 sheets.

R

rag paper Superior writing paper manufactured from rag pulp.

RAM (Random Access Memory) That part of a COMPUTER's memory that can be read from (offering no facility for user modification) or written to (interactive, enabling user modification). RAM is used to store data temporarily, whilst the computer is switched on. Discs or tapes are used to store data whilst a computer is switched off. As data can be accessed more quickly from RAM than from discs or tapes, frequently used data is kept in RAM whilst the computer is in use. See ROM (READ ONLY MEMORY)

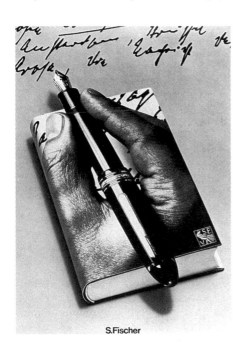

S.Fischer

Rambow/Lienemeyer/van de Sand promotional poster for the publisher S. Fischer Verlag, 1979.

Rambow/Lienemeyer/van de Sand Frankfurt graphic-design partnership. Originally founded as Rambow + Lienemeyer by Gunter Rambow (b.1938) and Gerhard Lienemeyer (b.1936) in Kassel (1960), after studying together at the Hochschule für bildende Kunst, Kassel, under Hans HILLMAN. The studio transferred to Stuttgart (1964) and to Frankfurt (1967), where they created the Kohlkunst Verlag publishing company (1967). Michael van de Sand (b.1945) studied photography and graphic design at Fachhochschule Niederrhein, Krefeld, 1963–68 and joined the practice as a designer in 1969, becoming a partner in 1973. The group produces book, corporate and exhibition design but is especially known for hard-hitting cultural, social and political posters that exploit photography and PHOTOMONTAGE to surreal effect. Its work includes the CORPORATE IDENTITY and an acclaimed series of promotional posters for the Frankfurt publisher S. Fischer Verlag 1976–83, award-winning theatre posters for the Schauspiel Frankfurt 1977–83, posters for the Frankfurt issue of the literary magazine *Der Neue Egoist,* posters for peace organizations (1982) and the Green Party (1983). The studio's *Othello* theatre poster (1978) was awarded a gold medal at the International Poster Biennale in Warsaw, 1980. Exhibited throughout Europe and in America at the Walker Art Center, Minneapolis, 1984. Rambow has been professor of graphic design and photography at Gesamthochschule, Kassel, since 1974.

Rand, Michael (b.1929) British magazine art director. Studied at University of London Goldsmiths' College of Art 1949–52. Worked as a freelance designer and then as a consultant designer to the *Daily Express* before becoming art editor of *The Sunday Times Magazine* (1963). The magazine quickly

THE CHEMICAL OLYMPICS

Double-page spread from *The Sunday Times Magazine,* 9 October 1988, by Michael **Rand**.

attracted acclaim for Rand's innovative use of photography and illustration. For a brief period he became design director and associate editor of *The Sunday Times* newspaper, returning to *The Sunday Times Magazine* as art director and managing editor. His numerous accolades include gold and silver awards from the DESIGNERS AND ART DIRECTORS ASSOCIATION, London and the 1989 Design Award from the International Centre of Photography, New York. He has designed and picture-edited a number of books, including *Homecoming*, and *Beirut: A City in Crisis* by Britain's distinguished war photographer, Don McCullin, and *Deeds of War* (1989) by the photographer James Nachtwey. In 1989 appointed as art director of *Mirabella* magazine, which was launched in the US.

Rand, Paul (1914–96) Seminal figure in American graphic design who explored the formal vocabulary of European avant-garde art movements including CUBISM, CONSTRUCTIVISM and DE STIJL and developed a unique, distinctly American graphic language. His work is characterized by wit, simplicity and a BAUHAUS approach to problem solving. Educated in New York at the Pratt Institute 1929–32, Parsons School of Design 1932–33 and the Art Students League 1933–34, with George GROSZ. Rand was a major force in editorial design, advertising and corporate graphics. Art director of *Esquire* and *Apparel Arts* magazines 1935–41, and designer of outstanding covers for the cultural journal *Direction* 1938–45. He joined the Weintraub Advertising Agency, New York, 1941–54 where his collaboration with Bill Bernbach (see DOYLE DANE BERNBACH), especially on the Orbach's department-store campaign, pioneered the closer integration of design and copy. From 1955 he freelanced, becoming design consultant to major companies like

Paul **Rand**'s 1960 symbol for the Westinghouse Electric Corporation.

IBM, Cummins Engine Company, Westinghouse Electric Corporation and NeXT. His masterly LOGOTYPE for IBM was created in 1956; logos for Westinghouse, United Parcel Service and ABC Television followed. He influenced successive generations of designers through his writings and his involvement in design education. His most important texts include *Thoughts on Design* (1947) and *Paul Rand: A Designer's Art* (1985). Lectured at the Cooper Union, Pratt Institute and appointed professor at Yale University, New Haven in 1956. His many awards include gold medals from AIGA and the ART DIRECTORS CLUB OF NEW YORK, joining their Hall of Fame in 1972. RDI and member of AGI.

Random Access Memory See RAM

ranged left/ragged right Typesetting format in which text lines of unequal length align on the left margin, with a ragged, UNJUSTIFIED effect on the right edge. This entry is set in 8/10 pt Gill Sans unjustified ranged left on a 60 mm column width.

> **ranged right/ragged left** Typesetting format in which text lines of unequal length align on the right margin, with a ragged, UNJUSTIFIED effect on the left edge. This entry is set in 8/10 pt Gill Sans unjustified ranged right on a measure of 60 mm.

Ravilious, Eric (1903–42) Artist, designer and illustrator. Born in London, he trained at Eastbourne School of Art and then at the Royal College of Art, London 1922–25. Quickly established reputation as a wood engraver, contributing to the revival of this craft in England before the Second World War. Inspired by Paul NASH, he was a contemporary and friend of Edward BAWDEN. Popular as a book and magazine illustrator, he produced WOOD ENGRAVING illustrations and delicately coloured LITHOGRAPHY for the GOLDEN COCKEREL PRESS, Nonesuch Press (see Sir Francis MEYNELL), Curwen Press (see Harold CURWEN), *Radio Times* and London Transport. His first major wood engraving commission was for Shakespeare's *Twelfth Night*, published and printed by the Golden Cockerel Press (1932). A versatile designer with a genius for decoration, Ravilious also designed furniture, glass, textiles, wallpapers and ceramics. From the mid-1930s he worked with Wedgwood, producing a superb series of designs for ceramic ware, which remained in production throughout the 1950s. Appointed official war artist in 1940, he was killed on active service in Iceland.

Lithograph poster by Man **Ray** for the London Underground (1932)

-KEEPS LONDON GOING

Hams, an illustration by **Ravilious** from *High Street* by J.M. Richards, 1938.

Ray, Man (1890–1977) Artist, designer and photographer. Born in Philadelphia, US, his early training was as a painter in New York. Much influenced by the 'Armory Show' of modern art in New York (1913). He met Marcel Duchamp and the photographer Alfred Stieglitz in 1915 and along with Duchamp and Francis Picabia, formed a New York DADA group in 1917. Moved to Paris in 1921 and at about this time created his most significant photographic images, which he called 'rayographs' (PHOTOGRAMS). Created without a camera, they were achieved by manipulating the light source projected on to objects placed on light-sensitive photographic paper. After 1923, along with a group of Dadaists led by André Breton, he became involved with SURREALISM. Thereafter experimented with photographic COLLAGE and photographic techniques like multiple exposure and SOLARIZATION. By the mid-1930s Ray was established as a successful photographer, collaborating with Picasso (1936) to produce a series of rayographs and working with Alexey BRODOVITCH at HARPER'S BAZAAR. He returned to the US in 1940, settling in Hollywood. Under Herbert BAYER's direction Ray contributed to the advertising and design programmes devised for the CONTAINER CORPORATION OF AMERICA. He returned finally to Paris in 1950. His autobiography, *Self Portrait,* was published in 1963.

RDI *See* ROYAL DESIGNERS FOR INDUSTRY

Read Only Memory *See* ROM

ream Traditional term for a quantity of paper, normally 500 sheets but may range from 480 to 516 sheets.

rebus Graphic device that uses pictures or symbols, in place of words or syllables, to represent a statement or idea. The 'sound' of the selected illustrations, when pronounced, can be modified by the addition or deletion of certain letters.

Rebus for IBM, designed by Paul Rand in 1981.

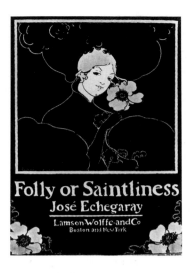

Reed's poster for José Echegaray's *Folly or Saintliness*, 1895.

Reed, Ethel (1876– ?) Poster designer. Born in Massachusetts, US. Working in a restrained ART NOU-VEAU style, incorporating dignified typography, she was the first American woman to establish a national reputation in graphic arts. Displaying a remarkably mature talent, some of her best posters were produced during her teenage years. However, after working in Boston throughout the mid-1890s (particularly for the publisher Lamson, Wolffe & Co.), Reed's whereabouts thereafter remain a mystery. She made a brief but significant contribution to the American Art Nouveau tradition established by Will BRADLEY, Edward PENFIELD and Louis RHEAD.

Reid, Jamie (b.1940) British graphic designer. Trained as a painter at Croydon School of Art 1964–68. Politically active from an early age, he co-founded the Suburban Press (1970–75), publishing amongst other things his own radical community newspaper (*The Suburban Press*) in the early 1970s. Established his reputation as art director of the PUNK rock group the Sex Pistols, managed by fashion and pop entrepreneur Malcolm McLaren (an art school contemporary of Reid). Reid designed all the visual paraphernalia associated with the Sex Pistols up to their demise in 1979 – record sleeves, advertising, posters, T-shirts, etc. Raw and aggressive, his designs brought him controversy and street credibility in equal measure. His COLLAGE technique, with random visual and typographic elements manipulated and distorted to powerful effect, created a new genre of anarchic graphics. Since 1980 he has collaborated with the Liverpool actress Margi Clarke. Involved in a number of radical film projects in Liverpool, whilst also maintaining an association with Malcolm GARRETT's Assorted images company in London. An exhibition of his work entitled 'Jamie Reid: The Rise of the Phoenix – Celtic Surveyor IV' was held in Liverpool in 1991.

Reiner, Imre (b.1900) Artist, engraver and letterer. Hungarian-born, he trained originally as a sculptor before moving to Germany in 1920 to study graphic arts under Ernst Schneidler in Stuttgart. A distinguished successor to the great German calligrapher Rudolf KOCH, his distinctive free-form technique elevated hand-drawn lettering to a new level of creative expression. Since settling in Switzerland in 1932, subsequently taking Swiss citizenship, he has produced numerous book and TYPEFACE designs. His book illustrations have been a major influence on the revival of the craft of WOOD ENGRAVING in the 20th c. A master at combining illustration and calligraphy with typography, his books on the craft of lettering include *Grafika* (1947), *Monograms* (1947), and *Lettering in Book Art* (1948, with his wife Hedwig). He has specialized in the design of informal SCRIPT typefaces, including Reiner Script (1951), Bazaar (1956), Mercurius (1957) and Corvinus (1929–34), a useful ROMAN for DISPLAY setting. His work has featured in many one-man exhibitions throughout the world.

relief printing Traditional printing process in which the image to be printed is raised above the non-image area. Ink is applied to the raised surface and the image transferred to the paper surface by application of pressure. See LETTERPRESS PRINTING

Record cover and poster for the Sex Pistols by **Reid** (1977).

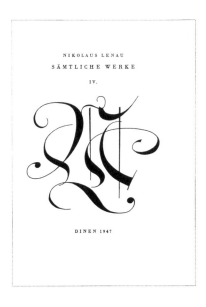

NIKOLAUS LENAU

SÄMTLICHE WERKE

IV.

DINEN 1947

One of a series of title pages from *Lettering in Book Art*
(1948) by Imre and Hedwig **Reiner**.

Fachschulen Bayerns (Technical Schools of Applied Arts of
Bavaria), a lithograph exhibition poster by **Renner**, 1928.

Renner, Paul (1878–1956) German book and TYPE-
FACE designer. Began as a painter after training in
Berlin, Karlsruhe and Munich. He gained experience
in book design with the Munich publisher Georg
Müller. In 1926 he became director of the Munich
School for Master Book Printers; his opposition to
National Socialism resulted in his dismissal in 1933.
His major achievement was the design of the classic
SANS SERIF typeface FUTURA (1927–30) for the Bauer
foundry. This functional typeface, which evolved
from a more severely geometric original design,
gained widespread acceptance throughout the 1930s.
Renner's experiments with sans serif lettering were a
manifestation of the NEW TYPOGRAPHY and followed in
the tradition established by Herbert BAYER's 'universal' alphabet (1925).

Reverb A Los Angeles–based consultancy with
particular focus on branding and strategic image
development. The five founding principals initially
worked as a collective/workshop before establishing
Reverb in 1991. The original partners included Somi
Kim (b.1962), Whitney Lowe (b.1958), Lisa Nugent
(b.1955), Susan Parr (b.1959) and on a part-time basis
designer, writer and educator Lorraine Wilde
(b.1953). Kim, Nugent and Parr remain as principals
and have built the branding, strategy and consumer-
research side of the practice. Kim and Nugent taught
for a number of years at Otis College of Art and Art
Center College of Design. The designers were among
the first generation to explore the potential of the
APPLE MACINTOSH in the creation of dynamic and highly
experimental design. Their output reveals diverse
styles and influences, reflecting the visual excitement

Pages from the IBM Summer Jam report designed by
Reverb, 1999.

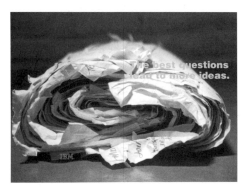

of Los Angeles and their fascination with books and typographic history. The practice began by working for such cultural organizations as California Institute of Arts (CalArts) and the Whitney Museum of Art, New York; its expanded client base now encompasses large corporate organizations like Nike, Netscape, IBM, Hewlett Packard. In 1995 Reverb received the Chrysler Award for Innovation in Design.

Rhead, Louis (1857–1926) Poster designer and illustrator, born in Staffordshire, England. Studied in England and Paris before emigrating to America (1883) where he was based in New York; his ART NOUVEAU designs continued to reveal a European influence. Travelled to Europe in his mid-thirties, staying for three years and acquiring a particular respect for the achievements and style of Eugène GRASSET. On returning to the US, his decorative and distinctively coloured posters and magazine covers gained widespread acclaim. Throughout the 1890s his eclectic European approach complemented the Art Nouveau output of Will BRADLEY and Edward PENFIELD.

Ricketts, Charles de Sousy (1866–1931) Artist, typographer and designer. Born in Geneva, he spent his early years in England, Italy and France. From 1882 he trained in WOOD ENGRAVING at the City & Guilds Art School, London. Quickly emerged as a leading engraver and book designer of the ARTS AND CRAFTS MOVEMENT, with his light, graceful style a contrast to the richness and luxuriance of the KELMSCOTT PRESS books produced by William MORRIS. His bindings, typography and illustrations for luxury books during the early 1890s acknowledged ART NOUVEAU and rivalled the originality and finesse of works by Aubrey BEARDSLEY. His design of Oscar Wilde's *The Sphinx* (1894), printed by The Ballantyne Press, is of particular note. Together with his friend Charles Shannon, he published the magazine *The Dial* (1889–97) and established the Vale Press in Chelsea (1896–1904). The Vale Press was more of a publishing house than a private press, with Ricketts using other printers and typesetters to achieve his own high standards of production. His TYPEFACE designs for the Press include Vale (1896), a heavy ROMAN based on VENETIAN proportions, and King's Fount (1903), another heavy roman with a mixture of UPPER and LOWER CASE characters making for poor legibility. The most successful Vale Press book is probably *The Marriage of Cupide and Psyche* (1897). His versatility extended to the design of jewelry, costumes and stage sets. As a painter, he was elected a member of the Royal Academy, London, in 1928.

Ricketts' woodcut title page for *Nimphidia* and *the Muses Elizium* by Michael Drayton (1896).

Symbol for Holman Scaffolding Ltd by **Roch**, 1988.

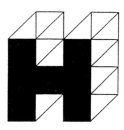

Roch, Ernst (b.1928) Canadian designer of CORPORATE IDENTITY programmes, books, postage stamps, posters and exhibitions. Born in Osijek, Yugoslavia, he trained in Austria at the Staatliche Meisterschule für Angewandte Kunst, Graz, 1948–53, then emigrated to Canada. After a period with Y&M Studio 1953–59 and at the Montreal offices of James Valkus Inc. 1960, founded Roch Design, Montreal 1960–65. With Rolf HARDER, he established Design Collaborative where he produced functional design solutions reflecting his

European roots. Re-established Roch Design in 1977. Major design achievements include Canadian postage stamps featuring Queen Elizabeth II (1963), a visual identity programme for the National Arts Center, Ottawa (1965), the official poster for the Montreal Olympics (1976) and the 'AGI Posters' exhibition, Montreal 1982. Member of AGI and AIGA.

Rock, Michael (b.1959) New York–based graphic designer, writer and educator. Studied literature, then graphic design at the Rhode Island School of Design, where he later lectured in design theory. Taught graphic design at Yale University, New Haven under Sheila Levrant de BRETTEVILLE. Rock met Susan Sellers (b.1967) at Rhode Island, where she was studying graphic design. After initial collaborations on writing projects, they moved to New York, joining Georgianna Stout (b.1967) to establish the studio 2x4 in 1995. Clients include the Museum of Modern Art, *The New York Times* and *ANY* (the New York architectural journal). In publications, including *EYE* magazine, Rock has contributed to the emergence of a critical writing on graphic design that challenges the traditional schism between practice and theory.

Rockwell Popular SLAB SERIF TYPEFACE with a disciplined, mechanistic character. Developed during the first half of the 19th c. along with other EGYPTIAN faces, the Rockwell family works well in DISPLAY and text settings.

Rockwell, Norman (1894–1978) Born in New York, he is the best-known American illustrator of the 20th c. Trained at the National Academy and then at the Art Students League, New York. Renowned for his idealized view of small-town America, he made his reputation working for the *Saturday Evening Post*, for whom he painted 322 covers between 1916 and 1963. His illustrations appeared in other leading magazines including *Life*, *Colliers* and *Look*. The US government used his evocative images in posters supporting the American war effort during the Second World War. A supreme draughtsman, his unique ability to give visual expression to the American Dream was employed in major advertising campaigns and two popular, long-running series of calendars for the publishers Brown & Bigelow. In 1960, he published his autobiography, *My Adventures as an Illustrator*.

Rock's book design for *Charette*, 1997.

Rockwell slab serif typeface.

ABCDEFGH
abcdefgh

Rodchenko, Alexander (1891–1956)
Artist, designer, photographer. Born in St Petersburg. From 1911 trained at the art school in Kazan, moving to Moscow in c.1914. Along with Vladimir Tatlin and El LISSITZKY, he was a leading figure of Russian CONSTRUCTIVISM. In 1921 he abandoned 'pure art' in favour of a visual communication that would serve the needs of society: his pioneering constructivist typography,

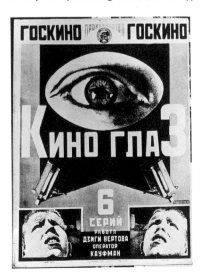

Rodchenko's poster for the film *Kino-Eye* directed by Dziga Vertov, 1928.

with its geometrical severity, heavy rules and bold, hand-drawn SANS SERIFS, was inextricably linked with the politics of revolution. In the early 1920s his utilitarian graphics were supplemented by overtly political PHOTOMONTAGE designs. He was active in many different areas, devising posters, book jackets, interiors, products, furniture and stage sets. In 1922 he designed animated film titles for Dziga Vertov's documentary newsreels, followed in 1923 by his art direction of *Lef*, a radical arts magazine edited by his friends Vladimir Mayakovsky and Osip Brik. His collaboration with Mayakovsky produced posters advertising state services like education; he also designed a number of Mayakovsky's poetry anthologies in the late 1920s. Shortly after the establishment of the Moscow Vkhutemas (1919) – the most progressive art school in the world at that time – he took charge of the metalwork department. About 1924 he started to take photographs, a development consistent with his desire to achieve a new objectivity by technical means. His versatility is demonstrated by designs for a reading room in a Workers' Club, exhibited in the Soviet Pavilion at the 1925 Paris 'Exposition Internationale des Arts Décoratifs et Industriels Modernes'. After 1928, Stalin's five-year plan constrained the creative activities of artists and designers. From the 1930s onwards Rodchenko worked as a typographer and photo-journalist, contributing to magazines like *USSR in Construction*.

Rogers, Bruce (1870–1957) American book and TYPEFACE designer, born in Lafayette, Indiana. After studying art at Purdue University, Lafayette, he pursued a brief career as a newspaper and book illustrator. Moved to Boston as designer of *Modern Art* magazine, before joining the Riverside Press of the Houghton Mifflin Co. 1896–1912. After an early period designing within the tradition of the ARTS AND CRAFTS MOVEMENT, he acquired a profound understanding of earlier typographic styles. When the Press established a department for limited-edition volumes (1900), his 'allusive' skills at recreating the typographic achievements of 15th- and 16th-c. Europe flourished. His reputation as one of America's greatest book designers (along with Daniel Berkeley UPDIKE and Frederic GOUDY) is confirmed by many of the books he created after leaving the Riverside Press in 1912. Working as a freelance consultant he advised the great university presses, including Cambridge, Oxford and Harvard. His most famous typeface, Centaur (1914), a VENETIAN ROMAN based on Jenson's roman of 1470, was originally designed as a titling FONT for the Museum of Modern Art, New York. It first appeared in *The Centaur* (1915) a book designed by Rogers. Following an unsuccessful collaboration with Emery WALKER in London during the First World War, he returned to England in the late 1920s where he created his masterpiece, the *Oxford Lectern Bible* (1935), which was set in Centaur.

Title page, hand-lettered by **Rogers**, for Stanley Morison's *Fra Luca De Pacioli* (1933).

Röling's self-portrait for *Het Parool* newspaper, 1976.

Röling, Marte (b.1939) Dutch artist, illustrator and designer. Trained at the Academy of Fine Arts, Amsterdam, 1956–62, where her father, Professor G.V.A. Röling, was teaching. Her designs range from huge sculptures for public and private buildings to postage stamps for the Dutch Postal and Telecommunications company (PTT), album covers for Philips/Fontana, posters, book jackets, fashion illustration, video and design for the theatre. Her state portrait of Queen Beatrix of the Netherlands has received international acclaim. She explores a diverse range of materials including glass, plastics, wood, concrete, metal, textiles, paint and photographs. Since 1959 she has exhibited in a large number of solo and group shows, alongside artists like Picasso, Lichtenstein, Keinholz and Warhol. Member of AGI.

Roller, Alfred (1864–1935) Member of VIENNA SECESSION. Designed posters for Secession exhibitions and contributed to *Ver Sacrum*, the Secession's innovative magazine. Designed the cover for the first issue (January 1898). His densely textured style became increasingly rectilinear, reflecting the influence of the Glasgow Four. See Charles Rennie MACKINTOSH

ROM (Read Only Memory) Software program that controls the routine functions of a COMPUTER. Whilst the data can be accessed and read, there is no facility for modification by the user. When the program is contained in the form of a compact disc (CD) it is called CD/ROM. See RAM (RANDOM ACCESS MEMORY)

Roman (a) Generic term to describe a wide range of TYPEFACE designs with SERIF forms. Roman typefaces have evolved from four distinct stages of development: VENETIAN, based on the incunabula models favoured by the printers of Venice; OLD FACE of the 16th and 17th c.; TRANSITIONAL of the 18th c.; and MODERN of the 19th c. The past five hundred years have produced endless experimentation with the size and shape of the serif and the relationship between thick and thin strokes. There has been a shift from a diagonal STRESS to a vertical stress. A rich source for typographers, Roman typefaces of all periods remain in frequent use for much current design and advertising. Classic Roman typefaces include BASKERVILLE, BEMBO, BODONI, GARAMOND. (b) Also casually used as a term to describe a typeface in its standard 'vertical' form, distinct from the ITALIC or BOLD versions.

Poster for *Secession XVI*, 1903, by **Roller**.

Roman numerals Numerical notation system developed by the Romans. Based on a combination of symbols and CAPITAL LETTERS, the system was subsequently replaced by the simpler ARABIC NUMERALS.

I	1
II	2
III	3
IV	4
V	5
VI	6
VII	7
VIII	8
IX	9
X	10
L	50
C	100
D	500
M	1000

Now rarely used apart from chapter and section headings.

Rosenwald, Laurie (b.1955) American designer and illustrator. Trained at the Rhode Island School of Design, graduating in 1977. New York–based, Rosenwald emerged as a creative influence on the East Coast during the early 1980s. She established her own studio, working as a publications designer, illustrator and COLLAGE artist. Her clients have included the *New York Times*, *GQ* magazine, Swatch Watches, Virgin and Warner Brothers records. She has produced book jacket designs for Alfred A. Knopf, Little, Brown and Company, Chronicle Books. Exoding vitality and visual wit, her work featured in a one-person exhibition in Tokyo in 1986. Typographic consultant with Condé Nast 1983–88. Designed the Paris '89 campaign that celebrated one hundred years of the Eiffel Tower. Her shopping bag for Bloomingdale's is included in the permanent collection of the Museum of Modern Art, New York. Member of AIGA.

Rosetti, Dante Gabriel (1828–82) Born in London. Poet and painter who exercised a major influence on the cultural life of Victorian England. Studied painting at the Royal Academy, London, 1845–47, with additional drawing instruction from Ford Madox Brown and Holman Hunt. In 1848, along with a group including Hunt and John Everett Millais, founded the Pre-Raphaelite Brotherhood. Met William MORRIS and Edward BURNE-JONES in 1856, subsequently becoming a partner in their decorating co-operative Morris, Marshall, Faulkner & Co. (established 1861). Rossetti remained with the firm until 1875, designing stained

Rosenwald designed this poster to celebrate the 100th anniversary of the Eiffel Tower, as part of the Paris '89 bicentenary celebrations.

Poster for the ballet at Zurich opera house, 1975, by **Rüegg**.

glass, bindings and furniture. He was one of a number of artists commissioned to illustrate a distinguished production of *Lord Tennyson: Poems* (1857) published in London by Edward Moxon: he contributed five highly acclaimed allegorical illustrations.

Royal Designers for Industry (RDI) Founded in 1936 by the Royal Society of Arts, London, the Faculty of Royal Designers for Industry has conferred the title of RDI on many of Britain's most distinguished designers. Embracing all design disciplines, membership of the faculty is restricted to a hundred at any one time. The title of Honorary Royal Designer for Industry (Hon RDI) can be conferred on significant designers from abroad. In 1986 the Faculty held a fiftieth anniversary exhibition, 'Eye for Industry', at the Victoria and Albert Museum, London.

Ruder, Emil (1914–70) Swiss typographer, graphic designer and educator. After an early training as a compositor in Zurich 1929–33, he pursued his design studies in Paris 1938–39 and at the Kunstgewerbe-schule, Zurich 1941–42. Taught at the Allgemeine Gewerbeschule, Basle 1942–70, the last five years as director. Director of the Kunstgewerbemuseum, Basle 1965–70. His work and writings were a major influence on Swiss design, contributing substantially to the systematic rationale of the INTERNATIONAL TYPOGRAPHIC STYLE. Using the GRID to unify disparate typographic elements, he stressed that clear typographic legibility was essential to effective visual communication. This philosophy was articulated further in *Typographie* (1967), his seminal design manual. An advocate of SANS SERIF letterforms, he initially demonstrated the design potential of UNIVERS in an important article in the professional journal *TM* (*Typografische Monatsblätter*, or *Typography Monthly*) in 1961.

Rüegg, Ruedi (b. 1936) Swiss designer and typographer educated at the Kunstgewerbeschule, Zurich 1959–62. Worked in Europe and America with the design masters Josef MÜLLER-BROCKMANN 1960–63, 1965–67 and Paul RAND 1963–64. In Japan he was a designer at the Nakamoto International Agency, Osaka 1964–65. Rüegg's output for advertising, corporate schemes, posters, books and exhibitions reflects a rational, functional Swiss ethic, enlivened by a lyrical use of type. Co-founder and a principal of the advertising and design agency Baltis & Rüegg 1977–89. In 1989 he established Buro Ruedi Rüegg. Since 1968, visiting professor at Ohio State University. Member of AGI and president of the AGI in Switzerland 1976–81.

Cover of **Ruder**'s design manual *Typographie* (1967).

'Stars in Motion' symbol for the 1984 Los Angeles Olympic Games, designed by **Runyan**.

Runyan, Robert Miles (b. 1925) American graphic designer and, since 1962, a principal of the Los Angeles practice Robert Miles Runyan & Associates, which specializes in annual reports and CORPORATE IDENTITY programmes – he has brought a boldness to annual reports through his use of photography and arresting imagery. Created the official 'Stars in Motion' SYMBOL for the 1984 Los Angeles Olympic Games. His dramatic and disturbing poster for the 17th ASPEN INTERNATIONAL DESIGN CONFERENCE is now in the New York Museum of Modern Art collection. A retrospective exhibition of his work in Japan (1984–85) was accompanied by the publication of the book *State of the Art of Robert Miles Runyan*.

saddle-stitching

S

saddle-stitching *See* BINDING METHODS

Sagmeister, Stefan (b.1962) New York–based graphic designer. Born in Austria, Sagmeister studied at the Hochschule für Angewandte Kunst (Academy of Applied Arts), Vienna. Thereafter, won a Fulbright scholarship to the Pratt Institute, New York (1985). Subsequently worked in Hong Kong (with the Leo Burnett Agency) before returning to New York to work briefly with Tibor KALMAN. Established his studio, Sagmeister Inc. in New York (1993). Often collaborating with Icelandic designer Hjalti Karlsson, Sagmeister is renowned for his meticulous, at times subversive, CD cover designs for the music industry. His clients have included David Byrne, Pat Metheny and The Rolling Stones. Created the graphics for a campaign by the lobbying group Business Leaders for Sensible Priorities, which sought to persuade the US government to spend a small percentage of its military budget on social causes (1999). *Sagmeister: Made You Look* (Booth-Clibborn Editions, 2001) is a compendium of his work.

Album cover for *Set the Twilight Reeling* by Lou Reed, designed by **Sagmeister** in 1999.

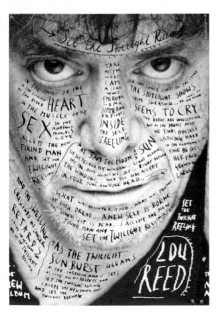

Sand, Michael van de *See* RAMBOW/LIENE-MEYER/VAN DE SAND

Sandberg, Willem (1897–1984) Dutch graphic and exhibition designer, influential in the design of museum publications and the presentation of contemporary art. Inspired by Piet ZWART and Hendrik WERKMAN, he was a post-Second World War practitioner of the NEW TYPOGRAPHY. Training at the State Academy of Art, Amsterdam, 1919–20, was followed in the late 1920s by a period studying psychology in Vienna, where Otto Neurath was developing ISOTYPE. Continued his psychology studies part-time in Utrecht and as assistant to F. Roels 1930–35. Began his design career in 1927 with calendars for the Ploegsma publishing company and the following year he was commissioned by the Stedelijk Museum to prepare pictorial statistical information for the exhibition 'Work for the Disabled'. Other pre-war clients included the Dutch Post Office (PTT), various government agencies and the publishers Nijgh en Van Ditmar. Appointed curator of modern art at the Stedelijk Museum, 1937–41. During the German occupation he worked with the Dutch resistance movement on the falsification of identity cards. Whilst in hiding he produced an explorative series of eighteen typographic works entitled *experimental typographica*, which were to inspire his later work. Director of the Stedelijk 1945–62 where he personally designed over three hundred catalogues and numerous posters. His bold work was characterized by asymmetrical layouts and contrasts of colour, texture and typographic scale. He had a particular liking for coarse, open-grained paper, large woodblock type and roughly torn letter forms, the latter often juxtaposed with crisp uniform type. Director of Fodor and Willet Museums, Amsterdam, 1949–62, and advisor for the building of cultural centres worldwide, including the Centre Georges Pompidou, Paris, and the Israel Museum, Jerusalem. Numerous awards include the Werkman Prize, Amsterdam, 1959 and the Erasmus Prize, Amsterdam, 1975.

ABCDEFGH
abcdefgh

News Gothic, a **sans serif** typeface.

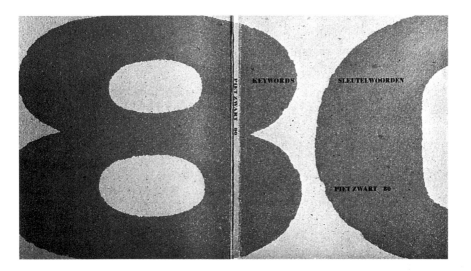

Sandberg's cover for *Keywords* (1966), a booklet that celebrated Piet Zwart's eightieth birthday.

Promotional poster for Air France (1956) by **Savignac**.

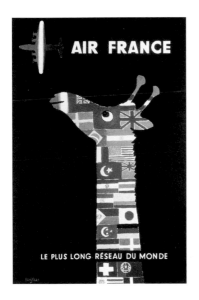

sans serif TYPEFACE characterized by letters without SERIF forms and with main strokes of consistent thickness.

Savignac, Raymond (b.1907) Parisian poster artist and cartoonist. Educated at the École Lavoisier, Paris. Met A.M. CASSANDRE c. 1935, collaborating with him for several years. His fluid style combined with an ability to convey a complex concept in a simple image brought him great success in the 1950s and 60s. Following a joint exhibition with his colleague Bernard VILLEMOT, Savignac sold his first major poster, *Mon Savon* (1949). His ensuing popularity enabled him to work for international organizations including Olivetti, Air France and UNICEF. His sharp humour has been used to great effect in support of social or political issues, such as his glowing 'thermal' cartoon figure for the French campaign to 'Utilisez le Coke' (1948) or his 1958 poster opposing an autoroute on the Left Bank in Paris. The powerful appeal of Savignac's work is confirmed by his nickname, 'l'homme de choc'.

Saville, Peter (b.1955) Graphic designer. Studied at Manchester Polytechnic, 1975–78. Established a design reputation within the British music industry, initially designing posters and album covers for the Manchester-based Factory Records. In 1979 became art director for Dindisc Records, a subsidiary of the Virgin Group. Winner of many awards during the early 1980s, his esoteric imagery and elegant typography led the *Los Angeles Times* to describe him as 'England's most influential rock graphics designer'. Along with the Canadian typographer Brett Wickens, founded Peter Saville Associates, London, 1983. Building on his music-industry reputation, he attracted a wide range of clients including London's Whitechapel Art Gallery, the fashion designer Yohji Yamamoto and the French Ministry of Culture. In October 1990 he disbanded his practice and joined the London Office of PENTAGRAM as a partner. Left Pentagram in 1993, thereafter working as an independent consultant in Europe and the US. In 1993 Saville moved to Los Angeles to become creative director at design agency Frankfurt Balkind. He returned to England in 1995 to set up a London office for German communications agency Meiré und Meiré, working for clients including ABC Television, Mandarina Duck, Christian Dior and the Swatch and Mercedes-Benz joint venture the Smart Car. In London Saville has also worked with photographer Nick Knight and the Barbican Arts Centre. He has acted as communications consultant to the facilities house The Mill (1999) and was appointed consultant to Selfridges & Co., the London department store (2000), to redesign its promotional magazine *Yellow*.

Front sleeve for *Coming Up* by Suede, designed by **Saville** in 1996.

Savoy, The An illustrated quarterly journal published by Leonard Smithers in London in January 1896. Aubrey BEARDSLEY was art editor. The first issue had contributions from George Bernard Shaw and Beardsley (featuring drawings for his own novel *Under the Hill*). The second issue reproduced his superbly decorative illustrations for *The Rape of the Lock*.

Renowned for its distinctive pink and black covers, *The Savoy* achieved excellent standards of editorial illustration during the eight volumes of its existence.

Scher, Paula (b.1948) New York–based graphic designer, educated at the Tyler School of Art, Philadelphia. During the 1970s, Scher art directed numerous record covers at Atlantic Records and CBS Records. The music industry provided opportunities for innovation and experimentation and Scher drew inspiration from her knowledge of 20th-c. art and design history, in particular Russian CONSTRUCTIVISM, FUTURISM and DADA. She also acknowledges the influence of Seymour CHWAST of PUSH PIN STUDIO in her playful appropriation of early letterforms. In 1984 she co-founded Koppel & Scher, in partnership with Terry Koppel. Joined PENTAGRAM as a principal (1991) where she has developed CORPORATE IDENTITIES, promotional literature, packaging and environmental graphics. She has taught at the New York School of Visual Arts and is a member of AGI. Scher's work is represented in numerous collections including New York's Museum of Modern Art, the Cooper-Hewitt, National Design Museum and the Centre Georges Pompidou, Paris.

Schleger, Hans (Zéró) (1898–1976) British poster, advertising and corporate designer. Born in Kempen, Germany. Trained at the Kunstgewerbeschule, Berlin, 1918–21, before becoming publicity and film set designer for Karl Hagenbeck, Berlin 1921–24. Moved to New York in 1924 where he contributed to the development of modern American advertising design. In 1926 established his own Madison Avenue studio, signing his work Zéró. Returned to Berlin 1929–32, working in the German office of W.S. Crawford advertising agency. Settled permanently in England in 1932, naturalized in 1938. His early poster design, particularly from the Second World War, was distinguished by wit and innovative techniques like PHOTOMONTAGE. His projects for design-conscious clients such as Shell and London Transport helped familiarize the public with the graphic design of MODERNISM. In 1935 he revised and refined the famous London Transport 'circle-and-bar' SYMBOL for use as a bus stop sign (see Edward JOHNSTON). Designed and contributed to the text of the influential book *The Practice of Design*, 1946. During the 1950s and 60s, along with F.H.K. HENRION, he pioneered CORPORATE IDENTITY in Britain, through his collaboration with the advertising agency Mather & Crowther and through Hans Schleger and Associates, founded in 1953.

Scher's poster for *Simpatico*, a play by Tom Shepard at The Public Theater, 1994.

Schleger (Zéró) designed this 1938 advertisement for Shell.

'The future belongs to Bauhaus wallpapers' is the slogan reflected in the metallic ball in this advertisement designed by Schmidt in 1931.

Produced enduring symbol designs for Sir Allen LANE, John Lewis Partnership, Design Centre, Finmar Furniture and the Edinburgh Festival. Member of AGI and an RDI. *Zero, Hans Schleger – A Life of Design*, by his partner and widow Pat Schleger, illustrates the diversity of his work and writings (2001).

Schmidt, Joost (1893–1948) German typographer, sculptor, advertising and exhibition designer at the BAUHAUS. Studied at the Academy, Weimar 1911–14. After military service and a period as a prisoner of war, he returned to the Bauhaus, Weimar, to study sculpture and typography (1919). His student poster for the 1923 Bauhaus exhibition reveals the influence of CONSTRUCTIVISM and DE STIJL. The school moved to Dessau in 1925 and he became head of the sculpture workshop and taught typography. In 1928 he succeeded BAYER as master of typography and graphic design. He was a pioneer of functional asymmetrical typography. Denounced as a 'cultural bolshevik' by the Nazis, he lost his studio in 1933. In 1945 he was appointed professor at the Hochschule für bildende Kunst, Berlin.

Schmoller, Hans (1916–85) German-born typographer and book designer. Apprenticed as a compositor at the book printing firm of Siegfried Scholem, Berlin 1933–37. Following a course in keyboarding and casting at the MONOTYPE Technical School, London, in 1937 he could neither return to a Germany ruled by Hitler, nor remain in England as an alien. Subsequently became assistant manager of the Morija Printing Works, a missionary press in Lesotho 1938–46. After becoming a naturalized British citizen he returned to England and joined the Curwen Press, Plaistow (see Harold CURWEN) as manager of the bindery and typographic assistant to the director, Oliver SIMON 1947–49. Designed many catalogues for the British Council and the Arts Council of Great Britain. Joined Penguin Books as a typographer in 1949, taking over from Jan TSCHICHOLD; became head of production (1956), a director 1960–76, and a consultant 1976–80 (see Sir Allen LANE). Developed the classical typographic standards in editorial style and typesetting established by Tschichold, he designed and supervised a number of major paperback series including *The Buildings of England* and *The Pelican History of Art*. *The Complete Pelican Shakespeare* (1969) demonstrates his mastery of typographically complex material and won a gold medal at the International Book Design Exhibition, Leipzig, 1971. President, DOUBLE CROWN CLUB, London 1968–69. Elected RDI, 1976.

Poster by **Schuitema**, 1932, urging support for the work of the General Dutch Union for Foreign Travel.

Pictogram figures form the roman numerals XXIII in **Schwartzman**'s symbol for the 1984 Los Angeles Olympics.

Schuitema, Paul (1897–1973) Graphic, exhibition and furniture designer, photographer, film maker, painter and teacher. Born in Groningen, Holland. Along with Piet ZWART, a pioneer of MODERNISM in DUTCH GRAPHIC DESIGN. Studied painting at the Academy of Art, Rotterdam 1915–20, with an interruption for military service, 1917–18. Turned to graphic design during the 1920s, working for the Berkel manufacturing company for whom he produced a unified design programme covering advertisements, booklets, stationery, exhibitions and a TRADEMARK. His powerful typographic design solutions relied solely upon the colours black, white and red and bold SANS SERIF type. He exploited the technique of overprinting and after 1926 photography and PHOTOMONTAGE became major devices in his work. Beginning in 1929 he made a series of three films dedicated to different aspects of movement. His other major clients included the Chevalier printing company, Philips and the Dutch Post Office (PTT). A committed socialist, he designed functionalist covers for left-wing books and magazines. Taught at the Royal Academy, The Hague 1930–62.

Schwartzman, Arnold (b.1936) Prolific graphic designer, illustrator and film maker. Born in London, he studied graphic design at Canterbury College of Art, Kent, 1953–55. For the first two decades of his career worked for British companies: Associated Rediffusion Television 1959–65 (producing graphics for the innovative pop show 'Ready, Steady, Go'), Erwin-Wasey Advertising 1965–68, Conran Design Group 1968–69 (as graphics director), then as a television commercials director with the Director's Studio, 1969–78. A restless, eclectic image-maker with an impressive repertoire of styles, he won three silver awards from the DESIGNERS AND ART DIRECTORS ASSOCIATION, London (1969, '71 and '75). Elected to AGI in 1974. Moved to US in 1978, becoming design director of Saul BASS Associates until 1979. Director of design for the 1984 Los Angeles Olympic Games 1982–83, since when he has been president of Arnold Schwartzman Productions, Hollywood, California. Awarded an Academy Award 'Oscar' for best documentary feature film, as producer, director and screenwriter of *Genocide* (1982).

Schwitters, Kurt (1887–1948) Artist, typographer and poet. Born in Hanover, Germany. From 1909–14 studied at the Academy of Dresden, followed by a brief period at the Academy in Berlin. He was a potent force in the development of German DADA, applying the principle of random choice to his Merz COLLAGE designs of ephemera and rubbish. First produced in 1919, these compositions enabled him to produce art from non-traditional art materials. In 1922 Schwitters took part in the International Congress of Constructivists and Dadaists in Weimar, a year later publishing the first issue of his famous Merz magazine. Featuring the work of progressive artists like Hans Arp, Théo van DOESBURG, Piet Mondrian, Man RAY, Walter GROPIUS, and El LISSITZKY, Merz ran for twenty-four issues up to 1932. Merz 11 (1924) featured typography in advertising. Throughout the 1920s he became increasingly influenced by the principles of CONSTRUCTIVISM, applying them to his art and his flourishing graphic design practice in Hanover. Along with Jan TSCHICHOLD and others formed the 'Ring neue Werbegestalter' (Circle of the New Advertising Typographer) in 1927. In 1929 worked as a typographer, under Gropius, on the Dammerstock modern housing exhibition in Karls-ruhe. Following persistent Nazi persecution he lost his post as advisor on typography and advertising to the City of Hanover in 1934. Three years later left Germany for Oslo, escaping to Scotland after the German invasion of Norway in 1940. Moved to the English Lake District in 1945, where he remained until his death.

screen printing Versatile printing process in which the image is created by forcing the printing ink through a fine screen of fabric or metal. A stencil of the image (coated manually or by photographic means) adheres to the surface of the screen, with the ink coming through the holes in the stencil on to the printed surface. Now capable of quality results at high speeds, screen printing evolved from the traditional 'silk screen' printing (serigraphy) favoured by fine art printmakers. Characterized by bright, opaque colours, screen printing can be applied to a wide range of surface textures e.g. paper, card, cloth, plastic and metal.

script Any TYPEFACE displaying the flowing curves and flourishes associated with handwriting.

Bernhard Cursive Bold, 1925, a **script** typeface.

section-sewn binding See BINDING METHODS

Schwitters' title pages from three issues of Merz magazine (January, April and July 1923).

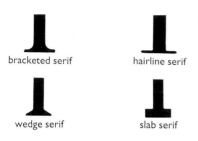

bracketed serif

hairline serif

wedge serif

slab serif

The four main types of **serif**.

Frederic Goudy's illustration of the space accorded to various letters in a **set** width.

S H A D E D

Shaded letters from the Gill Shadow Titling typeface.

serif Characteristic terminal stroke normally at the top and bottom of the main strokes of letters in a ROMAN TYPEFACE. There are four main types of serif: bracketed (e.g. TIMES NEW ROMAN), hairline (e.g. BODONI), slab (e.g. ROCKWELL), wedge (triangular shaped serifs used in the LATIN DISPLAY faces of the 19th c.).

set Measurement that indicates the relative width of a TYPEFACE. The 'set' width is determined by the widest character (normally a capital M or W), with all the other characters allocated a proportional unit of measurement.

Sezessionstil *See* VIENNA SECESSION

shaded letter (a) Alphabets given strong three-dimensional quality by use of heavy shadows on one side of main strokes. Shaded letters can either have SERIF forms or be SANS SERIF and often utilize the forms of OUTLINE LETTERS. (b) Letterforms that have the main strokes 'shaded' with horizontal or diagonal lines rather than solid.

Shahn, Ben (1898–1969) Artist, illustrator and letterer. Born in Lithuania of Jewish parents, moving to New York in 1906, where he trained in LITHOGRAPHY 1913–17. Thereafter travelled in Europe, returning to New York to work as a trade lithographer until c. 1930. His radical political beliefs underpinned his artistic activities. Ranging across fine and applied art, his social realist paintings and illustrations often attacked political and economic injustices in America. Produced two full-colour posters for the US Office of War Information in 1942. Many of America's leading magazines used his illustrations during the late 1940s and 50s, with William GOLDEN commissioning him to work on a number of advertising campaigns promoting CBS Television. A letterer of genius, he created unique brush and pen alphabets that reflect an understanding of different languages including Hebrew, Chinese and Japanese. Beautiful, irregular letterforms are used to convey a deeply personal response to language. His approach is superbly illustrated in *Love and Joy about Letters* (1964). Represented the US at the 1954 Venice Biennale.

side-stitching *See* BINDING METHODS

Poster by **Shahn** from the Container Corporation of America's 1950s and 60s campaign, 'Great Ideas of Western Man'.

signage Term for co-ordinated directional, instructional and information sign requirements associated with the urban environment, buildings and major events such as exhibitions. Signage is an integral component of many CORPORATE IDENTITY programmes.

silk screen process See SCREEN PRINTING

Silverstein, Louis (b.1919) Influential newspaper designer/journalist, renowned for his redesign of the *New York Times*. As assistant managing editor, his redesign evolved during the early 1970s, with many of his visual decisions being based on informed journalistic considerations. Head of the paper's promotion department since 1952, he utilized proven advertising techniques to transform the visual impact of the news and attract new readers. The design programme introduced a new page GRID, larger headlines, a stronger emphasis on photography, and more charts and maps. He pioneered the need for journalists and designers to overcome professional demarcation and work together on the presentation of news. His achievement is documented in the catalogue of an exhibition in New York at the Herb Lubalin Study Center of Design & Typography, *Louis Silverstein: Design and The New York Times 1952–86* (1988).

Simon, Oliver (1895–1956) British printer, book designer, typographer and writer who emphasized traditional skills and values in modern printing and typographic developments. Editor of *The FLEURON*, an influential review of historic and modern developments in typography, 1923–25. Founder member of the DOUBLE CROWN CLUB, London, in 1924. Editor and publisher of *Signature*, a publication devoted to the art and craft of printing, 1935–40 (a new series was published 1946–54). Enjoyed a long association with the Curwen Press, London, becoming chairman 1939–56 (see Harold CURWEN). Author of a classic text, *Introduction to Typography* (1945). His autobiography *Printer and Playground* was published in 1956.

slab serif Those TYPEFACE designs characterized by rectangular SERIF forms. The junction of the serif to the vertical can either be at right-angles (e.g. ROCKWELL) or bracketed (e.g. CLARENDON). See EGYPTIAN

small capitals Alternative set of capitals available with most TYPEFACE designs used for text setting. Smaller than standard capitals, they normally align with the alphabet's LOWER CASE X-HEIGHT.

SMALL CAPITALS

Two words beginning with full-size capitals and continuing with **small capitals**, all in the Garamond typeface.

Photograph produced by Man Ray in 1932 using **solarization**.

solarization Photographic technique that exposes a negative or print to an intense source of light during the development process to produce a partial reversal of 'normal' tonal values. Man RAY experimented with solarization techniques from the mid-1920s.

Solomon, Barbara Stauffacher (b.1932) Trained initially as a painter at the San Francisco Art Institute before moving to Switzerland to study design at the Basle Kunstgewerbeschule, 1957–61. Embracing the Swiss approach to design, she assimilated the geometric discipline associated with the INTERNATIONAL TYPOGRAPHIC STYLE. Worked briefly in Europe and New York before returning to San Francisco in 1962 to establish a design practice. Until the early 1970s she worked on a wide range of large-scale interior and exterior commissions from architects and landscape architects. Her architectural 'supergraphics' with their distinctive use of colour, strong diagonals and huge HELVETICA letterforms add drama to interiors, SIGNAGE, public spaces and exhibitions. Early commissions for the architect Charles Moore's Sea Ranch

The Sea Ranch Supergraphics interior, designed by **Solomon** for the Sea Ranch swim club in 1966.

Cover of The Penrose Annual, vol. 57, designed by **Spencer** (1964).

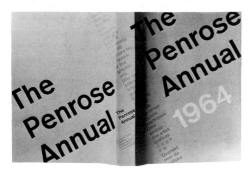

Still from Typemovie by Erik **Spiekermann**, designed for the Glasgow 1999 festival.

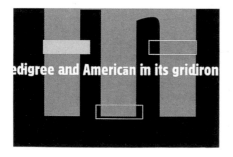

housing project in northern California and for Ghirardelli Square, San Francisco are of particular note. Increasingly involved as a landscape designer, her concern for the environment is outlined in her Green Architecture and Agrarian Gardens (1988).

Spencer, Herbert (1924–2002)

Typographic designer, photographer, author and educator, born in London. His major achievement from the early 1950s onwards has been the introduction of 'modern' European typographic developments to Britain. An admirer of Jan TSCHICHOLD, he encouraged an emerging generation of typographers and printers to explore new ways of presenting typographic information. Worked for London Typographical Designers 1946–47. Established his own practice in 1948 and thereafter pursued a diverse and productive career. Taught at the Central School of Arts and Crafts, London, 1949–55. Founded Typographica, a typography journal in 1949, editing it up to its demise in 1967. He began a long association with the printers Lund Humphries in 1950, becoming a director of their publishing division (1969) and design consultant up to 1975. Editor of the PENROSE ANNUAL 1964–73. Senior research fellow in charge of the Readability of Print Research Unit at the Royal College of Art, London, 1966–78, then professor of graphic arts 1978–85. His books, which have influenced generations of typographers, include Design in Business Printing (1952), The Visible Word (1969) (a research project in association with the RCA on the legibility of print) and Pioneers of Modern Typography (1969). International president of AGI 1971–74. Master of the Faculty of RDI 1979–81.

Spiekermann, Erik (b.1947) German typographer

and TYPEFACE designer. Studied English and Art History at Berlin University. Moved to England in 1973, teaching typography at the London College of Printing. Worked as a freelance designer in London throughout the 1970s, collaborating with consultancies like WOLFF OLINS and HENRION Design Associates. An advocate of computerized typesetting systems, he is a perceptive commentator on the changing relationship between the designer and new technologies. In addition to redrawing a number of existing text typefaces for the type manufacturer Berthold, Spiekermann is increasingly involved in creating typefaces for the APPLE MACINTOSH, including Meta, an elegant SANS SERIF available in three weights. Some of his typefaces have been specifically designed as components of CORPORATE IDENTITY programmes. A witty writer on typographic practice, his satirical Rhyme &

Reason – A Typographic Novel was published in 1982. Founder and principal of MetaDesign, Berlin, San Francisco and London (1983–2000), a consultancy specializing in corporate, information and web design. In the late 1980s he opened FontShop, Berlin, a mail-order company supplying typeface designs for PostScript printers. This was expanded into an international operation, with partners including Neville BRODY in London, Roger Black in the US and Ed Cleary in Canada.

Stankiewicz, Eugeniusz (b. 1942)
Born in Oszmiana, he studied architecture, then fine art at the Art Academy, Wroclaw, Poland. A versatile practitioner: his output ranges over posters, painting, silk screen prints, engraving and stage design. Committed to the production of posters with a radical social or political message, Stankiewicz and his partner from the late 1960s, Jan Jaromir ALEKSIUN, have contributed to a renaissance of Polish poster art. Many of his threatening images make an aggressive demand on the viewer's attention. A superb draughtsman, he is particularly adept at combining extravagant calligraphy with his meticulous illustrations. Awarded second prize at the Poster Biennale, Warsaw, 1975 for an innovative poster promoting the play *Exodus*. (The poster was in ten parts, which were assembled to form a cross, with the naked figure of a woman on one side and a man on the other.)

Stankowski, Anton (1906–98) German painter and graphic designer. His practice as a painter, particularly his explorations of colour and form, informs his solutions as a designer. Important in the field of CORPORATE IDENTITY where he was masterful at creating a visual symbol to communicate unseen scientific forces or processes. After an apprenticeship as a church decorator in Düsseldorf, 1921–26, he studied under Max Burchartz at the Folkwangschule, Essen, 1927–29. During the 1930s worked in Zurich and Stuttgart, exploring CONSTRUCTIVISM and BAUHAUS vocabulary and experimenting with photographic imagery including PHOTOMONTAGE. After wartime military service and a period as a prisoner of war, he returned to Stuttgart to become responsible for the layout and typography of the acclaimed picture magazine *Stuttgarter Illustrierte* 1949–51. During the 1950s and 60s he pioneered corporate design programmes for clients such as Standard Elektrik, Pausa AG and IBM. Commissioned by the city of Berlin in the late 1960s to develop a civic identity embracing printed publicity, architectural and street SIGNAGE; his solution included

the consistent use in publications of a long horizontal line with a short vertical rising from it – a symbol for a Berlin divided by the wall. Joined Karl Duschek and O.S. Rechenauer in the design practice Stankowski + Partner from 1970. He chaired the committee responsible for the visual design of the 1972 Munich Olympic Games. Numerous awards and retrospective exhibitions in Europe and America. In 1985 the Anton Stankowski Foundation and Prize was established in Stuttgart. Member of AGI.

Poster for a jazz concert by **Stankiewicz**, 1980.

Symbol for Deutsche Bank by **Stankowski**, 1974.

Starowieyski

Poster designed in 1970 by **Starowieyski** publicizing two plays by Harold Pinter, *The Lover* and *A Slight Ache*.

Steinlen produced this advertising poster for sterilized milk in 1894.

Starowieyski, Franciszek (Jan Byk) (b.1930)
Polish poster artist, book, stage and film set designer. Born in Krakow where he studied painting and graphic design at the School of Arts & Crafts 1949–52, and at the Academy of Art, Warsaw 1952–55. He was a major contributor to the group of designers that emerged during the 1960s with a determination to revitalize the waning Polish poster tradition. Along with Roman CIESLEWICZ, Waldemar SWIERZY and Jan LENICA he brought a new social and political awareness to poster imagery. His technically superb work displays an unsettling pathos resulting from a bizarre vision, as in his *Oni* (They) theatre poster, *c.*1983. A freelance poster artist from 1958, he has also tackled a diverse range of projects including books, calligraphy, murals, and sets for film, stage and television productions. Since 1974 he has been regularly invited to work in New York with the Kosciusko Foundation. A consistent winner of international awards, he is a member of AGI.

Steinberg, Saul (1914–99) Cartoonist. Born near Bucharest, Romania. During the early 1930s he studied sociology and psychology at the University of Bucharest and architecture at the University of Milan. Emigrated to US in 1941, naturalized 1943. For five decades his acerbic drawings have reflected and criticized the mores of contemporary America. An outstanding draughtsman, the linear tautness and variety of his drawings make them instantly recognizable. Since 1941, he has worked for *The New Yorker* magazine, also contributing to a great variety of periodicals and books worldwide. His own publications include *The Art of Living* (1949), *The Passport* (1954), *The Labyrinth* (1960), and *The Inspector* (1973). In 1978 the Whitney Museum, New York organized a major travelling retrospective of his work. Increasingly involved in the practice of fine art.

Steinlen, Théophile-Alexandre (1859–1923)
Swiss poster designer and illustrator. Born in Lausanne, he began his studies in Paris *c.*1881. Quickly established as a leading Parisian realist illustrator whose work offered radical comment upon poverty and the working classes. Responsible for a vast number of book, magazine and music sheet covers and posters. In 1885 he produced his first coloured posters, many printed by CHROMOLITHOGRAPHY. His dramatic, sensitively illustrated posters of the 1890s enjoyed a popularity that matched those by contemporaries like Jules CHÉRET, Georges AURIOL and Eugène GRASSET. Prolific throughout his career, towards the

end of his life he produced haunting posters highlighting the need for war relief in the aftermath of the First World War.

Stoecklin, Niklaus (1896–1982) Swiss poster artist, postage stamp designer, painter and printmaker. Trained at the Kunstgewerbeschule, Munich, before returning to his home town of Basle to continue his studies at the Allgemeine Gewerbeschule. His super-realist posters of the 1930s and 40s are characterized by a single, beautifully composed illustration, with lettering featuring only as an integral element on the drawing of the product. Striking for their simplicity and strength, his posters are forerunners of the photographic objectivity favoured by the succeeding generation of Swiss designers including Josef MÜLLER-BROCKMANN and Armin HOFMANN. A consistent winner in the Swiss best poster of the year award (1941, '42 and '45) he also designed a range of elegant stamps for the Swiss Postal Service.

Stone, Reynolds (1909–79) English designer-craftsman with a prolific output in the fields of lettering, book design and WOOD ENGRAVING. Studied history at Cambridge University, 1926–30. Apprenticed as a type compositor at the Cambridge University Press 1930–32, working within a typographic discipline influenced by Stanley MORISON. During this period he spent time with Eric GILL acquiring the fundamental skills of wood engraving. Became a freelance typographer and book designer from 1934. Major design achievements include: Victory commemorative stamp for the British Post Office (1946), £5 banknote for the Royal Mint (1961), lettering for many leading UK publishers, the TYPEFACE Minerva for LINOTYPE (1954), and the stone memorial tablet for Sir Winston Churchill at Westminster Abbey. For over forty years his superlative wood-engraved illustrations of the English countryside pursued a tradition developed by Thomas Bewick in the 18th c. Elected RDI in 1956.

Storch, Otto (b.1913) American art director and photographer. Educated in New York, working in the early 1930s as assistant art director at Dell Publishing. Took lessons in art direction from Alexey BRODOVITCH and on his advice left Dell to become a freelance designer. After the Second World War he joined the McCall's Corporation, working on *Better Living Magazine* as an assistant art director. In 1953 he was appointed art director of *McCall's*, the women's magazine. His reputation rests on his redesign of *McCall's* (1958) and his meticulous art direction of the

Poster for PKZ, men's outfitters (1934), by **Stoecklin**.

Wood-engraved frontispiece designed by **Stone** for Penguin Books, 1951.

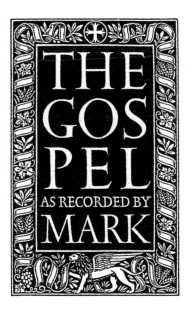

magazine over fifteen years. His innovative approach included powerful typography, provocative photography and illustration with images startlingly positioned on the page. One of a distinguished group of American art directors of the 1950s and 60s (including Bradbury THOMPSON, Henry WOLF, Allen HURLBURT and Leo LIONNI), he resigned from *McCall's* in 1967 to work as an editorial and advertising photographer.

stress The thicker parts of curved letters in a ROMAN alphabet are angled in a distinctive and discernible direction. This angle of stress, or shading, varies from the oblique (sloping diagonally to the left or right), e.g. BEMBO, to the vertical, e.g. BODONI.

Studio, The (1893–1988) Periodical of the fine and applied arts first published in London. Influential in promoting an international understanding of ART NOUVEAU, the first issue featured a cover by Aubrey BEARDSLEY. Gleeson White, the editor appointed to replace the founding editor C. Lewis Hind, gave *The Studio* a strong sense of direction with articles by and on Jan TOOROP, Walter CRANE, Liberty & Co., Christopher Dresser, Charles Voysey and Charles Rennie MACKINTOSH, etc. An American version was published from 1897. Special issues featuring specific aspects of the graphic arts were published regularly up to 1939. In the 1960s as *Studio International* it reasserted itself as a progressive magazine.

Suprematism Russian art movement created by the painter Kasimir Malevich (1878–1935) in *c.*1915. Evolving from Malevich's earlier support for FUTURISM and CUBISM, Suprematism espoused the expressive qualities of abstract, geometric shapes and pure colour. Suprematism's 'art for art's sake' philosophy provided a direct counterpoint to the utilitarian ethos of emergent CONSTRUCTIVISM.

Surrealism Art movement founded in Paris in 1924 by André Breton (1896–1966). Emerging from the aftermath of DADA, it challenged accepted concepts of the normal and rational. Attracted to the imaginative potential of dreams and the unconscious, Surrealists attached great significance to the theories of the psychoanalyst, Sigmund Freud. Surrealist imagery was diverse and included the organic forms favoured by Joan Miró and Hans Arp, the fantastic juxtapositions perfected by Salvador Dali and René Magritte, the COLLAGE designs of Max Ernst and the haunting photographs of Man RAY. The potency of Surrealist thinking had a positive and liberating effect on artists and writers; its fantasy and wit are evident in many current advertising campaigns, book jackets, record covers and animated films.

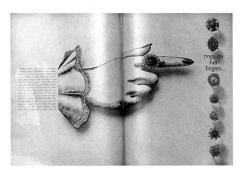

Double-page spread from *McCall's* magazine (1961) by **Storch**.

Angles of **stress** in capital letters from the Bembo and Bauer Bodoni typefaces.

Bembo   Bauer Bodoni

Cover of the first issue of *The Studio* (1893).

Sussman, Deborah (b.1931) American graphic designer, renowned for colourful environmental graphics applied to large architectural projects and public spaces. Studied in New York at Bard College, Annandale-on-Hudson 1948–50 and at the Institute of Design, Chicago, 1950–53. During the 1950s and 60s she produced publicity, packaging, exhibitions and films for the furniture designers Charles and Ray Eames. Established her own studio in 1968, which in 1980 evolved into Sussman/Prejza & Co., to include her husband Paul Prejza. The practice has developed visual identity programmes for department stores and large complexes including the Crocker (now the Wells Fargo) Center, Los Angeles. Achieved international recognition with the environmental graphics for the 1984 Los Angeles Olympics.

Sutnar, Ladislav (1897–1976) Czech-born graphic and exhibition designer, educator and writer, an important design innovator in both Europe and America. After training in Prague, he taught at the State School of Graphic Arts, Prague 1923–36, becoming director in 1929. Joined the publishing house of Družstevní Práce as design director 1929–39. An early interest in painting and stage design developed into the design of exhibitions during the 1930s. Travelled to America in 1939 as exhibition designer for the Czech Pavilion at the New York World's Fair; with the political crisis in Europe deepening, he decided to remain. A two-decade association with Sweet's Catalog Service resulted in the design of *Sweet's Files*, annual catalogues of architectural and industrial products conveying complex technical information. He structured this information in a rational, systematic manner using the GRID, SANS SERIF types, colour, contrast and lines to produce functional design solutions that allowed an accessible flow of information. His methods foreshadowed develop-

ments in 'information graphics' during the 1970s. He also produced early CORPORATE IDENTITY programmes, as in his work for Addox Business Machines. An important commentator on design, his books include *Package Design: The Force of Visual Selling* (1953), and *Visual Design in Action: Principles, Purposes* (1961).

swash characters Those ITALIC characters with extravagant calligraphic flourishes. Available in UPPER CASE and LOWER CASE, they provide decorative possibilities when combined with standard ROMAN or italic characters.

Jan van Krimpen designed these **swash characters**, part of the Lutetia Swash Caps typeface, in 1925.

Poster for the Thirteenth International Festival of Contemporary Music in Warsaw, September 1969, by **Swierzy**.

Sutnar's symbol for the technical annuals *Sweet's Files* (1942).

Swierzy, Waldemar (b.1931) Polish poster designer, illustrator and educator. Studied at the Krakow Academy of Fine Arts 1947–51, before moving to Warsaw in 1952. His mastery of painterly techniques, combined with a remarkable sensitivity to changing styles, has been applied to over 1,500 posters covering cultural, political and social themes. Since the mid-

1950s Swierzy (along with Roman CIESLEWICZ) has contributed to a new sense of direction in the renowned Polish poster tradition. Endlessly inventive in his representation of the human head, his work has featured in many exhibitions throughout the world. Since 1965 he has taught at the School of Fine Arts, Poznan. In 1978 he was appointed president of the Warsaw Biennale. Member of AGI.

Swift, Ian (b.1965) British designer, known as Swifty, specializing in typography and magazine design. After studying graphic design at the former Manchester Polytechnic, UK (1983–86) became assistant to Neville BRODY in London. Worked on *The Face* and *Arena* magazines before designing and art directing the British jazz-fusion magazine *Straight No Chaser* (1989). Swifty's flyers and covers for the jazz and club scenes (particularly his graphic s for the label Talkin Loud in the early 1990s) combine inventive typography, discordant colours and a profound understanding of American and European graphic styles of the 1950s and 60s. Established Swifty Typografix, London (1990). He is increasingly involved in the production of digitized versions of his customized fonts and the application of his typographic skills to mainstream advertising projects.

Swiss Style/Swiss graphic design
See INTERNATIONAL TYPOGRAPHIC STYLE

symbol Letter or sign designed to represent an activity, idea or object. Symbols can be pictorial or abstract and can be used within a cultural, social, political or commercial context. Effective symbols work across national boundaries, e.g. Otto Neurath's ISOTYPE system, and Otl AICHER's symbols for the 1972 Munich Olympic Games. See LOGOTYPE, PICTOGRAM, TRADEMARK

symmetric typography Traditional typographic style evolved over past centuries with each line centred on the central axis of the page. The relative importance of each line is emphasized by its position on the page combined with the weight and size of type selected. See ASYMMETRIC TYPOGRAPHY

T

tabular work Typesetting in the form of tables or columns of statistical information.

Talbot, William Henry Fox (1800–77) English pioneer of photography. Inventor of the photogenic drawing (1833) – a negative image that was produced when an object such as a piece of lace or a leaf was sandwiched between light-sensitive paper and glass, and then exposed to light. In 1839 he contact-printed the negative on to light-sensitive paper to create a positive image, making reproduction possible. He adapted his photogenic drawing technique for use in a camera, inventing a photographic process known as calotype in 1840 (talbotype). Talbot's book *The Pencil of Nature* (1844) was a landmark in publishing, being the first volume to be illustrated with photographs. *See* DAGUERROTYPE

Tanaka, Ikko (1930–2002) Japanese graphic and exhibition designer. Creator of sensitively coloured, clear design solutions which are characteristically Japanese while nevertheless acknowledging the vocabulary of European MODERNISM. Graduated from the City College of Fine Arts in Kyoto in 1950 before joining the Kenegafuchi Spinning Mills as a textile designer 1950–52. Graphic designer with Sankei Press 1952–57 and later with the Nippon Design Centre, Tokyo 1960–63, where he was largely engaged in automobile advertising. Established Tanaka Design Atelier 1963–76, since when he has been principal of Ikko Tanaka Design Studio, Tokyo. Inspired by the illustrations of Yoshio Hayakawa and by a passion for American jazz, he is responsible for numerous cultural posters and programmes for theatre and ballet, many for Kanze Noh Drama. In 1982 he designed an outstanding series of environmental posters for a campaign organized by *Asahi Journal*. Co-editor of *Japanese Coloring* (1982) which attempts to define a specifically Japanese attitude to colour. Has exhibited in Europe, America and Japan. Elected to the ART DIRECTORS CLUB OF NEW YORK Hall of Fame (1994). *Tanaka Ikko: Graphic Master* (1998) documents and contextualizes his work within the history of Japanese graphic design. Member of AGI.

Tattersfield, Brian
See MINALE, TATTERSFIELD & PARTNERS

Taylor, Fred (1875–1963) British poster artist, decorator and watercolourist. Studied briefly at Goldsmith's College, London where he was awarded a gold medal for his posters and a scholarship to study in Italy. He designed numerous fine posters for shipping and railway companies, particularly the London and North Eastern Railway and London Underground. His elegant and elaborate designs, which frequently refer to architectural subjects, are executed with outstanding draughtsmanship and subtly balanced colouring. As a decorator he is remembered for his ceiling paintings for the former Underwriting Room at Lloyd's, London, and murals for Austin Reed's Red Lacquer Room (1930).

Teige, Karel (1900–1951) Born in the former Czechoslovakia, Teige was a book designer and writer who during the 1920s and 30s was a zealous exponent of international MODERNISM. Untrained as a designer, Teige was convinced that the amateur practitioner brought innovation and experimentation to artistic activity. Leader of Devetsil (meaning 'nine forces'), a group of avant-garde artists, poets, architects, designers, musicians, dancers, who were enthusiastic about the new socialist order. Devetsil was founded in Prague in 1920 and grew to comprise some eighty members. Poetry was a core inspiration for the group. In 1924 Teige produced his manifesto *Poetism*. Between 1922 and 1938 he designed some hundred books and magazines that demonstrate his many evolving styles – the abstract elemental forms of CONSTRUCTIVISM, expressive typography, collage, montage and photographic images from silent movies. Teige believed that an accepted universal language of design would serve to ease the cultural divisions between capitalist America and communism in the former Soviet Union. In 1927 he wrote a typographic manifesto that proposed a standardized and rational approach to the design of books, intended to improve accessibility. He experimented with new letterforms, one of which was a version of Herbert BAYER's Universal TYPEFACE. Teige edited a number of magazines, such as *Disk*, *ReD*, *Stavba* and *Zeme Sovetu*. After the 1948 communist putsch, he lost favour with state authorities. Condemned for his cosmopolitanism, he was prevented from pursuing his activities as a designer or writer.

Telingater, Solomon (1903–69) Graphic designer and typographer. A champion of Russian CONSTRUCTIVISM during the 1920s and 30s. His typographical designs for books and posters and his PHOTOMONTAGE

Tanaka's poster for the Asian Performing Arts Institute 1981 tour.

London Transport poster from 1913, by **Taylor**.

Front and back covers for *Slovo Predostaliaetsia Kirsanova* (1930) by K. Kirsanov, designed by **Telingater**.

Barry Deck's typeface **Template Gothic**, 1990.

ABCDEFGHIJKLM
NOPQRSTUVWXYZ
abcdefghijklm
nopqrstuvwxyz

designs are witty and energetic, betraying the influence of DADA. Trained in Baku 1919–20 and at the Vkhutemas, Moscow 1920–21. He practised in Moscow from 1925, designing for printing houses and gaining a comprehensive knowledge of book production. Art director of the Communist Party publishing house, Partizdat 1933–41, which was awarded a gold medal for book design in the International Exhibition, Paris 1937. His respect for letterforms and the Russian printing tradition is evident in his highly successful TYPEFACE design Telingater's Job Work Type (1963), based on a handwritten Cyrillic script. Awarded the Gutenberg Prize in Leipzig, 1963.

Template Gothic Digitally created sans-serif typeface designed by Barry DECK in 1990, which rejects the regularity and predictability of traditional forms of typeface design. Inspired by the naivety of a stencilled sign in a local laundrette, this POST-MODERN typeface is characterized by inconsistent stroke width, variations of weight and a deliberate degradation of form, acknowledging the 'destructive ravages of photo-mechanical reproduction'.

Testa, Armando (1917–92) Graphic and advertising designer, a master of the Italian advertising poster. Photographer with the Italian Air Force 1940–43. His involvement with avant-garde art continually informs his graphic design practice. In 1937 he gained the first of many awards in poster competitions, for an abstract poster for the ICI printing ink company. In 1946 he founded the Armando Testa S.p.A advertising agency, which became one of Italy's largest agencies. His posters are dramatic, often surreal, with image taking primacy over text as he playfully juxtaposes incongruous elements. Designer of the official poster for the 1960 Rome Olympic Games. In 1962 he created Paulista and Papalla, animated plaster puppets for television. Awarded first prize in the Warsaw Poster Biennale, 1970, for his Plast 72 plastics exhibition poster, the first commercial poster to win this coveted award. In 1968 the Italian Ministry of Culture awarded Testa a gold medal for his important contribution to the visual arts.

Thompson, Bradbury (1911–96) Distinguished American graphic designer and art director. Born in Topeka, Kansas, where he graduated from Washburn College in 1934. After a period as art director with Capper Publishers 1934–38, he moved to New York. Designer and editor of *Westvaco Inspirations*, the arts journal of the West Virginia Pulp and Paper Company

Testa's 1954 Pirelli poster.

Bradbury **Thompson** produced this advertisement for the West Virginia Pulp and Paper Company.

Letters from the **Times New Roman** typeface.

ABCDEFGH
abcdefgh

1938–62. Thompson experimented with photographic reproduction, typography and colour, adopting an eclectic approach that combined the best of traditional design and MODERNISM. In 1958 he began designing the exemplary American Classic Book Series for Westvaco, a limited-edition series for distribution as a Christmas gift to customers. During the Second World War he was art director of the US Office of War Information. Post-war he became a freelance designer in New York working as art director of *Mademoiselle*, 1945–59, design director of *Art News* 1945–72, and also designing the formats of numerous other magazines, including *Smithsonian*. A prolific designer of over a hundred US postage stamps. In 1969 he began creating the beautiful *Washburn College Bible* (1982-83), which he illustrated with masterpieces of religious painting – the text is set RANGED LEFT/RAGGED RIGHT in phrase length lines, emphasizing the rhythm of the language. An inspirational teacher, he was visiting critic at Yale School of Art and Architecture, New Haven from 1956. Recipient of many honours from the ART DIRECTORS CLUB OF NEW YORK and AIGA. Member of AIGA and AGI.

Thompson, J. Walter One of the earliest American advertising agencies. Founded in New York in 1864, the company originated as a newspaper 'space' brokerage, buying white space at a discount rate from newspapers to resell to advertisers. By the mid-1880s JWT, like other major agencies at that time (see N.W. AYER & SON), extended their space-buying activities into a comprehensive service including design, copywriting and production. JWT was a major contributor to the development of Madison Avenue, New York, as the creative centre of world advertising. Growing dramatically after the Second World War, it became the biggest agency in the world in the 1960s and 70s. Part of the British owned WPP Communications conglomerate from 1987.

Times New Roman Popular ROMAN TYPEFACE, commissioned from MONOTYPE by *The Times* newspaper, London in 1931. Designed with short ASCENDER and DESCENDER forms to save space, its production was supervised by Stanley MORISON. Used exclusively by *The Times* for its first year of production, the Times New Roman family was made available to the printing trade in 1933, on a range of type-composing systems.

Tissi, Rosmarie *See* ODERMATT & TISSI

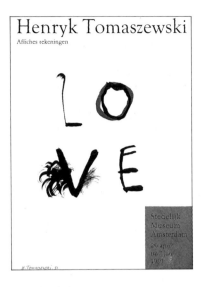

Henryk Tomaszewski
Affiches tekeningen

Tomaszewski created this advertisement for an exhibition of his posters and drawings, April–June 1991.

Image by **Tomato**, taken from their monograph *Process*, 1997.

Tomaszewski, Henryk (b.1914) Polish poster designer, illustrator and educator. Studied at the Academy of Fine Arts, Warsaw, 1934–39. Established himself as a freelance designer in Warsaw immediately after the Second World War. Since then he has emerged as the major influence on the celebrated Polish poster school. Acclaimed for the acerbic wit and potent simplicity of his imagery, he has produced political and cultural posters, book jackets, children's book illustrations, satirical illustrations and stage designs. His prolificacy and domination of Polish graphic design since the 1950s has been confirmed by many international exhibitions. In addition to numerous prizes at the Warsaw Poster Biennales, he was awarded first prize at the 1963 São Paulo Biennale and a gold medal at the 1965 Leipzig Book Fair. His preeminence as a practitioner is matched by his contribution to education as professor of graphic design at the Academy of Fine Arts, Warsaw, since 1955. Succeeding generations of Polish designers have benefited from his guidance, with his renowned work attracting many overseas admirers, including the original founders of the French group GRAPUS and the British-born illustrator Andrzej KLIMOWSKI. Elected Hon RDI London, 1975. Member of AGI.

Tomato London-based multidisciplinary studio and creative collective of designers, writers, typographers, film makers and musicians. Established in 1991, by Steve Baker, Dirk van Dooren, Karl Hyde, Richard Smith, Simon Taylor, John Warwicker and Graham Wood. Jason Kedgley joined in 1994 and Michael Horsham in 1996. Members of the collective are also part of the band Underworld. The studio quickly attracted an international reputation for its ability to generate expressive and emotional imagery across such a diverse range of media as print, film and television. In addition, Tomato is active in such areas as architecture, the fashion brand UACT, product design and exhibition work. Tomato's book projects include *mmm . . . skyscraper, I love you* (1994, Booth-Clibborn Editions), *Process* (1997, Thames & Hudson), *Bareback* (1999, Laurence King Publishing) and *Tycho's Nova* (Tomato/Gingko Press, 2001).

Toorn, Jan van (b.1932) Radical Dutch graphic and exhibition designer whose work offers a critique of the social and aesthetic influences underpinning mainstream graphic design. Trained in Amsterdam where he has freelanced since 1957. He has enjoyed important collaborations with several, mainly public sector, organizations. He produced posters, cata-

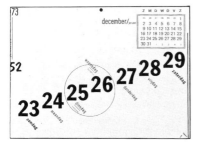

Pages from a 1973 calendar for the Dutch printer Mart. Spruyt, designed by van **Toorn**.

Poster for Delftsche Slaolie salad dressing by **Toorop**, 1895.

logues and exhibitions for Stedelijk van Abbemuseum in Eindhoven 1967–73, which rejected a glossy, rational house style in favour of a challenging informality, often relying on hand- or type-written texts and cheap paper. During the 1960s and 70s he designed sharply critical calendars for the printer Mart. Spruyt, Amsterdam, which focused on contemporary attitudes and events. His work for the Dutch Post Office (PTT) includes posters, reports and outstanding postage stamps that exploit cropped photography and dynamic typography. From 1980–88 he produced a series of posters for the De Beyerd visual arts centre, Breda, which all incorporate the same iconoclastic image of Sophia Loren and her son. During the 1980s he became increasingly involved with education, teaching in Holland and America. Appointed director of the Jan van Eyck Academy, Maastricht 1991. Member of AGI.

Toorop, Jan (1858–1928) Leading Dutch Symbolist painter, poster artist and illustrator. Born in Java of Norwegian and Oriental parents, his extravagant style was influenced by Aubrey BEARDSLEY and William MORRIS. Popular illustrator whose work appeared in ART NOUVEAU magazines of the period including *The STUDIO* and the Belgian arts journal *Van Nu en Straks*. His poster for the salad dressing Delftsche Slaolie (1895), with its flowing lines and dense repetition of patterns, contributed to the growing popularity of Belgian Art Nouveau.

Torrent, Pere See PERET

Total Design Influential multidisciplinary group founded in Holland in 1963. The original five partners included the graphic designers Wim CROUWEL and Benno Wissing and the industrial designer Friso Kramer. Renowned for their functionalist ethos and early commitment to the INTERNATIONAL TYPOGRAPHIC STYLE, Total designers were skilled at handling complex information design projects. During the 1960s they designed the innovative SIGNAGE scheme for Schiphol Airport, Amsterdam, a major CORPORATE IDENTITY for PAM Petrol, and posters and catalogues for the Stedelijk Museum. Crouwel remained with Total up to the mid-1980s, the other founding partners leaving earlier to pursue their own interests. The systematic approach of Total enabled the group to collaborate with Studio DUMBAR during the late 1970s and early 80s on the design of the corporate identity for the Dutch Post Office (PTT). In the last decade Total has favoured a more pluralistic design

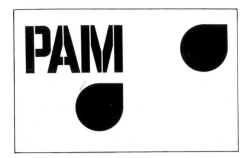

Logotype for PAM Oil products, devised by **Total Design** c. 1964.

Reine de Joie, 1892, a **Toulouse-Lautrec** poster advertising the book by Victor Joze.

Letters from the Bulmer typeface, an example of a **transitional type**.

ABCDEFGH
abcdefgh

philosophy, thereby ensuring that it remains a vital influence on contemporary DUTCH GRAPHIC DESIGN. In addition to attracting a new generation of designers, it has fostered diverse talents like Loek van der Sande, Frans Leishout and Anthon BEEKE. Ben Bos, a graphic designer who joined in the 1960s, emerged as a leading influence throughout the 1980s. He left in 1991, with Jelle van der Toorn Vrijthoff assuming the role of creative director.

Toulouse-Lautrec, Henri de (1864–1901) French poster artist, printmaker and painter. Although he designed only thirty-two posters and a small number of menu heads, book and music covers, Lautrec was a major force in the development of the modern poster. He turned to drawing after breaking both hips when he was thirteen, leaving him crippled and stunted in growth. Influenced by Jules CHÉRET and Degas, and a friend of Théophile-Alexandre STEINLEN, he began studying art in Paris in 1882, developing into an outstanding academic draughtsman. In 1891 designed his first startling poster for *La Goulue* at the Moulin Rouge, which brought instant recognition. Inspired by the compositional qualities of the Japanese print, his work is characterized by unusual placement of forms, flat simplified silhouettes, contrasting unmodulated colours and a vital expressive line, often achieved by drawing directly on to the lithographic stone (see CHROMOLITHOGRAPHY). He recorded the performers and patrons of the cabarets, cafés and circus, with his piercing caricatures presenting an unsentimental view of Parisian night-life.

trademark Identification device, in the form of a SYMBOL or LOGOTYPE, used to identify and/or unify the products or services provided by a particular manufacturer or supplier.

transitional type Any TYPEFACE design that emerged during the mid-18th c. with characteristics placing it in an interim stage of development between OLD FACE and MODERN. The fine SERIF forms, contrasting thick and thin strokes, and vertical STRESS are all pointers to the subsequent emergence of MODERN faces. *See* BASKERVILLE

Trickett & Webb Design consultancy founded in London in 1971 by graphic designers Lynn Trickett (b.1945) and Brian Webb (b.1945). Trickett trained at Chelsea School of Art, London 1962–66, Webb at Canterbury College of Art, Kent 1963–67. They met whilst working at the Derek Forsyth Partnership,

SIXTY YEARS PASSENGER SERVICE FOR THE CAPITAL

Sixty Years of Passenger Service poster, designed by **Trickett & Webb** for London Transport, 1993.

Troxler's poster for an American jazz evening in Willisau, 1978.

Trump Mediaeval, the most successful typeface designed by **Trump**.

ABCDEFGH
abcdefgh

London 1970–71. Their practice specializes in graphic design, packaging and exhibition design, with architectural projects undertaken in collaboration with Trickett Associates. Their design solutions have a visual sophistication informed by the partners' understanding of post-war British graphic design history. Elegant typography is often combined with images commissioned from leading illustrators and photographers. Recipients of DESIGNERS AND ART DIRECTORS ASSOCIATION silver awards for direct mail, CORPORATE IDENTITY, and book design, the International Package Design gold award in New York, and a medal in the first Poster Triennale at the Museum of Modern Art in Toyama, Japan. They have also designed stamps for the Royal Mail, London.

Troxler, Niklaus (b.1947) Swiss graphic designer and poster artist, best known for humorous and striking posters for the Jazz Festival, Willisau. Studied at the Kunstgewerbeschule, Lucerne 1968–71. Worked briefly as art director at Hollenstein Creation, Paris 1972–73 before founding his own studio in Willisau in 1973. Clients include the Little Theatre, Lucerne, the Kunstgewerbemuseum, Zurich, and the West German Industrial Design Association. Recipient of a host of annual awards for Best Swiss Poster as well as the Toulouse-Lautrec gold medal, Essen, 1987.

Trump, Georg (1896–1985) German book and TYPEFACE designer, illustrator and educator. Training at the Staatliche Kunstgewerbeschule, Stuttgart, was interrupted by army service during the First World War. Resumed his studies in Stuttgart 1919–23 under the inspirational teacher and typeface designer Professor Ernst Schneidler. Trump himself became an important educator and a designer of lively types, the best inspired by calligraphic forms. After three years as a ceramicist in Italy, he returned to Germany in 1926 to establish a graphic-design department at the Kunstgewerbeschule, Bielefeld, Westphalia. In 1929, invited by Paul RENNER to teach lettering and typography at the Meisterschule für Deutschlands Buchdrucker, Munich, alongside Jan TSCHICHOLD. Designed his first typeface in 1930 – an EGYPTIAN called City, which Paul RAND used in 1956 as the basis of the IBM LOGOTYPE. The BLACKLETTER Trump Deutsch followed in 1935. Taught in Berlin from 1931–34, succeeding Renner as head of the Munich School after Renner's dismissal by the Nazis. Simultaneously, he began a long association with the Stuttgart foundry of C.E. Weber, for which he produced his finest typefaces, including the Schadow family (1937–45), the

"ALL TOGETHER NOW: HAPPY BIRTHDAY USA"

Poster for America's bicentenary celebrations, designed in 1975 by **Tscherny** Davis-Delaney-Arrow Inc.

Title page of *Die neue Typographie* (1928), **Tschichold**'s first book.

JAN TSCHICHOLD

DIE NEUE TYPOGRAPHIE

EIN HANDBUCH FÜR ZEITGEMÄSS SCHAFFENDE

BERLIN **1928**

VERLAG DES BILDUNGSVERBANDES DER DEUTSCHEN BUCHDRUCKER

elegant calligraphic Delphin (1951–55) and his ROMAN masterpiece Trump Mediaeval (1954–60). He retired from teaching in 1953 and established a freelance practice creating new typefaces.

Tscherny, George (b.1924) Graphic designer and educator. Born in Budapest, Hungary, he spent his childhood in Berlin, emigrated to the US in 1941, becoming naturalized in 1943. After serving in the US Army during the Second World War, he trained at the Pratt Institute, New York, 1947–50. Began his professional career in New York with Donald Deskey and Associates 1950–53, and then with George Nelson and Associates 1953–55. Established his own studio in New York in 1956. His work is distinguished by a logical approach to visual communication with typography, photography and illustration used sparingly and for maximum effect. Worked on major CORPORATE IDENTITY schemes (e.g. W.R. Grace & Co., 1974), posters (e.g. for Mobil Oil Corporation, 1977, and the US Bicentennial poster for Davis-Delaney-Arrow in 1975), annual reports (e.g. for Johnson & Johnson, and SEI Corporation) stamps (e.g 1976 Telephone Centennial for the US Postal Service), advertising, packaging. A committed educator, he taught at the Pratt Institute 1956–57, the School of Visual Arts 1956–64, and in 1976 as Mellon Visiting Professor at Cooper Union. President of AIGA 1966–68. Silver medallist at the Warsaw Poster Biennale, 1976. In 1988 his consistent and elegant vision was recognized by the award of an AIGA medal. Selected for the ART DIRECTORS CLUB OF NEW YORK Hall of Fame in 1997. Member of AGI.

Tschichold, Jan (1902–74) German-born typographer, book and TYPEFACE designer and writer on design. Leading influence on the emergence of the NEW TYPOGRAPHY in Europe during the 1920s and 30s. Son of a sign writer, he trained originally as a teacher, before transferring to the Leipzig Academy for the Graphic Arts and Book Production Trade 1919–21. Worked in Leipzig as a freelance typographer up to 1925. Although not associated with the BAUHAUS, he visited the first Bauhaus exhibition in Weimar (1923); thereafter his work and ideas were influenced by Bauhaus principles. He wrote a major article entitled *elementare typographie* for a special issue of the journal *Typographische Mitteilungen* (1925). Taught typography and calligraphy at the German Master Printers' School in Munich 1926–33, under its director Paul RENNER. His contract with the School ended after harassment from the Nazis forced Tschichold and his family to move to Basle, Switzerland. In 1928 he published his first book *Die neue Typographie*, which established the importance of ASYMMETRIC typographic principles. This was followed by two useful design manuals, intended to make his typographic ideas accessible to printers and compositors: *Eine Stunde Druckgestaltung* (1930) and *Schriftschreiben für Setzer* (1931). From 1926–29 he designed an experimental single-alphabet SANS SERIF, much influenced by Herbert BAYER's proposal of 1925 (neither were put into production). His major text *Typographische Gestaltung* (1935) was published in Switzerland. In the same year an exhibition of his work, held at the London office of the publishers Lund Humphries, led to various commissions, including the design of the 1938 PENROSE ANNUAL. His stature and influence were acknowledged by an invitation to speak to the DOUBLE CROWN CLUB, London 1937. About this time Tschichold began to question, and eventually reject, the New Typography, which he came to identity with the dogma associated with German fascism. This volte-face led to his becoming a brilliant practitioner of classical typography. From 1940–70 he produced six scholarly works on Chinese colour printing. Engaged by Sir Allen LANE of Penguin Books, London, to redesign all Penguin publications 1946–49. Moved from Switzerland to London for this commission, designing over five hundred title pages and establishing the masterly 'Penguin Composition Rules'. (On his return to Switzerland he relinquished the design responsibility for Penguin to Hans SCHMOLLER.) Produced Sabon (1964–66), the first typeface to be designed for LINOTYPE, MONOTYPE and hand composition. A prolific practitioner, teacher and writer throughout his later years, he received the gold medal of the AIGA in 1954 and the Gutenberg Prize, Leipzig, 1965. Elected Hon RDI, London in 1965. Tschichold's typographic achievements and writings constitute a major contribution to the graphic arts of the 20th c.

type (a) Term applied to range of typographic output from any type composition system (e.g PHOTO-COMPOSITION). (b) Traditional term for unit of metal with raised typographic character. The face of a relief character is inked prior to printing by LETTERPRESS. Words are formed by joining individual metal characters together. The size of the metal body varies according to the size of the letter required. *See* TYPE NOMENCLATURE

Maximilien Vox created this **typeface classification** system.

typeface Alphabet created for the purpose of reproduction. The individual characters of a typeface are designed to work in different combinations and to remain consistent when reproduced by printing. Available in a wide variety of designs and sizes, typefaces offer a predictable outcome when specified by typographers, designers, printers, etc.

typeface classification The most convincing 20th-c. system for TYPEFACE categorization according to their period and design was evolved during the 1950s by the French typographer, Maximilien Vox (1894–1974). Vox created a series of new category headings:
Humane *(See* VENETIAN*)*
Garalde *(See* OLD FACE/OLD STYLE*)*
Reale *(See* TRANSITIONAL*)*
Didone *(See* MODERN FACE*)*
Mecane *(See* SLAB SERIF*)*
Lineale *(See* SANS SERIF*)*
Incise (types based on stone-cut lettering, including LATIN)
Scripte *(See* SCRIPT*)*
Manuaire (types formed by pen or brush, including BLACKLETTER)
Although not universally accepted, his system has been recognized and developed by the British Standards Institute and the ASSOCIATION TYPOGRAPHIQUE INTERNATIONALE. The shortcomings of this classification system, like all others to date, are exposed by the fact that many typefaces fall into more than one category.

ABCDEFGH
ABCDEFGH
ABCDEFGH
ABCDEFGH
ABCDEFGH
ABCDEFGH
ABCDEFGH
ABCDEFGH
ABCDEFGH

Granby **type family**: (top to bottom) Granby, italic, light, light condensed, condensed, bold condensed, bold, extra bold, elephant.

Type nomenclature in letterpress printing.

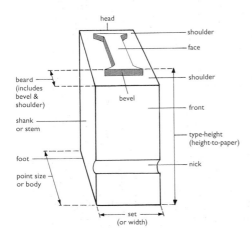

type family Generic term for the wide range of related variations (ITALIC, CONDENSED, expanded, BOLD, extra bold, medium, light, extra light, etc.) that may be available as alternatives to the standard version of any typeface.

type-height (height-to-paper) Term used in LETTERPRESS printing to describe the height of type from the printing bed to the printing surface (0.918in [2.3 cm] in UK and US). *See* TYPE NOMENCLATURE

type mark-up (TMU) Typesetting specification on copy or manuscript prepared by designer/typographer and supplied to compositor. The type mark-up would normally specify the TYPEFACE to be used, POINT SIZE, punctuation, spacing, spelling, rules, etc.

type measurement *See* ANGLO-AMERICAN POINT SYSTEM, DIDOT POINT SYSTEM, POINT

type nomenclature (for metal type) The traditional terms describing the parts of an individual unit of TYPE used in LETTERPRESS printing.

typographer (a) In UK, a designer who specializes in the use of TYPE for visual communication purposes. Highly skilled in TYPEFACE selection and specification. (b) In US, more often applied to the skilled operator who sets type using a type composition system (a 'compositor' in the UK).

Typographica (1949–67) British typographic journal founded and edited by Herbert SPENCER. Well-designed, it offered an informed and sympathetic assessment of 20th-c. European 'modern' typographers.

typography (a) Arrangement and specification of type in preparation for printing. Traditionally associated with printing from metal type (LETTERPRESS), now equally applied to typesetting produced by any type composition system. (b) Quarterly journal produced in UK (1936–39). Founded by Robert Harling, James Shand and Ellic Howe, *Typography* was renowned for its coverage of graphic design, typography and illustration. Precursor of *Alphabet and Image*, a similar publication edited by Robert Harling after the Second World War. (c) Classic typographic design manual by the Swiss typographer Emil RUDER. Originally published under the title *Typographie* (1967).

U

U&lc, U/lc (a) Typographic abbreviation for typesetting in UPPER CASE and LOWER CASE. Derives from a long-established practice in the printing trade whereby the upper case of type contains the CAPITALS and SMALL CAPITALS, with the lower case reserved for all other typographic sorts. (b) *U&lc* is a journal produced by the INTERNATIONAL TYPEFACE CORPORATION. First issued in 1973, with Herb LUBALIN as design director.

Ulm Hochschule für Gestaltung (1951–68) German design school. Founded in Ulm in 1949 from a fund established by Inge Aicher-Scholl in memory of her late sister and brother, murdered by the Nazis. Under its first director Max BILL, the philosophy of the Hochschule für Gestaltung (Technical College for Design) reflected functionalist BAUHAUS principles. Bill was succeeded in 1957 by the Argentinian painter Tomás Maldonado, who rejected the school's continued espousal of a pre-war design aesthetic in a post-industrial age and introduced subjects like sociology, psychology and cultural history into the curriculum. The school was eventually closed after a destructive period of disputes and criticisms.

Univers Influential SANS SERIF TYPEFACE designed by Adrian FRUTIGER in 1957. The simplicity and rationality of Univers, combined with an impressive range of co-ordinated variations, has made it one of the most popular post-war typefaces.

Part of the **Univers** 55 typeface.

ABCDEFGH
abcdefgh

unjustified (RANGED LEFT/RANGED RIGHT) Typesetting format in which only one margin of a piece of text is aligned (on the left or right), with the other side having a ragged effect due to each line making its own length. *See* JUSTIFIED

Updike, Daniel Berkeley (1860–1941) American printer, designer and scholar. Successor to Theodore Lowe de VINNE, and along with Frederic W. GOUDY and Bruce ROGERS a major influence on the American

Pages from *The Altar Book* (1896), designed by Bertram Goodhue for **Updike**'s Merrymount Press.

typographic revival during the early decades of the 20th c. He worked at the Riverside Press, Cambridge, Massachusetts, before establishing the Merrymount Press, Boston, in 1893. Books published by the Press were of great distinction and refinement, with many earlier productions acknowledging the achievements of William MORRIS and the KELMSCOTT PRESS. His two-volume seminal text, *Printing Types: their history, forms, and use* (1922), analyzed the evolution of typographic styles from the 15th c.

upper case Traditional typographic term for CAPITAL letters. *See* LOWER CASE, U&LC

ABCDEFGHI JKLMNOPQR STUVWXYZ

Upper case letters from the Bembo typeface.

V

Vale Press *See* RICKETTS, CHARLES

Valicenti, Rick (b.1951) Chicago-based graphic designer and photographer who initially trained as a painter at Ohio's Bowling Green State University before graduating from photography from the University of Iowa (1976). His interest in graphic design was awakened at the 1978 ICOGRADA Congress at Northwestern University, Illinois. After a period with Bruce Beck Design, he established his own practice (1982). In 1988 joined photographers Tom Vack and Corinne Pfister to form Thirst (3st), a design and photography collaborative. Valicenti's exuberant and controversial work emerges from his willingness to take risks in pursuit of self-expression. He has lectured at numerous universities and professional gatherings and exhibited in Japan and the US.

VanderLans, Rudy (b.1955) Trained and practised graphic design in the Netherlands before emigrating to America in 1981 to study photography at the University of California, Berkeley. Founder, editor and art director of the graphic-design magazine EMIGRE

(1984), which focuses on the social and cultural effects of graphic design on society. As a parallel interest VanderLans has photographed the California environment, resulting in a number of experimental photo books and exhibitions. His wife Zuzana LICKO runs the digital type foundry Emigre Fonts. Their company has received a number of awards including the Chrysler Award for innovation in design (1994), the Charles Nypels award for excellence in the field of typography (1998) and the American Institute of Graphic Arts Gold Medal Award (1997).

Velde, Henry Clemens van de (1863–1957) Belgian architect, painter, writer and versatile designer of furniture, metalwork, interiors and graphic design. Trained initially as a painter in Antwerp, 1881–84, and Paris under Carolus Duran, 1884–85. Abandoned painting for design in 1892. Influenced by Jules CHÉRET and the British ARTS AND CRAFTS MOVEMENT, van de Velde's early designs reflect the curvilinear organic forms of ART NOUVEAU. From 1893 he contributed titles and ORNAMENT to the advanced Belgian arts journal *Van Nu en Straks* (*Today & Tomorrow*). In 1898 he was commissioned by the food manufacturer Tropon to create advertising and packaging materials – an early example of modern professional design practice. Van de Velde's only poster design was for Tropon and it indicates his movement from representation towards abstraction. He made a lasting contribution as a design theorist through teaching and prolific writing. A founder member of DEUTSCHER WERKBUND, he initially embraced machine production and believed modern design should be true to its materials and modes of manufacture. A disagreement with Hermann Muthesius at the Cologne 1914 Deutscher Werkbund exhibition revealed van de Velde's inability to reconcile mechanization and individual creativity. Architect of the new Kunstgewerbe-schule in Weimar and professor of the school 1904–14. He recommended Walter GROPIUS as his successor, an appointment that eventually led to the establishment of the BAUHAUS. Van de Velde moved to Switzerland in 1917 and Holland in 1920 where he worked as an architect, teacher and writer.

Venetian Category of ROMAN TYPEFACE originating in Venice *c.* 1470–95. Typographic characteristics of Venetian typefaces include wide characters with a relatively small variation between the thin and thick strokes, strong bracketed SERIF forms, and a lower-case 'e' with a distinctly sloping crossbar.

Valicenti's editorial art for *ESPN* magazine, 2000.

Lithograph advertising poster for Tropon by van de **Velde** (1898).

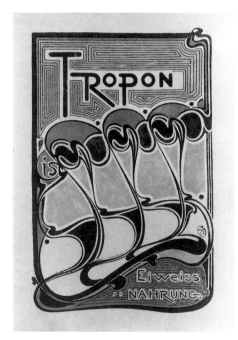

ABCDEFGH
abcdefgh

Cloister Old Style (c.1897), a **Venetian** typeface.

Venn diagram System for the visual presentation of information, perfected by John Venn during the 1880s. It uses overlapping circles and ovals that enable the viewer to identify connections between disparate groups of statistics.

Ver Sacrum See VIENNA SECESSION

Vermeulen, Rick See HARD WERKEN

Vienna Secession Organization formed on 3 April 1897 after younger members of the Künstlerhaus, the Viennese academic art society, rebelled over the exclusion of foreign artists from exhibitions. Led by Gustav KLIMT, the group included Kolomon MOSER, Alfred ROLLER and the architects Josef HOFFMANN and J.M. Olbrich. The graphic language of the Secessionists – known as Sezessionstil – evolved through Symbolist painting, French ART NOUVEAU and rapidly absorbed the influence of the Glasgow School (see Charles Rennie MACKINTOSH), which exhibited in the Eighth Secessionist Exhibition, Munich, 1900. Characteristics of mature Sezessionstil were flat, two-dimensional shapes, geometric designs using squares, rectangles and circles, the distortion of letterforms to fit geometric patterns and a great symmetrical unity. The journal of the Secession was *Ver Sacrum* (*Sacred Spring*; 1898–1903): a luxurious and innovative showpiece, even the advertisements were designed by Secessionists to maintain carefully the cohesion and integrity of the publication. See WIENER WERKSTÄTTE

Koloman Moser's cover design for *Ver Sacrum* (1899), the journal of the **Vienna Secession**.

Vignelli

A NEW WAVE OF AUSTRIAN ARCHITECTURE

Poster for the Institute for Architecture and Urban Studies, New York, by **Vignelli**, 1979–80.

Cover of the September 1958 issue of *Neue Grafik* magazine (New Graphic Design) by **Vivarelli**.

Vignelli, Massimo (b.1931) New York–based graphic, exhibition and product designer who trained as an architect in Milan, 1950–53, and Venice, 1953–57. Designed posters and graphics for the Venice Biennale (1962, '64) before moving to the US in 1965. Co-founder of Unimark International, Chicago, in 1965 where he created the CORPORATE IDENTITY for Knoll International, the furniture manufacturers (1966), and the LOGOTYPE for American Airlines (1967). Responsible for the SIGNAGE and maps for the New York subway, 1966, and the Washington Metro, 1968. In 1971 Vignelli and his architect wife Lella established Vignelli Associates, New York, designing corporate identity programmes, posters, publications, architectural graphics and exhibitions as well as furniture and other products. Lettering is an important element in Vignelli's graphic solutions; he contrasts type, colour and texture whilst retaining clarity of form through a reliance on the typographic GRID. Designed many books for Chanticleer Press and Rizzoli International Publications. The Vignellis' work is represented in the Museum of Modern Art, New York. Their design achievements are assessed in a collection of essays, *design: Vignelli* (1990). They were awarded the 1983 AIGA gold medal.

Villemot, Bernard (1911–89) French poster artist, stage designer and painter. Born in Trouville, the son of the cartoonist Jean Villemot, he studied painting at the Académie Julian and the École Paul Colin. Many of his posters address social and health issues, such as alcoholism, child care and the environment. His advertising clients include Air France, Bally, Perrier, Orangina and Bergasol. His finely balanced compositions are characterized by strong, joyful colours and fluid, contoured illustrations of the human form. Numerous one-man exhibitions, including one at the Bibliothèque Nationale in Paris, 1981. Member of AGI.

Vinne, Theodore Lowe de (1828–1914) Leading American LETTERPRESS printer of the 19th c. and author of a four-volume tome on *The Practice of Typography*, beginning with *Plain Printing Types* (1899). In 1894 De Vinne commissioned L.B. BENTON to cut the CENTURY typeface specifically for *Century* magazine.

Vivarelli, Carlo L. (b.1919) Swiss graphic designer and exponent of the systematic INTERNATIONAL TYPOGRAPHIC STYLE. Studied in Paris with Paul COLIN and worked briefly for Studio Boggeri, Milan, 1946 before returning to Zurich. Co-founder of the influential journal *NEUE GRAFIK*, 1958. Like his contemporary Josef

MÜLLER-BROCKMANN, Vivarelli demonstrated the potential of juxtaposing SANS SERIF alphabets and objective photography within the discipline of a mathematically precise typographic GRID.

Vogue International fashion journal celebrated for its exemplary editorial design standards. Established in the early 1890s, American *Vogue* only achieved significance following its acquisition by the publisher Condé Nast in 1909. British *Vogue* was established in 1916, followed by a French version in 1920. The early American covers demonstrate a commitment to contemporary developments in European art (e.g. ART DECO, SURREALISM). The illustrations of Georges Lepape and Eduardo Benito reflected the Jazz Age of the 1920s. Throughout the 1930s the fluent graphic style of Eric (Carl Erickson) was a dominant influence, superbly conveying the excitement of international *haute couture*. After the Second World War colour photographs were increasingly used on covers and for fashion reportage. Major editorial art directors who worked for *Vogue* include Mehemed Fehmy AGHA, Herbert BAYER, Alexander LIBERMAN and Cipe PINELES.

Vorticism British art movement, founded by Wyndham Lewis (1882-1957) in 1914, which sought to combine the dynamic compositional qualities of both CUBISM and FUTURISM. Lewis edited *Blast*, the movement's controversial paper. Vorticist illustrations and typography were intentionally unsettling, with harsh contrasts and jagged lines based on contrasting diagonals. The movement's demise coincided with the end of the First World War.

Vox Classification of Typefaces See TYPEFACE CLASSIFICATION

W

Walker, Emery (1851–1933) Book designer and printer, important in the 20th-c. revival of standards of typographic design and book production in England and Germany. Gained his knowledge of printing at Alfred Dawson's Typographical Etching Company, London, which he joined in 1873. In 1886 established Walker and Boutall, which became Walker and Cockerell, 1900, and Emery Walker Ltd, 1904. He was a founder of the ARTS AND CRAFTS EXHIBITION SOCIETY in 1888, president in 1927, and master of the ART WORKERS' GUILD in 1904. A close friend of William MORRIS whom he advised on the setting up of the KELMSCOTT PRESS. Along with T.J. Cobden-Sanderson (1840–1922), founded the Doves Press, Hammersmith, 1900. This product of the PRIVATE PRESS MOVEMENT eschewed ornamentation and illustration and relied upon fine typography, excellent presswork and quality materials to produce beautiful volumes. The press possessed a single ROMAN typeface, in one size: Doves Roman, cut by Edward Prince under Walker's supervision, was a modernized version of a 15th-c. VENETIAN type by Nicholas Jenson. The distinguished Doves *Bible* (1903) is a masterpiece of design and technical perfection. It includes a few initials by the calligrapher Edward JOHNSTON. In 1905 Walker brought the Doves style to Germany through his design of a series of classics for Insel-Verlag, with calligraphic title pages by Johnston and Eric GILL.

Cover of *Blast*, issue no. 2 (July 1915), designed by Wyndham Lewis, founder of **Vorticism**.

The Woman in White, the 1871 theatre poster by Frederick **Walker**.

Text from **Warde**'s broadsheet *This is a Printing Office* (1932).

> ## THIS IS
> ## A PRINTING OFFICE
>
> CROSSROADS OF CIVILIZATION
> REFUGE OF ALL THE ARTS
> AGAINST THE RAVAGES OF TIME
> ARMOURY OF FEARLESS TRUTH
> AGAINST WHISPERING RUMOUR
> INCESSANT TRUMPET OF TRADE
>
> FROM THIS PLACE WORDS MAY FLY ABROAD
> NOT TO PERISH ON WAVES OF SOUND
> NOT TO VARY WITH THE WRITER'S HAND
> BUT FIXED IN TIME HAVING BEEN VERIFIED IN PROOF
> FRIEND YOU STAND ON SACRED GROUND
> THIS IS A PRINTING OFFICE

Walker, Frederick (1840–75) English illustrator and painter. Walker's sole poster design is the famous *Woman in White* (1871) for the Olympic Theatre, London, incorporating a WOOD ENGRAVING by W.H. Hooper. This dramatic image represents a break in the long tradition of the typographic LETTERPRESS poster and heralds the dawn of the pictorial poster in England. He was highly revered by contemporaries like Sir John Everett Millais. Illustrated books for the novelist William Makepeace Thackeray.

Warde, Beatrice (1900–69) American typographer, writer and scholar who spent much of her working life in England. Educated at Barnard College, Columbia where she developed an interest in calligraphy and letterforms. From 1921–25 worked as assistant librarian with the AMERICAN TYPE FOUNDERS COMPANY, pursuing her research into typefaces and the history of printing. In 1925, after marriage to the type designer Frederic Warde, moved to Europe, subsequently working for *The* FLEURON, then edited by Stanley MORISON. Her reputation was established by a 1926 article in *The Fleuron*, written under the pseudonym of 'Paul Beaujon', which traced types mistakenly attributed to GARAMOND back to Jean Jannon of Sedan. In 1927 became editor of *The Monotype Recorder*, London (see MONOTYPE). A believer in the power of the printed word to defend freedom, Warde wrote and designed the famous Monotype broadsheet *This is a Printing Office* (1932), using Eric GILL's PERPETUA typeface. Rejected the avant-garde in typography as introspective, believing that classical typography provided a 'clearly polished window' through which ideas could be communicated. *The Crystal Goblet: Sixteen Essays on Typography* (1955) is an anthology of her writings.

Weingart, Wolfgang (b.1941) Self-taught graphic designer, typographer and influential teacher who pioneered POST-MODERNISM. Learned the skills of HOT METAL COMPOSITION as an apprentice in Germany. Moved to Basle where in 1968 began teaching at the Kunstgewerbeschule, alongside Armin HOFMANN. During the late 1960s he challenged the rational order and dogmatic rules of the INTERNATIONAL TYPOGRAPHIC STYLE (see ODERMATT & TISSI). Weingart's intuitive, expressive typographic 'experiments', appearing on poster and cover designs, utilized wide wordspacing and letterspacing, step rules, reversed type blocks, unpredictable contrasts of type weight, and diagonal or random placement of letterforms. During the mid-1970s he began exploring the graphic imagery made possible with PHOTOLITHOGRAPHY, incorporating

Poster for a 1981 exhibition of 'Calligraphy in German-speaking Switzerland 1548–1980', by **Weingart**.

Issue no. 9 of *The Next Call* (1926) carried this cover design by **Werkman**.

COLLAGE, enlarging and overlapping HALFTONE dot patterns and experimenting with the design elements to create uniquely dynamic solutions. Weingart taught numerous American students in Basle including April GREIMAN and Daniel FRIEDMAN and is a regular visiting lecturer at many US design schools. His work has had a profound influence on American graphic design, providing a dynamic alternative to the predictability of corporate design solutions based on systematic Swiss design principles. His visual memoir *Wolfgang Weingart: Typography* (2000) reveals his influences and philosophy. Member of AGI.

Werkman, Hendrik N. (1882–1945) Dutch printer, typographer, painter and printmaker. Acclaimed for the asymmetric typographic compositions he created whilst experimenting with printing materials and techniques. Werkman spent his early years working for printing houses and newspapers. Self-taught as a painter and designer. Beginning in 1908 he built up a substantial printing company, which he was obliged to sell in 1923 because of economic problems. Opened a small printing shop where he began publishing an experimental typographic magazine, *The Next Call,* which appeared in nine issues between 1923 and 1926. Werkman's unconventional printing techniques included the inking of wood blocks, type, even found objects, and pressing them directly on to the letterpress bed of an old hand press. His montage-like assembly of design elements, use of found materials and bold typographic configurations are reminiscent of DADA design practice. Also in 1923 Werkman began producing prints that he called 'druksels' and 'tiksels', many of which were abstract. During the 1930s his experiments included the application of inked rollers to the paper and extensive use of stencils. In occupied Holland during the Second World War he produced forty issues of a subversive broadsheet *The Blue Barge.* In 1945 he was executed by the Nazis, only days before liberation. Much of his work was destroyed at this time.

Why Not Associates London design consultancy formed, 1987, by Andrew Altman, David Ellis and Howard Greenhalgh, shortly after graduating from Royal College of Art, London. Influenced by Gert DUMBAR during his brief reign as professor at the RCA, the partners seek to challenge the conventions of mainstream graphic design. Their typographic solutions indicate an awareness of CONSTRUCTIVISM and also reflect the creative freedoms presented by the APPLE MACINTOSH (MAC) COMPUTER (e.g. Altman's

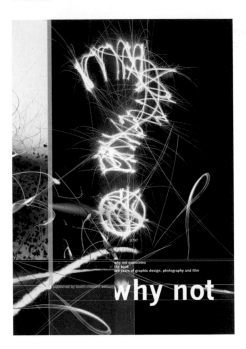

Poster designed by **Why Not Associates** to advertise their book, *Why Not?*, 1998.

Symbol design for the Centre Georges Pompidou, Paris (1974) by **Widmer**.

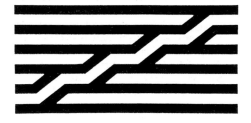

TYPEFACE for a Midland Bank press campaign (1991) combined classic PERPETUA with the mechanistic, SANS SERIF Din 17). Attracting clients in the UK, Europe, US and Japan, the versatility of Why Not is conveyed in their campaign for Smirnoff vodka (1990), and catalogue covers and section inserts for the fashion retailer Next (1990 and '91). Through their Why Not Films and Why Not Publishing offshoots the consultancy has produced pop videos and also published several unusual books. Their elegantly designed *Steel Works* (1990), by Julian Germain, records the decline of Consett, a town in northern England, following the demise of its steel industry. Designed Royal Mail stamps to commemorate 40th anniversary of the Queen's accession to the throne, 1992. The consultancy's innovation and experimentation across diverse media from postage stamps to exhibition design is demonstrated in their publication *Why Not?* (1998).

Widmer, Jean (b. 1929) Swiss-born graphic designer and typographer. Studied graphic design at the Kunstgewerbeschule, Zurich under Johannes ITTEN, 1945–50. This introduction to the discipline of SWISS GRAPHIC DESIGN was extended by further study at the École des Beaux Arts, Paris, 1952–55, after which he worked as art director with an advertising agency in Paris until 1959. From then until 1961 he worked with the Galeries Lafayette department store, Paris, before becoming art director of the magazine *Jardin des Modes* until 1970. Widmer then founded his own studio in Paris, establishing a reputation promoting cultural events and institutions. His functional and disciplined approach is enhanced by an ability to utilize typographic elements in a playful and unexpected manner. Widmer's high-profile projects include posters for the Centre de la Création Industrielle (CCI), CORPORATE IDENTITY schemes for the Centre Georges Pompidou, Paris (1983), and a SIGNAGE system for French motorways. This last project was a major undertaking, with over five hundred PICTOGRAMS designed to inform travellers of the cultural and geographical features in each French region. A retrospective exhibition of his work was held in 1991 in Villeurbanne, France. Member of AGI.

Wiener Werkstätte (Vienna Workshops) Co-operative of designers and craftworkers established in Vienna in 1903, originally to produce the SEZESSION-STIL designs of Josef HOFFMANN and Koloman MOSER. Based on the writings and workshops of William MOR-RIS and C.R. Ashbee in England, and financed by the industrialist Fritz Wärndorfer, it endeavoured to

Logotype for the **Wiener Werkstätte**, 1903.

Cover of the December 1958 issue of
Harper's Bazaar, designed by **Wolf**.

improve the functional and aesthetic standards of everyday objects. Although the overall quality of output was variable, the graphic designs in the aftermath of ART NOUVEAU were influential in establishing a geometric style with a sharp contrast between positive and negative forms. It offered a graphic-design service to private and industrial clients, covering posters, advertisements, LOGOTYPE design, monograms, bookplates, postcards, bookbindings, etc. The distinctive Wiener Werkstätte logotype was probably designed by Moser. Many of the printing and lettering projects were supervised by the distinguished letterer and teacher, Rudolf von Larisch. The Werkstätte was dissolved in 1932 because of financial problems.

windows Used with graphics-based computer interfaces, a window is a rectangular area of the screen in which the user of a computer performs a set of tasks such as using a word processor, spreadsheet, drawing package etc. Windows can be overlaid, shrunk, or enlarged, thereby allowing the user to perform several different tasks, each in its own window. Information can be transferred between windows by 'cutting and pasting' using a MOUSE.

Wolf, Henry (b.1925) One of the outstanding American magazine art directors of the 1950s; also advertising designer and photographer. Born in Vienna, he studied in France before emigrating to the US in 1941, where he received further training at the School of Industrial Art, New York (1941–42). After wartime service in the US army Wolf worked in advertising and design and as art director at the US State Department. Appointed art director of *Esquire* in 1952, he redesigned the magazine's format and heightened visual impact with increased exploitation of bold photography and white space. Succeeded BRODOVITCH at *HARPER'S BAZAAR* in 1958 where he experimented with page layout and typography and designed many subtle and witty photographic covers. Wolf commissioned illustrations from major artists like Ben SHAHN and Richard Lindner. Moved to the arts periodical *Show* in 1961; his inventive art direction matched the journal's progressive content. Wolf worked for advertising agencies from 1964–71 when he established Henry Wolf Productions Inc., New York, working in film as well as advertising and design. Since 1954 has taught in New York at Cooper Union, the School of Visual Arts and Parsons School of Design. Recipient of many awards including the AIGA gold medal in 1976. Inducted into the ART DIRECTORS CLUB OF NEW YORK Hall of Fame in 1980. Member of AGI. Elected Hon RDI in 1990.

Elements of the corporate identity scheme devised for the Bovis construction company by **Wolff Olins** in 1971.

Magazine cover designed in *c.* 1946 by **Wolpe**.

Wood engraving by Eric Gill for the double title page of *The Green Ship* by Patrick Miller, published by the Golden Cockerel Press in 1936.

Wolff Olins Consultancy formed in London in 1965 by graphic designer Michael Wolff (b. 1933) and design manager Wally Olins (b. 1930). Renowned for its innovative CORPORATE IDENTITY programmes, Wolff Olins has taken a lead in acknowledging the need for visual identity to be linked to the structure and marketing strategy of international organizations. Major design programmes have been produced for Bovis, Renault, BOC, P&O, BfG (a German bank), British Telecom, Prudential, Q8 (Kuwait Petroleum), ICI. Olins' writings, including *The Corporate Personality* (1978) and *Corporate Identity* (1989), have been influential in explaining the design process to the international business community. Michael Wolff left the company in 1983, becoming chairman of the London consultancy Addison in 1987. Wally Olins is now chairman of Wolff Olins. In 2001 the consultancy merged with the American communications group Omnicom.

Wolpe, Berthold (1905–89) Typographer, letterer and teacher. Trained as a metalworker, acquiring the skills of smithing, chasing and engraving that were to influence his later work. From 1924–28 he was a pupil of Rudolf KOCH at the Offenbach Kunstgewerbeschule, becoming a teacher and Koch's assistant in 1929. Simultaneously, from 1929 until 1933, Wolpe taught at the Frankfurt Kunstschule. During his first visit to England in 1932, Wolpe met Stanley MORISON who suggested that he create a TYPEFACE for the MONOTYPE Corporation. The face, a DISPLAY ROMAN based on his bronze inscriptions, was ALBERTUS, which provided the foundation for a type family he developed over the ensuing fifty years. In 1935 Wolpe left Nazi Germany to settle in England, working for the next four years at the Fanfare Press, London, where his work included some of the famous yellow book jackets for Gollancz. In 1940 joined Faber & Faber, London, designing a prodigious number of books, bindings and book jackets until retirement in 1975. Wolpe's type designs include Hyperion (1931), Tempest (1936), the Pegasus range (1937–84), Sachsenwald (1937), Decorata (1955), and an italic type commissioned by the London Transport Board (1973). He designed the masthead used by *The Times*, London from 1966 until 1970. Taught at the Camberwell School of Art (1948–53), Royal College of Art (1956–75) and The City & Guilds of London Art School. Elected RDI in 1959 and awarded an honorary doctorate by the Royal College of Art, London, in 1968.

woodcut Traditional technique in which illustrations or designs are cut into a block of wood. The surface is cut with a knife along the side grain of the wood. The non-printing areas are cut away, with the remaining, raised lines or solid areas becoming the printing surface. The image is then reproduced by RELIEF PRINTING.

wood engraving Technically sophisticated version of the WOODCUT, with the image cut on the harder, end grain of a block of wood. Using special tools, the engraver can create very fine lines and achieve a remarkable subtlety in the tonal range. As with the woodcut, reproduction is by RELIEF PRINTING.

wove paper Uncoated paper of even texture. Manufactured using a mould of finely meshed woven wire, the surface is devoid of the faint, horizontal lines associated with LAID PAPER.

Wright, Edward (1912–89) British typographer, graphic designer, educator and artist. Studied at Liverpool School of Art (1930–31) and Bartlett School of Architecture, London University (1933–36). Specialized in lettering for architectural environments. In 1961, with architect Theo Crosby (later a PENTAGRAM partner), Wright designed a mural with relief lettering for the International Union of Architects Congress on the South Bank, London. Also responsible for the famous rotating triangular sign for New Scotland Yard, London, 1968. In 1988 he designed the illuminated lettering for the Tate Gallery, Liverpool. Taught experimental typography at the Central School of Arts and Crafts, London in the early 1950s, joining the Royal College of Art, London, in 1956. In the 1970s became head of graphic design at Chelsea School of Art. Wright's graphic work and painting were celebrated by an Arts Council exhibition in London, 1985.

Wunderlich, Gert (b. 1933) Book designer, TYPEFACE designer, educator. After a trade apprenticeship as a typesetter, trained at the School for Graphic and Book Arts, Leipzig (1953–58). Worked as a book designer before becoming secretary of the International Book Exhibition, Leipzig in 1964. Since 1971 has lectured in book design and typography at the School for Graphic and Book Arts, Leipzig, becoming Professor in 1979. Wulnderlich's posters and books combine the rational principles of the INTERNATIONAL TYPOGRAPHIC STYLE with his fluent calligraphic and lettering skills. Designed Maxima, a photocomposition typeface for Typoart, Dresden. Regular exhibitor at the International Book Exhibition, Leipzig, Warsaw Poster Biennale and the Brno Biennale. Awarded the President's Prize, Brno in 1978, the Gutenberg Prize, Leipzig in 1979, and the DDR National Prize in 1986.

Alphabet designed by **Wright** for the 'House of the Future' exhibition at Olympia, London 1956.

Advertisement by **Wunderlich** for the 1986 Erfurt exhibition of the '100 Best Posters' from the previous year.

Wurman, Richard Saul (b.1935) American designer of guides, maps, charts, directories, etc. who addresses the problems of presenting complex information to the public in a rational and clear manner. Trained as an architect at the University of Pennsylvania, with Louis Kahn. Wurman was a principal in the architecture and town-planning practice of Murphy Levy Wurman, Philadelphia, from 1963–76, where he also designed exhibitions. In 1981 he established Access Press, New York & San Francisco, which has published user-friendly guide books to the great cities of America and Europe, and designs information on a diversity of subjects including medical topics, the Olympic Games and the *Wall Street Journal*. In 1990 Wurman developed a *US Road Atlas* that uses systematic changes of scale and colour coding to accommodate both the interstate driver and the downtown tourist. Wurman is also a respected teacher and writer on information design. He founded and organizes the annual TED conferences (Technology, Entertainment and Design), which are usually held in Monterey, California.

Wyman, Lance (b.1937) New York–based TRADE-MARK, LOGOTYPE and TYPEFACE designer and creator of large-scale environmental graphic systems, such as he produced for the Metro systems of Mexico City (1969) and Washington (1974), the National Zoo, Washington (1975) and Jeddah International Airport (1978). Trained at the Pratt Institute, New York from 1956–60. After a period in Detroit and New York, he established a practice in 1966 with English industrial designer Peter Murdoch. Wymall's benchmark's design programme for the 1968 Mexico Olympic Games used PICTOGRAM signs and colour coding to communicate across language barriers. His distinctive solutions drew upon the colours and patterns of contemporary Mexican and ancient Aztec culture. Wyman and Murdoch collaborated on the design of standard interchangeable elements for signs, kiosks, telephones, maps, etc. From 1971–79 he was president of Wyman & Cannan, New York. Consistently demonstrates his ability to combine originality and clarity of expression in corporate design systems. In 1979 became president of Lance Wyman Ltd., New York, where he has continued to produce such innovative design solutions as the new signage system for the American Museum of Natural History in New York, which uses floor maps, icons and photographs (1992).

WYSIWYG Acronym for 'What You See Is What You Get' a desirable technical connection between what the designer/operator sees on a VDU screen and what will emerge as the final output on film or in print.

X

x-height Body height of any LOWER CASE character that has neither ASCENDER nor DESCENDER (as typified by x, but also including a, c, e, i, m, n, o, r, s, u, v, w, z).

Lower-case letters from the Garamond typeface showing their **x-height**.

Some of the pictogram signs designed by **Wyman** for the 1968 Mexico Olympics.

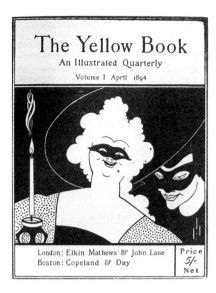

Cover design by Aubrey Beardsley for the first volume of **The Yellow Book**, April 1894.

Yokoo's theatre poster for a play entitled *John Silver*, 1967.

Y

Yellow Book, The (1894–97) Influential literary quarterly published in London by Elkin Mathews & John Lane, and in Boston by Copeland & Day. So named because of the bright yellow cover, the book ran for thirteen issues and achieved notoriety through the ART NOUVEAU illustrations, posters and cover designs produced by Aubrey BEARDSLEY. Art editor for the first four volumes, Beardsley was sacked in 1895 following allegations about his relationship with the disgraced writer Oscar Wilde.

Yokoo, Tadanori (b. 1936) Japanese graphic designer. Joined the Japanese Design Centre, 1960–64, leaving to establish a freelance practice. Yokoo created an alternative to the European MODERNISM that predominated in the work of the preceding generation of Japanese designers such as Yusaku KAMEKURA. His exotic and experimental posters and illustrations use COLLAGE, PHOTOMONTAGE and AIRBRUSH techniques to explore the impact of Western popular culture on Japanese society. His intuitive and potent mix of images from East and West has attracted international recognition. During the 1980s he increasingly focused on the practice of fine art.

Z

Zapf, Hermann (b. 1918) German TYPEFACE designer, calligrapher, book designer, educator. Self-taught, emerging at the end of the 1930s as a master craftsman with a sophisticated understanding of the work and writings of calligraphers like Rudolf KOCH and Edward JOHNSTON. Established freelance practice in 1938. Zapf's pre-eminence in type design is illustrated by his contribution to a number of international type compostron organizations: type director of the Stempel AG foundry, Frankfurt 1947–56, design consultant to Mergenthaler Linotype, New York 1957–74, vice-president of Design Processing International, New York 1977–86, and since 1987, chairman of Zapf, Burns & Co., New York. Zapf's prolific output as a typeface designer has extended over five decades. Of particular note are Palatino (1950), Melior (1952), OPTIMA (1958), ITC Zapf International (1977) and ITC Zapf Chancery (1979). His two editions of *Manuale Typographicum* (1954 and 1968) with their single-page quotations on typography are high

The whole duty of Typography, as of Calligraphy, is to communicate to the imagination, without loss by the way, the thought or image intended THOMAS JAMES COBDEN–SANDERSON *to be communicated by the Author.*

Page from *Manuale Typographicum* (1968), by **Zapf**.

Advertisement for NKF, c. 1925, by **Zwart**.

points of 20th-c. lettering and book design. *Hermann Zapf and his design philosophy*, published in 1987, provides an elegant overview of his career. Awarded the F.W. Goudy Award, Rochester, New York (1969) and the Gutenberg Prize, Mainz (1974). In addition to lecturing throughout the world, Zapf has, since 1960, held a number of senior teaching posts in America and Germany. Member of AGI, AIGA, and elected an Hon RDI, London in 1985.

Zéró See SCHLEGER, HANS

Zwart, Piet (1885–1977) Dutch typographer, photographer, industrial designer. Trained at Amsterdam School of Arts & Crafts 1902–7, then briefly at the technical school, Delft 1913–14. Worked for the DE STIJL architect Jan Wils from 1919, becoming assistant to the renowned Dutch architect H.P. Berlage in 1921. Zwart's involvement in typographic and advertising design, which had originated during his time with Wils, developed rapidly when Berlage introduced him to a major graphic-design client, the cable manufacturer N.V. Nederlandsche Kabelfabriek (NKF), Delft. Along with Paul SCHUITEMA, Zwart rejected traditional typographic conventions, choosing instead to apply the formal principles of CONSTRUCTIVISM and De Stijl to Dutch commercial design. By the time he was forty, Zwart's increasing involvement with graphic design enabled him to leave Berlage and establish his own practice. Zwart worked with NKF up to the late 1920s designing and writing hundreds of promotional items. Concerned to attract the attention of the consumer, Zwart's exuberant experimentation contributed to numerous advertisements and catalogues with bold SANS SERIF lettering, repetitive word patterns, strong diagonals, and an early use of PHOTO-MONTAGE. His intuitive and elegant manipulation of typographic elements, combined with a preference for the De Stijl primary colours, provides a contrast to the more formal, dogmatic approach of other contemporary exponents of the NEW TYPOGRAPHY. From 1929 Zwart developed a long creative association with the Dutch Post Office (PTT), producing many stamps and publicity booklets. In later years, before and after the Second World War, he turned increasingly to industrial design.

The evolution of graphic design

Bibliography

Sources of illustrations

The evolution of graphic design

1840   1860

Arts and Cra

art & design movements

---

influential designers

1840	1860
Owen Jones	Walter Crane
	Dante Gabriel Rossetti

---

developments & events

1840	1860
Pioneering work in photography by Louis Daguerre and William Henry Fox Talbot	The advertising agency N.W. Ayer & Son founded in US 1869

ovement

Wiener Werkstätte

Art Nouveau

Jugendstil

Plakatstil

Futurism

Dada

Constructivism

Cubism

De Stijl

Aubrey Beardsley
The Beggarstaff Brothers
Will Bradley
Edward Burne-Jones
Jules Chéret
Eugène Grasset
Gustav Klimt
William Morris
Alphonse Mucha
T.-A. Steinlen
Henri de Toulouse-Lautrec
Theodore Lowe de Vinne

Peter Behrens
Lucian Bernhard
Frederic W. Goudy
Josef Hoffmann
Ludwig Hohlwein
Edward Johnston
Maxfield Parrish
Daniel Berkeley Updike
Henry C. van de Velde

Century Guild formed 1882

Art Workers' Guild formed 1884

Linotype typesetting machine invented 1886

Monotype typesetting machine invented 1887

Kelmscott Press established 1891

Development of offset litho printing in US 1904

American Institute of Graphic Arts (AIGA)
founded 1914

Design and Industries Association (DIA)
founded 1915

The evolution of graphic design *continued*

1920   **1940**

art & design movements

Wiener Werkstätte

Art Deco

Internatio▸

Surrealism

Plakatstil

Dada

Constructivism

Bauhaus

New Typography

De Stijl

influential designers

Mehemed Fehmy Agha
Josef Albers
Théo Ballmer
Herbert Bayer
Henryk Berlewi
Jean Carlu
A.M. Cassandre
Paul Colin
William Addison Dwiggins
Eric Gill
Ashley Havinden
Edward McKnight Kauffer
El Lissitzky
László Moholy-Nagy
Stanley Morison
Tom Purvis
Man Ray
Alexander Rodchenko
Kurt Schwitters
Ladislav Sutnar
Jan Tschichold
Piet Zwart

Walter H. Allner
Lester Beall
Max Bill
Joseph Binder
Alexey Brodovitch
Will Burtin
Tom Eckersley
Abram Games
Yusaku Kamekura
Alvin Lustig
Herbert Matter
Josef Müller-Brockmann
Cipe Pineles
Paul Rand
Emil Ruder
Hans Schleger
Bradbury Thompson
Henry Tomaszewski

developments & events

Art Directors Club of New York founded 1920

Society of Industrial Artists and Designers (now Chartered Society of Designers) formed 1930

Federal Art Project 1935–39

Isotype devised

Royal Designers for Industry (RDI) founded 1936

Council of Industrial Design (now Design Council) founded 1944

Doyle Dane Bernbach formed 1949

Alliance Graphique Internationale (AGI) founded 1951

Festival of Britain 1951

Association Typographique Internationale (A Typ I) formed 1957

Emergence of phototype setting systems

pographic Style

Psychedelia

Post-Modernism

Punk

Otl Aicher	Neville Brody	Katherine McCoy
Saul Bass	Gert Dumbar	David Carson
Pieter Brattinga	Grapus	Daniel Friedman
Robert Brownjohn	April Greiman	Bruce Mau
Chermayeff & Geismar	Eiko Ishioka	Tomato
Seymour Chwast	Terry Jones	
Wim Crouwel	Tibor Kalman	
Lou Dorfsman	Peret	
Heinz Edelmann	Erik Spiekermann	
Willy Fleckhaus		
Alan Fletcher		
Adrian Frutiger		
Shigeo Fukuda		
Bob Gill		
Milton Glaser		
F.H.K. Henrion		
Armin Hofmann		
George Lois		
Herb Lubalin		
Odermatt & Tissi		
Ikko Tanaka		
Wolfgang Weingart		
Henry Wolf		
Hermann Zapf		

Letraset launched 1960	Apple Macintosh computer launched 1984	Development of website design and interactive design
ICOGRADA formed 1963		
Development of electronic typesetting system with digitally generated characters	Emergence of desktop publishing: proliferation of software programs enables designers to exploit the creative potential of computers	

Bibliography

Editions given are those consulted by the authors

Ades, D. (1984): *The 20th-Century Poster: Design of the Avant-Garde*, New York

Aldersey-Williams, H. (1988): *New American Design: Products and Graphics for a Post-Industrial Age*, New York

Allen, E.M. (1963): *Harper's Dictionary of the Graphic Arts*, New York

Amstutz, W. (ed.) (1982): *Who's Who in Graphic Art*, Zurich

Aynsley, J. (2000): *Graphic Design in Germany: 1890-1945*, London

Barnicoat, J. (1972): *Posters: A Concise History*, London

Berry Turner, W., A.F. Johnson and W.P. Jaspert (1962): *The Encyclopaedia of Type Faces*, 3rd revised edition, London

Blumenthal, J. (1973): *Art of the Printed Book, 1455–1955*, New York

Campbell, A. (1983): *The Designer's Handbook*, London

Carson, D. (2000): *The End of Print*, London

Carter, R., B. Day and P.B. Meggs (1985): *Typographic Design: Form and Communication*, New York

Carter, S. (1987): *Twentieth-Century Type Designers*, London

Cato, K. (1989): *First Choice*, Tokyo

Craig, J. and B. Barton (1987): *Thirty Centuries of Graphic Design*, New York

Darracott, J. and B. Loftus (1972): *Second World War Posters*, Imperial War Museum, London

—(1981): *First World War Posters*, 2nd edition, Imperial War Museum, London

DeNoon, C. (1987): *Posters of the WPA*, Los Angeles

Dreyfuss, H. (1972): *Symbol Sourcebook*, New York

Fairbanks, A. (1949): *A Book of Scripts*, London

Fifty Years Banhaus (1968): exhibition catalogue, Royal Academy of Arts, London

Fletcher, A., C. Forbes and B. Gill (1963): *Graphic Design: Visual Comparisons*, London

Friedman, M. and P. Freshman (ed.) (1989): *Graphic Design in America*, Walker Art Center, Minneapolis

Gerstner, K. (1959): *The New Graphic Art*, Teufen, Switzerland

—(1968): *Designing Programmes*, enlarged new edition, Teufen, Switzerland

Glaser, M. (1977): *The Milton Glaser Poster Book*, New York

Gluck, F. (ed.) (1969): *World Graphic Design: Fifty Years of Advertising Art*, New York

Heller, S. and S. Chwast (1988): *Graphic Styles from Victorian to Post-Modern*, London

Heller, S. and M. Ilic (2001): *Icons of Graphic Design*, London

Henrion, F.H.K. and A. Parkin (1967): *Design Coordination and Corporate Image*, London

Hillier, B. (1970): *The Decorative Arts of the Forties and Fifties: Austerity Binge*, London

Hofmann, A. (1965): *Graphic Design Manual*, Teufen, Switzerland

Hogben, L. (1949): *From Cave Painting to Comic Strip*, New York

Hollis, R. (1994): *Graphic Design*, London

Jackson, D. (1981): *The Story of Writing*, London and New York

Jervis, S. (1984): *The Penguin Dictionary of Design and Designers*, London

Jobling, P. and D. Crowley (1996): *Graphic Design: Reproduction and Representation Since 1800*

Julier, G. (1993): *The Thames and Hudson Encyclopaedia of 20th century Design and Designers*, London

Kelly, R.R. (1969): *American Wood Type: 1828–1900*, New York

Kepes, G. (1944): *Language of Vision*, Chicago

—(1966): *Sign, Image, Symbol*, New York

Kinross, R. (1992): *Modern Typography: An Essay in Critical History*, London

Lewis, J. (1963): *Typography: basic principles*, London

—(1967): *The Twentieth-Century Book*, London

—(1970): *Anatomy of Printing*, London

MacCarthy, F. (1979): *A History of British Design, 1830–1970*, London and Boston

MacCarthy, F. and P. Nuttgens (1986): *Eye for Industry: Royal Designers for Industry 1936–1986*, London

McDermott, C. (1987): *Street Style: British Design in the 80s*, London and New York

McLean, R. (1980): *The Thames and Hudson Manual of Typography*, London

McQuiston, E. (1988): *Women in Design: A Contemporary View*, London

McQuiston, E. and B. Kitts (1987): *Graphic Design Source Book*, London

Massey, J. (ed.) (1976): *Great Ideas*, Chicago

Meggs, P.B. (1983): *A History of Graphic Design*, London and New York

Meyer, S.E. (1978): *America's Great Illustrators*, New York

Modley, R. (1976): *Handbook of Pictorial Symbols*, New York

Moholy-Nagy, L. (1947): *Vision in Motion*, Chicago

Moran, J. (1971): *Stanley Morison*, London

Morison, S. (1963): *The Typographic Book, 1450–1935*, London

Naylor, G. (1968): *The Bauhaus*, London

Neumann, E. (1967): *Functional Graphic Design in the '20s*, New York

Neurath, O. (1939): *Modern Man in the Making*, New York

Newdigate, B. (1938): *The Art of the Book*, London

Packer, W. (1980): *The Art of Vogue Covers 1919–1940*, New York

Pevsner, N. (1960): *Pioneers of Modern Design*, revised edition, London

Poyner, R. (1994): *Typography Now: The Next Wave*, London

Printing and the Mind of Man (1963): exhibition catalogue, Earls Court, London

Rand, P. (1947): *Thoughts on Design*, New York

Remington, R.R. and B.J. Hodik (1989): *Nine Pioneers in American Graphic Design*, Cambridge, Massachusetts

Rowland, K. (1973): *A History of the Modern Movement*, New York

Scarfe, L. (1954): *Alphabets*, London

Schweiger, W.J. (1984): *Wiener Werkstätte: Design in Vienna*, New York

Simon, O. (1963): *Introduction to Typography*, 2nd revised edition, London

Sparke, P. (1987): *Design in Context*, London

—(1987): *Japanese Design*, London

Steinberg, S.H. (1955): *Five Hundred Years of Printing*, London

Sutton, J. and A. Bartram (1968): *An Atlas of Typeforms*, London

Tschichold, J. (1995): *The New Typography*, California

Twyman, M. (1970): *Printing, 1770 1970: An Illustrated History of its Development and Uses in England*, London

Weill, A. (1985): *The Poster: A Worldwide Survey and History*, Boston

Wilbur, P. and M. Burke (1999): *Information Graphics*, London

Wingler, H.M. (1969): *The Bauhaus: Weimar, Dessau, Berlin, Chicago*, Cambridge, Massachusetts

Sources of illustrations

Plate numbers (pl.) refer to colour illustrations.
All other references are to page numbers:
a above; *b* below; *l* left; *r* right; *m* middle.

Kunstgewerbemuseum, Prague pl.18
Mervyn Kurlansky, Pentagram 130*bl*
Lambie-Nairn & Company Limited pl.45
Olaf Leu 133
Library of Congress, Washington 84*a*
Leo Lionni pl.35
Bernard Lodge 138*a*
M&Co, New York 122*a*
McCall's Magazine 204*al*
Katherine McCoy pl.46
Edward McDonald 141
McGraw-Hill Information Systems, New York 205*bl*
Holger Matthies 148*b*
Peter Max Enterprise, Inc. 178
Me Company 149*b*
Mendell & Oberer 150*a*
Russell Mills 152*b*
Minale, Tattersfield & Partners Limited 153*al*, 153*bl*
The MIT Press 55*ar*, 103*b*
Jan Mlodozeniec 153*br*
Bruno Monguzzi 156*a*
Municipal van Abbemuseum, Eindhoven pl.10
Musée Air France, Paris (photo) 193*b*
Museum of Modern Art, New York 126*b*
National Film Archive, London (photo) 187*b*
Siegfried Odermatt 165*a*
Vaughan Oliver 166*am*, pl.53
Adam Opel 34*a*
Art Paul 169
Michael Peters Limited 172*a*
Sophie and Roger Pfund, Communication Visuelle 172*b*
Woody Pirtle, Pentagram 175*bl*
Poster Museum, Wilanow, Warsaw 134*b*
Princeton University Library, N.J. 217*b*
Private collection, pl.11 (Moscow), pl.20, pl.28
Alain le Quernec 180*b*
Michael Rand 181*r* (photo Kenneth Jarecke/Contact/
    Colorific)
Ernst Roch, Roch Design 186*b*
Marte Röling 188*r*
Laurie Rosenwald 190*ar*
Royal College of Art, London 18*a*
Ruedi Rüegg 190*br*
Robert Miles Runyan, Runyan Hinsche Associates 191*b*
John Rushworth and Vince Frost, Pentagram pl.56
St. Bride Printing Library, London (photo) 28*a*, 55*br*, pl.26
Peter Saville 194
Paula Scher, Pentagram 195*a*
Arnold Schwartzman 196*b*
Reproduced by kind permission of Shell U.K. Limited 28*m*,
    195*m*, pl.30
Some Bizarre/Virgin Records 40*b*
Herbert Spencer 200*m*, pl.42
Anton Stankowski, Stankowski and Duschek 201*b*
State Lenin Library, Moscow pl.12, pl.13
State Mutual Life Assurance 22*m*
Barbara Solomon Stauffacher 200*a*

Stedelijk Museum, Amsterdam 132*ar*, 193*a*
D. Stempel AG, Frankfurt am Main 130*al*
Tate Gallery, London 176*a*
Henryk Tomaszewski 210*a*
Jan van Toorn 211*a*, pl.44
Total Design 212*a*
Trickett & Webb 213*a*
Niklaus Troxler 213*m*, pl.55
George Tscherny 214*a*
Unimark International 164*b*
Verve/Polydor Records pl.39
Massimo Vignelli, Designer 220*a*
Virgin Records Limited 94*b*, 184*r*
Why Not Associates 224*a*
Wolff Olins Limited 226*a*
Gert Wunderlich 227*r*
Hermann Zapf 230*a*

The following illustrations are from books and journals:
Monotype Recorder, Volume 44, no. 1, Autumn 1970, 222*b*;
Otto Neurath, *Bildstatistik nach Wiener Methode in der
Schule*, Vienna, 1933, 118*b*